FIX-IT and Enjoy-It!™
COOKBOOK

FIX-IT and Enjoy-It!™

COOKBOOK

All-Purpose, Welcome-Home Recipes

By *The New York Times* bestselling author
Phyllis Pellman Good

Good Books

Intercourse, PA 17534
800/762-7171
www.GoodBks.com

Cover design and illustrations by Cheryl Benner
Design by Dawn J. Ranck

FIX-IT AND ENJOY-IT COOKBOOK
Copyright © 2006 by Good Books, Intercourse, PA 17534

International Standard Book Number-13: 978-1-56148-526-0 (paperback edition)
International Standard Book Number-10: 1-56148-526-8 (paperback edition)

International Standard Book Number-13: 978-1-56148-525-3 (comb-bound paperback edition)
International Standard Book Number-10: 1-56148-525-X (comb-bound paperback edition)

International Standard Book Number-13: 978-1-56148-527-7 (hardcover gift edition)
International Standard Book Number-10: 1-56148-527-6 (hardcover gift edition)

Library of Congress Catalog Card Number: 2005034069

Library of Congress Cataloging-in-Publication Data
Good, Phyllis Pellman
   Fix-it and enjoy-it cookbook : all purpose, welcome-home recipes / Phyllis Pellman Good.
      p. cm.
   Includes index.
   ISBN-13: 978-1-56148-527-7 (hardcover), ISBN-10: 1-56148-527-6 (hardcover)—
   ISBN-13: 978-1-56148-526-0 (pbk.), ISBN-10: 1-56148-526-8 (pbk.)—
   ISBN-13: 978-1-56148-525-3 (plastic comb), ISBN-10: 1-56148-525-X (plastic comb)
   1. Cookery, American. I. Title.
   TX715.G6366 2006
   641.5973—dc22   2005034069

Table of Contents

About *Fix-It and Enjoy-It Cookbook*

If I can cook, you can, too.

Let me be honest.

My mother tried to teach me, bless her persistent heart. But she had to make the kitchen more enticing than the books I was always trying to sneak off and read, and I couldn't be persuaded. I have a box full of *unstained* recipe cards—written in her hand and mine—to prove it.

I can still bring back the panic that flashed through me when I suddenly had to make a grocery list. Merle and I were married for two weeks and were settling into our grad-school housing in New York. Merle had volunteered to do the cleaning. I said I'd cook. Merle had far more experience in the kitchen than I did. He had been unable to duck the duty as one of seven sons (no daughters!), each of whom had to take his turn helping their mother with serious food preparation.

I was blithely naïve. I've learned since that Merle was earnestly hopeful. You see, in the masculine world of his upbringing, boys worked in the kitchen only when there was absolutely no alternative.

My roommate had given us a cookbook for a wedding gift. And somehow, I had brought my mother's favorite community cookbook along to our first home. Those two books, and the trusty box of recipe cards my mother had helped me to fill, must have been the source of my confidence when I agreed to cook.

When I read the community cookbook, but still couldn't figure out how to cook a chicken to get chicken broth, I realized I needed a very basic cookbook. And so I began reading cookbooks that spelled out every step. I tried stuff. Merle ate and cheered me on.

In fact, he started suggesting that we invite our visiting family and friends to stay for meals. (It did take me a while to figure out that I didn't need to wait until our guests had arrived to start preparing the food. I vividly remember chopping onions for my one reliable casserole in full view of our visitors—and only then realizing that I could have done that before they came and saved myself the pressure of observers.)

So here's what I've figured out since I started cooking:

1. Good cookbooks are godsends. Carefully enumerated steps can get you through. (These books can also be entertainment. Today, reading recipes and imagining their outcomes relaxes me.)

2. Sometimes you feel like cooking; sometimes you don't. But everybody always feels like eating. Or so it seems.

When I gained enough confidence to believe that Merle and I wouldn't starve with me in charge of meal-making, I started to like it. In fact, cooking became a great relief from grad-school reading assignments. Now it's a good foil to numbing computer screens.

Sometimes cooking is a real burden. My mother-in-law once confessed to me that she was sick and tired of cooking. I was shocked. She put amazing meals on the table without a whimper or a sigh. Then she reminded me that she had made three full meals a day for her farmer husband, seven sons, and a hired man for a good chunk of her life. Including baking dinner rolls, doughnuts, and pies, making from-scratch gravy and potatoes a dozen different ways, and serving up salads and a multitude of fresh vegetables pulled from her own garden. No wonder the woman was tired of cooking. But I was in a different life phase. I was still wide-eyed with wonder that Merle liked what I was trying, every other day or so a new recipe.

3. What would we do without the great practice of pass-it-on recipes?

I am utterly grateful for good cooks who happily share their recipes and hard-won wisdom. Sometimes they do it in the kitchen—I'm forever indebted to my mother who tried, and then sent her typed-up recipes along with me into life, knowing that I would someday come to my senses. (And she never said I-told-you-so when I called her with a dumb cooking question.)

This book is full of pass-it-on recipes. I started the sorting process with more than 3,000 recipes, and spent months selecting the more than 675 you find here.

Thank you to all the cooks who shared their family favorites. We name them alongside their recipes in honor of their good dishes, but also their generous spirits.

4. When you're squeezed for time— Look at three elements before you rip into one of these recipes:

1.) The Prep and Cooking/Baking Times, just above the list of ingredients for each recipe. They'll give you a pretty accurate sense of how long each recipe will take to prepare.

2.) The length of the list of ingredients. If that's short, good chance the recipe's a quickie to put together.

3.) The number of steps in the procedure. Again, if that's brief, the recipe likely won't take a lot of your time to fix.

5. If you don't know how or where to start—

1.) Choose a couple of recipes, each with a short list of ingredients and only a few steps in their procedures. Go with those recipes made from packaged and prepared ingredients. Not a bad way to start.

2.) Do you have the ingredients those recipes call for? If not, can you easily find them in your grocery store?

3.) Can you do what the recipes ask, and do you have the equipment they require?

4.) Do they sound good?

5.) Take a chance. It will be hard to fail with any of these, except for some of the bread recipes which are geared to more experienced cooks.

6. If you love to cook—You know what to do! You'll spot the from-scratch recipes. This is a collection of real treasures. And your family and friends will be very pleased.

May you enjoy this good, everyday food from some of the best cooks in the country—as you prepare it, and when you eat it!
— Phyllis Pellman Good

4

Appetizers and Snacks

Hot Virginia Dip

Sue Suter
Millersville, PA

Makes 4 cups

Prep Time: 20-30 minutes
Baking Time: 20-25 minutes

1 cup chopped pecans
2 Tbsp. butter
2 8-oz. pkgs. cream cheese,
   softened
4 Tbsp. milk
5 ozs. dried beef, chopped
1 tsp. garlic powder
1 cup sour cream
4 tsp. chopped onion

1. In skillet, saute pecans
in butter. Set aside.
2. Combine remaining
ingredients. Spread in greased
baking dish.
3. Sprinkle sauted pecans
over top.
4. Bake at 350° for 20-25
minutes.

Ham Dip

John D. Allen
Rye, CO

Makes 4 cups, or 8-10 servings

Prep Time: 15 minutes
Chilling Time: 8 hours,
   or overnight

8 ozs. finely chopped
   cooked ham
1 1/2 cups mayonnaise
1 1/3 cups sour cream
2 Tbsp. chopped onion
2 Tbsp. chopped fresh
   parsley
2 tsp. dill seed
2 tsp. Beau Monde
   Seasoning

1. Combine all ingredients
thoroughly.
2. Refrigerate for 8 hours.
3. Serve with crackers,
chips, or cocktail rye bread.

Sausage Bean Dip

Sherlyn Hess
Millersville, PA

Makes 6 cups, or about
12 appetizer-sized servings

Prep Time: 30 minutes
Cooking Time:
   15 minutes on stove-top,
   or 3 hours in slow cooker

1/2 lb. bulk sausage
1/2 lb. hot sausage,
   squeezed out of casing
2/3 cup chopped onions
2 16-oz. cans B&B beans
1 cup barbecue sauce
3 Tbsp. brown sugar

1. Brown sausage and
onions in skillet. Drain.
2. Combine all ingredients
in food processor or blender.
Blend until smooth.
3. Heat in slow cooker for
3 hours on low, or in a
saucepan on the stove for 15
minutes.
4. Serve warm with crack-
ers, nachos, or tortilla chips.

Baked Clam Dip

Barbara Lukan
Ridgewood, New York

Makes 1 cup

Prep Time: 5-8 minutes
Baking Time: 30 minutes

6.5-oz. can minced clams
1/4 cup bread crumbs
1 tsp. garlic powder
1 tsp. parsley
1/8 tsp. dried oregano
1/8 tsp. salt
1 tsp. chopped onion
2 Tbsp. oil
Parmesan cheese
crackers

1. Combine all but Parmesan cheese and crackers. Pour into small greased baking dish. Sprinkle with cheese.
2. Bake at 275° for 25-30 minutes.
3. Serve with crackers.

A Tip —

Keep spatulas, wire whisks, wooden spoons, etc. near the stove, within arms' reach.

Dilly Crab Dip

Joyce M Shackelford
Green Bay, Wisconsin

Makes 1 1/2 cups

Prep Time: 30 minutes
Chilling Time: 2 8 hours

1/2 cup mayonnaise or
   salad dressing
1/2 cup sour cream
1 cup flaked crabmeat,
   divided
1 tsp. dried dill weed
2 tsp. finely chopped
   onion *or* scallion
1/2 tsp. finely shredded
   lime peel
1 tsp. lime juice
dash of bottled hot pepper
   sauce
dash ground red pepper,
   optional
salt and pepper to taste

1. Stir together mayonnaise, sour cream, 2/3 cup crabmeat, dill weed, onion, lime peel, lime juice, hot pepper sauce, and red pepper. Season with salt and pepper to taste.
2. Refrigerate for 2 hours, or overnight.
3. Just before serving, sprinkle with reserved crabmeat.
4. Serve with warm or chilled artichokes or crackers.

Tip: Canned or frozen crab meat may be used.

Cheese and Shrimp Strudel

D. Fern Ruth, Chalfont, PA

Makes 16-18 slices

Prep Time: 20 minutes
Baking Time: 20-25 minutes
Cooling Time: 20 minutes

half a 17.25-oz. pkg.
   (1 sheet) frozen puff
   pastry, thawed
1 1/2 cups (6 ozs.) shredded
   Swiss cheese
1/2 cup sour cream
1/4 cup thinly sliced green
   onion
1 cup (4 ozs.) cooked
   shrimp, chopped,
   or 4.5-oz. can shrimp,
   rinsed, drained, and
   chopped
1 egg, beaten

1. On a lightly floured surface, roll the thawed puff pastry to a 10 x 18 rectangle.
2. Place rectangle of pastry on lightly greased, large baking sheet.
3. In a medium-sized bowl, stir together cheese, sour cream, onion, shrimp, and half the beaten egg (about 2 Tbsp.).
4. Spread the mixture lengthwise down half of the rectangle. Brush edges of pastry (using pastry brush) with some of the remaining beaten egg.
5. Carefully fold dough over the filling and seal edges with the tines of a fork. Brush top and sides of strudel with remaining egg.

6. Bake at 400° for 20-25 minutes, or until golden.

7. Remove from oven and cool 20 minutes before slicing.

8. With a very sharp knife, slice slightly on the diagonal.

Tip: You can also make this with crabmeat, or a combination of shrimp and crab.

This is part of our late-evening meal of oyster stew and varied appetizers and desserts at our family homestead, following Christmas Eve services at church.

Salmon Spread
Erma Brubaker
Harrisonburg, VA

Makes 1½ cups, or 6-8 servings

Prep Time: 5 minutes

2 6-oz. cans salmon (without bones or black skin)
8 ozs. light cream cheese
1 Tbsp. dried onion
1 Tbsp. light hickory smoke
1 Tbsp. Worcestershire sauce
1 Tbsp. lemon juice
1 Tbsp. horseradish

1. In mixing bowl, mix together salmon, cream cheese, onion, hickory smoke, Worcestershire sauce, lemon juice, and horseradish.

2. Beat together for 2 minutes or until smooth.

3. Serve with your favorite crackers.

Raspberry Bean Dip
Nancy Wagner Graves
Manhattan, KS

Makes 2½ cups

Prep Time: 5 minutes
Baking Time: 20-30 minutes

15.5-oz. can black beans, drained
8 ozs. cream cheese, sliced thin
1 small red onion, chopped
½ jar (15.75-oz. size) Roasted Raspberry Chipotle sauce*
8 ozs. Monterey Jack cheese, shredded

1. In 9 x 9 greased baking dish, layer ingredients in order given above.

2. Bake at 325° for 20-30 minutes, or until bubbly.

*Look for this in the hot sauce and steak sauce aisle of the grocery store. If you can't find this sauce (made by Bronco Bob's), look for Raspberry Chipotle Grilling Sauce (by Harry & David), or for raspberry salsa.

Texas Caviar
Reita F. Yoder
Carlsbad, NM

Makes about 8 cups, or about 20 appetizer-sized servings

Prep Time: 20 minutes
Cooling Time: Overnight

2 15-oz. cans black-eyed peas, drained
15-oz. can white hominy, drained
1 medium onion, chopped
2 jalapeños, minced
2 cloves garlic, minced
½ tsp. black pepper
¼ cup minced parsley
1 large tomato, chopped
8-oz. bottle Italian salad dressing

1. Combine all ingredients and refrigerate overnight.

2. Drain before serving.

3. Serve with corn chips.

Bleu Cheese Cheesecake

Shari Jensen, Fountain, CO

Makes 12 servings

Prep Time: 10 minutes
Baking Time: 48-53 minutes
Chilling Time: 3-24 hours

2 8-oz. pkgs. cream cheese,
    at room temperature
8 ozs. bleu cheese,
    crumbled, at room
    temperature
2 cups sour cream, *divided*
3 large eggs
2 Tbsp. dried parsley
2 Tbsp. dried onion flakes
1 tsp. garlic salt
1/4 tsp. white pepper
a variety of crackers and/or
    sliced French bread

1. In a large mixing bowl, cream together the cheeses.
2. When thoroughly creamed, add 2/3 cup sour cream, eggs, parsley, onion flakes, garlic salt, and pepper. Beat well.
3. Pour into 9" springform pan. Bake at 300° for 40-45 minutes, until a toothpick inserted in center comes out clean.
4. Remove from oven. Cool on rack 5 minutes.
5. Carefully spread remaining sour cream on top of cheesecake to within 1/2" of edge.
6. Return to oven and bake 8 minutes longer. Don't let the sour cream topping brown.

7. Remove from oven. Cool completely without removing from pan. Cover with plastic wrap and chill in refrigerator for 3-24 hours.
8. Remove from refrigerator. Open the springform pan, using a knife to slip around the edge of the pan to loosen if necessary.
9. Place on platter. Surround with a variety of crackers and/or slices of French bread.

Tips:

1 You can serve this sliced into 12 wedges for a first course, along with a tossed green salad. Or serve it on a platter with a knife for spreading the crackers.

2. Don't worry if the top cracks after baking. It will be covered with sour cream.

3. Melt down leftovers and thin with a bit of milk. Use it as a topping for baked potatoes, steaks, or veggies.

4. The baked cheesecake freezes well. Cut it into quarters. Place the quarters on a cookie sheet. Freeze. Remove from freezer, wrap each quarter in plastic wrap while frozen and then in freezer wrap. You can keep it in the freezer for up to 6 weeks.

Hot Cheese Dip

Renee D. Groff
Manheim, PA

*Makes about 7 cups,
or 10-12 servings*

Prep Time: 10 minutes
Baking Time: 25 minutes

2 cups shredded
    mozzarella cheese
2 cups shredded cheddar
    cheese
2 cups mayonnaise
1 medium-sized onion,
    chopped
4-oz. can chopped green
    chilies, drained
1 1/2 ozs. sliced pepperoni
1/2 cup sliced black olives

1. Combine cheeses, mayonnaise, onion, and green chilies.
2. Pour into greased 8 x 12 baking dish or 9" or 10" pie pan.
3. Top with pepperoni and black olives.
4. Bake at 325° for 25 minutes.
5. Serve warm with crackers and/or corn chips.

Spinach Dip

Karen Stoltzfus
Alto, MI

Makes 4½ cups

Prep Time: 10-15 minutes

1 envelope dry vegetable
  soup mix
8 ozs. sour cream
1 cup mayonnaise
10-oz. pkg. frozen chopped
  spinach, thawed and
  squeezed dry
8-oz. can water chestnuts,
  drained and chopped

1. Combine all ingredients.
2. Serve with crackers.

Dill Weed Dip for Vegetables

Hannah D. Burkholder
Bridgewater, VA

Makes 1 ¼ cups

Prep Time: 15 minutes

⅔ cup sour cream
⅔ cup mayonnaise
1 Tbsp. fresh chopped
  parsley
1 Tbsp. grated onion
1 Tbsp. dried dill weed
¼ tsp. dry mustard

1. Mix all ingredients
together; then refrigerate
until ready to serve.

2. Serve with cut-up fresh
vegetables.

Tip: If you think of it, prepare
this a day or two before you
plan to use it. The flavors are
enhanced by some time
together!

Healthy Hummus

Barbara Forrester Landis
Lititz, PA

Makes 1½ cups, or 8 servings

Prep Time: 15 minutes

1½ cups drained canned
  Great Northern beans
¼ red onion, chopped
1 tsp. fresh minced garlic
1 tsp. fresh rosemary,
  finely chopped
1 tsp. Kosher salt, or to
  taste
1 tsp. black pepper, or to
  taste
½ cup extra-virgin olive oil

1. In a food processor,
puree beans until they are
halfway between chunky and
smooth.
2. Add onion, garlic, rosemary, salt, and pepper.
3. Puree while drizzling in
olive oil.
4. Add more or less olive
oil, salt, and pepper to taste.
5. Serve with crackers or
pita chips. Or spread in tortilla wraps with roasted vegetables, or with cheese and
salsa.

Note: The hummus should be
spreadable.

Fresh Fruit Dip

**Christie Detamore-
Hunsberger**
Harrisonburg, VA

Makes 1 cup

Prep Time: 5 minutes

8 ozs. sour cream *or*
  vanilla yogurt
1 Tbsp. sugar
½ tsp. pumpkin pie spice
¼ tsp. vanilla

Combine all ingredients
and chill.

A Tip —

When you find a recipe
that you love, make a
notation in the cookbook
that it is a great recipe.

Peanut-Buttery Fresh Fruit Dip

Mary Jane Musser
Manheim, PA

Makes 3 cups

Prep Time: 5 minutes

1 cup peanut butter
8-oz. pkg. cream cheese,
   softened
1 cup brown sugar
1/4 cup milk

1. Mix all ingredients together until well blended. Chill.
2. Serve with sliced apples.

Fruit Dip

Wanda Marshall
Massillon, OH

Makes 2 cups

Prep Time: 10-15 minutes

1 pint sour cream
1/4 cup brown sugar
12 macaroon cookies,
   crushed or broken

1. If the cookies are hard, crush with a rolling pin. If softer, break into small pieces.
2. Mix together sour cream and brown sugar. If using hard cookies, stir in small pieces and allow to stand for 5 hours or longer. If using soft cookies, stir in cookie pieces just before serving.
3. Serve as a dipping sauce for bite-sized chunks of pineapple, cantaloupe, kiwi, and watermelon.

Cranberry Appetizer

Christie Detamore-Hunsberger
Harrisonburg, VA

Makes 8 cups, or 12-14 servings

Prep Time: 5-10 minutes
Cooking Time: 20 minutes
Cooling Time: 1 hour

1 cup water
1 cup sugar
8- or 12-oz. pkg. fresh
   cranberries
1/2 cup apricot preserves
2 Tbsp. lemon juice
1/3 cup toasted slivered
   almonds
8-oz. pkg. cream cheese

1. In saucepan over medium heat, bring sugar and water to a boil without stirring. Boil 5 minutes.
2. Add cranberries and cook until the berries pop, about 10 minutes. Remove from heat.
3. Add preserves, lemon juice, and almonds. Cool.
4. Place cream cheese block on a serving dish. Pour cranberry mixture over cheese. Serve with crackers.

Zingy Cheese Spread

Lois Gae E. Kuh
Penfield, NY

Makes 2 cups

Prep Time: 5-7 minutes

10-oz. jar pineapple
   marmalade
10-oz. jar applesauce
5 1/2-6-oz. jar white
   horseradish
3 Tbsp. dry mustard
2 8-oz. pkgs. cream cheese

1. Combine marmalade, applesauce, horseradish, and dry mustard until well mixed.
2. Place blocks of cheese on a serving plate. Pour zingy mixture over cream cheese.
3. Refrigerate until ready to serve.
4. Serve with cut-up fresh vegetables or a variety of snack crackers.

Chocolate Chip Cheese Ball

Carol Sommers
Millersburg, OH
Carisa Funk
Hillsboro, KS

Makes 2 cups

Prep Time: 15-20 minutes
Chilling Time: 3 hours

8-oz. pkg. cream cheese, softened
1/2 cup butter (no substitutes), softened
1/4 tsp. vanilla extract
2 Tbsp. brown sugar
3/4 cup confectioners sugar
3/4 cup miniature semi-sweet chocolate chips
3/4 cup finely chopped pecans
graham crackers *or* graham cracker sticks

1. In mixing bowl, beat the cream cheese, butter, and vanilla until fluffy.
2. Gradually add brown sugar and confectioners sugar, and beat just until combined. Stir in chocolate chips by hand.
3. Cover and refrigerate for 2 hours.
4. Place cream cheese mixture on a large piece of plastic wrap. Shape into a ball and refrigerate for at least 1 hour.
5. Just before serving, roll cheese ball in pecans.
6. Serve with graham crackers.

Artichoke Appetizer

Joyce Bowman
Lady Lake, FL

Makes 10 servings

Prep Time: 30 minutes
Baking Time: 8-10 minutes

14-oz. can artichokes, drained
3/4 cup mayonnaise (light or regular)
3/4 cup Parmesan cheese
1 tube refrigerated biscuits, 10-biscuit size

1. Cut artichokes in pieces. Set aside.
2. Mix mayonnaise and Parmesan cheese together. Set aside.
3. Snip or cut each biscuit in thirds and press each lightly into a square shape. Spread mayonnaise mixture on each biscuit piece. Top each with a piece of artichoke.
4. Place on lightly greased baking sheet.
5. Bake at 400° for 8-10 minutes. Watch carefully so they don't burn.

Note: After the biscuits have been baked, you can cool them and then place them in freezer bags and store them in the freezer until you need them. To serve, heat them in the microwave.

Crab-Stuffed Mushrooms

Kim Stoll, Abbeville, SC

Makes 6 servings

Prep Time: 30 minutes
Baking Time: 15 minutes

12 large, fresh mushrooms
1 tsp. melted butter
1/2 cup crabmeat, chopped fine
1/4 cup cream cheese, at room temperature
1/2 cup Monterey Jack cheese, grated
dash of pepper
1/2 tsp. garlic powder

1. Clean mushrooms and remove stems.
2. Mix remaining ingredients together in a bowl.
3. Dip mushrooms in melted butter and place each one in a muffin tin cup, bottom-side up.
4. Fill mushrooms with crab-cheese mixture.
5. Bake at 400° for 15 minutes.

Variations:
1. You can substitute other cheese for the Monterey Jack, such as Colby or mozzarella.
2. Instead of using mushroom caps, cut slices of bread into quarters, dip in the melted butter, and push down into the individual cups in a mini-muffin pan. Fill the center of each bread cup with the crab mixture. Bake according to directions above.

Stuffed Mushrooms

Hannah D. Burkholder
Bridgewater, VA

*Makes 20 mushrooms,
or enough for 5 servings*

Prep Time: 30 minutes
Cooking Time: 5 minutes

2 ozs. (about 1½ cups)
  Swiss cheese, shredded
1 hard-cooked egg, finely
  chopped
3 Tbsp. fine bread crumbs
½ clove garlic, finely
  chopped
½ stick (4 Tbsp.) butter,
  softened
1 lb. fresh mushrooms,
  stems removed
1 stick (8 Tbsp.) butter,
  melted

1. In mixing bowl, combine cheese, egg, bread crumbs, garlic, and ½ stick softened butter. Blend thoroughly.
2. Dip each mushroom cap in 1 stick melted butter; then fill each with cheese mixture. Place in long baking pan, stuffed side up.
3. Broil for 5 minutes or until the caps sizzle.

A Tip —

Don't put cold water in a hot pan. It can cause a pan to warp.

Hot Buffalo Wing Dip

Barbara Kuhns
Millersburg, OH

Makes about 8 cups

Prep Time: 15 minutes
Baking Time: 45 minutes

2 8-oz. pkgs. cream cheese,
  at room temperature
8 ozs. Ranch dressing
12 ozs. hot wing sauce
3 cups grilled chicken,
  cubed
2 cups cheddar cheese,
  shredded

1. Combine cream cheese, Ranch dressing, and hot wing sauce. Mix well.
2. Add chicken and cheddar cheese. Pour into greased baking dish.
3. Bake at 350° for 45 minutes.
4. Serve warm with tortilla chips or celery.

Chicken Wraps

Marlene Fonken, Upland, CA

Makes 3 cups

Prep Time: 30 minutes
Chilling Time: 2 hours

Wraps:
2 large chicken breasts
1¾ cups chicken broth
¼ cup soy sauce
1 Tbsp. Worcestershire
  sauce
1 lb. large leaves of fresh
  spinach

Dip:
1 cup sour cream
2 tsp. toasted sesame seeds
½ tsp. ground ginger
4 tsp. soy sauce
2 tsp. Worcestershire sauce

1. To make the wraps, combine chicken, broth, ¼ cup soy sauce, and 1 Tbsp. Worcestershire sauce in a skillet or saucepan. Simmer until chicken is just cooked. Cool and cut meat into chunks.
2. Wash spinach. Pour boiling water over the leaves. Immediately drain and cool.
3. Place a chunk of chicken on stem end of spinach leaf. Roll leaf over. Fold ends in and continue to roll. Secure with toothpick and chill.
4. To make dip, mix together all dip ingredients and chill.
5. Serve stuffed leaves with dip.

Tip: To toast sesame seeds, spread in a single layer on a cookie sheet. Bake at 350° for 15 minutes.

Variation: If you prefer less Worcestershire sauce, reduce the amount in the wraps to 1 tsp., and in the dip to 1 tsp.

Party Pinwheels
Della Yoder, Kalona, IA

Makes 36 pieces

Prep. Time: 20-25 minutes
Chilling Time: 2 hours

1-oz. packet Original Hidden Valley Ranch Dressing Mix
2 8-oz. pkgs. cream cheese, softened
2 green onions, minced
4 12" flour tortillas
4-oz. jar diced pimentos, drained
4-oz. can diced green chilies, drained
2.25-oz. can diced black olives, drained

1. Mix together ranch mix, cream cheese, and green onions. Spread onto tortillas.
2. Sprinkle equal amounts of vegetables over cream cheese mixture.
3. Roll up tortillas tightly. Refrigerate for at least 2 hours.
4. Cut tortillas into 1" slices. Discard ends. Serve with spirals facing up.

Crab Delight
Renee D. Groff
Manheim, PA

Makes 12-15 servings

Prep Time: 15 minutes
Cooking Time: 5 minutes

9 slices white bread
7.5-oz. can crabmeat, flaked
1 small onion, finely chopped
1 cup grated cheddar cheese
1 cup mayonnaise
1 tsp. dill weed
1/2 tsp. salt

1. Cut crusts off bread. Cut each slice into 4 squares, strips, or triangles.
2. Mix crabmeat, onion, cheese, mayonnaise, dill weed, and salt. Spread on bread.
3. Place spread bread on lightly greased cookie sheet. Broil several minutes until golden and bubbly.

Tip: For parties I use cookie cutters to create shapes to fit the occasion. Freezing the bread first makes for easier cutting.

Feta Bruschetta
Lena Sheaffer
Port Matilda, PA

Makes 10 servings

Prep Time: 15 minutes
Baking Time: 20 minutes

1/4 cup butter, melted
1/4 cup olive or vegetable oil
10 slices French bread, cut 1" thick
4-oz. pkg. crumbled feta cheese
2-3 garlic cloves, minced
1 Tbsp. chopped fresh basil, or 1 tsp. dried basil
1 large tomato, seeded and chopped

1. Combine butter and oil. Brush on both sides of bread. Place on baking sheet.
2. Bake at 350° for 8-10 minutes, or until lightly browned.
3. Combine feta cheese, garlic, and basil. Sprinkle over toast. Top with tomato.
4. Bake 8-10 minutes longer, or until heated through. Serve warm.

Variation: Mix chopped red pepper into Step 3, along with any other of your favorite herbs.

Garlic Bread

Barbara Yoder
Christiana, PA

Makes 10 servings

Prep Time: 15-20 minutes
Baking Time: 40 minutes

1 loaf unsliced Italian
   bread
10-12 slices of Colby,
   cheddar, Swiss, *or*
   Monterey Jack cheese
1 tsp. minced garlic
1/2 tsp. seasoning salt
1/2 tsp. lemon juice
1 1/2 tsp. poppy seeds
1/4 cup butter
1 cup chopped
   mushrooms, *optional*
1 small onion finely
   chopped

1. With a very sharp knife,
cut down diagonally through
the loaf, making slices
approximately 1" apart. Do
not cut through the bottom of
the loaf. Then cut slits on the
diagonal in the opposite
direction, also about 1" apart,
also without cutting com-
pletely through the bottom of
the loaf.
2. Place loaf on large piece
of foil. Place slices of cheese
in grooves going the one
direction.
3. Place remaining ingredients in microwave-safe bowl.
Stir until well mixed. Cover
and microwave on high for 2
minutes.
4. Spoon evenly over
bread.

5. Wrap loaf in foil, pinching closed so no ingredients
ooze out while baking. Place
on a cookie sheet to catch
any drippings. Bake at 350°
for 40 minutes.

Ham and Cheese Sticky Buns

Rosanne Weiler
Myerstown, PA

Makes 12 servings

Prep Time: 10 minutes
Baking Time: 20 minutes

24 party-size potato rolls
1 lb. sliced Swiss cheese
1/2 lb. sliced ham
1 cup butter
1/3 cup brown sugar
2 Tbsp. Worcestershire
   sauce
2 Tbsp. prepared mustard
2 Tbsp. poppy seeds

1. Slice rolls in half and
place bottoms in 9 x 13 pan.
2. Layer on cheese and
ham, and top with roll tops.
3. Melt butter and add
sugar, Worcestershire sauce,
mustard, and poppy seeds.
Bring to boil and let boil 2
minutes.
4. Immediately pour over
rolls and bake at 350° for 20
minutes.

*Tip: These can be made ahead
and heated when ready to
serve.*

*When I serve these as an
appetizer, everyone comes back
for seconds!*

Tangy Ham and Cheese Wraps

Cheryl Lapp, Parkesburg, PA

*Makes 8 appetizer servings,
or 4 main-dish servings*

Prep Time: 20-30 minutes

4 10" flour tortillas
8-oz. container onion and
   chive cream cheese
   spread
4-oz. jar apricot jam,
   optional
1 cup shredded carrots
1 cup Monterey Jack
   cheese, shredded
1 lb. thinly sliced ham
leaf lettuce

1. Spread tortillas with
cream cheese and apricot
jam.
2 Top with carrots and
shredded cheese.
3. Layer on ham and let-
tuce.
4. Roll up and wrap in
plastic wrap. Refrigerate for
at least 30 minutes.
5. Cut in half, or serve
whole.

*Tip: You can make these up to
12-14 hours ahead of your serving time.*

*Variation: If you prefer less
meat, 1/2 lb. ham works well.*

Breakfast and Brunch Dishes

Blueberry Streusel Cornbread

Judi Janzen
Salem, OR

Makes 9 servings

Prep Time: 20-30 minutes
Baking Time: 45-50 minutes

2 pkgs. corn-muffin mix
2 eggs
2/3 cup milk
2 Tbsp. flour
2 cups fresh blueberries

Streusel Topping:
3 Tbsp. butter *or*
    margarine, softened
3/4 cup sugar
1/2 cup flour
3/4 tsp. cinnamon

1. Mix corn-muffin mix, eggs, milk, and flour in a medium-sized mixing bowl for 30-60 seconds, using an electric mixer.

2. Fold in blueberries. Pour into greased 9 x 9 baking dish.

3. In a small mixing bowl, using a pastry blender, combine streusel ingredients until mixed into fine crumbs. Spoon over cornbread mixture in pan.

4. Bake at 350° for 45-50 minutes, or until a toothpick stuck into the center comes out clean. Serve warm.

Cinnamon Coffee Cake

Janice Burkholder
Richfield, PA

Makes 16 servings

Prep Time: 15 minutes
Baking Time: 70 minutes

1 cup butter *or* margarine,
    softened
2 3/4 cups sugar, *divided*
2 tsp. vanilla
4 eggs
3 cups flour
2 tsp. baking powder
1 tsp. baking soda
1 tsp. salt
2 cups (16 ozs.) sour cream
2 Tbsp. cinnamon
1/2 cup chopped walnuts

1. In a large mixing bowl, cream butter and 2 cups sugar together with a mixer until fluffy. Blend in vanilla.

2. Add eggs one at a time, beating well after each addition.

3. Combine flour, baking powder, soda, and salt in a separate bowl and add to egg mixture, alternating with sour cream.

4. Spoon 1/3 of the batter into a greased 10" tube or bundt pan.

5. Combine cinnamon, nuts, and remaining sugar. Layer 1/3 of this mixture over batter. Repeat layers two more times.

6. Bake at 350° for 70 minutes, or until toothpick inserted in center of cake comes out clean.

7. Remove from pan and cool on a wire rack.

Rhubarb Coffee Cake

Mary Lou Mahar
Williamsfield, IL

Makes 12 servings

Prep Time: 10 minutes
Baking Time: 40 minutes

1 stick (1/2 cup) butter *or*
　margarine, at room
　temperature
2 cups brown sugar, *divided*
1 egg
1 tsp. vanilla
1 cup milk
2 cups flour
1 tsp. baking soda
pinch of salt
1 cup milk
2 cups chopped rhubarb
1/2 tsp. cinnamon

1. With an electric mixer, cream together butter and 1 1/2 cups brown sugar. Add egg and vanilla and mix thoroughly.

2. In a separate mixing bowl, stir together flour, baking soda, and salt.

3. Add dry ingredients to creamed ingredients alternately with milk.

4. When well blended, mix in rhubarb by hand. Pour batter into greased 9 x 13 glass baking pan.

5. Sprinkle with 1/2 cup reserved brown sugar and cinnamon.

6. Bake at 350° for 40 minutes.

Raspberry Custard Kuchen

Tabitha Schmidt
Baltic, OH

Makes 10-12 servings

Prep Time: 30 minutes
Baking Time: 40-45 minutes

1 1/2 cups flour, *divided*
1/2 tsp. salt
1 stick (1/2 cup) cold butter
　or margarine
2 Tbsp. evaporated milk
1/3-1/2 cup sugar, according
　to your taste preference
3 cups fresh raspberries, *or*
　2 pints frozen rasp-
　berries, thawed and
　drained

Topping:
1 cup sugar
2 Tbsp. flour
2 eggs, beaten
1 cup evaporated milk
1 tsp. vanilla

1. In a medium-sized bowl, combine 1 cup flour and salt. Cut in butter with pastry cutter until coarse crumbs form. Stir in evaporated milk.

2. Pat into a greased 9 x 13 baking pan.

3. Combine sugar and remaining flour (1/2 cup) and sprinkle over crust. Arrange raspberries over crust.

4. For topping, combine sugar and flour in a mixing bowl. Stir in eggs, evaporated milk, and vanilla. Pour gently over berries, being careful not to scatter them.

5. Bake at 375° for 40-45 minutes, or until lightly browned. Serve warm or chilled. Store any leftovers in refrigerator.

Variation: Substitute whipping cream for evaporated milk.

Note: This is great for breakfast, or served with ice cream for a dessert.

A Tip —

　Don't get hung up on exact measurements. Yes, they are important for some recipes, but most are very forgiving. I often guess, adding new flavors, herbs, and other seasonings. Remember, years ago people measured by pinch, teacup, and ladle, and they were good cooks!

Peach Cobbler Coffee Cake

Jean Butzer
Batavia, NY

Makes 15-20 servings

Prep Time: 20 minutes
Baking Time: 60-70 minutes
Cooling Time: 30 minutes

21-oz. can peach pie filling
16-oz. can sliced peaches, drained well
1 cup brown sugar
4 cups flour, *divided*
1/2 cup dry quick oats
3 sticks (1 1/2 cups) butter, softened and *divided*
1 cup sugar
1 1/4 cups sour cream
2 eggs, slightly beaten
1 Tbsp. vanilla
1 tsp. baking powder
1 tsp. baking soda
1/2 tsp. salt
1 cup confectioners sugar
1-2 Tbsp. milk

1. In a medium-sized mixing bowl, stir together pie filling and sliced peaches. Set aside.

2. In another mixing bowl, mix together brown sugar, 1 cup flour, and oats. Cut in 1 stick (1/2 cup) butter with a pastry cutter until mixture resembles coarse crumbs. Set aside to use as topping.

3. In a large electric mixer bowl, beat together 2 sticks (1 cup) butter and sugar until creamy. Add sour cream, eggs, and vanilla. Beat until well mixed.

4. Reduce speed to low and gradually add 3 cups flour, baking powder, baking soda, and salt. Beat until well mixed.

5. Spread half the batter into a greased 9 x 13 deep baking pan. Spoon peach filling evenly over batter. Drop spoonfuls of remaining batter over filling. (Do not spread.)

6. Sprinkle with topping. Bake at 350° for 60-70 minutes, or until toothpick comes out clean.

7. Cool 30 minutes. Meanwhile, stir together confectioners sugar and enough milk to make glaze. Drizzle over cooled coffee cake.

Tips:

1. You may use any fruit (pie filling and canned fruit) of your choice. Just be sure the sliced fruit is well drained.

2. Use a deep pan (at least 2 1/4") since this recipe fills it right to the top.

Apple Coffee Cake

Tabitha Schmidt
Baltic, OH

Makes 12-18 servings

Prep Time: 40 minutes
Baking Time: 35-40 minutes

2 cups sugar
2 eggs, beaten
3/4 cup oil
1 tsp. vanilla
2 1/2 cups flour
2 tsp. baking powder
1 tsp. baking soda
1 tsp. salt
1 tsp. cinnamon
4 cups apples, peeled and finely diced
1 1/2 cups chopped nuts, *optional*

Topping:
1/2 cup brown sugar
1/2 cup chopped nuts, *optional*
1/2 tsp. cinnamon
1/4 tsp. nutmeg

1. Combine sugar, beaten eggs, oil, and vanilla in a large mixing bowl. Mix until creamy.

2. In a separate bowl, combine flour, baking powder, baking soda, salt, and cinnamon. Add to sugar-egg mixture and mix well. Batter will be crumbly.

3. Fold in apples, and nuts, if desired. Pour into a greased and floured 9 x 13 baking pan.

4. In the mixing bowl, mix topping ingredients together well, and sprinkle over batter.

5. Bake at 350° for 35-40 minutes, or until tooth pick inserted into center comes out clean.

Tips:

1. Granny Smith, or other crisp, apples are especially good in this cake.

2. Skip peeling the apples, and save time and add fiber to your diet!

3. Chopped pecans are a tasty nut to use here.

Sticky Buns

Elaine Rineer, Lancaster, PA

Makes 12 servings

Prep Time: 20 minutes
Chilling Time:
  8 hours, or overnight
Baking Time: 35 minutes

1 stick (1/2 cup) butter,
  divided
1/2 cup brown sugar
1/2 cup corn syrup
1/4 cup + 2 Tbsp. sugar
2 Tbsp. cinnamon
2 loaves frozen bread
  dough, thawed

1. Melt half a stick (1/4 cup) of butter on stovetop or in microwave. Stir in brown sugar and corn syrup until well blended. Pour into a 9 x 13 baking pan.

2. Melt remaining half stick (1/4 cup) butter in microwave or on stovetop. Set aside.

3. In a small mixing bowl, combine sugar and cinnamon.

4. Break off golf-ball-sized pieces of bread dough, 12 per loaf. Dip each in melted butter and then roll in sugar-cinnamon mixture. Place coated balls in baking pan.

5. Cover and refrigerate for 8 hours, or overnight.

6. Remove from refrigerator and let stand for 30 minutes before baking.

7. Bake uncovered at 325° for 35 minutes. Turn out of pan immediately onto serving platter.

Variation: Add 1/2-3/4 cup chopped pecans to mixture in pan (Step 1).

Maple Twists

Marcella Heatwole
North Lawrence, OH

Makes 16-18 servings

Prep Time: 2 hours
Rising Time: 21/2-3 hours
Baking Time: 18-22 minutes

Dough:
3/4 cup milk
1/2 stick (1/4 cup) butter
23/4-3 cups flour, *divided*
3 Tbsp. sugar
1/2 tsp. salt
1 pkg. yeast
1 tsp. maple extract
1 egg
3/4 cup butter, melted and
  divided

Filling:
1/2 cup brown sugar
1/3 cup nuts
1 tsp. cinnamon
1 tsp. maple extract

Glaze:
2 Tbsp. butter, melted
1 Tbsp. milk
1/2 tsp. maple extract
1 cup confectioners sugar

1. In small pan, heat milk and butter until it just reaches the boiling point.

2. In large electric mixer bowl, blend warm liquid, 1 cup flour, 3 Tbsp. sugar,

salt, yeast, 1 tsp. maple extract, and egg at low speed until moistened. Beat 2 minutes at medium speed.

3. By hand, add remaining flour to form soft dough.

4. Place on floured surface and knead until smooth and elastic. Place dough in greased bowl. Cover and let rise until double, about 11/2-2 hours.

5. Grease 12" pizza pan. Divide dough into 3 balls. Roll out 1 ball of dough to cover pan. Brush with 1/4 cup melted butter.

6. Sprinkle with 1/3 of filling, made by combining brown sugar, nuts, cinnamon and 1 tsp. maple extract in a small bowl.

7. Repeat two more layers: rolled-out dough, melted butter, and filling. (Press last layer of filling down into dough to prevent it from falling off during Step 8.)

8. With scissors, mark 16 or 18 evenly spaced wedges in the circle. Cut from outside edge of circle into wedges. Carefully twist each wedge 5 times.

9. Lay twists on a jelly roll pan. Cover. Let rise for 45-60 minutes, or until almost double in size.

10. Bake at 375° for 18-22 minutes.

11. Cool to room temperature. Drizzle with glaze made by combining 2 Tbsp. butter, milk, 1/2 tsp. maple extract, and powdered sugar. Add 1 Tbsp. more milk if needed to make of pouring consistency.

Fresh Apple Pockets

Janet Groff
Stevens, PA

Makes 8 servings

Prep Time: 30-40 minutes
Resting/Rising Time:
  40 minutes
Baking Time: 20-25 minutes

Dough:
2-2½ cups flour, *divided*
1 pkg. (1 Tbsp.) fast-rising
  yeast
2 tsp. sugar
½ tsp. salt
⅔ cup water
½ cup oil

Filling:
2 cups thinly sliced apples
  (about 2 apples)
½ cup sugar
2 Tbsp. flour
½ tsp. cinnamon

Frosting:
1½ cups confectioners
  sugar
water, enough to make the
  frosting of drizzling
  consistency

1. In large bowl, combine 1 cup flour, undissolved yeast, sugar, and salt. Add very warm water (120 – 130°).
2. Stir in oil and enough additional flour to make a soft dough.
3. On floured surface, knead 4 minutes.
4. Cover and let rest 10 minutes.
5. Meanwhile, make filling in a mixing bowl by combining dry ingredients. Toss with apples. Set aside.
6. Divide dough in half. On lightly floured surface, roll each half into a 10" square. Cut each square into 4 squares.
7. Place ¼ cup filling onto center of each square. Bring corners up over filling, making a triangular-shaped "pocket." Pinch to seal.
8. Transfer to greased baking sheet. Let rise until double, about 30 minutes.
9. Bake at 350° until golden brown, about 20-25 minutes. Cool on wire rack.
10. Drizzle with frosting.

Apple Nut Ring

Naomi Cunningham
Arlington, KS

Makes 10 servings

Prep Time: 10 minutes
Baking Time: 25-30 minutes

2 7.5-oz. pkgs. refrigerated
  buttermilk biscuits
¼ cup butter *or*
  margarine, melted
⅔ cup sugar
2 Tbsp. ground cinnamon
3-4 medium-sized apples
⅓ cup nuts, chopped

1. Separate biscuits.
2. In a saucepan, melt the butter or margarine.
3. Combine sugar and cinnamon in a small bowl.
4. Dip biscuits in butter, and then roll in sugar mixture. Arrange biscuits, so that they overlap, around the edge and into the center of a greased 9 x 13 baking pan.
5. Peel, core, and slice the apples. Cut slices in half crosswise. Place an apple slice between each biscuit and around the outer edge of the baking dish.
6. Mix the nuts with any remaining sugar mixture. Sprinkle over top of biscuits and apples.
7. Bake at 400° for 25-30 minutes, or until biscuits are a deep golden brown.

Country Brunch

Esther J. Mast
Lancaster, PA
Barbara Yoder
Christiana, PA
Ruth Ann Gingrich
New Holland, PA
Lafaye Musser
Denver, PA

Makes 12-15 servings

Prep Time: 30 minutes
Chilling Time: 8 hours,
  or overnight
Baking Time: 45-60 minutes
Standing Time: 10-15 minutes

16 slices firm white bread
1³/4-2 lbs. (2¹/2 cups) cubed
  ham *or* browned
  sausage, drained
1 lb. (3 cups) shredded
  cheddar cheese
1 lb. (3 cups) shredded
  mozzarella cheese
8 eggs, beaten
3¹/2 cups milk
¹/2 tsp. dry mustard
¹/4 tsp. onion powder
¹/2 tsp. seasoning salt
1 Tbsp. parsley

Topping:
3 cups uncrushed
  cornflakes
¹/2 cup butter, melted

1. Trim crusts from bread
and cut slices in half.
2. Grease a 10 x 15 baking
dish.
3. Layer ingredients in this
order: cover bottom of pan
with half the bread, top with
half the ham, then half the
cheddar cheese, and then half
the mozzarella cheese.
4. Repeat layers once
more.
5. In large mixing bowl,
combine eggs, milk, dry mustard, onion powder, seasoning
salt, and parsley. Mix well
and pour over layers.
6. Cover and refrigerate
for 8 hours, or overnight.
7. Remove from refrigera-
tor 30 minutes before baking.
8. Combine cornflakes and
butter and sprinkle over
casserole.
9. Cover loosely with foil
to prevent over-browning.
Bake at 375° for 45 minutes.
10. Remove from oven and
let stand 10-15 minutes
before cutting into squares.

Overnight Breakfast Casserole

Hannah D. Burkholder
Bridgewater, VA
Esther S. Martin
Ephrata, PA

Makes 8-10 servings

Prep Time: 45 minutes
Chilling Time: 8 hours,
  or overnight
Baking Time: 1 hour

1 lb. fresh bulk sausage
4 cups cubed day-old
  bread
2 cups shredded sharp
  cheddar cheese
1 tsp. dry mustard
10 eggs, slightly beaten
4 cups milk
1 tsp. salt
freshly ground pepper to
  taste
¹/4 cup chopped or grated
  onion
¹/2 cup peeled, chopped
  tomatoes, *optional*
¹/2 cup diced green and red
  peppers, *optional*
¹/2 cup sliced fresh
  mushrooms, *optional*

1. Cook the sausage in a
skillet until browned. Drain
and break up the meat into
small pieces. Set aside.
2. Place bread in buttered
9 x 13 baking dish. Sprinkle
with cheese.
3. Combine the next 6
ingredients. Pour evenly over
the bread and cheese.
4. Sprinkle cooked sausage
and chopped tomatoes, peppers, and mushrooms over
the top.
5. Cover and chill in refrigerator for 8 hours, or overnight.
6. Preheat over to 325°.
Bake uncovered for 1 hour.
Tent with foil if top begins to
brown too quickly.

Breakfast Pizza

Jessica Hontz
Coatesville, PA

Makes 8 servings

Prep Time: 10 minutes
Baking Time: 20-25 minutes

10-oz. refrigerated pizza
   crust
8 eggs
1/4 cup milk *or* cream
6 slices bacon, cooked
   crisp and crumbled
2 cups shredded cheddar,
   or Monterey Jack,
   cheese

1. Unroll pizza crust onto baking sheet.
2. Bake at 425° for 10 minutes.
3. Whisk together eggs and milk in a large mixing bowl.
4. Cook in skillet until eggs start to congeal, about 3-4 minutes. Spoon onto crust.
5. Top with bacon and cheese.
6. Bake an additional 10 minutes until eggs are set and crust is golden brown.

A Tip —

Be sure to read a recipe the whole way through before beginning to cook, so you are certain you have all the ingredients you need.

Eggs California

Vonda Ebersole
Mt. Pleasant Mills, PA
Judy Gonzales
Fishers, IN
Esther Gingerich
Parnell, IA

Makes 10 servings

Prep Time: 20 minutes
Baking Time: 40-45 minutes

10 eggs
2 cups cottage cheese
1/2 cup flour
1 tsp. baking powder
1/2 tsp. salt
1/2 cup melted butter
1 lb. grated cheddar, Swiss,
   or Monterey Jack cheese
1 *or* 2 4-oz. cans chopped
   green chilies, depending
   upon your taste
   preference

1. In a mixing bowl, beat together eggs, cottage cheese, flour, baking powder, salt, and butter.
2. Stir in cheese and green chilies.
3. Pour into a greased 9 x 13 baking dish.
4. Bake at 350° for 40 to 45 minutes, or until set.

Tips:
   1. Garnish with chopped avocado, sour cream, or salsa.
   2. Add steamed and cut-up shrimp, fried and crumbled bacon, or fully cooked, cubed or chipped ham to Step 2.

Greek Eggs

Mrs. Rosanne Hankins
Stevensville, MD

Makes 4 servings

Prep Time: 15 minutes
Cooking Time: 20 minutes

2 garlic cloves, sliced
1/4 cup sliced white onion
1 Tbsp. oil
10-oz. pkg. frozen chopped
   spinach, thawed and
   squeezed as dry as
   possible
8 eggs, beaten, *or* 16 ozs.
   eggbeaters
1/2-1 tsp. dried oregano,
   according to your taste
   preference
4 ozs. feta cheese

1. In large skillet, saute garlic and onion in oil for 3-4 minutes.
2. Stir in spinach.
3. Pour eggs and oregano into hot skillet.
4. Cook, turning 2-3 times until eggs are lightly cooked, about 5 minutes.
5. Turn off heat, crumble cheese over top of spinach-egg mixture. Cover and let set for 2 minutes, or until cheese melts into eggs.

Variations:
   1. For added color and flavor, stir half a sweet red bell pepper, chopped, into Step 1.
   2. For additional flavor, add 1/4 tsp. black or white pepper and 1/8 tsp. salt in Step 3.

Mushroom Oven Omelet

Elaine Patton
West Middletown, PA

Makes 4 servings

Prep Time: 20 minutes
Baking Time: 20 minutes

1/2 lb. fresh mushrooms,
  cleaned and sliced
2 Tbsp. butter
2 Tbsp. flour
6 eggs
1/3 cup milk
1/8 tsp. pepper
1/4 cup chopped onions,
  optional
1/4 cup chopped green
  pepper, *optional*
1 1/2 cups shredded cheddar
  cheese, *divided*
1/2 cup real bacon bits

1. In a small skillet, saute mushrooms in butter until tender. Drain. Set aside.
2. In a bowl, combine flour, eggs, milk, and pepper until smooth. Add chopped vegetables if you wish.
3. Stir in 1 cup cheese, bacon, and mushrooms.
4. Pour into a greased 8"-square baking dish.
5. Baked uncovered at 375° for 18-20 minutes, or until eggs are completely set.
6. Sprinkle with remaining cheese, return to warm oven for 1 minute, and then serve.

Eggs ala Shrimp

Willard E. Roth
Elkhart, IN

Makes 6-8 servings

Prep Time: 10 minutes
Baking Time: 20 minutes

2 Tbsp. butter *or* oil
12 eggs
1/4 cup evaporated milk
1 onion, chopped fine
1/2 cup celery leaves
4 ozs. precooked shrimp
  (can be frozen)
3 Tbsp. white wine
4 ozs. frozen peas
seasoning to taste

1. Preheat electric skillet to 375° and melt butter in it.
2. While skillet is heating and butter is melting, toss eggs with milk in a mixing bowl. Set aside.
3. When butter is melted, saute onion and celery leaves in it.
4. Add shrimp and wine to skillet. Cover and cook for 2 minutes.
5. Pour egg-milk mixture into skillet and stir in frozen peas.
6. Turn the skillet down to 325°, and stir contents gently as they cook.
7. When eggs are set, but not hard, serve on warm platter.

I developed this recipe to share with my first formal cooking classmates at Patchwork Quilt Country Inn in 1976.

Breakfast Burritos

Arleta Petersheim
Haven, KS

Makes 6-8 servings

Prep Time: 35-40 minutes
Baking Time: 15 minutes

1/2 lb. bulk sausage
2 large potatoes, peeled
  and grated
1 green pepper, chopped
1/2 cup chopped onion
2 Tbsp. butter
8 eggs, beaten
1/2 tsp. salt
1/4 tsp. pepper
8" flour tortillas
2 cups shredded cheddar
  cheese
salsa, *optional*

1. Brown sausage in skillet over low heat. Drain all but 1 Tbsp. drippings and set sausage aside.
2. Cook potatoes, chopped pepper, and onions in skillet over medium heat, stirring occasionally.
3. When potatoes are soft, add butter, eggs, salt, and pepper. Continue cooking until eggs are set. Add sausage.
4. Divide meat/egg mixture onto individual tortillas and roll up. Place in lightly greased 9 x 13 pan. Cover tightly with foil.
5. Bake at 375° for 10 minutes. Sprinkle with cheese. Cover again and bake 5 more minutes.
6. Serve with salsa if you wish.

These burritos are a great main dish for brunch. I usually make them a day ahead and refrigerate them (covered) overnight so I can just pop them in the oven the next morning. They will need to bake 10 minutes longer if you put them in the oven cold.

Scrambled Egg Muffins

Julia Horst, Gordonville, PA
Mary Kay Nolt
Newmanstown, PA

Makes 12 servings

Prep Time: 20 minutes
Baking Time: 20-30 minutes

1/2 lb. bulk sausage
12 eggs
1/2 cup chopped onion
1/4 cup chopped green pepper
1/2 tsp. salt
1/4 tsp. pepper
1/4 tsp. garlic powder
1/2 cup shredded cheddar cheese

1. In a skillet, brown sausage. Drain.
2. In a bowl, beat the eggs.
3. Add onion, green pepper, salt, pepper, and garlic powder to the eggs and blend well. Stir in sausage.
4. Spoon by 1/3-cupfuls into greased muffin cups.
5. Bake at 350° for 20-30 minutes, or until knife inserted near centers comes out clean.

Bacon Quiche

John D. Allen
Rye, CO

Makes 6-8 servings

Prep Time: 25 minutes
Baking Time: 35 minutes

9" pie shell, unbaked
8 slices bacon
3 large eggs
3 large egg yolks
1 cup milk
1 cup heavy cream
1/2 tsp. salt
1/2 tsp. pepper
pinch of grated nutmeg
1/2 cup (4 ozs.) grated Gruyere cheese

1. Jag pie shell with fork over the bottom and along the sides. Bake at 400° for 10 minutes.
2. While shell is baking, fry bacon in skillet to crispy stage. Drain thoroughly and crumble coarsely.
3. In large mixing bowl, whisk together remaining ingredients, except cheese.
4. Spread cheese in bottom of warm pie shell.
5. Top with crumbled bacon.
6. Pour egg mixture to within 1/2 inch of top of crust.
7. Bake at 375° until lightly golden brown, about 32-35 minutes, and until knife blade comes out clean when inserted one inch from the edge. Cool on rack.
8. Serve warm or at room temperature.

Note: It is easier to place the crust on the oven rack and fill it there than to fill it and try to move it to the oven.

Asparagus Quiche

Moreen Weaver
Bath, NY

Makes 4-6 servings

Prep Time: 10-15 minutes
Baking Time: 40-50 minutes
Standing Time: 10 minutes

2-3 cups asparagus, cut in small pieces, depending upon how much you love asparagus
2 cups sharp cheddar cheese, shredded
1 cup mayonnaise
2 tsp. lemon juice
9" unbaked pie crust

1. In a mixing bowl, combine asparagus, cheese, mayonnaise, and lemon juice. Mix thoroughly.
2. Spoon into pie crust.
3. Bake at 350° for 40-50 minutes.
4. Let stand 10 minutes. Serve warm.

Add-What-You-Like Quiche

Rosaria Strachan
Fairfield, CT

Makes 8 servings

Prep Time: 10-15 minutes
Baking Time: 40-45 minutes
Standing Time: 10 minutes

2 cups (1/2 lb.) grated Swiss
   cheese
1/2 cup milk
1/2 cup mayonnaise
2 Tbsp. flour
1/4 cup minced onions
2 eggs
1 optional ingredient listed
   below
9" or 10" baked pie shell

1. Combine cheese, milk
mayonnaise, flour, onions, and
eggs, and one of the optional
ingredients, if you wish.
2. Pour into pie shell.
3. Bake at 350° for 40-45
minutes, or until well browned
and set in the middle. (Check
by inserting knife blade into
center. If it comes out clean,
the quiche is finished.)
4. Allow quiche to stand for
10 minutes before slicing and
serving.

*You may add 1 of the following
to Step 1, if you wish:*
4 ozs. crabmeat
4-oz. can fully cooked ham
   chunks
1 1/2 cups chopped fresh
   broccoli
6 strips bacon, cooked and
   crumbled

1 1/2-2 cups fresh spinach,
   chopped

Variations:
*1. Mix first 6 ingredients in a
blender.*
*2. Do not use a pie crust.
Instead place 3/4 cup all-purpose
baking mix, along with the first
6 ingredients, in a blender and
mix. Stir in optional ingredient if
you wish, and pour into greased
pie plate. Continue with Step 3.*

Baked Peach French Toast

Lynette Nisly
Lancaster, PA

Makes 6 servings

Prep Time: 20-30 minutes
Baking Time: 15-25 minutes

10-14 slices, 1"-thick French
   or Italian bread
tub of cream cheese,
   softened
15-oz. can peach slices,
   drained
1/2-3/4 cup chopped pecans,
   optional
3 eggs
1/4 cup milk
1/3 cup maple syrup
2 Tbsp. butter *or*
   margarine, melted
1 Tbsp. sugar
1 tsp. cinnamon
1 tsp. vanilla

1. Spread cream cheese on
both sides of bread slices.
2. Place bread in a greased

9 x 13 baking pan. Prick each
bread slice 3-4 times with a
fork.
3. Top bread with peach
slices and sprinkle chopped
pecans over peaches, if
desired.
4. In mixing bowl, beat
eggs, and then combine with
milk, maple syrup, butter,
sugar, cinnamon, and vanilla.
Whisk together. Pour egg mixture over bread.
5. Bake at 400° for 15-25
minutes, or until egg mixture
is set.
6. Serve with syrup, if you
wish.

*Tip: You can prepare this the
night before you want to serve
it. Cover and refrigerate it
overnight. If you put it in the
oven cold, be sure to uncover it
and bake it for 35 minutes, or
until brown, and until a knife
inserted in the center comes out
clean.*

Baked French Toast

Susan Wenger
Lebanon, PA
Nancy Funk
North Newton, KS

Makes 8 servings

Prep Time: 20 minutes
Chilling Time: 4 hours,
or overnight
Baking Time: 35-45 minutes

1 stick (1/2 cup) butter
1 cup brown sugar
2 tsp. molasses
8-10 slices sturdy white
   bread
peanut butter, *optional*
5-6 eggs
1 1/2-2 cups milk
1 tsp. cinnamon

1. In a saucepan, heat butter, brown sugar, and molasses together until sugar is dissolved and butter is melted. Stir occasionally to prevent sticking. When melted and blended together, pour into a 9 x 13 baking pan.

2. If you wish, spread peanut butter on one side of each slice of bread and then lay the bread on the syrup, peanut-butter side down. If you don't include peanut butter, simply lay the bread in a single layer on top of the syrup.

3. In a mixing bowl, mix eggs, milk, and cinnamon together, and then pour on top of bread.

4. Cover and refrigerate for at least 4 hours, or overnight.

5. Bake at 350° for 35-45 minutes, or until browned.

Variations:
Esther Nafziger, Bluffton, OH
1. Instead of 1 cup brown sugar and 2 tsp. molasses, use 1/2 cup brown sugar and 1/2 cup pure maple syrup.

2. Immediately after Step 1, sprinkle 1/2-1 cup coarsely chopped pecans over the syrup. (Drop the peanut butter in Step 2.)

3. Instead of milk, use half-and-half. And add 1 tsp. vanilla to Step 3.

Variations: After Step 1, add a layer of the following mixture, tossed lightly together: 3 tart apples, peeled, cored, and thinly sliced; 1/2 cup raisins; 2 tsp. cinnamon. Continue with Step 2, without the peanut butter.
— **Diann J. Dunham**
State College, PA

A Tip —

Often on a Saturday morning, I make a double or triple recipe of pancakes, then freeze the leftovers on a cookie sheet. After they are frozen, I put them in an airtight container. They make a quick, healthy breakfast on a school morning. You can heat them easily in the microwave or toaster oven.

Light Buttermilk Pancakes

Mary Lynn Miller
Reinholds, PA

Makes 4 servings

Prep Time: 10 minutes
Cooking Time: 10-15 minutes

1 cup flour
1 Tbsp. sugar
1 1/2 tsp. baking powder
1/2 tsp. salt
1/2 tsp. baking soda
1 Tbsp. oil
1 cup buttermilk*
1 egg, beaten

1. Combine dry ingredients in mixing bowl.

2. Combine oil, buttermilk, and egg in a separate bowl. Add to dry ingredients, stirring just until flour mixture is moistened.

3. Fry on griddle until bubbly on top. Flip and continue cooking until bottom is lightly browned.

If you don't have buttermilk, make your own by placing 1 Tbsp. lemon juice in a one-cup measure. Fill cup with milk. Mix well.
— **Linda E. Wilcox**
Blythewood, SC

Mom's Oatmeal Pancakes

Donna Treloar
Hartford City, IN

Makes about 24 pancakes

Prep Time: *15 minutes*
Cooking Time: *3-5 minutes*
per skillet- or griddle-full

1½ cups buttermilk
1 cup quick or regular
    oats, uncooked
¼ cup brown sugar
½ stick (¼ cup) butter,
    melted
2 eggs, slightly beaten
1 cup flour
1 tsp. baking soda
1 tsp. salt
⅓ cup applesauce
¼ tsp. cinnamon, *optional*

1. In a medium-sized mixing bowl, place oats in buttermilk and let stand for several minutes.
2. Stir in brown sugar.
3. In a separate bowl, add melted butter into eggs and then stir into oat mixture.
4. In the now-empty butter-egg bowl, mix together flour, baking soda, and salt. Add to oat mixture, stirring just until blended.
5. Gently stir in applesauce, and cinnamon if you wish.
6. Spoon batter onto lightly greased skillet or griddle. Cook until golden brown.
7. Top with butter and your favorite syrup.

Tip: Store leftover pancakes in a resealable plastic bag and refrigerate. When ready to serve, pop in the toaster.

Pumpkin Pancakes

Stacy Schmucker Stoltzfus
Enola, PA

Makes 4-6 servings

Prep Time: *5-10 minutes*
Cooking Time: *4 minutes*
per batch

2 heaping cups flour
3½ tsp. baking powder
1 tsp. cinnamon
1 tsp. nutmeg
3 eggs, beaten
1 cup sugar
1 cup milk
¾ cup oil
1 tsp. vanilla
1¼ cups canned pumpkin
1 cup coconut, *optional*

1. Whisk together flour, baking powder, cinnamon, and nutmeg in a small bowl.
2. In a large bowl, beat together eggs, sugar, milk, oil, vanilla, and pumpkin.
3. Add dry ingredients and coconut to pumpkin mixture, stirring just until moistened. A few lumps are okay.
4. Preheat oven to Warm (150-200°). Preheat large skillet or griddle pan over medium-high heat.
5. Pour desired amount of batter onto hot griddle and turn heat down to medium.

Cook until edges are dry and pancake is bubbly. Flip over and cook 1-2 minutes more.
6. Place pancake in warm oven* and continue making remaining pancakes. (*This keeps the pancakes warm, but will not dry them out, unless you forget they're there!)
7. Serve hot with maple syrup, vanilla yogurt, and/or toasted pecans.

Variations:
1. Use half whole wheat flour; half all-purpose flour.
2. Use ½ cup brown sugar; ½ cup granulated sugar.

Strawberry Pancakes

Becky Frey
Lebanon, PA

Makes 15 medium-sized pancakes, or 4-5 servings

Prep Time: *10-15 minutes*
Cooking Time: *10 minutes*

2 eggs
1 cup buttermilk
1 cup crushed
    strawberries*
¼ cup oil
1 tsp. almond extract
2 cups whole wheat
    (*or* white) flour
2 Tbsp. brown sugar
2 tsp. baking powder
1 tsp. baking soda

1. In large mixing bowl beat eggs until fluffy.

2. Stir buttermilk, strawberries, oil, and almond extract into eggs.

3. In a separate bowl, combine flour, brown sugar, baking powder, and baking soda. Add to wet ingredients. Beat together with whisk just until smooth.

4. Heat skillet or griddle until a few drops of water sizzle when sprinkled on top. Fry pancakes until bubbly on top. Flip and continue cooking until browned.

Strawberries can scorch, so keep checking to make sure they're not burning. Turn the heat lower if necessary.

You can use fresh or frozen berries. If frozen, thaw them and drain them well before mixing into batter.

Notes:

1. I have a tough time getting small pancakes to turn out nicely. I make one "plate-size" pancake at a time. It can easily be cut into wedges to serve to those with smaller appetites.

2. Top finished pancakes with vanilla yogurt and fruit sauce and serve for breakfast, brunch, a light lunch or supper, or as a dessert.

Chocolate Pancakes

Cassandra Ly
Carlisle, PA

Makes 30 pancakes

Prep Time: 5-7 minutes
Cooking Time: 5 minutes per batch

2 cups chocolate milk
2 eggs, slightly beaten
2 cups flour
1 tsp. baking soda
1 tsp. baking powder
1 Tbsp. sugar
2 Tbsp. butter *or* margarine, melted
mini M&Ms
syrup, *optional*
vanilla or plain yogurt, *optional*

1. Mix all ingredients together in a large mixing bowl, except M&Ms and optional ingredients.

2. Pour by 1/4-cupfuls onto a hot non-stick griddle to make pancakes 3 inches in diameter. Place a few mini M&Ms on each pancake.

3. Flip pancakes when bubbles formed on their tops begin to break. Remove pancakes from griddle when the bottoms are golden brown.

4. Serve with syrup or yogurt.

Apple Puff Pancake

Wilma Stoltzfus
Honey Brook, PA

Makes 8 servings

Prep Time: 20 minutes
Baking Time: 50 minutes

4 Tbsp. butter
2 large apples, peeled and thinly sliced
3 Tbsp. brown sugar
1 tsp. cinnamon
6 eggs
1 1/2 cups milk
1 cup flour
3 Tbsp. sugar
1 tsp. vanilla extract
1/2 tsp. salt
1/2 tsp. cinnamon
confectioners sugar
syrup, *optional*

1. Melt butter in a 9 x 13 pan. Arrange apples over butter. Mix brown sugar and cinnamon in small bowl and sprinkle over apples.

2. Bake at 375° about 10 minutes, or until apples soften.

3. Combine in blender, eggs, milk, flour, sugar, vanilla, salt, and cinnamon. Blend thoroughly and pour over apples.

4. Return to oven and bake 40 minutes.

5. Sprinkle with confectioners sugar and serve immediately. Serve with syrup if you like.

Fluffy Waffles and Cider Syrup

Jan McDowell
New Holland, PA
Phyllis Peachey Friesen
Harrisonburg, VA

Makes 12-14 waffles

Prep Time: 15 minutes
Cooking Time: 5-6 minutes
per waffle

Waffles:
2 cups flour
3 tsp. baking powder
1 Tbsp. sugar
1 tsp. salt
2 eggs, separated
1 2/3 cups milk
6 Tbsp. butter, melted

Syrup:
1 cup sugar
2 Tbsp. cornstarch
1/4 tsp. cinnamon
1/4 tsp. nutmeg
2 cups apple cider
2 Tbsp. lemon juice
1/2 cup butter

1. To make waffles, mix flour, baking powder, sugar, and salt together in a medium-sized bowl.

2. In a separate bowl, beat together egg yolks, milk, and melted butter. Add to dry ingredients and mix well.

3. In a third bowl, beat egg whites until stiff. Gently fold into above mixture.

4. Bake in waffle iron.

5. To make syrup, mix sugar, cornstarch, cinnamon, and nutmeg in saucepan.

6. Stir in cider and lemon juice.

7. Heat to boiling, stirring constantly. Boil 1 minute or until slightly thickened.

8. Blend in butter and serve warm.

My mother used to make these waffles for our Sunday night supper.

— Jan McDowell

Tip: Vanilla pudding, vanilla yogurt, and fresh or canned fruit are all good toppings for these waffles at any time of the day. Or cover them with chicken or sausage gravy and serve them for lunch or dinner.

— Phyllis Peachey Friesen

Oatmeal Breakfast Scones

Suzanne Nobrega
Duxbury, MA

Makes 6 servings

Prep Time: 15 minutes
Baking Time: 10-15 minutes

1 1/4 cups flour
1/4 cup sugar
2 tsp. baking powder
1/4 tsp. salt
6 Tbsp. cold butter
1 cup regular *or* quick dry oats
1/4 cup dried fruit, i.e. raisins, craisins, cherries, etc., *optional*
1 egg, lightly beaten
1/4-1/3 cup milk

1 egg beaten with 1 Tbsp. water
confectioners sugar

1. Sift flour, sugar, baking powder, and salt into large bowl. Stir well.

2. Divide cold butter into 1/4" cubes and mix into flour mixture with pastry blender or fingers until mixture becomes coarse crumbs.

3. Stir in the oats and the dried fruit, if you wish.

4. Beat together 1 egg and milk and add to dry ingredients, mixing until just moistened.

5. Turn dough onto lightly floured surface and knead 4-5 times into a ball.

6. Gently roll out to a 6-7 inch circle and cut into six pie shaped wedges.

7. Place slightly apart on parchment-lined cookie sheet. Brush tops with egg/water mixture. Sprinkle with confectioners sugar, if desired.

8. Bake at 400° for 10-15 minutes or until lightly browned.

9. Serve warm with raspberry, or your favorite, jam.

Tip: This can be used for breakfast, brunch, or an afternoon tea.

Baked Oatmeal

Lena Sheaffer
Port Matilda, PA
Susie Nissley
Millersburg, OH
Esther Nafziger
Bluffton, OH
Katie Stoltzfus
Leola, PA
Martha Hershey
Ronks, PA

Makes 4-6 servings

Prep Time: 10 minutes
Baking Time: 30 minutes

1/2 cup oil
1 cup honey *or* brown
 sugar
2 eggs
3 cups rolled *or* quick
 oatmeal, uncooked
2 tsp. baking powder
1 cup milk
1/2 tsp. cinnamon *or*
 nutmeg, *optional*
1 cup chopped nuts,
 raisins, apples, or other
 fruit*

1. Combine oil, honey or
brown sugar, and eggs in a
large mixing bowl.
2. Add dry oatmeal, baking
powder, and milk. Mix well.
3. Add nuts and/or fruit.
Mix well.
4. Pour into a greased 8"
square baking pan.
5. Bake at 350° for 30 minutes.
6. Serve hot, cold, or at
room temperature with milk.

**Add any or all of these: 1/2 cup
dried cherries, 1/2 cup dried
cranberries, 1/2 cup cut-up apricots.*

— **Annabelle Unternahrer**
Shipshewana, IN

*Variation: For a lower calorie
version, use only 1 egg and 1/2
cup sugar, use skim milk, and
use 1/2 cup applesauce instead
of 1/2 cup oil.*

— **Evie Hershey**
Atglen, PA

Peach Baked Oatmeal

Bertha Burkholder
Hillsville, VA

Makes 10 servings

Prep Time: 10 minutes
Baking Time: 35 minutes

1 cup oil
4 eggs
1 1/2 cups sugar
3 cups dry quick oats
4 tsp. baking powder
2 tsp. salt
2 tsp. vanilla
1 pint canned peaches,
 chopped (reserve liquid)
2 cups milk

1. In large mixing bowl,
combine oil, eggs, and sugar.
Add dry quick oats, baking
powder, salt, and vanilla.
2. Drain peaches, reserving
juice. Add water to peach
juice to make 2 cups.

3. Add chopped peaches,
peach juice, and milk to oatmeal mixture.
4. Pour into a greased
9 x 13 pan. Bake at 350° for
35 minutes. Serve warm with
milk.

Overnight Oatmeal

Barbara Forrester Landis
Lititz, PA

Makes 10-11 servings

Prep Time: 5 minutes
Baking Time: 6-7 hours

1 cup dry steel-cut oats
1 cup dried cranberries
1 cup chopped, dried
 apricots
3 cups water
1 1/2 cups milk

1. In a slow cooker, com-
bine all ingredients and set
on low.
2. Cover and cook for 6-7
hours.

Tips:
*1. Make this before you go
to bed, and it will be ready in
the morning.*
*2. Serve topped with vanilla
or plain yogurt.*
*3. Heat any leftovers in the
microwave before eating.*

29

Grits Casserole

Sue Williams
Gulfport, MS

Makes 6 servings

Prep Time: 15 minutes
Baking Time: 15-20 minutes

1 cup quick-cooking grits
4 cups water
1 tsp. salt
1 stick (1/4 lb.) butter
1/4 lb. sharp cheddar
   cheese, grated
2 eggs, beaten

1. Cook grits in boiling, salted, water for 5 minutes. Add butter and cheese. Stir until well mixed. Cool.
2. Add beaten eggs and mix thoroughly.
3. Pour mixture into a greased pan or casserole dish.
4. Bake at 400° for 15-20 minutes, or until lightly browned.
5. Serve hot.

A Tip —

Always ask for advice from older and more experienced cooks. They will be glad to share their knowledge!

New Guinea Granola

Kate Good
Lancaster, PA
Marian Good
Lancaster PA

Makes 8 cups

Prep Time: 10 minutes
Baking Time: 20 minutes

3 cups dry quick oats
3 cups dry regular oats
1/2 cup dry oat bran
1/2 cup dry powdered milk
2/3 cup honey
2/3 cup vegetable oil
1 tsp. vanilla
cinnamon
3/4 cup slivered almonds
1/2 cup sunflower seeds
3/4 cup craisins and/or
   raisins

1. Mix all ingredients, except cinnamon, nuts, seeds, and fruit, together in a large mixing bowl.
2. Place on a lightly greased cookie sheet. Sprinkle with cinnamon.
3. Bake at 325° for 20 minutes.
4. After the first 5 minutes of baking, stir in slivered almonds, sunflower seeds, craisins, and/or raisins, and continue baking.
5. Continue stirring every 5 minutes.
6. Cool, stirring every 10 minutes, breaking up granola into the size chunks you like.
7. When thoroughly cool, stir in an airtight container.

Peanut Butter and Banana Roll-Up

Clarice Williams
Fairbank, Iowa

Makes 4 servings

Prep Time: 5 minutes

1/4 cup applesauce
1/4 cup peanut butter
2 tsp. honey
4 8"-10" flour tortillas
2 firm medium-sized
   bananas

1. In small bowl, combine applesauce, peanut butter, and honey. Mix well.
2. Spread tortillas with mixture to within 1/4" of their edges.
3. Peel bananas. Cut each banana in half lengthwise. Place 1 banana half at edge of each tortilla. Roll up jelly-roll fashion.
4. Serve.

Breads

French Bread

Martha Ann Auker
Landisburg, PA
Joan Miller
Wayland, IA

Makes 3 loaves

Prep Time: 30 minutes
Standing/Rising Time:
60-75 minutes
Baking time: 20 minutes

2 pkgs. dry yeast
3/4 Tbsp. sugar
1/2 cup warm (120-130°)
   water
2 cups boiling water
2 Tbsp. shortening
2 Tbsp. sugar
2 tsp. salt
6-6 1/2 cups flour
1 egg white
1 tsp. sesame seeds

1. Dissolve 2 pkgs. yeast and 3/4 Tbsp. sugar in 1/2 cup warm water. Set aside.

2. In large mixing bowl, mix together boiling water, shortening, 2 Tbsp. sugar, and salt. Stir and let cool.

3. When cooled to room temperature, add yeast mixture. Add as much flour as you can by hand, mixing well. Let stand 10 minutes.

4. Place dough on floured surface and knead in remaining flour. Cover dough on floured surface and allow to stand for 10 minutes.

5. Knead again for 5 minutes, until dough becomes smooth and elastic. Repeat standing/kneading 3 more times.

6. After the final kneading, cut the dough into 3 pieces. Roll out each piece and then roll each one up into a long roll. Shape each into a long French-bread-shaped loaf. Place on 1 or 2 greased cookie sheets, with at least 4 inches between the loaves.

7. Cover and let rise 10-15 minutes. Cut diagonal marks 1/4" deep, spaced every 2 inches across the top of each loaf.

8. Brush tops with egg white and sprinkle with sesame seeds.

9. Bake at 400° for 20 minutes, or until lightly golden.

A Tip —

When making breads, be careful that the liquid you mix with the yeast is neither too cool, nor too hot. It must be lukewarm. Allow the dough to rise in a warm place where there are no drafts. Watch it double in size.

Sunflower Oatmeal Bread

Orpha Herr
Andover, NY

Makes 1 loaf

Preparation time: 30 minutes
Rising time: 2-3 hours
Baking time: 30 minutes

2¼ tsp. dry yeast
1 cup, plus 2 Tbsp., warm (120-130°) water
¼ cup honey
2 Tbsp. butter *or* margarine
1½ tsp. salt
½ cup dry quick-cooking oats
3 cups flour
2 Tbsp. dry milk powder
½ cup salted, roasted sunflower seeds

1. In small bowl, dissolve yeast in warm water. When thoroughly mixed, add honey.

2. In a large mixing bowl, combine remaining ingredients. Add yeast mixture and blend thoroughly.

3. Knead with bread hook for 8 minutes.

4. Put dough in greased bowl, turning once to grease both sides. Cover and let rise until double, about 1-1½ hours.

5. Punch down. Shape into loaf. Place in greased 9 x 5 bread pan. Cover and let rise until double, about 1-1½ hours.

6. Bake at 350° for 30 minutes, or until lightly browned.

7. After removing from oven let stand 5 minutes. Remove from pan and cool on cooling rack.

Barb's Multi-Grain Bread

Dawn Ranck
Lansdale, PA

Makes 2 loaves

Prep Time: 35 minutes
Rising/Resting time: 70 minutes
Baking time: 30-35 minutes

2-2½ cups flour, *divided*
2⅓-3 cups whole-grain wheat flour, *divided*
½ cup dry rolled oats
½ cup flaxseed
½ cup dry wheat bran
½ cup instant dry powdered milk
1 Tbsp. dry yeast
2½ cups water
¼ cup honey
2 tsp. salt
3 Tbsp. butter *or* margarine

1. In large electric mixer bowl, combine 1 cup flour, 1½ cups whole wheat flour, oats, flaxseed, wheat bran, dry milk, and yeast.

2. In a saucepan, heat together water, honey, salt, and butter until just warm (115-120°), stirring constantly to melt butter.

3. Add to dry mixture. Beat with electric mixer on low speed for 30 seconds, scraping sides of bowl constantly. Then beat 3 minutes on high speed.

4. By hand, stir in enough of remaining flours to make a moderately stiff dough.

5. Turn dough onto lightly floured surface. Knead until smooth (5-7 minutes), kneading in as much remaining flour as you can.

6. Place dough in large greased bowl. Turn once to grease surface of dough. Cover and let rise until double, about an hour.

7. Punch down. Divide dough in half. Cover and let rest 10 minutes.

8. Shape each portion into a loaf. Place in 2 greased 9 x 5 loaf pans.

9. Bake at 400° for 30-35 minutes.

10. Remove from pans. Cool on wire racks.

Whole Wheat Walnut Bread

Kathy Hertzler
Lancaster, PA

Makes 3 loaves

Prep Time: 20-30 minutes
Rising and Standing Time:
1 hour and 50 minutes
Baking Time: 40-45 minutes

3 cups warm (120-130°)
   water
2 scant Tbsp. dry yeast
3/4 cup honey
1/2 stick (1/4 cup) butter,
   melted
4 cups whole wheat flour,
   stone-ground if possible
5-6 cups bread flour,
   divided
1 1/4 tsp. salt
2 cups walnuts, coarsely
   chopped
1 Tbsp. butter, melted

1. Place 3 cups warm water in large electric mixer bowl. Whisk in yeast by hand. Let stand 5 minutes.
2. Add honey and melted butter.
3. Add whole wheat flour and one cup bread flour. Mix with dough hook.
4. Stir in salt and walnuts. Mix well.
5. Add remaining flour. Mix with dough hook for 5 minutes.
6. Place dough on lightly floured surface. Knead for a few strokes by hand, adding a few tablespoons of flour if dough is very sticky.
7. Place dough in greased bowl. Rotate dough to grease it all over. Cover bowl and let dough rise for about 60 minutes, or until double.
8. Cut dough in thirds. Form into loaves. Place in greased 8 x 5 loaf pans.
9. Allow to rise until the dough just reaches the top of the pans, about 45 minutes.
10. Bake at 350° for 40-45 minutes, or until crusty and golden brown.
11. Remove loaves from oven and brush tops with butter.

Note: Using a dough hook cuts the kneading time in half. You can also knead the bread by hand for 8-10 minutes.

Variation: Substitute maple syrup for the honey, and pecans for the walnuts.

A Tip —

Check the bread recipe carefully before you begin preparing it to be sure that you have enough yeast. The small store-bought packets of yeast hold only 1-2 tsp., and recipes often call for 1 Tbsp. of yeast. You may find it useful to buy yeast in bulk and keep it in the freezer.

Homemade White Bread

Cathy Farren
Bridgewater, VA

Makes 5 loaves

Prep Time: 30 minutes
Rising and Standing Time:
3-4 1/2 hours
Baking Time: 45 minutes

2 Tbsp. yeast
5 cups lukewarm water
12 cups flour, *divided*
3/4 cup sugar
2 Tbsp. salt
3 Tbsp. shortening

1. Dissolve yeast in water in a large mixing bowl.
2. Add 3 cups flour. Mix to make a soft dough.
3. Add sugar, salt, and shortening. Mix well.
4. Stir in remaining flour. Knead dough until smooth and elastic.
5. Place in greased bowl. Let rise until double in size, about 1-1 1/2 hours.
6. Knead well and let rise again until double in size, about 1-1 1/2 hours.
7. Form into 5 loaves. Place in greased 8 x 5 or 9 x 5 loaf pans. Let rise until double in size, about 1-1 1/2 hours.
8. Bake at 325° for 45 minutes.

Arle's Anadama Bread

Diane Ralston
Port Angeles, WA

Makes 1 loaf

Preparation Time: 15 minutes
Rising Time: 2¹/₂ hours
Baking Time: 40-45 minutes

1¹/₂ cups water
1 tsp. salt
¹/₃ cup yellow cornmeal
¹/₃ cup molasses
1¹/₂ Tbsp. shortening
1 cake compressed yeast
¹/₄ cup lukewarm water
4-4¹/₂ cups sifted flour
1 Tbsp. melted butter
cornmeal

1. In saucepan, bring 1¹/₂ cups water and salt to a boil.
2. Stir in cornmeal and bring to a boil again. Immediately remove from heat and pour into a large bowl.
3. Stir in molasses and shortening. Cool to lukewarm.
4. Crumble yeast and add to ¹/₄ cup lukewarm water. Mix well, and then add to cornmeal mixture.
5. Add 4 cups flour and mix well.
6. Place dough on a floured surface and knead until smooth, adding up to ¹/₂ cup more flour.
7. Place in large greased bowl, cover, and and let rise until double (about 1¹/₂ hours).
8. Punch down, shape into a loaf, and put into a greased 9 x 5 loaf pan.
9. Let rise until double (about 1 hour).
10. Brush with melted butter and sprinkle with a little cornmeal before baking.
11. Bake at 375° for 40-45 minutes.

Bread Machine Challah

Sheila Raim
Oxford, IA

Makes 1 large or 2 small loaves

Preparation Time: 10 minutes,
plus 1¹/₂ hours knead cycle
Rising Time: 1-1¹/₂ hours
Baking Time: 20 minutes for
loaves; 45 minutes for the
braid

1¹/₄ cups water
¹/₄ cup oil
¹/₄ cup honey
1¹/₂ tsp. salt
2¹/₂ cups whole wheat flour
2 cups flour
1¹/₂ Tbsp. quick-rising dry yeast
1 Tbsp. gluten
1 egg white, *for braid only*
2 Tbsp. sesame seeds, *for braid only*

1. Measure ingredients into bread pan in order listed. Use dough setting. Adjust flour as needed so dough cleans the side of the pan as it kneads.
2. At the end of the dough cycle, form dough into two loaves. Place in lightly greased 9 x 5 loaf pans and cover. Let rise until double, about 1-1¹/₂ hours.
3. Bake for 20 minutes at 350°, or until golden brown.

Variation: To form the dough into braids, break off half of dough after the dough cycle ends and form into 3 8"-long ropes. Braid and seal ends.

Divide the rest of the dough into 3 equal parts. Form into 14"-long ropes and braid, sealing ends.

Place long braid on lightly greased baking sheet. Lay short braid on top of long braid. Press down gently to make braids adhere to each other.

Cover, and let rise until double, about 1-1¹/₂ hours.

Brush with egg white and sprinkle with sesame seeds before baking. Bake at 325° for 45 minutes.

A Tip —

Keep nuts, coconut, and whole wheat flour in airtight containers in the freezer in order to retain their freshness and flavor.

Italian Bread

Tabitha Schmidt
Baltic, OH

Makes 6 servings

Prep Time: 25 minutes
Rising Time: 20 minutes
Baking Time: 15 minutes

2¹/₂ cups flour
1 tsp. salt
1 tsp. sugar
1 Tbsp. dry yeast
1 cup warm (120-130°)
   water
1 Tbsp. oil

Topping:
¹/₄-¹/₃ cup Italian salad
   dressing
¹/₄ tsp. salt
¹/₄ tsp. garlic powder
¹/₄ tsp. dried oregano
¹/₄ tsp. dried thyme,
   optional
dash of pepper
1 Tbsp. grated Parmesan
   cheese
¹/₂ cup grated mozzarella
   cheese

1. In a large mixing bowl, combine flour, salt, sugar, and yeast.
2. In a separate bowl, mix water and oil together. Add to flour mixture.
3. Stir well. Add more flour, if needed, to form soft dough.
4. Place dough on lightly floured surface, and knead for 1-2 minutes, or until smooth. Place in a greased bowl. Cover and let rise for 20 minutes.
5. Knead dough down. Then place on a 12" pizza pan. Roll or pat into a 12" circle.
6. Brush with salad dressing.
7. Combine seasonings and sprinkle over top. Sprinkle with cheeses.
8. Bake at 450° for 15 minutes, or until golden brown.
9. Cover with foil tent to prevent over-browning if necessary.
10. Cut into narrow wedges and serve warm.

Buttery Soft Pretzels

Mary Sommerfeld
Lancaster, PA

Makes 12 pretzels

Preparation Time: 20 minutes
Standing and Rising Time:
   70 minutes
Baking Time: 8 minutes

4 tsp. dry yeast
1 tsp., plus ¹/₂ cup, sugar,
   divided
1¹/₄ cups warm (110°)
   water
5 cups flour
1¹/₂ tsp. salt
1 Tbsp. vegetable oil
¹/₂ cup baking soda
4 cups hot water
salt

1. Dissolve yeast and 1 tsp. sugar in warm water. Let stand 10 minutes.
2. In large mixing bowl, mix flour, ¹/₂ cup sugar, and salt. Make a well in the center.
3. Add yeast mixture and oil to dry ingredients. Mix well. If dry, add several tablespoons water.
4. Knead dough 7-8 minutes, until elastic. Place in oiled bowl and cover. Let rise in a warm, draft-free place until double, about 1 hour.
5. Preheat oven to 450°.
6. Dissolve baking soda in hot water in large bowl.
7. Divide dough into 12 pieces. Roll each into a long, thin rope—about 20" long—on an unfloured surface. Shape each into a pretzel.
8. Dip in soda-water solution and place on greased baking sheet. Sprinkle with salt.
9. Bake 8 minutes until browned. Brush with butter.

Cheese-Filled Ring

Gwendolyn Chapman
Gwinn, MI

Makes 12-14 slices

Prep Time: 30-40 minutes
Rising Time: 60-70 minutes
Baking Time: 30-35 minutes

16-oz. pkg. hot roll mix
3/4 cup warm
(120-130°) water
1 tsp. dried oregano
1 tsp. dried basil
1 large egg, slightly beaten
1 cup coarsely shredded
sharp cheddar cheese
4 Tbsp. grated Parmesan
cheese, *divided*
2 tsp. parsley flakes
1/8 tsp. paprika
1 egg yolk, beaten
2 tsp. milk *or* cream

1. In a mixing bowl, dissolve yeast from hot roll mix in 3/4 cup warm water.

2. Add herbs, whole egg, and flour mixture (from hot roll mix).

3. Turn onto slightly floured board and knead until smooth.

4. Place dough back in cleaned and slightly greased mixing bowl. Cover and let rise 30 minutes.

5. Turn onto floured board and knead again until smooth.

6. Roll into 10 x 15 rectangle.

7. Sprinkle with cheddar cheese, 2 Tbsp. Parmesan cheese, parsley flakes, and paprika.

8. Starting along the 15" side, roll the dough tightly to form a log.

9. Place on a greased baking sheet, seam down. Shape into a 7"-diameter ring, pinching ends securely together.

10. Cut 1/2"-deep slashes at 2" intervals along the top of the roll.

11. Cover and let rise 30-40 minutes.

12. In a small mixing bowl, combine egg yolk and milk or cream. Brush over dough ring.

13. Sprinkle with 2 Tbsp. Parmesan cheese.

14. Bake at 350° for 30-35 minutes. (Tent with foil if the top begins to get too brown before end of baking time.)

15. Remove from oven and cool slightly before slicing and serving.

Tomato Bread

Betty Hostetler
Allensville, PA

Makes 2 loaves

Prep Time: 35-40 minutes
Rising Time: 70-100 minutes
Baking Time: 20-25 minutes

2 cups tomato juice
2 Tbsp. butter
3 Tbsp. sugar
1 tsp. salt
1/2 tsp. dried basil
1/2 tsp. dried oregano
1/4 cup ketchup
1/4 cup grated cheese
1 pkg. dry granulated yeast
1/4 cup warm water (110-115°)
7 cups bread flour, sifted

1. In saucepan, heat tomato juice and butter together until butter is melted.

2. Stir in sugar, salt, herbs, ketchup, and cheese. Cool to lukewarm.

3. In a large electric mixer bowl, sprinkle yeast on warm water. Stir to dissolve.

4. Add tomato mixture and 3 cups flour to yeast. Beat at medium speed for 2 minutes or until smooth.

5. Gradually add enough remaining flour to make soft dough that leaves the sides of the bowl.

6. Turn onto slightly floured board. Knead for 8-10 minutes, until elastic and smooth.

7. Place in lightly greased bowl, turning once. Cover and let rise in warm place until double, about 1-1 1/2 hours.

8. Punch down. Divide in half. Cover and let rest 10 minutes.

9. Shape into loaves. Place in greased loaf pans. Cover and let rise until doubled, about 1 hour.

10. Bake at 375° for 15 minutes. Cover with foil and bake an additional 10 minutes.

60-Minute Dinner Rolls

Dolores Horst
Hinton, VA

Makes 2 dozen rolls

Prep Time: 12-15 minutes
Rising Time: 30-35 minutes
Baking Time: 20 minutes

2 pkgs. dry yeast
¼ cup sugar
1½ cups warm (120-130°) milk
1 tsp. salt
¼ cup butter, melted
4 cups flour

1. In a large mixing bowl, add yeast and sugar to warm milk. Stir to dissolve. Let stand 15 minutes.

2. Stir in remaining ingredients. Mix well.

3. Cover and let stand in warm place for 15-20 minutes, or until double in size.

4. Form 24 rolls, each the size of an egg. Place on greased cookie sheets.

5. Bake at 375° for 20 minutes.

Easy Nut Bread

Betty B. Dennison
Grove City, PA

Makes 18 servings

Prep Time: 45 minutes
Rising Time: 5-10 hours
Baking Time: 25-30 minutes

2 pkgs. dry yeast
1 cup milk, warmed to 120-130°
1¾ cups sugar, *divided*
½ tsp. salt
4 eggs, separated
1 cup shortening, melted
4 cups flour
4 cups ground nuts, any kind
maple *or* walnut flavoring
1 egg, beaten

1. In small mixing bowl, stir yeast into warm milk until dissolved.

2. Add ¾ cup sugar and salt to yeast mixture. Let cool.

3. In a large bowl, beat egg yolks (reserve whites). Add melted shortening, cooled yeast mixture, and 2 cups flour. Stir until well blended.

4. Place dough on floured surface and knead in as much of the remaining flour as needed to make a soft dough. Cover and place in refrigerator at least 3 hours, or overnight.

5. Meanwhile, beat the egg whites until stiff. Set aside.

6. Make the filling in a large bowl by mixing together ground nuts, 1 cup sugar, stiffly beaten egg whites, and flavoring.

7. When dough is thoroughly chilled, divide into 3 balls. Roll out one at a time into circles, each about 12" in diameter.

8. Spread each circle with ⅓ of the filling, then roll each into a long loaf.

9. Place all 3 loaves on 1 or 2 slightly greased cookie sheets. Let stand for 2 hours in a warm place.

10. Brush tops with 1 egg beaten well.

11. Bake at 350° for 25-30 minutes.

12. When cooled, slice and serve.

A Tip —

When baking bread, always stir in less flour than called for. Then as you knead the dough, you can knead in the flour you haven't yet used. The temperature and humidity will affect the amount of flour you use. When I first made bread I stirred in the whole stated amount, and my loaves were like bricks . . . hard enough to dent the floor if dropped! You will learn by "feel."

Refrigerator Butterhorns

Becky Frey, Lebanon, PA

Makes 36-48 rolls

Prep Time: 15-20 minutes
Rising Time: 7-9 hours
Baking Time: 10-12 minutes

1 Tbsp., *or* 1 pkg., **fast-rise, dry yeast**
1/2 **cup sugar**
1 **tsp. salt**
6 **cups flour**
3/4 **cup butter** *or* **margarine, cut in pieces, at room temperature**
2 **cups warm (120-130°) milk**
1 **egg, beaten**
2 **Tbsp. water**

1. In a large mixing bowl, combine yeast, sugar, salt, and flour.
2. In a separate bowl, add butter to warm milk. Stir until butter melts. Beat in egg and water.
3. Pour liquid into flour mixture. Mix well, but do not knead. Dough will be sticky.
4. Cover with well-greased waxed paper. Refrigerate 4-5 hours.
5. Divide dough into three parts. Roll each into a 9"-10" circle on a lightly floured counter.
6. Cut each circle into 12-16 wedges. Roll each wedge up, beginning with the point and rolling toward the wide end, as you would to make a butterhorn. Place on greased cookie sheets, about 2 inches apart from each other.
7. Cover with waxed paper. Let rise 3-4 hours, or until double in size.
8. Bake at 375° for 10-12 minutes, or until golden brown.

Variations:

1. For whole wheat rolls: Replace flour with whole wheat flour. Add 1 Tbsp. wheat gluten to dry ingredients (in Step 1). Add 1 Tbsp. liquid soy lecithin to wet ingredients (in Step 2).

2. For part-whole wheat rolls: Use 3 cups white flour and 3 cups whole wheat flour.

Note: You do not have to refrigerate the dough. I'm usually in a hurry for them. Just let the dough rise until double. Roll out and shape. Let rise again until double and bake. The rising times are much shorter when the dough is warm.

Oatmeal Dinner Rolls

Martha Bender, New Paris, IN

Makes 18-20 rolls

Prep Time: 30-35 minutes
Rising and Resting Time: about 2 hours
Baking Time: 20-25 minutes

2 **cups water**
1 **cup dry quick oats**
3 **Tbsp. butter** *or* **margarine**
1 **pkg. dry yeast**
1/3 **cup warm (120-130°) water**
1/3 **cup packed brown sugar**
1 **Tbsp. sugar**
1 **tsp. salt**
43/4-51/4 **cups flour**

1. In a saucepan bring 2 cups water to boil. Add oats and butter. Cook and stir 1 minute. Remove from heat. Cool to lukewarm.
2. In a large mixing bowl, dissolve yeast in 1/3 cup warm water. Add cooled oats mixture, sugars, salt, and 4 cups flour. Beat until smooth. Add enough remaining flour to form a soft dough.
3. Turn onto floured board and knead 6-8 minutes, kneading in more flour, until smooth and elastic.
4. Place in greased bowl, turning once to grease top. Cover and let rise in warm place until doubled, about 1 hour.
5. Punch down. Allow to rest 10 minutes.
6. Shape into 18 balls. Place in greased 9" round baking pan. Cover. Let rise until double, about 45 minutes.
7. Bake at 350° for 20-25 minutes until golden brown. Remove from pan to wire racks to cool.

Whole Wheat Cottage Cheese Rolls

Janelle Myers-Benner
Harrisonburg, VA

Makes 2 dozen rolls

Prep Time: 20-30 minutes
Rising Time: 2-3 hours
Baking Time: 12-15 minutes

3 1/2–4 cups whole wheat
   flour, *divided*
2 Tbsp. dry yeast
1/2 tsp. baking soda
1 1/2 cups cottage cheese
1/2 cup water
1/4 cup brown sugar
2 Tbsp. oil
2 tsp. salt
2 eggs

1. In large electric mixer bowl, stir together 2 cups whole wheat flour, yeast, and baking soda.

2. In a saucepan, heat together cottage cheese, water, sugar, oil, and salt until very warm (130°).

3. Add wet ingredients to dry mixture, along with eggs.

4. Beat vigorously for 3-4 minutes with electric mixer—1/2 minute on low, and 3 minutes on high.

5. Stir in enough remaining flour to make a stiff dough. Knead dough on lightly floured surface for 8-10 minutes.

6. Place in a greased bowl turning once to grease all sides.

7. Cover and let rise until double (1-1 1/2 hours).

8. Shape into 24 rolls. Place in lightly greased muffin tins, or on a lightly greased cookie sheet.

9. Let rise until nearly double (1-1 1/2 hours).

10. Bake at 350° for 12-15 minutes.

Tips:

1. This recipe is a great way to use up cottage cheese that may have soured. It won't hurt the rolls!

2. This recipe works well with Bronze Chef flour, a high protein flavorful flour.

3. Try a different presentation and form each roll by first making 3 small balls. Put all 3 into one muffin tin and you'll have a 3-leaf clover roll.

Bread Machine All-Bran Rolls

Sheila Raim
Oxford, IA

Makes 16 servings

Preparation Time: 10 minutes,
   plus 1 1/2 hour dough cycle
Rising Time: 1 hour
Baking Time: 15 minutes

1 cup warm (120-130°)
   water
1/2 cup dry All-Bran cereal
1/4 cup oil
1/4 cup honey
3/4 tsp. salt
1 egg

1 1/2 cups whole wheat
   flour
2-2 1/4 cups unbleached
   flour
2 tsp. dry fast-rising yeast
1 Tbsp. wheat gluten
3 Tbsp. butter, melted

1. Add all ingredients except 3 Tbsp. butter to bread pan in order listed. Allow All-Bran to soak in the water until it is soft before beginning the dough cycle.

2. Adjust the amount of flour as needed so that the dough cleans the sides of the bread pan as it kneads. Use the dough setting on the bread machine.

3. At the end of the cycle, divide the dough in half. Roll out each half into a 10" circle.

4. Spread the circles with a thin coat of melted butter. Then cut each circle into 8 pie-shaped wedges.

5. Roll up each wedge, starting from the wide edge.

6. Place wedges on baking sheets, about 2 inches apart, and let rise until double, about an hour.

7. Bake at 350° for 15 minutes, or until golden brown.

Bread Sticks

Janice Burkholder, Richfield, PA

Makes 6 servings

Prep Time: 15 minutes
Rising Time: 1-1½ hours
Baking Time: 10-15 minutes

1½ cups warm (120-130°)
    water
1 Tbsp. dry yeast
1 Tbsp. oil
1 Tbsp. salt
1 Tbsp. sugar
3 cups whole wheat flour
1 cup flour
¼ cup butter, melted
3 Tbsp. vegetable *or*
    olive oil
3 Tbsp. Parmesan cheese
1 tsp. garlic powder
2 Tbsp. dried parsley
1 tsp. dried oregano

1. In large mixing bowl, dissolve yeast in warm water.
2. Add oil, salt, and sugar.
3. In separate bowl mix flours together.
4. Stir flour into wet ingredients until dough becomes stiff.
5. Place dough on lightly floured surface and knead in flour, if some remains, for several minutes until smooth and elastic.
6. Place dough in greased bowl. Turn dough to grease all over, and then cover. Allow to rise until double in size, about 1-1½ hours.
7. On a flat, lightly floured surface, roll dough out into a 15" square.

8. Cut in half with a pizza cutter, and then cut each half into 1" strips. Lay strips on a lightly greased cookie sheet.
9. In a small bowl, combine butter, oil, Parmesan cheese, garlic powder, parsley, and oregano. Brush strips of dough with the mixture.
10. Bake at 400° for 10-15 minutes or until golden brown.
11. Serve with cheese dip or warm pizza sauce.

Butter-Dipped Bread Sticks

Lori Newswanger
Lancaster, PA

Makes 32 sticks

Prep Time: 15-20 minutes
Baking Time: 12-15 minutes

⅓ cup butter *or* margarine
2½ cups flour
1 Tbsp. sugar
3½ tsp. baking powder
1½ tsp. salt
½-1 cup grated cheese
1 cup milk

**Toppings: sesame seeds,
    garlic powder, celery
    seed, your favorite herbs**

1. In a saucepan, or in the microwave, melt butter. Set aside.
2. In a mixing bowl, combine flour, sugar, baking powder, salt, and cheese.

3. Add milk and stir slowly with a fork. When dough clings together, turn onto a well-floured board. Roll dough to coat with flour. Knead gently 10 times.
4. Roll dough into a 12 x 8 rectangle, ½" thick. Cut dough in half to form 2 12 x 4 rectangles. Cut each rectangle into 16 ¾"-wide strips.
5. Dip strips in melted butter. Lay in rows in lightly greased 9 x 13 baking pan. Sprinkle with your choice of toppings.
6. Bake at 450° for 12-15 minutes. Serve immediately.

Weinerbrod (Danish Pastry)

Phyllis E. Wykes
Plano, IL

Makes 24 servings

Preparation Time: 30 minutes
Standing and Rising Time:
    3 hours and 10 minutes
Baking Time: 10 minutes

1 pkg. dry yeast
¼ cup warm (120-130°)
    water
1 cup cold milk
1 egg
10 cardamom seeds
1½ Tbsp. sugar
½ tsp. salt
3 cups flour
2 sticks (1 cup) butter, at
    room temperature
½ stick (4 Tbsp.) butter,
    melted

1 egg white
2 cups confectioners sugar

1. In a small bowl, sprinkle yeast over warm water and let stand 10 minutes.

2. In a large mixing bowl, combine milk, egg, cardamom seeds, sugar, and salt. Mix well. Stir in yeast-water and blend well.

3. Stir in the flour until a dough forms that is stiff enough to knead.

4. Place the dough on a floured surface and roll into a 12" square. Place 2 sticks of butter in the center of the square and fold the sides and ends over the center. Roll out and fold in this manner 6 times.

5. Place in the refrigerator for at least 2 hours. Remove from fridge 2 hours before ready to bake.

6. Roll out lightly into a 15 x 6 rectangle.

7. Cut dough into 24 strips. Make each into a twist or figure-eight. Place on 2 greased baking sheets and let rise for an hour in a warm room.

8. Brush with melted butter and bake at 400° for 10 minutes.

9. Meanwhile, make a thick frosting of 1 egg white and 2 cups confectioners sugar. When well mixed, brush over the pastries while still hot. (Thin frosting with a bit of water if it is too stiff to brush.)

Holiday Almond Ring

Christina Ricker
Gordonville, PA

Makes 12 servings

Prep Time: 30 minutes
Rising Time: 3½ hours
Baking Time: 25-30 minutes

2 pkgs. yeast
2 cups scalded milk
½ cup sugar
2 tsp. salt
2 eggs, well beaten
7–7½ cups flour, *divided*
½ cup melted shortening

Filling:
1½ cups brown sugar
1½ cups flour
1½ sticks (12 Tbsp.) butter, cold
1½ tsp. almond extract

Icing:
1½-2 cups confectioners sugar
2-3 Tbsp. warm milk

1. In a large mixing bowl, add yeast to cooled (lukewarm) scalded milk. Add sugar and salt. Stir until dissolved.

2. Stir in beaten eggs and 3½ cups flour. Beat until smooth.

3. Beat in cooled, melted shortening. Add remaining flour and stir until you've blended it as well as you can.

4. Turn dough out onto floured surface. Cover with bowl and let rest for 10 minutes.

5. Knead dough until smooth and elastic.

6. Place in large greased bowl, cover with towel, and let rise for 2 hours.

7. Punch down, cover, and let rise again for 45 minutes.

8. While dough is rising, make filling. In mixing bowl, mix sugar and flour together. Cut in butter with pastry cutter until mixture becomes crumbly. Gently stir in almond extract. Set aside.

9. After dough has risen for 45 minutes, punch it down again, shape it into a ball, and then divide it into 3 equal parts.

10. On lightly floured surface, roll each piece into a large circle and spread with ⅓ of the filling. Roll up into a long roll.

11. Place each in a pie pan, forming a ring. Seal the ends together by using a few drops of water. Repeat for each ring.

12. Let rise for 35 minutes. Bake at 350° for 35 minutes.

13. While rings are baking, mix together icing ingredients in a small bowl until of spreading consistency.

14. Remove baked rings from oven and, while they are still warm, drizzle with icing.

Tip: *This takes time, but it's worth it!*

Cheesy Flat Bread

Clarice Williams
Fairbank, IA

Makes 8 servings

Thawing Time: 8 hours,
* or overnight*
Prep Time: 10 minutes
Rising Time: 30 minutes
Baking Time: 20-25 minutes

1 loaf frozen bread dough
3 Tbsp. butter, softened
2-3 tsp. paprika
1/2 tsp. dried oregano
1/2 tsp. dried basil
1/2 tsp. garlic powder
1 cup shredded mozzarella
  cheese

1. Allow frozen dough to thaw in the fridge for 8 hours, or overnight.

2. Pat thawed bread dough onto bottom and up the sides of a greased 14″ pizza pan or 15″ baking pan, forming a crust.

3. Spread with butter and sprinkle with herbs.

4. Prick the crust; then sprinkle with cheese.

5. Cover and let rise in warm place for 30 minutes.

6. Bake at 375° for 20-25 minutes, or until golden.

7. Top with your favorite pizza sauce and toppings, and bake until heated through. Or serve as is for dipping into soup or spaghetti sauce.

Monkey Bread

Sheila Heil
Lancaster, PA

Makes 12 servings

Prep Time: 20 minutes
Baking Time: 30 minutes
Cooling Time: 10 minutes

1/2 cup sugar
1 tsp. cinnamon
3 7.5-oz.-cans refrigerated
  buttermilk biscuits
1 cup brown sugar
3/4 cup butter *or*
  margarine, melted

1. Heat oven to 350°. Lightly grease a 12-cup fluted tube, or bundt, pan.

2. Mix sugar and cinnamon together in plastic bag.

3. Separate dough into 30 biscuits. Cut each into quarters.

4. Shake 3 or 4 biscuit pieces at a time in the bag to coat.

5. Arrange coated pieces in pan.

6. In a small mixing bowl, mix brown sugar and butter together and pour over biscuit pieces.

7. Bake 28-32 minutes, or until golden brown and no longer doughy in center.

8. Cool in pan for 10 minutes.

9. Turn upside down onto a serving plate. Serve warm, allowing each person at the table to pull off pieces to eat.

Apricot Bread

Lauren Eberhard
Seneca, IL

Makes 10 servings

Prep Time: 10-15 minutes
Baking Time: 60 minutes

1 stick (1/2 cup) butter,
  softened
2 eggs
1 cup sugar
1/2 cup milk
1 tsp. orange extract
2 1/4 cups flour, *or* 1 cup
  whole wheat flour and
  1 1/4 cups flour
1 tsp. baking soda
1 cup chopped apricots,
  canned *or* dried
1/2 cup chopped nuts

1. In a large mixer bowl, cream together butter, eggs, and sugar.

2. Add milk and orange extract. Mix well.

3. Blend in flour and baking soda. Mix well.

4. Fold in apricots and nuts.

5. Pour into a greased 9 x 5 loaf pan.

6. Bake at 325° for 60 minutes, or until toothpick comes out clean.

7. Cool in pan 10 minutes. Remove from pan and place bread on wire rack.

Banana Nut Bread

Leona Yoder
Hartville, OH
Lilia Foltz
Pico Rivera, CA
Jennifer A. Crouse
Mt. Crawford, VA

Makes 1 loaf, or about 10 slices

Prep Time: 15-20 minutes
Baking Time: 45-50 minutes

1 scant cup sugar
1 stick (1/2 cup) butter, at
  room temperature
2 eggs
3 bananas, mashed
pinch of salt
1 tsp. baking soda
1/2 tsp. baking powder
1 3/4 cups flour
1 tsp. vanilla
1 cup broken nuts, *optional*

1. In a large mixing bowl,
beat together sugar and butter. When well mixed, beat in
eggs. Stir in mashed bananas.
2. In a separate bowl, stir
together salt, baking soda,
baking powder, and flour. Stir
into wet ingredients and mix
until well blended.
3. Stir in vanilla and nuts,
if you wish.
4. Pour into a greased 9 x
5 loaf pan.
5. Bake at 350° for 45-50
minutes, or until tester
inserted in center comes out
clean.
6. Allow to cool 10 min-
utes in pan. Then remove and
continue cooling on wire
rack.

Banana Bread

Margaret Moffitt
Bartlett, TN

Makes 1 loaf, or about 10 slices

Preparation Time: 30 minutes
Baking Time: 30 minutes

3/4 cup butter, softened
1 cup sugar
3 bananas, mashed
1 cup jam (blackberry
  works well)
2 eggs, well beaten
2 cups flour
1 tsp. baking soda
3/4 cup chopped pecans

1. In a large mixing bowl,
cream butter and sugar
together. Add mashed
bananas, jam, and eggs, and
blend well.
2. In a separate bowl, sift
flour and baking soda
together. Add to wet ingredients. When well mixed, stir
in nuts.
3. Line the bottom of a 9 x
5 loaf pan with waxed paper.
4. Bake at 350° for approximately 30 minutes, or until
tester inserted in center of
top of loaf comes out clean.
5. Allow to cool in pan for
10 minutes. Then remove loaf
and continue cooling on wire
rack.

A Tip —

Freeze over-ripe
bananas. Use them for
smoothies or in banana
bread.

Blueberry Bread

Renee Baum
Chambersburg, PA

Makes 1 loaf

Prep Time: 10-15 minutes
Baking Time: 1 hour

1 egg
1 cup sugar
2 Tbsp. vegetable oil
2/3 cup orange juice
2 cups flour
1 1/2 tsp. baking powder
1/2 tsp. baking soda
1/2 tsp. salt
1 cup fresh *or* frozen
  blueberries

1. Place egg in large mixing bowl and beat well.
2. Add sugar, oil, and
orange juice, and continue
beating till well mixed.
3. In a separate bowl, sift
together flour, baking powder,
baking soda, and salt. Add to
wet ingredients and mix well.
4. Gently stir in blueberries. (If you use frozen blueberries, gently mix them with
1 Tbsp. flour in a separate
bowl before adding to batter.)
5. Pour into greased 9 x 5
loaf pan.
6. Bake at 350° for 1 hour.

*This recipe came from my
husband's Home Economics
class.*

43

Lemon Tea Bread

Irene Klaeger, Inverness, FL

Makes 6 servings

Prep Time: 15 minutes
Baking Time: 50 minutes

3 Tbsp. butter, melted
1 cup sugar
2 eggs, at room temperature
1 1/2 cups flour
1 tsp. baking powder
1 tsp. salt
3/4 cup fresh lemon juice, *divided*
2 Tbsp. lemon zest, grated, *divided*
1/2 cup sifted confectioners sugar

1. Pour butter into mixing bowl and stir in sugar. When well blended, beat in eggs.
2. In separate mixing bowl stir together flour, baking powder, and salt.
3. Stir dry ingredients into wet ingredients. Mix well.
4. Add 1/2 cup lemon juice and 1 Tbsp. lemon zest.
5. Pour batter into a greased and floured 9 x 5 loaf pan.
6. Bake at 350° for 50 minutes. Remove from oven and cool 10 minutes.
7. While bread is baking, mix confectioners sugar with remaining 1/4 cup lemon juice and 1 Tbsp. lemon zest in a small bowl.
8. Cool bread for 10 minutes in pan. Remove from pan, place on a serving dish, and pour glaze over top.

Harvest Quick Bread

Lorraine Pflederer
Goshen, IN

Makes 12 slices

Prep Time: 20-30 minutes
Baking Time: 70 minutes

1/2 cup cut-up, pitted prunes
2 Tbsp. water
1 cup fresh *or* frozen cranberries, chopped
1 cup grated apple
1/2 cup apple juice
1 Tbsp. grated lemon peel
2 egg whites, lightly beaten
2 cups flour
1/2 cup sugar
1/2 cup brown sugar, firmly packed
1 tsp. baking powder
1/2 tsp. baking soda
1/2 tsp. cinnamon
1/2 tsp. nutmeg
1/2 cup chopped walnuts, *optional*

1. Place prunes and water in blender and puree.
2. Mix together prune puree, cranberries, apple, apple juice, lemon peel, and egg whites in a bowl.
3. In a separate large bowl, combine flour, sugar, brown sugar, baking powder, baking soda, cinnamon, nutmeg, and nuts, if you wish.
4. Stir the wet ingredients into the dry ingredients until just moistened. Transfer to a 9 x 5 loaf pan.
5. Bake at 350° for 1 hour

and 10 minutes, or until toothpick inserted in center comes out clean. Cool in the pan for 10 minutes. Remove and finish cooling on a wire rack.

Tip: To reduce the baking time, bake in 2 smaller loaf pans. Bake 45-50 minutes, and then check with toothpick to see if the loaves are fully baked. If they are not, bake longer, checking every 5 minutes with a toothpick to see if they are finished.

Green Chili Bread

Jeanne Allen
Rye, CO

Makes 12-15 servings

Prep Time: 20-30 minutes
Baking Time: 40-60 minutes

3 cups yellow cornmeal
1 1/2 tsp. baking powder
1 tsp. sugar
2 tsp. salt
1 cup vegetable oil
3 eggs, beaten
1 3/4 cups milk (whole *or* evaporated)
1 cup chopped onion
1 cup cream-style corn
4-oz. can chopped green chilies, drained
1 1/4 cups grated cheddar cheese

1. In a large mixing bowl, combine cornmeal, baking powder, sugar, and salt.
2. In a separate bowl, mix

together oil, eggs, and milk. Pour wet ingredients into dry ingredients and blend well.

3. Stir in onion, corn, chilies, and cheese. Mix gently until vegetables and cheese are well distributed.

4. Spoon mixture into a greased 9 x 13 baking pan.

5. Bake at 350° for 40-60 minutes, or until tester inserted in bread comes out clean.

Sour Cream Corn Bread

Ida H Goering
Dayton, VA

Makes 12 servings

Prep Time: 10-15 minutes
Baking Time: 20-22 minutes

3/4 **cup yellow cornmeal**
1 **cup flour**
1 **tsp. baking soda**
1 **tsp. cream of tarter**
1 **tsp. salt**
3 **Tbsp. sugar**
1 **egg, well beaten**
1 **cup sour cream**
1/2 **cup milk**
3 **Tbsp. butter, melted**

1. Preheat oven to 400°.

2. Grease a 9 x 9, or 7 x 11, baking pan.

3. Measure cornmeal into a mixing bowl and sift into it the flour, baking soda, cream of tarter, salt, and sugar.

4. In a separate bowl, beat egg well, and then add sour

cream, milk, and melted butter.

5. Pour wet ingredients into flour mixture. Stir just until well mixed.

6. Pour into baking pan.

7. Bake at 400° for 20-22 minutes, or until tester inserted in center of bread comes out clean.

8. Serve hot.

Tips:

1. Leftovers can be split into pieces, buttered lightly, and placed under the broiler until browned. Delicious!

2. For breakfast, serve the corn bread with sausage gravy and fried apples on the side. For a main meal, serve it with smoked sausage, steamed cabbage, pinto beans, and applesauce.

Pineapple Nut Bread

Esther Hartzler
Carlsbad, NM

Makes two loaves, or about 20 slices

Prep Time: 15-20 minutes
Baking Time: 45-60 minutes

1 1/2 **cup dry quick oats**
2 1/2 **cups flour**
2 **tsp. salt**
2 **tsp. baking soda**
4 **eggs**
1 1/2 **cups sugar**
2 1/2-3 **cups crushed pineapple** *or* **pineapple chunks, drained, but with** *juice reserved*
1 **cup grated coconut**
1 1/2 **cups chopped or broken pecans**

1. Grease and flour two 9 x 5 loaf pans.

2. In a large mixing bowl, stir together dry oats, flour, salt, and baking soda.

3. In a separate bowl, beat eggs. Then stir in sugar until well blended.

4. Stir wet ingredients into dry ingredients.

5. Gently stir in drained pineapple, coconut, and pecans. If mixture seems too dry, add several tablespoons of reserved pineapple juice.

6. Pour into loaf pans. Bake at 350° for 45-60 minutes, or until tops of loaves brown, and a toothpick inserted in the middle of the tops of the loaves comes out clean.

45

Pumpkin Bread

Jan McDowell
New Holland, PA
Janet Derstine
Telford, PA

Makes 3 loaves, or about 30 slices

Prep Time: 15-20 minutes
Baking Time: 1 hour

3 cups sugar
2/3 cup water
1 cup vegetable oil
4 eggs, beaten
2 cups (15-oz. can)
    prepared pumpkin
3½ cups flour
1½ tsp. salt
1 tsp. cinnamon
½ tsp. nutmeg
2 tsp. baking soda
2 cups raisins, *optional*
2 cup chopped walnuts *or*
    pecans, *optional*

1. In a large mixing bowl, dissolve sugar in water and oil. Add eggs and pumpkin and mix well.
2. In a separate bowl, combine all dry ingredients. Add to pumpkin mixture. Mix until all ingredients are just moistened.
3. If you wish, stir in raisins and nuts.
4. Divide into 3 greased and floured 9 x 5 loaf pans.
5. Bake at 350° for 1 hour.
6. Allow to cool in pan for 10 minutes. Remove from pan and let cool completely on wire rack before slicing.

Tip: This is very moist pumpkin bread. Serve it with warm apple cider on a cool autumn evening. Or slice it thin, spread each slice with whipped cream cheese, and top it with another slice. Cut "sandwiches" into quarters.

Strawberry Bread

Sally Holzem
Schofield, WI

Makes 2 loaves

Prep Time: 20 minutes
Baking Time: 45-60 minutes

3 cups flour
2 cups sugar
1 tsp. baking soda
1 tsp. salt
1 tsp. cinnamon
4 eggs beaten
1¼ cups vegetable oil
2 10-oz. pkgs. frozen
    strawberries, thawed
    and chopped, *or 2 cups
    fresh strawberries,
    chopped*
1 cup chopped pecans,
    optional

Frosting:
half an 8-oz. block of
    cream cheese, softened
1 tsp. vanilla
9–10 Tbsp. butter,
    softened
1½ cups confectioners
    sugar
chopped nuts, *optional*

1. In a large bowl, combine flour, sugar, baking soda, salt, and cinnamon. When well mixed, form a well in the center of the mixture.
2. In a separate bowl, combine beaten eggs, vegetable oil, strawberries, and chopped pecans. Pour into well in dry ingredients and stir until evenly mixed.
3. Spoon mixture into 2 greased and floured 9 x 5 loaf pans.
4. Bake at 350° for 45-60 minutes, until a tester inserted in the center of the tops of the loaves comes out clean.
5. Let loaves cool in pans for 10 minutes. Remove to wire racks and let cool completely.
6. To make the frosting, beat cream cheese, vanilla, and butter together until creamy in a medium-sized bowl. Gently stir in confectioners and chopped nuts until well distributed. Spread frosting over cooled bread.

Tip: This bread freezes well.

A Tip —

To get the best height and texture when making muffins, remember that the batter should be lumpy and the ingredients just moistened uniformly. In other words, don't over-stir the batter.

Apple Cranberry Muffins

Wendy B. Martzall
New Holland, PA

Makes 12 muffins

Prep Time: 10-20 minutes
Baking Time: 20 minutes

1¾ cups flour
¼ cup sugar
2½ tsp. baking powder
¾ tsp. salt
½ tsp. cinnamon
1 egg, well-beaten
¾ cup milk
⅓ cup vegetable oil
1 cup apple, peeled and finely chopped
½ cup chopped frozen cranberries

1. In a large mixing bowl, stir together flour, sugar, baking powder, salt, and cinnamon. When well mixed, make a well in the center of the dry ingredients.
2. In a separate bowl, blend together egg, milk, oil, apple, and cranberries.
3. Add all at once to dry ingredients. Stir just until moistened.
4. Fill paper-lined or greased muffin cups about ⅔ full.
5. Bake at 400° for 15-20 minutes, or until tops are lightly browned, and toothpick inserted in center of muffins comes out clean. Cool in tins for 10 minutes. Then remove and continue cooling on wire rack.

Tip: I've used dried cranberries as well with good results. Granny Smith apples are my choice, but other baking apples work, too.

Apple Pumpkin Muffins

Yvonne Kauffman Boettger
Harrisonburg, VA

Makes 18-20 muffins

Prep Time: 15-20 minutes
Baking Time: 35-40 minutes

2½ cups flour
2 cups sugar
1 Tbsp. pumpkin pie spice
1 tsp. baking soda
½ tsp. salt
2 eggs
1 cup canned *or* cooked pumpkin
½ cup vegetable oil
2 cups finely chopped, peeled apples

Streusel:
⅓ cup sugar
3 Tbsp. flour
½ tsp. ground cinnamon
4 tsp. butter *or* margarine, at room temperature

1. In a large mixing bowl, combine flour, sugar, spice, baking soda, and salt.
2. In another bowl, combine eggs, pumpkin, and oil. Stir into dry ingredients, just to moisten.
3. Fold in apples. Fill paper-lined muffin cups ⅔ full.
4. In a small bowl, combine sugar, flour, and cinnamon for streusel topping. Cut in butter until crumbly. Sprinkle over top of each muffin.
5. Bake at 350° for 35-40 minutes, or until golden brown, and toothpick inserted in muffin tops comes out clean.
6. Cool 5 minutes before removing from pans to wire racks.

A Tip —

Tunnels in muffins, peaks in their centers, and a soggy texture are caused from over-mixing.

Banana Wheat Germ Muffins

Terry Stutzman Mast
Lodi, California

Makes 12 muffins

Prep Time: 15-20 minutes
Baking Time: 18-20 minutes

1 1/2 cups flour
1 cup toasted wheat germ
1/2 cup brown sugar
1 Tbsp. baking powder
1 tsp. salt
3/4 tsp. ground nutmeg
2 eggs, beaten
1/2 cup milk
1/4 cup melted butter
1 cup (2 large) mashed ripe
  bananas
1/2 cup chopped walnuts

1. Preheat oven to 425°.
2. Lightly grease the muffin tins or line them with baking papers.
3. In a large mixing bowl, combine flour, wheat germ, sugar, baking powder, salt, and nutmeg. Blend well.
4. In a separate bowl, beat eggs into milk. Add melted butter and banana, continuing to beat until smooth.
5. Add banana mixture to dry ingredients, just until blended. Be careful not to over-mix.
6. Gently stir in nuts.
7. Spoon batter into muffin cups, filling 2/3 full. Bake 18-20 minutes, until muffins become a rich brown.
8. Allow to cool for 10 minutes in muffin cups, then remove and serve, or place on wire rack until completely cool and ready to be stored.
9. Serve warm or cold.

Tip: This is a perfect, healthy use for those ripe uneaten bananas that can be found every now and then in the kitchen.

All kids love these. It's fun to see my kids, and the neighbor kids, gobble them up for snacks!

Blueberry Muffins

Lois Stoltzfus
Honey Brook, PA

Makes 12-16 muffins

Prep Time: 20 minutes
Baking Time: 20 minutes

2 cups flour
1/2 cup sugar
2 tsp. baking powder
1/2 tsp. baking soda
1/2 tsp. salt
2 eggs
1 cup vanilla *or* lemon
  yogurt
1/4 cup oil
1 cup blueberries,
  fresh *or* frozen*

Crumbs:
4 Tbsp. sugar
2 Tbsp. flour
1 Tbsp. butter, at room
  temperature

1. In a large mixing bowl, mix dry ingredients together.
2. In another bowl, beat eggs. Add yogurt, oil, and blueberries. Gently add to dry ingredients until just moistened.
3. Place batter in greased, or paper-lined muffin tins, filling each 2/3 full.
4. Using one of the mixing bowls you've just emptied, blend crumb ingredients with a pastry blender or fork and sprinkle on top of muffins.
5. Bake at 400° for 20 minutes, or until tester inserted in tops of muffins comes out clean.

* If using frozen berries, first toss them in a separate bowl with 1 Tbsp. flour before stirring them into the batter.

Bran Flax Muffins

Ruth Fisher, Leicester, NY

Makes 15 muffins

Prep Time: 20 minutes
Baking Time: 15-20 minutes

1 1/2 cups flour
3/4 cup flaxseed meal
3/4 cup oat bran
1 cup brown sugar
2 tsp. baking soda
1 tsp. baking powder
1/2 tsp. salt
2 tsp. cinnamon
1 1/2 cups carrots, shredded
2 apples, peeled and
  shredded, *or* chopped
  fine

1/2 cup raisins, *optional*
1 cup chopped nuts
3/4 cup milk
2 eggs, beaten
1 tsp. vanilla

1. In a large bowl, mix together flour, flaxseed meal, oat bran, brown sugar, baking soda, baking powder, salt, and cinnamon.

2. Stir in carrots, apples, raisins, and nuts.

3. In a separate bowl, combine milk, eggs, and vanilla. Pour liquid ingredients into dry ingredients and stir just until moistened. Do not overmix.

4. Fill lightly greased muffin tins 3/4 full. Bake at 350° for 15-20 minutes.

Tips:
1. You can buy flaxseed meal at bulk food or health-food stores.
2. Flaxseed is a major source of fiber.

Double Chocolate Muffins

Janet Groff, Stevens, PA

Makes 12 muffins

Prep Time: 15 minutes
Baking Time: 30 minutes

1/2 cup dry quick oats
1/3 cup milk
1 cup flour
1/2 cup whole wheat flour
2 Tbsp. bran

1/2 cup sugar
1/4 cup brown sugar
1/3 cup cocoa powder
1/4 tsp. salt
1 rounded tsp. baking powder
1 egg
1/4 cup vegetable oil
1 cup milk
1 Tbsp. vanilla
3/4 cup chocolate chips

Glaze:
1-2 Tbsp. peanut butter
1 1/2 cups confectioners sugar
water

1. In a microwavable container, combine quick oats and 1/3 cup milk. Microwave on high 1 1/2 minutes. Set aside.

2. In a large bowl, combine flours, bran, sugars, cocoa powder, salt, and baking powder.

3. In a separate bowl, stir together oats mixture, egg, oil, milk, vanilla, and chocolate chips.

4. Gently fold wet ingredients into dry ingredients, mixing just until moistened.

5. Spoon batter into 12 greased muffin cups, making each 3/4 full.

6. Bake at 350° for 30 minutes, or until toothpick inserted in muffin tops comes out clean. Allow muffins to cool for 10 minutes before removing from tins.

7. To make glaze: Combine peanut butter and powdered sugar in a small bowl. Add water to desired consistency and stir until smooth. Drizzle over warm muffins.

Low-Fat Chocolate Muffins

Teresa Martin
Gordonville, PA

Makes 12 servings

Prep Time: 15-20 minutes
Baking Time: 15-20 minutes

1 1/2 cups flour
3/4 cup sugar
1/4 cup baking cocoa
2 tsp. baking powder
1 tsp. baking soda
1/2 tsp. salt
2/3 cup fat-free vanilla yogurt
2/3 cup skim milk
1/2 tsp. vanilla
confectioners sugar, *optional*

1. In a large mixing bowl, combine flour, sugar, baking cocoa, baking powder, baking soda, and salt.

2. In a separate bowl, stir together yogurt, milk, and vanilla until well mixed.

3. Stir wet ingredients into dry ingredients, just until moistened.

4. Fill greased muffin tins 2/3 full.

5. Bake at 400° for 15-20 minutes, or until toothpick inserted in centers of muffins comes out clean.

6. Cool for 5 minutes before removing from pan to wire rack.

7. Dust with confectioners sugar, if you wish.

Tip: These muffins freeze well.

Coconut Muffins

Vicki Hill
Memphis, TN

Makes 12 muffins

Prep Time: 10-15 minutes
Baking Time: 20-25 minutes

4 Tbsp. butter, softened
1 cup sugar
2 eggs
1/2 cup milk
1 tsp. coconut extract
1 1/2 cups flour
1 tsp. baking powder
1/4 tsp. salt
2/3 cup grated coconut

1. In a large mixing bowl beat butter and sugar together until thoroughly mixed.
2. Stir in eggs, milk, and extract and blend well.
3. In a separate bowl, stir together flour, baking powder, salt, and coconut.
4. Gently stir dry ingredients into wet ingredients until dry ingredients are moistened.
5. Spoon into greased muffin tins or muffin paper cups, filling each about 2/3 full.
6. Bake at 350° for 20-25 minutes, or until toothpick inserted in muffin tops comes out clean.

A Tip —
   Keep nuts in the freezer so you'll have them when you need them.

Morning Glory Muffins

Mary Jane Hoober
Shipshewana, IN

Makes about 36 muffins

Prep Time: 25-30 minutes
Baking Time: 20 minutes

3 eggs
1 cup vegetable oil
2 tsp. vanilla
1 1/4 cups sugar
2 cups, plus 2 Tbsp., flour
2 tsp. baking soda
2 tsp. cinnamon
1/2 tsp. salt
2 cups grated carrots
1 cup raisins
1/2 cup nuts, chopped
1/2 cup grated coconut
1 apple, peeled, cored, and grated, *or* chopped finely

1. In a large mixing bowl beat eggs. Then add oil, vanilla, and sugar and combine well.
2. In a separate mixing bowl, stir together flour, baking soda, cinnamon, and salt. When well mixed, add remaining ingredients.
3. Pour dry-fruit ingredients into creamed ingredients. Blend just until everything is moistened.
4. Fill greased muffin tins 2/3 full. Bake at 350° for 20 minutes, or until tester inserted in center comes out clean.

Pumpkin Chip Muffins

Julia Horst
Gordonville, PA
Sherri Grindle
Goshen, IN

Makes 36 muffins

Prep Time: 10 minutes
Baking Time: 17 minutes

4 eggs
2 cups sugar
15- or 16-oz. can pumpkin
3/4 cup vegetable oil
3/4 cup plain yogurt
3 cups flour
2 tsp. baking soda
2 tsp. baking powder
1 tsp. cinnamon
1 tsp. salt
2 cups chocolate chips

1. In a large bowl, beat eggs, sugar, pumpkin, oil, and yogurt until smooth.
2. In a separate bowl, combine flour, baking soda, baking powder, cinnamon, and salt.
3. Add dry ingredients to pumpkin mixture and mix just until moistened.
4. Fold in chocolate chips.
5. Fill paper-lined muffin cups 3/4 full.
6. Bake at 400° for 17 minutes, or until tester inserted in center of muffin tops comes out clean.

Soups, Stews, and Chilis

Creamy Asparagus Soup

Mary E. Riha
Antigo, WI

Makes 4 servings

Prep Time: 30 minutes
Cooking Time: 15-20 minutes

1/4 cup sesame seeds
2 Tbsp. olive oil
1 medium onion, chopped
2 medium potatoes, cubed
4 cups chicken stock,
    divided
1 lb. raw asparagus,
    broken in 1″ pieces
1 tsp. salt
dash of pepper
2 cups chicken stock
dash of nutmeg
sour cream
salted sunflower seeds,
    optional

1. In stockpot, sauté sesame seeds in olive oil until brown. Add onions and potatoes. Cook and stir until potatoes begin to stick.

2. Add 2 cups stock, asparagus, salt, and pepper. Bring to boil. Reduce heat and simmer until potatoes are done.

3. Carefully pour one-fourth of hot mixture into blender. Cover and blend until smooth. (Hold the lid on with a potholder to keep the heat from pushing it off.)

4. Put pureed soup back in stockpot. Continue blending cooked soup, one-fourth at a time. Continue to add pureed soup back into stockpot.

5. When all soup has been pureed, add 2 more cups chicken stock to soup in stockpot. Heat thoroughly.

6. Add a dash of nutmeg.

7. Top each serving with a dollop of sour cream and a sprinkling of sunflower seeds.

A Tip —

Write in your cookbook the date when you tried a particular recipe and whether or not you liked it. Develop a rating system for each recipe you try (Excellent, Good, Yummy, Okay). Write notes about what might be a good addition or deletion the next time you make it.

Southwest Bean Soup

Kathy Keener Shantz
Lancaster, PA

Makes 6-7 servings

Prep Time: 15-20 minutes
Cooking Time: 20-30 minutes

2 Tbsp. oil
1 onion, diced
4 garlic cloves, minced
2 tsp. cumin
1 tsp. salt
1 tsp. chili powder
1/4 tsp. ground red pepper
2 15-oz. cans corn, drained
2 15-oz. cans diced
   tomatoes
15-oz. can black beans,
   drained
15-oz. can kidney beans,
   drained
4 cups chicken broth
chopped fresh cilantro
blue or white corn chips
plain yogurt *or* sour cream

1. In large saucepan, sauté onion, garlic, and seasonings in oil.
2. Stir in corn, tomatoes, beans, and chicken broth. Bring to boil. Reduce heat. Cover and simmer for 20-30 minutes.
3. Serve topped with fresh cilantro, crushed corn chips, and yogurt.

Black Bean Sweet Potato Soup

Carisa Funk
Hillsboro, KS

Makes 4 servings

Prep Time: 10-15 minutes
Cooking Time: 20 minutes

1 Tbsp. oil
1 medium onion, chopped
2 garlic cloves, minced
2 medium-sized raw sweet
   potatoes, peeled and
   diced
1 Tbsp. chili powder
16-oz. jar salsa
1 cup water
2 15-oz. cans black beans,
   drained
sour cream
fresh cilantro

1. In large saucepan, sauté onion and garlic in oil for 4 minutes.
2. Stir in sweet potatoes, chili powder, salsa, and water. Heat to boiling. Reduce heat and cook 12-15 minutes, or until potatoes are fork tender.
3. Add beans. Cook 3 more minutes.
4. Garnish individual servings with sour cream and fresh cilantro.

> **A Tip —**
>
> Adding salt to dry beans before they are cooked soft will prevent them from getting soft.

Bean Soup with Turkey Sausage

Dorothy Reise
Severna Park, MD
D. Fern Ruth
Chalfont, PA

Makes 4 servings

Prep Time: 15-20 minutes
Cooking Time: 15-20 minutes

8 ozs. turkey kielbasa
4 cups chicken broth
2 15-oz. cans cannelloni
   beans, drained and
   rinsed
1/2-1 cup onion, chopped
1 tsp. dried basil, crushed
1/4 tsp. coarsely ground
   pepper
1 clove garlic, minced
1 carrot, peeled and sliced,
   or 1 cup baby carrots
half a red, yellow, *or*
   orange bell pepper,
   sliced
3 cups fresh spinach,
   cleaned, *or* 10-oz. pkg.
   frozen spinach
fresh parsley, chopped

1. Cut turkey kielbasa lengthwise, and then into 1/2" slices. Sauté in Dutch oven or large saucepan until browned, stirring occasionally so it doesn't stick.
2. Combine all ingredients in pan except spinach and parsley.
3. Bring to boil, and then reduce heat. Cover and simmer 10-15 minutes, or until onion and carrots are tender.

4. If you're using frozen spinach, add it to the soup and let it thaw in the soup pot. Stir occasionally to break up spinach and to have it heat through.

5. If you're using fresh spinach, remove stems from fresh spinach, stack, and cut into 1" strips. Remove soup from heat and stir in spinach and parsley until spinach wilts.

6. Serve immediately.

Variation: For a thicker soup, remove 1 cup of hot soup after Step 3 and carefully process in firmly covered blender or food processor until smooth. Stir back into soup and continue with Step 4.

Cheesy Broccoli Cauliflower Soup

Marcia S. Myer
Manheim, PA

Makes 5-6 servings

Prep Time: 20 minutes
Cooking Time: 40-45 minutes

6 Tbsp. butter
1/4 cup chopped onion
1/2 cup flour
2 cups milk
1 cup (4 ozs.) cubed
   Velveeta *or* American
   cheese
2 14-oz. cans chicken broth
2 cups chopped broccoli,
   fresh *or* frozen

2 cups chopped
   cauliflower, fresh *or*
   frozen
1/4 cup finely chopped *or*
   grated carrots
1/4 cup chopped celery
salt to taste
1/4 tsp. pepper

1. Melt butter in large saucepan. Stir in onion and sauté until just tender.

2. Stir in flour until well blended. Slowly add milk over medium heat, stirring constantly until thickened and smooth.

3. Stir in cheese, continuing to stir until cheese melts. Set aside.

4. In a separate saucepan, simmer broccoli, cauliflower, carrots, and celery in chicken broth until almost tender.

5. Season with salt, if you wish, and pepper.

6. Pour cheesy sauce into vegetables and heat through.

Variations:

1. Instead of chicken broth, use 2 chicken bouillon cubes and 1¾ cups water in Step 4.

2. Instead of cauliflower, use 2 additional cups broccoli, fresh or frozen.

— **Mary Jane Musser**
Manheim, PA

Broccoli Chowder

Ruth E. Martin
Loysville, PA

Makes 6 servings

Prep Time: 15-20 minutes
Cooking Time: 20 minutes

2 cups diced potatoes,
   peeled or unpeeled,
   your choice
1/2 cup water
2 cups chopped broccoli,
   fresh, *or* 10-oz. pkg.
   chopped broccoli, frozen
2 Tbsp. onion
1 cup corn
1/4-1/2 cup cooked, diced
   ham, *optional*
3 cups milk
1/2 tsp. salt, *optional*
1/8 tsp. pepper
1 tsp. powdered chicken
   bouillon, *or* 1 chicken
   bouillon cube
1/2 cup Velveeta cheese,
   cubed

1. In medium-sized saucepan, cook potatoes in water. When potatoes are almost soft, add broccoli and onion. Cook until tender.

2. Add corn, ham, if you wish, milk, seasonings, and bouillon. Heat, but do not boil.

3. Turn off and add cubed cheese. Let cheese melt for about 3-4 minutes. Stir and serve.

Cheesy Chowder

Ruth Ann Gingrich
New Holland, PA
Mary Kay Nolt
Newmanstown, PA
Pat Unternahrer
Wayland, IA
Maryann Markano
WIlmington, DE

Makes 6 servings

Prep Time: 10 minutes
Cooking Time: 20 minutes

2 cups water
2 cups diced potatoes,
    peeled or unpeeled,
    your choice
1/2 cup carrots, diced *or*
    shredded
1/4 cup onions, diced
1/2 cup diced celery,
    optional
1 tsp. salt
1/4 tsp. pepper

White Sauce:
1/4 cup butter
1/4 cup flour
2 cups milk
2 cups grated cheddar
    cheese
1 cup cubed ham

1. In a large saucepan,
combine water, potatoes, carrots, onions, celery, if you
wish, salt, and pepper.
Simmer, covered, for 10-12
minutes, or until vegetables
are tender.
2. While vegetables cook,
in medium-sized saucepan,
melt butter. Add flour and
stir until smooth.

3. Slowly add milk, stirring
continuously, and cook until
thickened.
4. Add cheese and stir over
low heat until melted.
5. Add cubed ham to
cheesy sauce.
6. When vegetables are
tender, gently stir white sauce
mixture into the undrained
vegetables.
7. Serve when thoroughly
mixed together.

*Tip: You can adjust the thick-
ness of the soup by pouring
some of the cooking water off
the vegetables before adding the
cheesy sauce.*

*Variation: Make Cheesy
Chicken Chowder by making
the following substitutions:*
*1. Use 3 cups chicken broth
instead of 2 cups water.*
*2. Use 1 cup diced carrots
instead of 1/2 cup and 1/2 cup
diced onion instead of 1/4 cup.*
*3. Use 2 cups diced cooked
chicken instead of 1 cup cooked
ham.*

— **Nancy Funk**
North Newton, KS

Tomato Mushroom Soup

D. Fern Ruth
Chalfont, PA

Makes 4-6 servings

Prep Time: 15 minutes
Cooking Time: 30 minutes

2 cups sliced fresh
    mushrooms
1/3 cup chopped onion
2 garlic cloves, minced
4 Tbsp. butter
6 Tbsp. flour
2 14.5-oz. cans chicken
    broth
2 14.5-oz. cans diced
    tomatoes, undrained
4 Tbsp. chopped, fresh
    basil leaves, *or* 1 1/2 Tbsp.
    dried basil
1 Tbsp. sugar
1 tsp. salt
1/4 tsp. pepper

54

1. In a large saucepan, sauté mushrooms, onion, and garlic in butter until tender. Remove vegetables from pan and set aside. Leave as much of the drippings as you can in the pan.

2. In the same pan, combine flour and chicken broth with drippings until smooth. Bring to boil and stir 2-4 minutes, or until thickened.

3. Return mushroom mixture to saucepan and stir into thickened chicken broth.

4. Add tomatoes, basil, sugar, salt, and pepper. Cook over medium heat 10-15 minutes, stirring occasionally.

5. Remove from heat. Cool slightly. Then puree in tightly covered blender (1/4 of the mixture at a time) until smooth.

6. Garnish with basil leaves and serve hot.

Tips:

1. Flavors blend nicely when you make the soup a day ahead and allow it to stand overnight.

2. Use fresh tomatoes in season.

A Tip —

Remember to use leftover cooked vegetables from your refrigerator when making soup.

Fresh Vegetable Soup

Sandra Chang, Derwood, MD

Makes 4-6 servings

Prep Time: 25-30 minutes
Cooking Time: 60-70 minutes
Standing Time: 1 hour

4 Tbsp. butter
1/2 cup of each:
  diced celery
  diced onions
  small chunks of peeled carrots
  chopped cabbage
  diced zucchini
  fresh *or* frozen whole-kernel corn
  fresh *or* frozen cut-up green beans
2 cups canned whole tomatoes
4 cups beef stock
2 Tbsp. sugar
salt to taste
pepper to taste
1/2 cup fresh *or* frozen petite peas

1. In 4-quart saucepan, melt butter. Sauté celery, onions, carrots, cabbage, and zucchini in butter until vegetables are soft but not brown.

2. Add rest of ingredients, except 1/2 cup peas.

3. Simmer gently for 30-45 minutes, or until vegetables are cooked but not mushy.

4. Take pan off heat and stir in peas. Allow soup to stand for one hour before serving.

5. Reheat just until heated through and serve.

Spicy, No-Salt Hamburger Soup

Jane Frownfelter
Grand Blanc, MI

Makes 8-10 servings

Prep Time: 30 minutes
Cooking Time: 2 hours and 10 minutes

2 lbs. ground beef
5 3/4 cups (46 ozs.) V-8 juice
14.5-oz. can stewed tomatoes, undrained
1 bay leaf
1 Tbsp. garlic powder
2 cups chopped celery
1 cup sliced carrots
2 cups green beans
2 cups sliced *or* shredded cabbage
1 tsp. dried basil
1/2 tsp. dried oregano
2 tsp. onion flakes
7-oz. can sliced *or* chopped mushrooms, drained
1 Tbsp. Worcestershire sauce

1. In large saucepan, brown beef. Drain well.

2. Add all other ingredients to beef in saucepan.

3. Simmer, covered, for 2 hours.

Variation: Instead of green beans, use 2 large potatoes, chopped.

— Louise Bodziony
Sunrise Beach, MO

Cheeseburger Soup

Marcella Heatwole
North Lawrence, OH
Jean Hindal, Grandin, IA
Beverly High, Ephrata, PA
Sherlyn Hess, Millersville, PA

Makes 8 servings

Prep Time: 30 minutes
Cooking Time: 20-30 minutes

1/2 lb. ground beef
3/4 cup chopped onions
3/4 cup shredded carrots
3/4 cup diced celery
1/4 tsp. dried basil
1 tsp. dried parsley flakes
4 Tbsp. butter *or*
   margarine, *divided*
3 cups chicken broth
2 cups diced potatoes,
   peeled or unpeeled,
   your choice
1/4 cup flour
1 1/2 cups milk
3/4 tsp. salt
1/4-1/2 tsp. pepper
8 ozs. cheddar cheese,
   grated
1/4 cup sour cream

1. In saucepan, brown beef. Drain. Set aside.
2. In same saucepan, sauté onions, carrots, celery, basil, and parsley in 1 Tbsp. butter until vegetables are tender.
3. Add broth, potatoes, and beef. Bring to boil. Reduce heat, cover, and simmer for 10-12 minutes, or until potatoes are tender.
4. While meat and potatoes cook, in small skillet melt 3 Tbsp. butter. Stir in flour until smooth. Cook and stir 3-5 minutes.
5. Reduce heat to low. Add milk, salt, and pepper. Stir until mixture thickens and becomes smooth.
6. Slowly stir in grated cheese, about 1/2-cupful at a time. Continue to stir until cheese is fully melted and blended into white sauce.
7. Blend in sour cream. Heat, but do not boil.
8. When vegetables are tender and cheesy white sauce is finished, pour the white sauce into the vegetable mixture and gently stir together.
9. When well mixed and heated through, serve.

Hearty Beef Barley Soup

Karen Gingrich,
New Holland, PA

Makes 4-5 servings

Preparation Time: 5-10 minutes
Cooking Time: 35 minutes

1 lb. beef tips
2 cups sliced fresh
   mushrooms
1/4 tsp. garlic powder
32-oz. can (3 1/2 cups) beef
   broth
2 medium-sized carrots,
   sliced
1/4 tsp. dried thyme
dash of pepper
1/2 cup quick-cooking
   barley

1. Cook beef in nonstick saucepan until browned and juices evaporate, about 10 minutes, stirring often.
2. Add mushrooms and garlic powder and cook until mushrooms begin to wilt, about 5 minutes.
3. Add broth, carrots, thyme, and pepper.
4. Heat to boiling. Stir in barley. Cover and cook over low heat for 20 minutes, or until barley is tender.

Beef Barley Soup

Jan Rankin
Millersville, PA

Makes 6 servings

Prep Time: 15 minutes
Cooking Time: 90 minutes

2-2 1/2-lb. chuck roast
2 cups tomato, *or* V8, juice
1 rib celery, finely chopped
2 carrots, diced
water
1 cup quick-cooking barley

1. In large saucepan, place meat, tomato juice, celery, and carrots. Add water to cover.
2. Cook until meat is soft and tender, approximately an hour.
3. Remove meat. Cut into small pieces and return to pot.
4. Add barley. Cook 15-30 minutes more, or until barley is tender.

Chopped Beef Potpourri
Becky Frey
Lebanon, PA

Makes 4-6 servings

Prep Time: 20 minutes
Cooking Time: 65-70 minutes

3/4 lb. ground beef
3 medium-sized onions, chopped
1/3 cup pearl barley
2 cups tomato juice, *or* diced tomatoes
1 tsp. salt
1/4 tsp. pepper
3 carrots, diced
3 potatoes, diced, peeled or unpeeled, your choice
3 ribs celery, diced
1 qt. water

1. Brown beef and onions in large pan. Drain off meat drippings.
2. Add remaining ingredients.
3. Cover and simmer 60 minutes, or until vegetables and barley are tender.

Variation: Add 2 cups broken green beans and 2 cups sliced cabbage to Step 2, if you wish.
— **Wilma Haberkamp**
Fairbank, IA

Pasta Fagioli Soup
Stacie Skelly, Millersville, PA

Makes 8-10 servings

Prep Time: 20 minutes
Cooking Time: 90 minutes

1 lb. ground beef
1 cup diced onions
1 cup julienned carrots
1 cup chopped celery
2 cloves garlic, minced
2 14.5-oz. cans diced tomatoes, undrained
15-oz. can red kidney beans, undrained
15-oz. can Great Northern beans, undrained
15-oz. can tomato sauce
12-oz. can V-8 juice
1 Tbsp. vinegar
1 1/2 tsp. salt
1 tsp. dried oregano
1 tsp. dried basil
1/2 tsp. pepper
1/2 tsp. dried thyme
1/2 lb. ditali pasta*

1. Brown ground beef in a large stockpot. Drain off drippings.
2. To browned beef, add onions, carrots, celery, and garlic. Sauté for 10 minutes.
3. Add remaining ingredients, except pasta, and stir well. Simmer, covered, for 1 hour.
4. About 50 minutes into cooking time, cook pasta in a separate saucepan, according to the directions on the package.
5. Add drained pasta to the large pot of soup. Simmer for 5-10 minutes and serve.

If you can't find these short tubes, you can substitute elbow macaronis.

Spaghetti Soup
Brenda J. Hochstedler
East Earl, PA

Makes 8 servings

Prep Time: 15 minutes
Cooking Time: 50 minutes

1 lb. ground beef
1 medium-sized onion, chopped
1 Tbsp. oil
1 Tbsp. Worcestershire sauce
1/2 cup ketchup
14-oz. *or* 16-oz. can pork and beans
3 qts. water
1 Tbsp. salt
1/8 tsp. pepper
1/4 lb. uncooked spaghetti

1. In large stockpot, brown ground beef and onion in oil.
2. Add Worcestershire sauce, ketchup, pork and beans, water, salt, and pepper. Bring to boil, and then simmer, covered, for 5 minutes.
3. Break spaghetti into small pieces and add to simmering mixture.
4. Cook for 30 minutes, stirring occasionally to keep spaghetti suspended in mixture.

Chicken or Turkey Vegetable Barley Soup

Esther J Mast
Lancaster, PA

Makes 10-12 servings

Prep Time: 45 minutes
Simmering Time: 70 minutes
(if using pre-cooked chicken or turkey)

5 qts. fresh chicken *or* turkey broth, fat skimmed off
2 cups diced celery
2 cups sliced carrots
2 cups green beans
1 onion, chopped
3/4 cup pearl barley
2-3 cups cooked chicken *or* turkey, diced
salt and pepper to taste
fresh parsley, if desired

1. In soup pot, combine broth, celery, carrots, green beans, onion, and barley. Simmer approximately 1 hour, or until vegetables and barley are tender but not mushy.
2. Add cooked diced chicken, salt and pepper to taste, and heat thoroughly.
3. Serve piping hot, garnished with fresh parsley.

Tips:

1. Use 2 cups diced potatoes instead of barley.
2. For a tasty variation on the traditional chicken-broth flavoring, tie into a cheesecloth bag 1 bay leaf, 10 kernels whole black peppercorns, and 1 whole star anise. Place bag of spices in water while cooking a whole chicken. Simmer slowly for about 2 hours, until chicken is tender and broth is well flavored. Debone chicken and reserve for Step 2 above.

A Tip —

Don't be afraid to invite friends in for a meal. They will accept your cooking freely, especially if you don't apologize for the food.

Chicken Tortellini Soup

Mary Seielstad
Sparks, NV

Makes 4-6 servings

Prep Time: 10 15 minutes
Cooking Time: 25 minutes

1 Tbsp. butter *or* margarine
4 cloves garlic, minced
5 cups chicken broth
9-oz. pkg. frozen cheese tortellini
1 1/2 cups diced cooked chicken
14-oz. can stewed tomatoes
10-oz. pkg. frozen spinach
1/2 tsp. pepper
1 tsp. dried basil
1/4 cup grated Parmesan cheese

1. In large saucepan, melt butter and sauté garlic for 2 minutes over medium heat.
2. Sir in broth and tortellini and bring to a boil. Cover, reduce heat, and simmer 5 minutes.
3. Add cooked chicken, tomatoes, frozen spinach, pepper, and basil and simmer 10-15 minutes. Stir every 3 minutes or so, breaking up frozen spinach and blending it into the soup.
4. Serve when soup is heated through, along with Parmesan cheese to spoon over individual servings.

Chicken Noodle Soup

Josephine A. Earle
Citronelle, AL

Makes 12 servings

Prep Time: 30-40 minutes
Cooking Time: 55-60 minutes

1 cup chopped celery
1 cup chopped onion
1/4 cup butter *or* margarine
12 cups water
1 cup diced carrots
3 Tbsp. chicken-flavored instant bouillon, *or* 3 chicken bouillon cubes
1/2 tsp. dried marjoram leaves, *optional*
1/4-1/2 tsp. pepper
1 bay leaf
4 cups cut-up cooked chicken
half a 12-oz. pkg. medium-sized egg noodles
1 Tbsp. chopped parsley

1. In a large Dutch oven, cook celery and onion in butter until tender.
2. Add water, carrots, bouillon, marjoram, pepper, and bay leaf. Cover. Bring to a boil. Reduce heat and simmer, covered for 30 minutes. Remove bay leaf.
3. Stir in chicken. Add noodles and parsley.
4. Cook 10 minutes longer until noodles are tender, stirring occasionally.

Variations:

1. Instead of cooked chicken called for above, cut up 2 lbs. uncooked skinless chicken breast, and add it to the soup in Step 2.
— Helen A. Roselle
Ellisville, IL

2. Instead of cooked chicken in the recipe above, put a whole chicken (weighing 3-4 lbs.) in Dutch oven in Step 2 above. (Eliminate bouillon.) Cook for 45-60 minutes, or until chicken is falling off the bones. Remove chicken from pot. Debone.
Return chicken meat to pot and continue with Step 3. Add 8 ozs. sliced, fresh mushrooms to Step 3, along with noodles and parsley.
— **Kara Maddox,**
Independence, MO

Surprise Gumbo

Brenda J Marshall
St. Marys, ON

Makes 6-8 servings

Prep Time: 20-30 minutes
Cooking Time: 30-40 minutes

1 1/4 lbs. cooked chicken, cubed*
2 medium-sized onions, cut in wedges
1 medium-sized green bell pepper, cut in narrow strips
28-oz. can whole tomatoes, undrained
1/4 cup Worcestershire sauce

2 Tbsp. prepared mustard
2 Tbsp. garlic cloves, minced
1 tsp. dried thyme
1 tsp. dried rosemary
1/4 tsp. pepper
1/2 lb. precooked shrimp
6 cups hot cooked rice

1. In large saucepan, combine chicken, onions, green pepper, tomatoes, Worcestershire sauce, mustard, garlic, thyme, rosemary, and pepper. Simmer for 25 minutes.
2. Add shrimp and cook 5 minutes more.
3. Serve over scoops of cooked rice in individual serving bowls.

If you don't have cooked chicken, cut up 1 whole skinless chicken breast (1 1/4-lbs.) and cook lightly in microwave. Or place raw chunks in saucepan along with just the tomatoes and simmer gently over medium heat for about 10 minutes, or until meat is losing its pinkness. Then continue with Step 1 above, adding the other ingredients listed there, and continuing to simmer them and the chicken.

Chicken Taco Soup

Mary Puskar
Forest Hill, MD

Makes 4 servings

Prep Time: 25 minutes
Cooking Time: 40 minutes

2 chicken breast halves
3 cups water
2 stalks celery
1 medium-sized onion
2 carrots
2 Tbsp. vegetable *or* canola oil
1 Tbsp. chili powder
1 Tbsp. cumin
4.5-oz. can green chilies
14-oz. can chicken broth
14-oz. can beef broth
14.5-oz. can diced tomatoes, undrained
1 Tbsp. Worcestershire sauce
tortilla chips, broken
Montery Jack cheese, grated

1. In a large stockpot, cook chicken breasts in water until tender. Remove meat, reserving cooking water. When chicken is cool enough to handle, chop into bite-sized pieces. Set aside.
2. Chop celery and onion. Grate carrots.
3. In stockpot used for cooking chicken, sauté vegetables in oil.
4. Combine all ingredients in stockpot, except the cooked chicken. Cover and simmer 15 minutes.

5. Add diced chicken. Heat through.
6. Top each serving with broken tortilla chips and grated cheese

Scrumptious White Chili

Gloria L. Lehman
Singers Glen, VA
Lauren Bailey
Mechanicsburg, PA

Makes 6 servings

Prep Time: 20-25 minutes
Cooking Time: 25 minutes

1½ Tbsp. oil
1 large onion, chopped
2 cloves garlic, minced
2 cups chopped cooked chicken*
4-oz. can chopped mild green chilies
½-1 Tbsp. diced jalapeno pepper, *optional*
1½ tsp. ground cumin
1 tsp. dried oregano
10.5-oz. can condensed chicken broth
1 soup can water
15-oz. can Great Northern beans
½ tsp. cayenne, *or* to taste
salt to taste
6 ozs. shredded Monterey Jack cheese
½ cup low-fat sour cream
chopped green onions, *optional*
fresh cilantro, *optional*

1. In large stockpot, sauté onion and garlic in oil over medium heat.
2. Add chicken, chilies, jalapeno pepper, if you want, cumin, oregano, chicken broth, water, and beans to stockpot and stir well. Bring to a boil, reduce heat, and simmer, covered, 10-15 minutes.
3. Just before serving, add cayenne, salt, cheese, and sour cream. Heat just until cheese is melted, being careful not to let the soup boil.
4. Serve at once, garnished with chopped green onions and fresh cilantro, if desired.

* *If you don't have cooked chicken, cut up 1½ lbs. skinless chicken breasts (about 1½ breasts) into 1" chunks. Follow Step 2 and proceed with the directions as given, being sure to simmer until the chicken is no longer pink.*

Plum Good Chili

Susan Guarneri
Three Lakes, WI

Makes 6 servings

Prep Time: 30 minutes
Cooking Time: 2¼-2½ hours

1½ garlic cloves, minced
1 Tbsp. oil
2 lbs. ground round beef
3 large onions, sliced
2 large green peppers, sliced

1 1/2 (16-oz. size) cans
stewed tomatoes,
undrained
2 16-oz. cans red kidney
beans, drained
6-oz. can tomato paste
2 Tbsp. chili powder
1/2 tsp. white vinegar
2 dashes cayenne pepper
2 whole cloves
1/2 bay leaf
1/4 cup plum preserves *or*
grape jelly
1/4 cup sugar
salt and pepper to taste

1. In a large skillet, cook garlic in oil until golden. Add crumbled pieces of beef and cook 10 minutes until evenly browned. With a slotted spoon, remove beef and garlic from skillet and place in a large stockpot or saucepan. Reserve drippings in skillet.

2. Cook onions and green peppers in beef drippings in skillet until tender.

3. Add to cooked meat, along with tomatoes, beans, tomato paste, chili powder, vinegar, cayenne pepper, cloves, bay leaf, jelly, sugar, salt, and pepper.

4. Cover and cook over low heat for 2 hours. If too dry, add additional tomatoes. If too much liquid, uncover and simmer longer.

5. Stir every 15 minutes to prevent chili from sticking or scorching. (It smells so good that you'll probably stir it more often.)

Black Bean Chili
Rita Steffen
Wellsboro, PA

Makes 12 servings

Prep Time: 20-25 minutes
Cooking Time: 40-70 minutes

---

1 lb. ground beef
1 large onion, chopped
2 medium green peppers,
chopped
3 cloves garlic, minced
1-lb. can baked beans (I
like Bush's)
1 *or* 2 1-lb. cans cooked
black beans, undrained
28-oz. can diced tomatoes,
undrained
1/2 tsp. cumin
2 tsp. chili powder
1 1/2 tsp. salt

1. In a large saucepan, brown beef together with onions, peppers, and garlic.

2. Add both kinds of beans, tomatoes, cumin, chili powder, and salt.

3. Simmer for 30-60 minutes, until flavors mingle and the chili is heated thoroughly.

4. Serve hot.

A Tip —

Put a handful of dry quick oats into your beef barbecue, chili, or spaghetti sauce to thicken it.

Chili Soup with Potatoes
Ruth Ann Hoover
New Holland, PA

Makes 8-10 servings

Prep Time: 15-30 minutes
Cooking Time: 1 hour
and 20 minutes

---

2 lbs. ground beef
1 medium onion, chopped
1 cup chopped celery
2 tsp. salt
2 10-oz. cans baked beans
1 qt. tomato juice
1/4 tsp. pepper
1 tsp. chili powder
1/4 cup brown sugar
4 medium-sized potatoes,
cooked, chilled, and
shredded

1. In a large stockpot, brown together beef, onion, celery, and salt.

2. Add beans, tomato juice, pepper, chili powder, and sugar.

3. Simmer 1 hour.

4. Meanwhile, cook 4 medium potatoes. Peel. Chill and shred. (Chilling makes the potatoes easier to shred.) Add to chili mixture at the end of one hour of simmering. Heat thoroughly.

Baked Potato Soup

Flo Quint, Quinter, KS
Susan Nafziger, Canton, KS

Makes 6-8 servings

Prep Time: 30 minutes
Cooking Time: 15-20 minutes

2/3 cup butter
2/3 cup flour
7 cups milk
4 cups baked potatoes
    (about 5 large potatoes),
    peeled and cubed
4 green onions, sliced thin
8-12 strips bacon
    (according to your taste
    preferences), cooked and
    crumbled
1 1/4 cups shredded cheese
8 ozs. sour cream, *optional*
3/4 tsp. salt, *optional*
1/4 tsp. pepper, *optional*

1. Melt butter in large
stockpot. Add flour and stir
until smooth over medium
heat.

2. Add milk, stirring often
until thickened. Be careful
not to scorch.

3. Add potatoes and onions
and bring to a boil. Reduce
heat and simmer 5 minutes,
stirring often.

4. Remove from heat and
add bacon, cheese, and sour
cream. Stir until melted.

5. Add seasonings and
blend thoroughly.

*Variation: Instead of 7 cups
milk, you can use 4 cups milk
and 3 cups chicken broth.*

Easy Creamy Potato and Ham Soup

Lori Klassen
Mountain Lake, MN

Makes 12 servings

Prep Time: 15 minutes
Cooking Time: 30 minutes

6 cups water
7 tsp. chicken bouillon
    granules
2 8-oz. pkgs. cream cheese,
    cubed
1 1/2 cups cubed ham, fully
    cooked
32-oz. pkg. frozen cubed
    hash brown potatoes
1/2 cup chopped onions
1 tsp. garlic powder
1 tsp. dill weed

1. Combine water and
chicken bouillon granules in a
large soup pot over heat. Stir
until granules are dissolved.

2. Add cream cheese and
stir until melted.

3. Add all other ingredi-
ents and simmer 20 minutes,
or until vegetables are tender.

*Tip: To reduce calories, use
low-fat cream cheese.*

French Onion Soup Made Light

Tanya Miseo
Bridgewater, NJ

Makes 6 servings

Prep Time: 15 minutes
*Cooking Time: 2 hours and
    20 minutes*

8 cups Vidalia onions,
    sliced
2 Tbsp. oil
10 cups beef stock
1 tsp. salt
1 tsp. pepper
1/2 tsp. garlic powder
1 cup white wine
6 thick slices Italian, *or*
    sourdough, bread
1/2 cup shredded
    mozzarella cheese

1. In large stockpot, slice
onions and sauté in oil until
they caramelize, about 40
minutes.

2. Add beef stock, salt,
pepper, and garlic powder to
onions. Cover, bring to boil,
and simmer for 1 hour.

3. Add white wine and
simmer for another 30 minutes.

4. Ladle into oven-safe
serving bowls. Float a piece
of bread on top of soup.
Sprinkle with cheese.

5. Broil for about 2 min-
utes until cheese melts. Serve
immediately.

Mushroom Stew

Lauren Bailey
Mechanicsburg, PA

Makes 10 servings

Prep Time: 20 minutes
Cooking Time: 30-35 minutes

5 Tbsp. butter, *divided*
1 Tbsp. oil
2 bay leaves
1 large onion, chopped
2 cloves minced garlic (use
    more if you wish)
2 Tbsp. flour
1 cup chicken broth
1 cup tomato juice, *or*
    fresh puree
2 cups cut-up tomatoes,
    fresh *or* canned
1 tsp. dried thyme
1½ lbs. fresh mushrooms,
    chopped
salt and pepper to taste
1½ cups red wine

1. In medium-sized saucepan melt 2 Tbsp. butter and oil. Add bay leaves and onion. Sauté until onions are golden. Stir in garlic and sauté one more minute.

2. Stir in flour and lower the heat. Cook several minutes on low, stirring constantly.

3. Add broth and tomato juice. Stir with whisk to remove all lumps. Add cut-up tomatoes.

4. In larger pot, sauté mushrooms in 3 Tbsp. butter. Add thyme over high heat. Add tomato mixture, salt and pepper. Lower heat and simmer for 20 minutes.

5. Add wine and stir for one minute.

A Tip —

Create a family tradition by putting a spin on a usual recipe. Add interesting complementary ingredients or a garnish. For example, cut out turkey shapes from toasted bread and put them on top of a stuffing casserole as a garnish.

Sausage-Lentil Soup

Esther J. Mast
Lancaster, PA

Makes 8-10 servings

Prep Time: 10-15 minutes
Cooking Time: 45 minutes

1 lb. fresh pork sausage
2 medium onions, chopped
1 garlic clove, minced
2 cups dry lentils
½ tsp. dried basil
½ tsp. cumin
½ tsp. dried marjoram
16-oz. can stewed tomatoes
1 qt. tomato juice
1 qt. water
4 beef bouillon cubes

1. In large kettle, brown sausage. Remove from kettle and drain, reserving ¼ cup drippings.

2. When sausage is cool enough to handle, cut into ½"-thick slices. Set aside.

3. Add onions and garlic to drippings in kettle. Cook 5 minutes, or until onions and garlic are tender.

4. Stir in lentils, basil, cumin, marjoram, tomatoes, tomato juice, water, bouillon cubes, and browned sausage. Simmer 30 minutes, or until lentils are tender.

This has become a favorite soup of our family. Even the grandchildren love it!

Sausage Tomato Soup

Teresa Martin
Gordonville, PA

Makes 6 servings

Prep Time: 10-15 minutes
Cooking Time: 25-30 minutes

1/2 lb. bulk Italian sausage, sweet *or* hot, *or* turkey sausage
1 medium-sized onion, chopped
1 small green *or* red pepper, chopped
28-oz. can diced tomatoes, undrained
14 1/2-oz. can beef broth
8-oz. can tomato sauce
1/2 cup picante sauce *or* salsa
1/2 tsp. dried oregano
1 tsp. dried basil
1 1/2 tsp. sugar
1/2-3/4 cup shredded mozzarella cheese

1. In large saucepan, cook sausage, onion, and pepper over medium heat until meat is no longer pink. Stir often with a wooden spoon to break up sausage chunks. Drain off drippings.

2. Stir in tomatoes, broth, tomato sauce, picante sauce, oregano, basil, and sugar. Bring to a boil. Reduce heat. Cover and simmer for 10 minutes.

3. Sprinkle with cheese before serving.

Italian Sausage Soup

Esther Porter
Minneapolis, MN

Makes 6-8 servings

Prep Time: 15-25 minutes
Cooking Time: 65-70 minutes

1 lb. Italian sausage, casings removed
1 cup chopped onions
2 large garlic cloves, sliced
5 cups beef stock, *or* 3 14.5-oz. cans beef broth
2 cups chopped *or* canned tomatoes
8-oz. can tomato sauce
1 1/2 cups zucchini, sliced
1 carrot, thinly sliced
1 medium-sized green bell pepper, diced
1 cup green beans, frozen *or* fresh
2 Tbsp. dried basil
2 Tbsp. dried oregano
8-10-oz. pkg. cheese tortellini
salt to taste
pepper to taste
freshly grated Parmesan cheese for topping

1. Sauté sausage in heavy Dutch oven over medium heat until cooked through, about 10 minutes, breaking it up as it browns with a wooden spoon.

2. Using a slotted spoon, transfer sausage to a large bowl. Pour off all but 1 Tbsp. drippings from Dutch oven. Add onions and garlic to the 1 Tbsp. drippings and sauté until clear, about 5 minutes.

3. Return sausage to pan. Add beef stock, tomatoes, tomato sauce, zucchini, carrot, pepper, green beans, basil, and oregano. Simmer 30-40 minutes, or until vegetables are tender.

4. Add tortellini and cook 8-10 minutes. Season to taste with salt and pepper.

5. Ladle hot soup into bowls and sprinkle with Parmesan cheese.

Variations:
1. Use leftover meat and vegetables from your refrigerator, instead of the sausage and the vegetables listed above.
2. Substitute V-8 juice for half of the beef stock or tomatoes.
3. When you're in a hurry, use Italian-style frozen vegetables instead of fresh beans, carrot, and zucchini.
4. Instead of tortellini, use 1/2-lb. package small pasta shells, uncooked.

— **Michelle Scribano**, Harrisonburg, VA

Aunt Marie's Tortellini Soup

Samantha Sorrentino
Tinton Falls, NJ

Makes 6 servings

Prep Time: 10 minutes
Cooking Time: 35 minutes

1/4 cup chopped onions
2 cloves garlic, chopped
2 Tbsp. olive oil
14-oz. can diced tomatoes, undrained
2 14-oz. cans chicken broth
2-3 soup cans water
2 tsp. Italian seasoning
salt and pepper to taste
8-oz. pkg. refrigerated cheese tortellini
8-9 ozs. fresh spinach, *or* 10-oz. pkg. chopped frozen spinach, thawed

1. In large stockpot, sauté onions and garlic in olive oil for 3 minutes.
2. Add diced tomatoes, chicken broth, water, and seasonings. Simmer 20 minutes.
3. Add tortellini and simmer 8 minutes.
4. Stir in spinach and simmer 2 more minutes.

Wild Rice and Ham Chowder

Doloris Krause
Mountain Lake, MN

Makes 8 servings

Prep Time: 30 minutes
Cooking Time: 60-90 minutes

---

3 cups water, *or* more
3/4 cup uncooked wild rice, rinsed
1/2 cup chopped onions
3 garlic cloves, minced
1/4 cup butter *or* margarine
1/2 cup flour
4 cups water
4 chicken-flavored bouillon cubes
1 1/2 cups chopped, peeled potatoes
1/2 cup chopped carrots
1/2 tsp. dried thyme
1/2 tsp. nutmeg
1/8 tsp. pepper
1 bay leaf
15-oz. can whole-kernel corn, undrained
2 cups half-and-half
3 cups (1 lb.) cubed ham, fully cooked
2 Tbsp. parsley

1. In a medium-sized saucepan, combine 3 cups water and wild rice. Bring to a boil. Reduce heat, cover, and simmer 35-40 minutes, or until tender. (Check after 20 minutes, and then again after 30 minutes, to make sure the rice isn't cooking dry and scorching. Add more water if needed.)
2. Meanwhile, in a large saucepan, cook onions and garlic in butter until crisp-tender. Stir in flour. Cook 1 minute, stirring constantly.
3. Gradually stir 4 cups water and bouillon into onion and garlic. Add potatoes, carrots, thyme, nutmeg, pepper, and bay leaf.
4. Bring vegetable mixture to a boil. Reduce heat, cover, and simmer 15-30 minutes.
5. Add corn to vegetables. Cover and simmer for an additional 15-20 minutes.
6. Stir in half-and-half, ham, cooked wild rice, and parsley. Cook over low heat until heated through.
7. Remove bay leaf and serve.

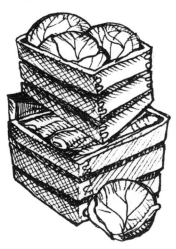

Pumpkin Soup

Sara Harter Fredette
Goshen, IN

Makes 8-9 servings

Prep Time: 10-15 minutes
Cooking Time: 20 minutes

1 large onion, chopped
3/4 tsp. cumin
1/2 tsp. cinnamon
1/2 tsp. ground ginger
2 chicken bouillon cubes
13/4 cups water
29-oz. can pumpkin
2 cups milk
1 Tbsp. honey
1 tsp. salt
2 Tbsp. butter *or* margarine
shake of Tabasco
shake of liquid smoke

1. In large saucepan, sauté onion in oil until soft. Stir in cumin, cinnamon, and ginger, and continue heating until spices are fragrant.
2. In a small saucepan, heat the water to boiling. Add bouillon cubes and stir until dissolved. Add to saucepan.
3. Add pumpkin and simmer mixture for 10-15 minutes. Remove from heat.
4. Stir in milk, honey, salt, butter, Tabasco, and liquid smoke.
5. When mixture has cooled to room temperature, puree in blender, 2 cups at a time.
6. Reheat before serving.

Butternut Squash Soup

Stephanie O'Conner
Cheshire, CT

Makes 6-8 servings

Prep Time: 15-20 minutes
Cooking Time: 35 minutes

1 shallot, finely chopped
4 Tbsp. butter
3-lb. butternut squash, peeled and cubed
11 whole leaves of fresh sage, washed, *divided*
4 cups chicken stock
1/2 tsp. salt
1/4 tsp. pepper
1/3 cup heavy cream
1/2 cup light brown sugar
1 tsp. ground cinnamon
pinch of nutmeg

1. In stockpot, sauté the shallot in butter over medium heat.
2. Add squash, 3 sage leaves, chicken stock, salt, and pepper. Cover and bring to a boil. Simmer, covered, for 20-30 minutes, until squash falls apart when stuck with a fork.
3. Puree soup by portions in a firmly covered blender, 2 cups at a time. When you've finished, return pureed mixture to stockpot.
4. Stir in cream, brown sugar, cinnamon, and nutmeg over low heat. Taste the soup to determine whether or not to add more cinnamon, sugar, salt, and pepper.
5. Serve garnished with whole leaves of fresh sage.

Matt's Spicy Peanut Soup

Dawn Ranck
Lansdale, PA
Esther Nafziger
Bluffton, OH

Makes 6 servings

Prep Time: 25 minutes
Cooking Time: 30 minutes

2 Tbsp. oil
1 large onion, minced
2 garlic cloves, crushed
1 tsp. mild cayenne pepper
2 red bell peppers, seeded and chopped
11/2 cups finely chopped carrots
11/2 cups finely chopped potatoes
3 celery ribs, sliced
33/4 cups vegetable stock
6 Tbsp. crunchy peanut butter
2/3 cup whole-kernel corn
salt to taste
freshly ground pepper to taste
roughly chopped peanuts

1. In large stockpot, sauté onion and garlic in oil for 3 minutes. Add cayenne pepper. Cook 1 minute.
2. Add red peppers, carrots, potatoes, and celery. Stir well. Cook 4 minutes, stirring occasionally.
3. Add stock, peanut butter, and corn. Mix well.
4. Season with salt and pepper. Cover and bring to boil.

5. Simmer about 20 minutes, or until vegetables are tender.

6. Garnish with peanuts when serving.

Creamed Crab and Corn Soup

Shari Jensen
Fountain, CO

Makes 8 servings

Prep Time: 15 minutes
Cooking Time: 25-30 minutes

1 lb. lump crabmeat
half a stick (1/4 cup) butter
1 1/2 cups finely chopped
   onions
2 Tbsp. flour
8 cups corn (freshly cut
   from cob is best*)
4 cups heavy cream
2 cups chicken broth
1/4 tsp. thyme
salt and white pepper, to
   taste
2 Tbsp. chopped parsley
grated cheddar cheese

1. Pick over crabmeat to remove any shell or cartilage. Set aside.

2. In large stockpot, melt butter. Add onions and sauté until clear and tender.

3. Blend in flour. Add corn kernels. Cook for 5 minutes, stirring frequently.

4. Add cream, broth, thyme, salt, and pepper. Cook over medium heat for 10 minutes, or until corn is tender. Stir often to prevent broth from scorching.

5. Add crabmeat and parsley and cook until meat is thoroughly heated.

6. Serve hot. Garnish with cheddar cheese.

Tip:
1. One good-sized ear of sweet corn will yield 1-1 1/2 cups corn kernels.

2. Don't use high heat or cream will scald.

A Tip —

Soups which include cream should never be boiled. The cream will curdle.

Egg Drop Soup

Susan Guarneri, Three Lakes, WI

Makes 6-7 servings

Prep Time: 10 minutes
Cooking Time: 25 minutes

2 Tbsp. cornstarch
6 cups chicken stock
2 Tbsp. soy sauce
3 Tbsp. white vinegar
1 small onion, minced
3 eggs, beaten
salt and pepper
sweet pepper flakes,
   optional

1. In stockpot, mix cornstarch with 1/2 cup cold chicken stock. When smooth, gradually add remaining chicken stock over medium heat, stirring continuously to keep cornstarch suspended and mixture smooth. Turn heat to low.

2. Add soy sauce, vinegar, and onion. Bring to low simmer (barely boiling).

3. Quickly stir in beaten eggs, swirling the broth and eggs in a circular motion to create "egg threads" in the soup. When all eggs are in the broth, allow to cook without stirring for 1 minute.

4. Remove pan from heat. Add salt and pepper to taste. Add sweet pepper flakes, if desired, before serving.

Crab Bisque

Jere Zimmerman
Reinholds, PA

Makes 4 servings

Prep Time: 15 minutes
Cooking Time: 20 minutes

1 stick (1/2 cup) butter,
  divided
1/2 cup finely chopped
  onions
1/2 cup finely chopped
  green pepper
2 green onions, finely
  chopped
1/4 cup fresh parsley,
  chopped
8 ozs. fresh mushrooms,
  chopped
1/4 cup flour
2 cups milk
1 tsp. salt
1/4 tsp. pepper
3 cups half-and-half
16-oz. can (2 1/2 cups) claw
  crabmeat
grated carrot for color,
  optional

1. Melt half a stick of butter in stockpot. Add onion,
green pepper, green onions,
parsley, and mushrooms.
Cook until tender. Remove
vegetables from heat and set
aside.

2. In the same stockpot,
melt remaining half stick of
butter over low heat. Add
flour and stir until smooth.
Add milk, stirring until thickened.

3. Add reserved vegetable
mixture, salt, pepper, half-
and-half, crabmeat, and
grated carrot, if desired.

4. Heat through over low
heat, but do not boil.

Great Fish Soup

Willard E. Roth
Elkhart, IN

Makes 6 servings

Prep Time: 15 minutes
Cooking Time: 1 hour

3 Tbsp. oil
1 onion, chopped
2 cloves garlic, minced
1/4 tsp. pepper
2 tsp. salt
1 bay leaf
1/4 tsp. dried thyme
1 lb. pollock, cut into
  chunks
1 lb. red snapper, cut into
  chunks
1/2 lb. tilapia, cut into
  chunks
5 cups water
1 cup white wine
1 lb. scallops
1 cup small pasta shells
12-oz. can evaporated milk

1. Combine oil, onion, and
garlic in large stockpot. Sauté
until onion and garlic begin
to soften. Stir in pepper, salt,
bay leaf, and thyme.
Combine well.

2. Stir in pollock, red snapper, and tilapia. Simmer gently for about 10 minutes.

3. Add water and wine.
Bring to a boil. Simmer for 10
more minutes.

4. Add scallops and pasta
shells. Cook about 15 minutes, or until shells are just-
tender.

5. Stir in milk.

Tip: Use your imagination to
determine which seafood to use,
depending on what's available
and what you and your diners
like best.

You can also use fresh herbs
if they're available.

Variation: If you'd like a
thicker soup, melt 3 Tbsp. butter in a small saucepan. Stir in
3 Tbsp. flour. Continue cooking
over low heat, stirring constantly for 2 minutes. Stir this
paste into hot soup in Step 5,
continuing to stir until paste is
well distributed and broth
thickens slightly. Adjust seasonings.

A Tip —

An enameled (outside
and inside) cast-iron casserole or kettle is a good
investment for making
stews, roasts, and soups.
Splurge and get a good
one. You'll use it for many
dishes!

Seafood Soup
Wafi Brandt
Manheim, PA

Makes 10 servings

Prep Time: 15 minutes
Cooking Time: 45 minutes

2 cups water
1 cup (¹/₂ lb.) small veined
   shrimp (salad shrimp)
1 cup (¹/₂ lb.) small bay
   scallops
1 cup (¹/₂ lb.) crabmeat
   (can be imitation)
1 small onion, chopped
   (about 1 cup)
1 carrot, peeled and
   chopped
4-6 cups chopped potatoes
   (about 6 medium)
1¹/₂ tsp. garlic salt
1¹/₂ tsp. garlic powder
1 Tbsp. Old Bay seasoning
1 Tbsp. chives
1 Tbsp. dill weed
1 Tbsp. rosemary
3 cups milk, *divided*
¹/₄ cup flour

1. Place the water and the 3 kinds of seafood in a large stockpot. Begin cooking over medium heat.

2. Add chopped onion, carrot, and potatoes. Simmer until desired tenderness.

3. Add garlic salt, garlic powder, Old Bay seasoning, chives, dill weed, and rosemary.

4. Shake together the flour and 1 cup milk in a jar. Add to soup, stirring until thickened.

5. Add remaining 2 cups milk. (More milk may be added for a thinner soup or to stretch it for more servings.)

Oyster Stew
Dorothy Reise
Severna Park, MD

Makes 4 servings

Prep Time: 10-15 minutes
Cooking Time: 15 minutes

2-3 doz. fresh oysters in
   liquid
2 Tbsp. butter
1 Tbsp. onion, chopped
3 Tbsp. flour
3 cups milk
1 tsp. salt
¹/₂ tsp. pepper
¹/₂ tsp. parsley, chopped
pinch of celery seed,
   optional
dash of paprika, *optional*

1. In a small skillet over medium heat, pre-cook oysters in their own liquid until edges curl and oysters become plump. Set aside.

2. In large stockpot, melt butter, add onion, and sauté until soft.

3. Over medium heat, add flour and stir until smooth.

4. Slowly add milk, stirring constantly until thickened.

5. Add the pre-cooked oysters and liquid, salt, pepper, parsley, and celery seed and paprika if you wish. Mix well.

6. Heat thoroughly and serve.

Italian Clam Chowder

Susan Guarneri
Three Lakes, WI

Makes 8 servings

Prep Time: 30 minutes
Cooking Time: 4-5 hours

2 lbs. sweet Italian sausage
1 onion, chopped
4 medium potatoes,
   unpeeled and cubed
2 12-oz. cans beer
2 cups water *or* chicken
   broth
1 pint cream
1/2 cup non-fat dry milk
1 dozen large fresh clams,
   chopped, *or* 61/2-oz. can
   clams
8-oz. can minced clams
1/2 tsp. salt
1/4 tsp. pepper
1 tsp. dried basil

1. Cut sausage into 1/2"
slices. Place in large Dutch
oven and brown until no longer
pink. Set sausage aside.
2. Reserve 2 Tbsp. drip-
pings in Dutch oven. Add
onion, potatoes, beer, broth,
cream, dry milk, clams, salt,
pepper, and basil. Stir until
well mixed.
3. Place Dutch oven in the
oven. Bake at 275° for 4-5
hours. (Do not increase the
temperature or the chowder
may boil and then the cream
will curdle.)
4. One hour before the
end of the baking time, stir in
the reserved sausage.

*I got this recipe from my Italian
neighbor when I lived in
Baltimore, Maryland. Fresh
clams were easy to get and this
filled up the entire family with
leftovers for lunch. The chowder
is even better the next day.*

Salmon Chowder

Ruth C. Hancock
Earlsboro, OK

Makes 8 servings

Prep Time: 25 minutes
Cooking Time: 70 minutes

1/2 cup chopped celery
1/2 cup chopped onions
1/2 cup chopped green
   pepper
1 clove garlic, minced
3 Tbsp. butter *or*
   margarine
14.5-oz. can chicken broth
1 cup uncooked diced
   potatoes
1 cup shredded carrots
11/2 tsp. salt
1/2 tsp. pepper
1/4 tsp. dill weed
15-oz. can creamed corn
2 cups half-and-half
15-oz. can salmon,
   deboned and broken
   into small chunks, *or*
   2 cups frozen salmon,
   cooked*

1. In large saucepan, sauté
celery, onions, green pepper,
and garlic in butter until tender.
2. Add broth, potatoes, carrots, salt, pepper, and dill
weed.
3. Bring to a boil, reduce
heat, cover, and simmer 40
minutes, or until vegetables
are nearly tender.
4. Stir in creamed corn,
half-and-half, and salmon.
Simmer 15 minutes.

* *You can use salmon frozen in
vacuum-sealed packages.
Microwave according to directions on the package. When
done, cut corner off package,
drain liquid, break up the
salmon, and add it to the chowder.*

*I found this recipe while
waiting for my husband who
was having an MRI. I was
pleasantly surprised the first
time I made it. My husband,
who doesn't like chowders,
loves this one. It is one of my
favorites!*

Main Dishes

Beef Main Dishes

Pot Roast and Wine

Christina Ricker
Gordonville, PA

Makes 4-6 servings

Prep Time: 15-20 minutes
Roasting Time: 1½-2 hours
Standing Time: 20 minutes

6-lb. eye round roast
1-2 Tbsp. olive oil
1 cup finely chopped celery
1 cup finely chopped onions
1 bottle white cooking wine
salt and pepper to taste

1. In a large skillet, brown roast on all sides in 1-2 Tbsp. olive oil. Then place in a large roasting pan or Dutch oven.

2. Sprinkle chopped celery and onion over and around roast.

3. Pour white wine over all. Sprinkle salt and pepper over meat and vegetables to taste.

4. Cover and roast at 325° for 1½-2 hours, until tender.

5. While meat roasts, check liquid level to be sure the pan juices haven't all cooked off. Add ½ cup water if you can't see any liquid in the pan. Baste meat occasionally with juices.

6. Allow to stand for 20 minutes before slicing and serving with pan juices.

A Tip —

Don't salt meat or a roast as you're browning it. Instead, add salt to taste at the end of the browning. The meat will stay more moist, since salt draws out moisture.

Savory Sweet Roast

Marie Hostetler
Nappanee, IN

Makes 6-8 servings

Prep Time: 20 minutes
Roasting Time: 2 hours
Standing Time: 20 minutes

3-4 lb. beef roast
1-2 Tbsp. olive oil
1 medium-sized onion, chopped
10.75-oz. can cream of mushroom soup
1/2 cup water
1 tsp. prepared mustard
2 tsp. salt
1/4 cup vinegar
1/4 cup sugar
1 tsp. Worcestershire sauce

1. In a large skillet, brown roast on all sides in olive oil.
2. Meanwhile, in a mixing bowl, blend together all other ingredients.
3. When roast is browned, place in roasting pan. Pour sauce ingredients over meat.
4. Cover and bake at 350° for 2 hours, or until tender.
5. Let meat stand for 20 minutes. Slice and serve with sauce.

Tips:
1. The sauce that the roast is cooked in makes a succulent gravy. Serve over the meat, and over potatoes, rice, or pasta, if you've made one of them as a go-along.
2. I like to cut potato wedges and place them on top of the meat before roasting it. I like to

do the same with julienned carrot sticks. Either of those combinations gives you a good meal all in one pan.

Pounded Swiss Steak in a Yummy Sauce

Robbin Poetzl
Springfield, OR

Makes 6-8 servings

Prep Time: 20-30 minutes
Browning/ Baking Time: 50 minutes

4-5 lbs. skirt *or* flank beef steak, about 1/2" thick
1 1/2-2 cups flour
1 Tbsp. Italian seasoning
1 tsp. garlic powder
1 tsp. pepper
1 tsp. onion powder
1 tsp. pepper herb seasoning
1/4 cup oil

Sauce:
2 tsp. oil
1/2 tsp. crushed garlic
1/2-1 cup red wine
1/3 cup teriyaki sauce
1 tsp. Italian seasoning
1 1/2 cups fresh mushrooms, sliced
1 cup celery, chopped
2 14.5-oz. cans diced tomatoes, undrained

1. Cut the steak into serving-size pieces. Pound each piece to about 1/4" thick. In a

small bowl, mix flour with seasonings. Flour all sides of pounded steak pieces.
2. Brown floured meat, a few pieces at a time, in hot oil in a large skillet. Brown 2-3 minutes on one side and then the other side for 2-3 minutes. Place browned steak in a shallow baking dish.
3. To make the sauce, heat 2 tsp. oil in a large, heavy skillet over medium-high heat. Stir in garlic. When garlic begins to "pop" add the wine.
4. Simmer for 2-3 minutes. Then add the teriyaki sauce, Italian seasoning, mushrooms, celery, and canned tomatoes. Bring to a light boil.
5. Turn down heat and continue to cook the sauce, uncovered, until it thickens. Pour the sauce over prepared steaks.
6. Cover and bake at 350° for 15 minutes. Remove lid and bake an additional 15 minutes.

Tips: For the sauce, use canned tomatoes with chopped jalapenos for a spicier flavor.

Simply Elegant Steak
Judy DeLong
Burnt Hills, NY

Makes 6 servings

Prep Time: 20 minutes
Cooking Time: 30 minutes

1½ lbs. tender sirloin
  steak
1½ Tbsp. olive oil
2 large onions, sliced into
  rings
10.75-oz. can cream of
  mushroom soup
½ cup dry sherry
4-oz. can sliced
  mushrooms (reserve
  liquid)
½ tsp. garlic salt
3 cups cooked rice

1. Cut steak into thin
strips. Place in large skillet
and brown in oil over high
heat. Add onions and sauté
until tender-crisp.
2. In mixing bowl, blend
soup, sherry, mushroom liquid, and salt. Pour over steak.
Top with mushrooms.
3. Reduce heat, cover, and
simmer for 15-30 minutes
until steak is tender, but not
overdone.
4. Serve over rice.

*Tips: For ease in slicing the
steak into strips, place the meat
in the freezer for 30 minutes;
then slice.*

Sirloin or Chuck Steak Marinade
Susan Nafziger
Canton, KS

Makes marinade for 4 steaks

Prep Time: 15 minutes

1 cup olive oil
1 cup soy sauce
¼ cup wine vinegar
½ cup chopped onions
⅛ tsp. garlic powder
¼ tsp. ground ginger
½ tsp. pepper
½ tsp. dry mustard

1. Mix all ingredients
together, either by whisking
together in a bowl, or
whirring the mixture in a
blender.
2. Place sirloin or chuck
steak in marinade mixture
and marinate for at least 1
hour per 1-inch thickness of
meat.
3. When ready to grill or
broil meat, drain off marinade and discard. Cook steak.

A Tip —

Keep a supply of cream
of mushroom soup in your
pantry. It is a quick and
convenient staple for beef,
veal, and pork roasts and
casseroles. It makes a good
sauce or gravy, with just a
few additional seasonings
or some sour cream.

Barbeque Beef Strips
Doris Ranck
Gap, PA

Makes 10 servings

Prep Time: 30 minutes
Cooking Time: 40-45 minutes

2 lbs. steak *or* London
  broil
2 Tbsp. vegetable oil
1 medium-sized onion,
  chopped
2 cups ketchup
⅓ cup water
3-4 Tbsp. brown sugar,
  according to your taste
  preference
1 Tbsp. prepared mustard
1 Tbsp. Worcestershire
  sauce

1. Slice steak into strips
about 3" long and ⅛" wide.
2. Place oil in large skillet.
Add strips of meat and
chopped onions. Brown
quickly over high heat, stirring so that all sides of beef
brown well. Pour off all but 2
Tbsp. drippings.
3. Combine remaining
ingredients in a mixing bowl.
When well mixed, pour over
beef strips and onions in skillet.
4. Cover and cook slowly
for 35-40 minutes, or until
beef is tender. Stir occasionally.
5. Serve over cooked rice
or pasta.

Flavorful Beef Stroganoff

Susan Guarneri, Three Lakes, WI

Makes 6 servings

Prep Time: 25 minutes
Cooking Time: 80 minutes

2 lbs. boneless chuck
1/4 cup flour
1 tsp. salt
2 Tbsp. butter
1 medium-sized onion, chopped
1 clove garlic, crushed
10.75-oz. can cream of mushroom soup
1/2 tsp. cinnamon
1/4 tsp. allspice
1 cup water
4-oz. can sliced mushrooms, undrained
1 pint sour cream

1. Cut chuck in strips 1/2" thick.
2. Mix flour and salt. Dredge meat in flour/salt mixture.
3. Melt butter in large skillet. Brown flour-coated meat in butter over high heat. Stir often so that meat browns on all sides.
4. When meat is browned, turn down heat and add onion, garlic, soup, cinnamon, allspice, and water.
5. Cover and simmer 1 hour.
6. Reduce heat and stir in mushrooms and sour cream. Do not allow to boil, but simmer, covered, until heated through. Serve over egg noodles.

Glazed Meat Loaf

Doris Beachy
Stevens, PA

Makes 10 servings

Prep Time: 10 minutes
Baking Time: 1 hour
Standing Time: 5 minutes

1 1/2 lbs. ground beef
3/4 cup dry quick oats
2 eggs, beaten
1/4 cup chopped onions
2 tsp. salt
1/4 tsp. pepper
1 cup tomato juice

Sauce:
1/4 cup ketchup
1 Tbsp. prepared mustard
2 Tbsp. brown sugar

1. In a large mixing bowl, combine ground beef with next 6 ingredients. Mix thoroughly and pack firmly into a greased 9 x 5 loaf pan.
2. In a small mixing bowl, combine sauce ingredients and pour over meat mixture.
3. Bake at 350° for 1 hour.
4. Let stand 5 minutes before slicing.

Variations:
1. In meat loaf, replace 1 cup tomato juice with 1/3 cup ketchup and 3/4 tsp. prepared mustard.
2. Add 2 tsp. Worcestershire sauce to sauce.
— **Monica Yoder**
Millersburg, OH

3. After the meat loaf is mixed and shaped (Step 1 above), place loaf in the center of a greased 9 x 13 baking pan. Surround the meat with a layer of peeled and sliced potatoes (from 3 medium-sized potatoes), followed by a layer of carrot slices (from 3 medium-sized carrots), and a layer of onion quarters or slices (from 3 medium-sized onions). Top the vegetables with 2 tsp. dried parsley flakes, 1 tsp. salt, and a dash of pepper. Cover pan tightly with foil. Bake at 375° for 1 hour covered, then for 10 minutes uncovered.
— **Jane Frownfelter**
Grand Blanc, MI

Cheesy Meat Loaf

Jean Turner
Williams Lake, BC

Makes 8 servings

Prep Time: 20-30 minutes
Baking Time: 1 1/2 hours

1/2 cup chopped onions
1/2 cup chopped green pepper
1 tsp. butter
8-oz. can tomato sauce
2 eggs, beaten
1 cup shredded white cheddar cheese
1 cup soft bread crumbs
1 tsp. salt
dash of pepper
1/4 tsp. dried thyme
1 1/2 lbs. ground beef
1/2 lb. ground pork

1. In a small saucepan, sauté onions and green pepper in butter just until tender.

2. In large mixing bowl, combine all ingredients and mix well.

3. Shape into a loaf. Place in greased 9 x 5 loaf pan.

4. Bake at 350° for 1½ hours.

10-Minute Meat Loaf

Esther J. Yoder, Hartville, OH

Makes 6 servings

Prep Time: 10 minutes
Cooking Time: 10 minutes in the microwave; 45 minutes in the oven
Standing Time: 10 minutes, if cooked in the microwave

1 lb. ground beef
1 egg
½ cup bread crumbs
¼ cup milk
1 Tbsp. dry onion soup mix
2 Tbsp. ketchup
2 Tbsp. soy sauce
½ cup shredded cheddar cheese *or* Swiss cheese, *or* a combination of the two

1. In a mixing bowl thoroughly combine all ingredients and shape into a round flat loaf, like a giant hamburger.

2. Place round loaf in a lightly greased 8" glass pie plate.

3. Cover with waxed paper and microwave for 10 minutes on high. Drain. Cover with foil and let stand for 10 minutes. (This standing time is very important!)

Variation:
If you prefer oven-baked meat loaf, bake at 350° for 45-60 minutes, uncovered.

Bacon Beef Roll

Susan Nafziger, Canton, KS
Ruth Ann Penner, Hillsboro, KS

Makes 12 servings

Prep Time: 30 minutes
Baking Time: 45-60 minutes

1 cup shredded cheddar cheese
1 cup coarse cracker crumbs
½ cup chopped onions
1 cup milk
2 Tbsp. ketchup, *or* barbecue sauce
1 tsp. salt
¼ tsp. pepper
¼ celery salt
¼ cup brown sugar
2 lbs. ground beef
12 slices bacon

1. Mix cheese, cracker crumbs, onions, milk, ketchup, salt, pepper, celery salt, and brown sugar in a large bowl.

2. Add ground beef and mix well.

3. Form into 12 "logs," each approximately 1" x 4".

Wrap 1 slice of bacon around each log, and fasten with a toothpick. Place side-by-side in a greased 9 x 13 baking dish.

4. Bake at 350° for 45 minutes. If bacon is not browned, turn oven to 375° and bake an additional 15 minutes.

Tips:
1. This recipe can be made a day ahead of time and then served to company. I have found a very easy way to make uniform rolls. On a cutting board, spread the meat mixture into a rectangular shape approximately the size of a 9 x 13 baking pan, and 1 inch thick. Divide it into 12 equal-size pieces by cutting down the center, and then lengthwise across 6 times. Shape each piece into a "log."

2. You can make this mixture into meatballs, without the bacon.

A Tip —

Place cooked hamburger in a strainer and rinse it under hot water to eliminate extra fat.

BBQ Meatballs

Jolene Schrock
Millersburg, OH
Sara M. Miller
Uniontown, OH
Rebecca Meyerkorth
Wamego, KS
Doris Beachy
Stevens, PA
Martha Belle Burkholder
Waynesboro, VA
Audrey L. Kneer
Williamsfield, IL
Pam McAllister
Wooster, OH

Makes about 24 medium-sized meatballs

Prep Time: 15-20 minutes
Baking Time: 1 hour

Meatballs:
12-oz. can evaporated milk
2 cups dry quick oats
2 eggs
1 cup chopped onions
2 tsp. salt
1/2 tsp. pepper
2 tsp. chili powder
3 lbs. ground beef

Topping:
1 cup brown sugar
1/2 cup chopped onions
1 cup ketchup
1 cup bottled barbecue
  sauce

1. In a large mixing bowl, mix all meatball ingredients together thoroughly. Shape into 24 balls and place in one layer in a greased 9 x 13 baking dish. (If your pan gets full, use an additional shallow baking pan or pie plate.)

2. In another mixing bowl, mix sauce ingredients together and pour over meatballs.

3. Bake at 350°, uncovered, for 1 hour.

Variations:
1. Use 1 cup quick dry oats and 1 cup cracker crumbs instead of 2 cups dry oats.
2. Use 2 lbs. ground beef and 1 lb. bulk sausage instead of 3 lbs. ground beef.
— Katie Stoltzfus
Leola, PA

3. For topping, use 2 cups ketchup, instead of 1 cup ketchup and 1 cup barbecue sauce, and add 1/2-1 tsp. liquid smoke if you wish.

Creamy, Spicy Meatballs

Sherlyn Hess, Millersville, PA

Makes 4-5 servings

Prep Time: 15 minutes
Baking Time: 40 minutes

1 lb. ground beef
1/2 lb. hot Italian sausage,
  squeezed out of its
  casing
1/2 cup fine dry bread
  crumbs
1 egg
1/2 cup chopped onions
1/2 tsp. salt
10.75-oz. can golden
  mushroom soup
1/4 cup water

1 clove garlic, minced
1/4 tsp. dried oregano

1. In a large mixing bowl, combine beef, sausage, bread crumbs, egg, onions, and salt. Form into golf-ball-sized balls.

2. Place meatballs in a single layer in a greased 9 x 13 baking pan.

3. Bake at 350°, uncovered, for 30 minutes.

4. Meanwhile, in a saucepan combine soup, water, garlic, and oregano. Bring to a boil. Pour over meatballs.

5. Return meatballs to oven and continue baking at 350°, uncovered, for an additional 10 minutes.

Chuck Roast Beef Barbecue

Helen Heurich
Lititz, PA

Makes 20 servings

Prep Time: 30-40 minutes
Baking Time: 3 hours

3-lb. chuck roast
2/3 cup hot ketchup, *or*
  barbecue sauce
1 1/4 cups ketchup
3 Tbsp. lemon juice
2 Tbsp. Worcestershire
  sauce
2 Tbsp. brown sugar
1 1/2 tsp. prepared mustard
3 Tbsp. vinegar, *optional*
1-2 medium-sized onions,
  chopped
3-4 ribs celery, chopped

1. Place beef in roast pan. Add 1/2" water and cover. Roast at 350° for about 2 hours, until the beef is tender.

2. Cool. Pull apart with two forks until beef is shredded.

3. While the beef is roasting, combine the remaining ingredients in a medium saucepan. Cover and cook until heated through.

4. Pour sauce over shredded meat.

5. Return to oven and roast for 1 hour at 350°.

6. Serve on hamburger rolls.

Teriyaki Burgers
Susan Kasting
Jenks, OK

Makes 4 servings

Prep Time: 10 minutes
Cooking Time: 10 minutes

1 lb. ground beef
2 Tbsp. soy sauce
1 Tbsp. peeled fresh
  ginger, grated
1 garlic clove, minced
1/4 cup chopped green
  onions
pinch of pepper

1. Combine all ingredients in bowl.

2. Form into 4 patties.

3. Grill or broil for 10 minutes, flipping to brown both sides.

Stuffed Hamburgers
Penny Feveryear
Narvon, PA

Makes 4 servings

Prep Time: 10-15 minutes
Baking Time: 30 minutes

1 lb. ground beef
1/3 cup bread crumbs
3 Tbsp. minced onions
1/4 cup tomato sauce
1 tsp. Worcestershire sauce
1 tsp. salt
1/4 tsp. pepper

Stuffing:
1/2 cup sliced mushrooms
1/2 cup celery, chopped
1 Tbsp. minced onions
2 Tbsp. butter
2 Tbsp. milk
1/4 cup bread crumbs

1. In a mixing bowl, blend together beef, bread crumbs, onions, tomato sauce, Worcestershire sauce, salt, and pepper. Form into 4 large cup-shaped portions and place in greased shallow baking pan.

2. To prepare stuffing, sauté mushrooms, celery, and onions in butter in skillet for 5 minutes. Remove from heat and stir in milk and bread crumbs.

3. Fill centers of beef cups with equal parts of stuffing, pushing sides up to form finished cups.

4. Bake at 350° for 30 minutes.

Pizza Cups
Barbara Smith
Bedford, PA

Makes 6 servings

Prep Time: 20 minutes
Baking Time: 12-15 minutes

3/4 lb. ground beef
6-oz. can tomato paste
1 Tbsp. minced onions
1/2 tsp. salt
1 tsp. Italian seasoning
1 tube refrigerated biscuits
1/2-3/4 cup shredded
  mozzarella cheese

1. In skillet, brown beef. Drain.

2. Stir in tomato paste, onions, and seasonings.

3. Cook over low heat for 5 minutes, stirring frequently. Mixture will thicken.

4. Meanwhile, place biscuits in greased muffin tins. Press them in so they cover the bottom and sides of each cup.

5. Spoon about 1/4 cup meat mixture into each biscuit-lined cup. Sprinkle with cheese.

6. Bake at 400° for 12-15 minutes, or until brown.

This has often been our Friday-night, once-a-month-supper-with-a-movie.

Bierrocks (Pocket Sandwiches)

Andrea Cunningham
Arlington, VA

Makes 30 bierrocks

Prep Time: 45-60 minutes
Rising Time: 75 minutes
Baking Time: 20-30 minutes

Bread:
2 cups warm (120-130°)
   water
2 pkgs. dry yeast
1/4 cup sugar
1 1/2 tsp. salt
1 egg
1/4 cup butter, softend
6-6 1/2 cups flour, *divided*

Meat Mixture:
1 1/2 lbs. ground beef
1/2 cup chopped onions
3 cups cabbage, finely
   chopped
1 1/2 tsp. salt
1/2 tsp. pepper
dash Tabasco sauce
1/4-1/2 cup water, if needed
8 slices American cheese

1. In a large mixing bowl, mix yeast with water until dissolved. Add other dough ingredients except flour. Mix well.

2. Add 5 cups flour and beat thoroughly by hand or mixer. Stir in additional cup of flour. Turn dough onto floured board and knead until smooth and elastic, about 10-12 minutes.

3. Place dough in large greased mixing bowl. Rotate dough until greased on all sides. Cover and let rise until nearly double, about 1 hour.

4. Meanwhile, brown meat and onion in a large skillet or saucepan. Add remaining meat ingredients (except cheese). Cover skillet and continue to cook until cabbage is tender. If mixture begins to cook dry, stir in water to moisten.

5. Punch down dough and roll out into thin sheets. Cut into 30 5" squares.

6. Place 2 Tbsp. meat mixture on each square. Add 1/4 slice of cheese. Pinch edges of squares together and place pinched-side down on a greased cookie sheet.

7. Let rise 15 minutes.

8. Bake at 350° for 20-30 minutes, or until nicely browned.

Zucchini Lasagna

Ruth Ann Hoover
New Holland, PA

Makes 6-8 servings

Prep Time: 20 minutes
Cooking/Baking Time:
   55 minutes

6 cups sliced raw zucchini,
   unpeeled
1 lb. ground beef
6-oz. can tomato paste
1/2 tsp. dried basil
1/2 tsp. dried oregano
1/2 tsp. salt
1/4 tsp. garlic powder
1 cup cottage cheese
1 egg, beaten
1/4 cup dry bread crumbs,
   plain or herb-flavored
1 cup shredded cheddar
   cheese
1 cup shredded mozzarella
   cheese

1. Spread slices of zucchini into a long microwave-safe dish. Sprinkle with 2 Tbsp. water. Cover, and cook on high for 3 1/2 minutes. Stir. Cover and return to microwave and cook on high an additional 3 1/2 minutes. Stir. Cover and return to microwave and cook on high 1 1/2 minutes more. Drain zucchini and set aside.

2. Meanwhile, in large stockpot, brown ground beef. Drain off drippings.

3. Add tomato paste, basil, oregano, salt, garlic powder, cottage cheese, egg, bread crumbs, cheddar cheese, and cooked zucchini to browned beef in stockpot. Stir gently together until well mixed.

4. Spoon mixture into greased 7 x 11 baking dish.

5. Bake uncovered at 350° for 25 minutes.

6. Sprinkle mozzarella cheese over lasagna. Return to oven and continue baking 20 more minutes.

Variations:
   1. Instead of ground beef, use ground venison.
   2. Instead of ground beef, use 1/2 lb. ground turkey and 1/2 lb. ground venison.

Mexican Lasagna

Marcia S. Myer, Manheim, PA

Makes 12 servings

Prep Time: 25 minutes
Cooking/Baking Time:
* 55 minutes*

1 lb. ground beef
15-oz. can corn, drained
15-oz. can tomato sauce
1 cup picante sauce,
   or hot salsa, if you want
   more kick
1 Tbsp. chili powder
1½ tsp. cumin
16-oz. carton cottage
   cheese
2 eggs, slightly beaten
¼ cup Parmesan cheese
1 tsp. dried oregano
½ tsp. garlic salt
12 corn tortillas
1 cup (4 ozs.) shredded
   cheddar cheese
chopped cilantro
2 chopped green onions
chopped lettuce
chopped tomatoes

1. In a large skillet, brown ground beef. Drain off drippings.

2. Add corn, tomato sauce, picante sauce or hot salsa, chili powder, and cumin. Simmer for 5 minutes.

3. In a medium-sized mixing bowl, combine cottage cheese, eggs, Parmesan cheese, oregano, and garlic salt. Mix well.

4. Arrange 6 tortillas on the bottom and up the sides of a greased 9 x 13 baking pan, overlapping as necessary. Top with half the meat/vegetable mixture.

5. Spoon cheese mixture over meat. Arrange remaining tortillas over cheese mixture. Top with remaining meat mixture.

6. Bake at 375° for 30 minutes or until bubbly. Remove from oven.

7. Top with cheddar cheese. Return to oven to melt cheese. Let stand 10 minutes before serving.

8. Just before serving top with cilantro, green onions, lettuce, and tomatoes.

Variations:

1. Use 16-oz. can of diced tomatoes instead of 15-oz. can of corn in Step 2.

2. Add 1 tsp. black pepper and ¼ tsp. red pepper to Step 2.

3. Add ¼ cup sliced black olives to the toppings in Step 8.

   — Mable Hershey
   Marietta, PA

Mild Indian Curry

Vic and Christina Buckwalter
Keezletown, VA

Makes 4-6 servings

Prep Time: 10 minutes
Cooking Time: 15-20 minutes

1 lb. ground beef
1 onion, chopped
3 garlic cloves, finely
   chopped
½ tsp. ground ginger
2 tsp. coriander
2 tsp. cumin
1 tsp. turmeric
¼ tsp. ground cloves
¼ tsp. cayenne pepper
¾ cup tomato sauce
2 tsp. salt
2 Tbsp. sugar
¼ cup plain yogurt
cooked basmati rice
topping options: grated
   cheeses; chopped fresh
   onions; orange sections;
   sliced bananas; chopped
   papaya, mango, and/or
   tomatoes; peanuts;
   raisins

1. In a large skillet, brown beef, onions, and garlic together. Drain off any drippings.

2. Add ginger, coriander, cumin, turmeric, ground cloves, and cayenne pepper to beef mixture. Cook 1 minute.

3. Stir in tomato sauce, salt, and sugar. Cook 10 minutes.

4. Just before serving, blend in yogurt.

5. Serve over basmati rice.

6. Send small bowls of each topping that you choose around the table after the rice and curry have been passed.

We picked up this recipe while living in East Africa. It brings back memories of the Swahili Coast.

A Tip —

   Find easy-to-prepare recipes so you always have something in mind to fix for unexpected guests.

Beef Lombardi

Lucille Amos, Greensboro, NC

Makes 6-8 servings

Prep Time: 15 minutes
Cooking/Baking Time:
75 minutes

1 lb. ground beef
10-oz. can tomatoes with
chilies
14-oz. can chopped
tomatoes
2 tsp. sugar
2 tsp. salt
1/4 tsp. pepper
6-oz. can tomato paste
1 bay leaf
1/2-lb. pkg. egg noodles
6 green onions, sliced
1 cup sour cream
1 cup grated sharp cheese
1 cup grated Parmesan
cheese
1 cup grated mozzarella
cheese

1. Brown beef in large skillet. Drain off drippings.
2. Stir into beef, both cans of tomatoes, sugar, salt, and pepper. Cover and cook for 5 minutes.
3. Add tomato paste and bay leaf. Cover and simmer 30 minutes.
4. Meanwhile, cook noodles in a saucepan according to package directions. Drain.
5. Return noodles to their saucepan and mix in sliced green onions and sour cream. Place creamy noodles in a lightly greased 9 x 13 baking pan.

6. Top with beef mixture. Sprinkle with cheeses.
7. Cover and bake at 350° for 30 minutes.
8. Uncover and bake an additional 5 minutes.

Tip: Prepare the recipe in two smaller baking dishes. Freeze one for later or give it to a friend.

Quickie Dinner

Velma Stauffer
Akron, PA

Makes 4 servings.

Prep Time: 15 minutes
Cooking Time: 30 minutes

1 lb. ground beef
1/4 cup dried minced
onions
2 14.5-oz. cans stewed
tomatoes
1 tsp. salt
1 tsp. chili powder
1/4 tsp. pepper
1/4 tsp. sugar
1 cup uncooked macaronis

1. In a large skillet or saucepan, brown ground beef and onions. Drain off drippings.
2. Add tomatoes and seasonings and bring mixture to a boil.
3. Reduce heat, cover, and simmer for five minutes.
4. Add macaronis and cover; then simmer for 15 minutes.

5. Uncover and simmer until macaroni is tender and sauce is thickened.

Tip: I sometimes add a can of corn or peas for a complete meal.

Hamburger-Potato-Carrot Bake

Eleya Raim
Oxford, IA

Makes 6-8 servings

Prep Time: 15-20 minutes
Baking Time: 60-90 minutes
Standing Time: 5-10 minutes

1 lb. ground beef
1/2 tsp. onion powder,
or 1 Tbsp. dried onion
soup mix
1/2 tsp. salt, *divided*
1/8 tsp. pepper
1/2 cup ketchup
4 medium-sized potatoes,
peeled and sliced
4 carrots, peeled and sliced
2 Tbsp. water
6 slices Velveeta cheese

1. Press uncooked ground beef into the bottom of a lightly greased 9" square pan. Sprinkle with onion powder, 1/4 teaspoon salt, and 1/8 teaspoon pepper.
2. Spread ketchup over top.
3. Arrange sliced potatoes on top of ground-beef layer. Sprinkle with remaining salt.

4. Arrange carrots on top of potato layer. Sprinkle with water.

5. Cover tightly with foil and bake at 350° for 1-1½ hours, or until vegetables jag tender.

6. Remove from oven. Top with cheese slices. Cover and let stand 5-10 minutes until cheese has melted.

Beef & Salsa Burritos

Joyce Shackelford
Green Bay, WI

Makes 8 servings

Prep Time: 10 minutes
Cooking Time: 15 minutes

1¼ lbs. ground beef
1½ Tbsp. chili powder
1½ Tbsp. cumin, *optional*
½ tsp. salt
¼ tsp. pepper
10-oz. pkg. frozen chopped spinach, thawed and squeezed dry
1¼ cups chunky salsa
1 cup shredded cheddar cheese
8 medium-sized flour tortillas, warmed

1. In a large skillet, brown ground beef. Pour off drippings. Season meat with chili powder, cumin, if you wish, salt, and pepper.

2. Stir in spinach and salsa. Heat through.

3. Remove from heat, stir in cheese.

4. Spoon about ½ cup beef mixture into center of each tortilla. Fold bottom edge up over filling. Fold sides to center. Serve.

Taco Tortilla Tower

Christine Lucke
Aumsville, OR

Makes 6 servings

Prep Time: 30 minutes
Cooking/Baking Time:
25-35 minutes

1 lb. ground beef
half an envelope dry taco seasoning mix
½ cup chopped onions
16-oz. can refried beans
½ cup sour cream
5 10″ flour tortillas
2 cups shredded cheddar cheese
6-oz. can black olives, sliced, drained
¼ cup sliced green onions
vegetable oil
2 cups shredded lettuce
1 medium-sized tomato, chopped
sour cream
salsa

1. In a large skillet, brown ground beef. Drain off drippings.

2. Stir in taco seasoning and chopped onions. Cook until onions are transparent. Remove from heat.

3. Add refried beans and sour cream. Mix well.

4. Place one tortilla on a pizza pan or stone. Spread one-quarter of meat mixture over the tortilla. Sprinkle with ½ cup cheese and one-quarter of olives and green onions.

5. Place another tortilla on top. Repeat layering 3 more times. Top with remaining tortilla. Brush with vegetable oil for a crunchy top.

6. Bake at 375° for 20-30 minutes, or until bubbly and browned.

7. Slice into 6 wedges.

8. Pass shredded lettuce, chopped tomato, sour cream, and salsa as toppings.

Tip: I like this recipe because you can make it ahead, bake it, and serve it without the fuss and flurry of making tacos for each person.

A Tip —

Get out all ingredients for a recipe before you start cooking, and put them away as soon as you use them.

Enchilada Pie

Arlene Leaman Kliewer
Lakewood, CO

Makes 8 servings

Prep Time: 30 minutes
Cooking/Baking Time:
* 55 minutes*
Standing Time: 10 minutes

2 lbs. ground beef
1 small onion, chopped
small can of chopped
    black olives, drained
2 cups tomato sauce
1-lb. can chili con carne,
    or Mexican-style beans,
    undrained
18 corn tortillas
2-lb. box Velveeta cheese,
    cubed or shredded
1 cup beef broth

1. Brown beef and onion together in large skillet. Drain off drippings.
2. Stir in olives, tomato sauce, and beans. Cover and simmer until hot.
3. In a greased 9 x 13 baking pan, layer half the tortillas, followed by a layer of half the ground beef mixture, and a layer of one-third of the cheese. Repeat the layers, ending with cheese.
4. Pour broth over all.
5. Bake at 350°, uncovered, for 45 minutes.
6. Allow to stand for 10 minutes before serving.

Creamy Mexican Casserole

Sharon Eshleman
Ephrata, PA

Makes 6-8 servings

Prep Time: 30 minutes
Cooking/Baking Time:
* 35-40 minutes*

1 lb. ground beef
10.75-oz. can tomato soup
10.75-oz. can cream of
    chicken soup
10.75-oz. can cream of
    mushroom soup
1 Tbsp. chili powder
1 lb. cheddar cheese,
    grated
9-oz. pkg. flour tortillas,
    cut into quarters

1. Brown beef in a large skillet or saucepan. Drain off drippings.
2. Mix in all other ingredients except cheddar cheese and tortillas.
3. Line the bottom of a greased 9 x 13 baking pan with half the quartered tortillas.
4. Spoon half the meat mixture over the tortillas. Cover with half the grated cheese.
5. Repeat the layers.
6. Bake uncovered at 350° for 25-30 minutes, or until well browned.

Variations:
  1. Use 2 cups cooked, cut-up chicken instead of the ground beef.

  2. Add a 15-oz. can kidney beans, drained, and an 11-oz. can corn, drained, to Step 2.
  3. Add a 15-oz. can refried beans, in addition to, or instead of, the kidney beans, in Step 2.
  4. For added zip, stir in a couple of cut-up jalapena peppers in Step 2.

Cheeseburger Casserole

Sherri Mayer
Menomonee Falls, WI

Makes 4 servings

Prep Time: 15-20 minutes
Cooking/Baking Time:
* 35-40 minutes*

1 lb. ground beef
1/2 cup chopped onions
1/4 cup chopped green
    pepper
8-oz. can tomato sauce
1/4 cup ketchup
1/8 tsp. pepper
1/2 lb. sliced American
    cheese, *or* your choice
4-oz. can refrigerated
    biscuits

1. In a large skillet, brown ground beef with onions and green pepper. Drain off drippings.
2. Blend in tomato sauce, ketchup, and pepper. Cook on low heat about 5 minutes.
3. In greased 2-qt. casserole dish, alternate layers of ground beef mixture and slices of cheese.

4. Arrange biscuits on top.

5. Bake at 400° 20-25 minutes, until biscuits are golden brown.

Meatball Sub Casserole

Rhoda Atzeff
Harrisburg, PA

Makes 6-8 servings

Prep Time: 30-35 minutes
Baking Time: 50 minutes

1/3 **cup chopped green onions**
1/4 **cup seasoned bread crumbs**
3 **Tbsp. grated Parmesan cheese**
1 **lb. ground beef**
1 **lb. loaf Italian bread, cut into 1"-thick slices**
8-oz. **pkg. cream cheese, softened**
1/2 **cup mayonnaise**
1 **tsp. Italian seasoning**
1/4 **tsp. pepper**
2 **cups shredded mozzarella cheese, *divided***
28-oz. **jar spaghetti sauce**
1 **cup water**
2 **garlic cloves, minced**

1. In a large mixing bowl, combine onions, crumbs, and Parmesan cheese. Add beef and mix well.

2. Shape into 1" balls. Place on a rack in a shallow baking pan.

3. Bake at 400° for 15-20 minutes, or until meat is no longer pink.

4. Meanwhile, arrange bread in a single layer in an ungreased 9 x 13 baking dish.

5. Combine cream cheese, mayonnaise, Italian seasoning, and pepper. Spread over the bread and sprinkle with 1/2 cup mozzarella cheese.

6. Combine spaghetti sauce, water, and garlic. Add meatballs. Pour over bread-cheese mixture. Sprinkle with remaining mozzarella cheese.

7. Bake, uncovered, at 350° for 30 minutes, or until heated through.

Variations:

1. If you prefer a less cheesy dish, reduce cream cheese by half.

2. To save time, use already-prepared meatballs.

A Tip —

Save the end pieces of loaves of bread in a bag in the freezer. When you have a bag full, run them through a food processor or blender to make bread crumbs. (My children love to do this.) Use the crumbs for breading chicken, in meat loaf, or with melted butter as a topping for macaronis and cheese.

Peppy Peppers

Susie Nisley
Millersburg, OH

Makes 6 servings

Prep Time: 30-40 minutes
Cooking/Baking Time:
75 minutes

1 **large green pepper, diced**
1 **lb. ground beef**
1 **tsp. salt**
1/4 **tsp. pepper**
1 **cup dry long-grain rice**
1 **qt. tomato juice**
1 **envelope dry taco seasoning**
Velveeta cheese, cubed

1. Place pepper in greased 2-qt. casserole.

2. In skillet, brown ground beef. Drain off drippings. Season meat with salt and pepper. Spread seasoned beef over green pepper.

3. Sprinkle rice over ground beef.

4. In a saucepan, or the skillet in which you browned the beef, combine tomato juice and taco seasoning. Bring to a boil. Pour over rice and beef.

5. Cover. Bake at 350° for 60 minutes. Top with Velveeta cheese. Return to oven until cheese melts.

Asian Beef and Noodles

Renee D. Groff
Manheim, PA

Makes 6-8 servings

Prep Time: 15 minutes
Cooking Time: 25-30 minutes

1¼ lbs. ground beef
2 3-oz. pkgs. Oriental-
  flavored ramen noodles,
  divided
2 cups water
2 cups frozen broccoli, *or*
  mixed vegetables
2 Tbsp. thinly sliced green
  onions

1. In a large skillet, brown
ground beef. Remove beef
from skillet with slotted
spoon. Season beef with one
seasoning packet from ramen
noodles. Set aside. Drain drippings out of skillet.

2. In the same skillet, combine 2 cups water, vegetables,
noodles (broken up), and the
remaining seasoning packet.

3. Bring to a boil. Reduce
heat. Cover and simmer 3
minutes, or until noodles and
vegetables are tender, stirring
occasionally.

4. Return beef to skillet.
Add green onion.

5. Heat thoroughly. Serve
immediately.

Main Dish Popover

Renee D. Groff
Manheim, PA

Makes 6-8 servings

Prep Time: 20 minutes
Baking Time: 30-35 minutes

1 lb. ground beef
½ cup chopped onions
8-oz. pkg. cream cheese,
  softened
¼ cup water
½ tsp. salt
½ tsp. dried oregano

Batter for crust:
2 eggs, beaten
¾ cup flour
½ tsp. salt
¾ cup milk
1 Tbsp. cornmeal
1 chopped tomato, *optional*

1. In a large skillet or
saucepan, brown ground beef
and onions together. Drain off
drippings.

2. To meat and onions in
pan, stir in cream cheese and
water. Stir over low heat until
cream cheese is melted.

3. Stir in salt and oregano
and set aside.

4. Combine eggs, flour,
salt, and milk in a small plastic container with a lid. Shake
until smooth. (You may need
to beat it with a fork to
remove lumps.) Or mix in a
mixing bowl with a whisk.

5. Pour batter into a
greased 9" pie plate. Sprinkle
with cornmeal.

6. Spoon meat mixture
over batter, leaving ½ inch
space around edges.

7. Bake at 400° for 35 minutes.

8. Top with chopped
tomato, if you wish, and
serve.

Pizza Casserole with Macaroni Crust

Dorothy Hess
Willow Street, PA

Makes 8 servings

Prep Time: 35 minutes
Cooking/Baking Time:
40-50 minutes

2 lbs. ground beef
1 onion, chopped
10.75-oz. can tomato soup
28-oz. jar pizza sauce
1 Tbsp. sugar
½-¾ lb. dry macaronis
1 egg, beaten
½ cup milk
4-oz. bag grated sharp
  cheddar cheese
8-oz. bag grated mozzarella
  cheese

1. In a large skillet, brown ground beef and onion. Drain off drippings.

2. To beef in skillet add tomato soup, pizza sauce, and sugar. Simmer, covered, for 10 minutes.

3. Meanwhile, cook macaronis in boiling water in saucepan for 7 minutes. Drain well. Return cooked macaronis to saucepan.

4. In a small bowl, combine egg and milk. Pour over cooked macaronis. Mix well.

5. Pour macaronis into bottom of a greased 9 x 13 baking pan.

6. Spread meat sauce over macaronis.

7. Sprinkle with cheddar and mozzarella cheeses.

8. Bake at 350° for 20-30 minutes, or until heated through and cheese is melted.

A Tip —

Brown ground beef in the microwave, using a microwavable cooker/ steamer. Stir and break up the meat every 2-3 minutes. The grease drains through the steamer basket, leaving fine, well-drained meat.

Seven Layer Dinner with Rice

Jere Zimmerman, Reinholds, PA

Makes 6 servings

Prep Time: 20-30 minutes
Baking Time: 1½ hours

1 cup uncooked minute rice
1 cup canned whole-kernel corn, drained
salt and pepper to taste
2 8-oz. cans tomato sauce, *divided*
¾ cup water, *divided*
½ cup chopped onions
½ cup chopped green pepper
¾ lb. uncooked ground beef
4 strips bacon, cut in half

1. Place rice in the bottom of a greased 2-qt. casserole dish.

2. Cover with drained corn. Sprinkle with salt and pepper.

3. In a small mixing bowl, blend 1 can tomato sauce and ½ cup water. Pour over corn.

4. Top with onions and green peppers.

5. Crumble uncooked ground beef over top. Sprinkle with salt and pepper.

6. Mix second can of tomato sauce with ¼ cup water and pour over meat.

7. Top with bacon slices.

8. Cover and bake at 350° for 1 hour. Uncover and bake ½ hour longer, until bacon is crisp.

Zucchini-Hamburger Bake

Linda Overholt
Abbeville, SC

Makes 6 servings

Prep Time: 20 minutes
Cooking Time: 45-55 minutes

1 lb. hamburger
1 small onion, chopped
½ tsp. salt
¼ tsp. pepper
2 cups pizza sauce
½ cup raw long-grain rice
4 cups zucchini, peeled and cubed
1½ cups water
¾ cup grated mozzarella cheese

1. In a large skillet or stockpot, brown hamburger and onion together. Drain off drippings. Season meat and onion with salt and pepper.

2. Add remaining ingredients, except cheese, and stir together. Cover and simmer over low heat until rice is soft, approximately 35-45 minutes.

3. Top with cheese and allow to melt before serving.

Tips:

1. An electric skillet works well for making this casserole.

2. You can double the amount of zucchini if you want.

Reuben Casserole

Joleen Albrecht
Gladstone, MI

Makes 8-10 servings

Prep Time: 25 minutes
Baking Time: 25 minutes

1 1/2 cups Thousand Island
    salad dressing
1 cup sour cream
1 Tbsp. minced onions
12 slices dark rye bread,
    cubed, *divided*
1 lb. sauerkraut, drained
1 1/2 lbs. corned beef, sliced
    and cut into bite-sized
    pieces
2 cups shredded Swiss
    cheese
1/4 cup butter *or*
    margarine, melted

1. In a mixing bowl, stir
together dressing, sour
cream, and onions. Set aside.

2. Arrange bread cubes in
a greased 9 x 13 baking dish,
setting aside approximately
1 cup cubes for the top.

3. Top the bread with a
layer of sauerkraut, followed
by a layer of corned beef.

4. Spread dressing mixture
over corned beef. Sprinkle
with Swiss cheese.

5. Top with remaining
bread cubes. Drizzle with
melted butter.

6. Cover and bake at 350°
for 15 minutes. Uncover and
continue baking for about 10
minutes or until bubbly.

Reuben Stromboli

Andrea Cunningham
Arlington, KS

Makes 6-8 servings

Prep Time: 15-20 minutes
Rising Time: 15 minutes
Baking Time: 25 minutes
Standing Time: 10 minutes

3 1/4-3 3/4 cups flour, *divided*
1 pkg., *or* 1 Tbsp., quick-
    rise yeast
1 Tbsp. sugar
1 Tbsp. butter, softened
1 tsp. salt
1 cup warm (120-130°)
    water
1/2 cup Thousand Island
    salad dressing
6 ozs. thinly sliced corned
    beef
4 ozs. sliced Swiss cheese
8-oz. can sauerkraut,
    drained
1 egg white, beaten
caraway seeds

1. In a large mixing bowl,
combine 2 1/4 cups flour,
yeast, sugar, butter, and salt.
Stir in warm water. Mix until
a soft dough forms. Add
remaining flour if necessary.

2. Turn onto a lightly
floured surface. Knead until
smooth, about 4 minutes.

3. On a greased baking
sheet, roll dough to a 14 x 10
rectangle.

4. Spread dressing down
center third of dough. Top
with layers of beef, cheese,
and sauerkraut.

5. Make cuts from filling
to edges of dough, 1" apart on
both sides of the filling.
Alternating sides, fold the
strips at an angle across filling.

6. Cover filled dough and
let rise in a warm place for
15 minutes.

7. Brush with egg white
and sprinkle with caraway
seeds.

8. Bake at 400°, uncov-
ered, for 25 minutes, or until
lightly browned.

9. Let stand for 10 min-
utes. Cut into 3/4" slices with
a sharp knife.

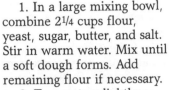

> ## A Tip —
>
> I often double a recipe.
> I freeze the one portion
> and serve the other. Then
> some night when I come
> home tired from work, I
> have a meal that needs
> only to be heated.

Pork Main Dishes

Tuscan-Style Pork Ribs with Balsamic Glaze

J.B. Miller, Indianapolis, IN

Makes 6-8 servings

Prep Time: 30 minutes
Standing (or Chilling) Time:
2-8 hours
Baking Time: 2 hours, 15 minutes

2 Tbsp. olive oil
2 Tbsp. chopped fresh
  rosemary leaves, *or*
  1 tsp. dried rosemary
1½ Tbsp. kosher salt
1½ Tbsp fennel seeds,
  or 1½ tsp. ground
  fennel
2 tsp. pepper
2 tsp. fresh chopped sage,
  or 1 tsp. dried sage
2 tsp. fresh chopped thyme,
  or ½ tsp. dried thyme
2 tsp. paprika
1 tsp. crushed red pepper,
  optional, depending on
  how much heat you like

1 tsp. ground coriander
½ tsp. ground allspice
6 lbs. pork ribs
3 Tbsp. balsamic vinegar

1. In a small bowl, combine olive oil, rosemary, salt, fennel seeds, pepper, sage, thyme, paprika, red pepper, coriander, and allspice.

2. Rub spice paste all over ribs and let stand at room temperature for 2 hours, or refrigerate overnight.

3. Preheat oven to 325°.

4. Arrange ribs on a large, rimmed baking sheet or roasting pan, meaty side up.

5. Roast ribs uncovered for 2 hours or until tender.

6. Preheat broiler. Brush meaty side of ribs with balsamic vinegar and broil 6 inches from heat until browned, about 2 minutes.

7. Let stand for 5 minutes, then cut between ribs, or serve in slabs.

Tip: You can use this glaze on pork chops, lamb chops, and cuts of chicken.

Finger-Lickin' Spareribs

Susan Guarneri, Three Lakes, WI

Makes 4 servings

Prep Time: 25 minutes
Cooking Time: 85 minutes

¼ cup oil
2 lbs. spareribs, cut in
  pieces

¼ cup chopped onions
¼ cup chopped green
  pepper
1 cup pineapple juice
¾ cup vinegar
¾ cup water
2 Tbsp. ketchup
1 Tbsp. soy sauce
¼ tsp. Worcestershire
  sauce
1 medium clove garlic,
  minced
½ cup brown sugar
2 Tbsp. cornstarch

1. Brown spareribs in oil in large skillet. Remove meat and pour off all but 2 Tbsp. drippings.

2. Add onions and green pepper to drippings and cook until tender. Stir in juice, vinegar, water, ketchup, soy sauce, Worcestershire sauce, and garlic. Bring to boil.

3. Blend brown sugar and cornstarch together and quickly stir into boiling mixture until thickened (a minute or two).

4. Reduce heat to low simmer and add meat. Cook uncovered for 1 hour, or until tender. Stir occasionally so the sauce and meat do not burn.

5. Check meat—it may take less time to cook to fork tender.

Variation: Add 1 cup pineapple chunks plus 1 cup juice for a heartier dish.

These were favorite "finger-lickin" favorites of my kids when they were growing up. They fought for the last morsels of the sauce.

Pork Chops with Apples and Stuffing

Louise Bodziony
Sunrise Beach, MO

Makes 6 servings

Prep Time: 15 minutes
Cooking/Baking Time:
75-85 minutes

6 boneless pork loin chops,
  1"-thick
1 Tbsp. oil
21-oz. can apple-pie filling
  with cinnamon
6-oz. pkg. crushed stuffing
  mix, prepared

1. In skillet, brown chops
in oil over medium-high heat.
(Do this in several batches so
as not to crowd the skillet.
The chops will brown better
if the pan isn't too full.)
2. Spread pie filling in a
greased 9 x 13 baking pan.
3. Place pork chops on top.
4. Spoon stuffing over
chops. Cover.
5. Bake at 350° for 55-65
minutes. Uncover and bake
10 minutes longer, or until
meat thermometer reads
160°.

A Tip —

Follow recipes exactly
until you've gained confidence and experience.
Remember to try, try
again!

Sweet Pork Chops

Angie Clemens
Dayton, VA

Makes 6 servings

Prep Time: 15 minutes
Cooking/Baking Time:
75 minutes

2 Tbsp. oil
6 boneless pork chops
1 onion, sliced
1 green pepper, sliced into
  rings
6 Tbsp. brown sugar
6 Tbsp. ketchup
6 Tbsp. lemon juice

1. Brown pork chops in oil
in large skillet. (Do not crowd
the skillet. The chops will
brown more fully if they're
not squeezed in the pan.)
Place browned chops in a
greased 9 x 13 baking dish.
2. On top of each chop,
place 1 onion slice and
1 green pepper slice.
3. In a small mixing bowl,
combine brown sugar,
ketchup, and lemon juice.
Top each chop with about
3 Tbsp. of the mixture.
4. Cover and bake at 350°
for 30 minutes. Uncover and
bake 30 minutes more.
5. Baste occasionally during the final 30 minutes.

*Tips: I like to put any extra
onions and green pepper pieces
around the edges of the baking
dish before putting the meat in
the oven.*

Spiced Pork Chops

Mary Jane Hoober
Shipshewana, IN

Makes 4 servings

Prep Time: 15 minutes
Cooking/Baking Time:
75 minutes

1/2 cup flour
1 1/2 tsp. garlic powder
1 1/2 tsp. dry mustard
1 1/2 tsp. paprika
1/2 tsp. celery salt
1/4 tsp. ground ginger
1/8 tsp. dried oregano
1/8 tsp. dried basil
1/8 tsp. salt
pinch of pepper
4 pork loin chops,
  approximately 3/4"-thick
1 to 2 Tbsp. oil
1 cup ketchup
1 cup water
1/4 cup brown sugar,
  packed

1. In a medium-sized mix-
ing bowl, combine the first 10
ingredients (through pepper).
2. Dredge pork chops on
both sides in dry mixture.
3. Heat oil in a skillet.
Brown chops on both sides.
(Do not crowd the skillet. The
chops will brown better if
they're not tight against each
other.) Place in a greased
9 x 13 baking dish.
4. In a small bowl, com-
bine ketchup, water, and
brown sugar. Pour over
chops.
5. Bake uncovered, at 350°
for 1 hour, or until tender.

Baked Pork Chops with Gravy

Margaret Jarrett
Anderson, IN

Makes 4 servings

Prep Time: *15 minutes*
Cooking/Baking Time:
75 minutes

1 Tbsp. oil
4 pork chops
10.75-oz. can cream of
   mushroom soup
3/4 cup water
1/2 tsp. ground ginger
1/4 tsp. rosemary
1 can onion rings
1/4 cup sour cream

1. Brown pork chops in oil in skillet. (Reserve the drippings.) Lay the browned chops in a lightly greased baking dish.

2. In a small mixing bowl, mix the mushroom soup, water, ginger, and rosemary together. Pour over the chops.

3. Cover and bake at 350° for 50 minutes.

4. Uncover and spread onion rings over top. Bake 10 more minutes.

5. While the chops are baking, make a gravy by heating the drippings. Stir in the sour cream and heat without boiling. Serve with the baked chops.

Pork Chops and Cabbage

Shirley Hedman
Schenectady, NY

Makes 4 servings

Prep Time: *10 minutes*
Cooking Time: *1-2 hours*

4 pork chops
2 Tbsp. oil
dash of salt
dash of pepper
dash of garlic powder
1 medium-sized head of
   cabbage, shredded
8-oz. can tomato sauce
1/4 cup water

1. In a large skillet or saucepan, brown pork chops on one side in oil. Turn.

2. Season with salt, pepper, and garlic powder.

3. Top chops with cabbage.

4. In a small bowl, mix together tomato sauce and water until smooth. Pour over cabbage. Cover pan.

5. Cook slowly over low heat for 1½ hours, stirring occasionally, until chops and cabbage are tender, but not overdone.

Cranberry-Glazed Pork Roast

Cova Rexroad, Kingsville, MD

Makes 6 servings

Prep Time: *15 minutes*
Baking Time: *2 hours*
Standing Time: *25-30 minutes*

2½-3-lb. pork roast
1 tsp. salt
1/2-1/4 tsp. pepper
16-oz. can whole-berry
   cranberry sauce
1/2 cup orange juice
1/4 cup brown sugar

1. Rub the pork roast with salt and pepper. Bake uncovered at 350° for 1½ hours.

2. Meanwhile, combine cranberry sauce, orange juice, and brown sugar in a small saucepan. Cook over low heat until mixture comes to a boil, making a thin sauce.

3. After the meat has baked, brush 1/4 of the sauce over the roast and bake uncovered another 30 minutes.

4. Remove the roast from the pan and place it on a serving platter. Cover with foil and allow to stand for 25-30 minutes. Slice thinly and serve with the remaining sauce.

Variation: *For the glaze, use 1/4 cup honey, 1 tsp. grated orange peel, 1/8 tsp. cloves, and 1/8 tsp. nutmeg, instead of orange juice and brown sugar.*
— **Chris Peterson**
   Green Bay, WI

Pear Pork Stir-Fry

Polly Anna Glaser
New Ulm, MN

Makes 4 servings

Prep Time: 5 minutes
Cooking Time: 20-25 minutes

16-oz. can pear slices,
  drained (reserve liquid)
12 ozs. lean pork loin, cut
  into julienned strips
2 Tbsp. vegetable oil
3 carrots, cut in 1/2"-thick
  slices
1 medium-sized onion,
  diced
1 red pepper, diced
3 Tbsp. brown sugar
3 Tbsp. red wine vinegar
1 Tbsp. cornstarch
2 Tbsp. soy sauce
dash of pepper

1. Cut pears slices in half.
Set aside.
2. In a skillet, sauté pork
over high heat in oil until
lightly browned, stirring constantly.
3. Add the vegetables and
cook just until tender-crisp,
about 5 minutes, stirring frequently.
4. In a small bowl, com-
bine pear liquid with brown
sugar, vinegar, cornstarch,
soy sauce, and pepper. When
smooth, stir into pork and
vegetables.
5. Add pears. Cook, stir-
ring gently 1-2 minutes, until
sauce thickens.
6. Serve over rice.

Pork Thai Stew

Marilyn Mowry, Irving, TX

Makes 6-8 servings

Prep Time: 15 minutes
*Cooking Time: 3 hours and
15 minutes*

2 lbs. pork tenderloin,
  cubed
2 Tbsp. oil
2 garlic cloves, minced
2 cups sliced red bell
  pepper
2 Tbsp. white wine *or* rice
  wine vinegar
1/4 cup teriyaki sauce
1 tsp. crushed red pepper
  flakes
1/2 cup water
1/4 cup creamy peanut
  butter
sliced green onions
chopped peanuts

1. In large skillet, brown
meat in oil.
2. Add remaining ingredi-
ents, except water, peanut
butter, onions, and chopped
peanuts.
3. Simmer, covered, 1 1/2
hours on stove. Stir in 1/2 cup
water. Cover and continue
simmering over low heat for
another 1 1/2 hours, or until
meat is very tender.
4. Remove skillet from
heat. While meat is still in
skillet, shred the meat using
2 forks to pull it apart. Stir in
peanut butter.
5. Serve over rice. Garnish
with chopped green onions
and chopped peanuts.

Mother's Baked Ham

Dawn Ranck
Lansdale, PA

Makes 6-8 servings

Prep Time: 10 minutes
Baking Time: 60-75 minutes

2 1-lb. slices ham steaks,
  each 1 1/4" thick
1 tsp. dried mustard
4 Tbsp. brown sugar
milk to cover ham

1. Place ham in large baking pan.
2. Rub with mustard.
3. Sprinkle with sugar.
4. Add enough milk to
barely cover ham. (Pour milk
in along the side of the meat
slices so as not to wash off
the mustard and sugar.)
5. Cover with foil.
6. Bake at 325° for 60-75
minutes, or until milk is
absorbed.

A Tip —

Oven meals are espe-
cially good for company if
you're a new cook. For
example, baked beef stew,
served with a salad and
garlic bread, takes the
pressure off last-minute
preparation.

Pineapple Glaze for Ham

Starla Kreider
Mohrsville, PA

Makes 4 cups

Prep Time: 5 minutes
Cooking Time: 10 minutes

¼ cup water
1½ cups brown sugar
1½ Tbsp. ketchup
1½ Tbsp. soy sauce
1½ tsp. dry mustard
1½ cups crushed
  pineapple, drained
2¼ Tbsp. cornstarch
½ cup water

1. Combine first 6 ingredients in a saucepan. Bring to a boil.
2. In a small mixing bowl, combine cornstarch and ½ cup water until smooth. Add to boiling mixture. Stir continuously and cook until clear.
3. Spoon over ham slices before baking. Or serve as a topping for cooked sweet potatoes or for cooked rice.

Variation: Use only ¾ cup of brown sugar if you prefer a tangier sauce.

Ham Loaf

Inez Rutt, Bangor, PA

Makes 6-8 servings

Prep Time: 20-30 minutes
Baking Time: 1-1¼ hours

¾ lb. ground ham
¾ lb. ground pork
1 egg
¼ cup minced onions
½ cup cracker crumbs
½ cup milk
pepper to taste

Glaze:
½ cup brown sugar
1 Tbsp. dry mustard
¼ cup vinegar

1. In a large mixing bowl, mix ham, pork, egg, onions, cracker crumbs, milk, and pepper together until well blended. Form into a loaf, and then place in greased loaf pan.
2. Make glaze by mixing brown sugar, dry mustard, and vinegar together until smooth.
3. Pour glaze over top of ham loaf.
4. Bake at 350° for 1-1¼ hours, or until well browned. Baste occasionally with glaze during baking.

Variation: Add 8-oz. can crushed pineapple and juice to the glaze.
   — **Mary E. Wheatley**
     Mashpee, MA
   — **Janice Yoskovich**
     Carmichaels, PA

Potato, Ham, and Cheese Casserole

Vera Martin
East Earl, PA

Makes 6 servings

Prep Time: 10-15 minutes
Baking Time: 40-45 minutes
Standing Time: 10 minutes

4 or 5 eggs, beaten
1 cup shredded cheese of
  your choice
½ cup milk
pinch of onion salt
2 medium-sized raw
  potatoes, peeled and
  shredded, about 2 cups-
  worth
½ cup chipped ham

1. In a bowl, combine eggs, cheese, milk and onion salt. Then add the shredded potatoes and the chipped ham.
2. Stir everything together well, and put into a greased 9 x 9 baking dish, or a 10" glass pie plate.
3. Bake at 350° for about 40-45 minutes, or until set, and knife inserted in center comes out clean.
4. Allow to stand 10 minutes before cutting to serve.

We like this dish for breakfast or for a light lunch.

Scalloped Potatoes and Ham

Sandra Chang, Derwood, MD

Makes 4 servings

Prep Time: 15 minutes
Cooking Time: 30 minutes
Standing Time: 5 minutes

4 medium-sized potatoes, peeled and sliced
1/4 cup onions, chopped
1 Tbsp. flour, *divided*
1 tsp. salt, *divided*
1/8 tsp. pepper
1 cup cooked ham, diced
1 2/3 cups milk
1 Tbsp. butter *or* margarine
1/2 cup (2 ozs.) shredded cheddar cheese
sprinkle of paprika

1. Arrange half of potatoes in greased 2-qt. microwavable casserole dish.
2. Sprinkle with onions, 1 1/2 tsp. flour, 1/2 tsp. salt, and pinch of pepper.
3. Layer remaining potatoes into dish. Add a layer of ham. Sprinkle with remaining flour, salt, and pepper.
4. Pour milk over top. Dot with butter.
5. Cover and microwave at 50% power for 30 minutes, or until potatoes are tender. Rotate dish one-quarter turn every 8 minutes.
6. Sprinkle with cheese and paprika.
7. Microwave, uncovered, at 50% power for 2 minutes, or until cheese is melted.

8. Cover and let stand for 5 minutes before serving.

Ham and Pea Casserole

Marcia S. Myer
Manheim, PA

Makes 6-8 servings

Prep Time: 35-40 minutes
Baking Time: 30 minutes

10.75-oz. can cream of celery *or* mushroom soup
1 soup can of milk
1/2 tsp. garlic powder
2 cups cooked ham, cubed
1 cup frozen peas, thawed
2 cups cooked macaronis
1/4 lb. Velveeta cheese, cubed
2 slices torn bread
3 Tbsp. melted butter

1. In a large mixing bowl, whisk together soup, milk, and garlic powder until smooth.
2. Gently stir in ham, peas, macaronis, and cheese cubes.
3. Spoon into a greased 2-qt., 7 x 11, or a 9 x 13, baking dish.
4. In the mixing bowl, combine the bread and butter. Spoon over casserole.
5. Bake at 350°, uncovered, for 30 minutes, or until heated through and bread topping is browned.

Pork Fried Rice

Sarah M. Balmer, Manheim, PA

Makes 6 servings

Prep Time: 30-45 minutes
Cooking Time: 30 minutes

1/2 lb. fresh pork, cubed
2 Tbsp. oil, *divided*
3"-piece smoked sausage, cut into 1/4" slices
1/2 cup diced carrots
1/2 cup finely chopped broccoli
1/2 cup chopped onions
1/2 cup chopped green pepper
1/2 cup canned corn, drained
3 cups cooked rice
2 eggs, beaten
3-4 Tbsp. soy sauce
1/4 tsp. garlic powder
1/8 tsp. ginger

1. In large skillet or wok, sauté pork in 1 Tbsp. oil over high heat until browned.
2. Stir in sausage, carrots, broccoli, onions, green pepper, and corn and cook for 3-4 minutes. Remove from skillet.
3. Add 1 Tbsp. oil to skillet. Heat cooked rice in skillet over low heat. Form well in center of rice. Pour eggs into well. Cook until set, stirring eggs occasionally. Then stir eggs into rice.
4. Add vegetables and meat, soy sauce, garlic powder, and ground ginger. Mix until well distributed. Continue heating, covered,

for a few minutes, or until heated through.

Smoked Sausage Oriental

Ruth Feister, Narvon, PA

Makes 6 servings

Prep Time: 10-15 minutes
Cooking Time: 10-15 minutes

1-1 1/2 lbs. smoked sausage, cut into 3/4" thick chunks
1 Tbsp. butter
1 medium-sized onion, chopped
3 small tomatoes, chopped
1 Tbsp. cornstarch
1/2 tsp. ginger
1 Tbsp. vinegar
1 Tbsp. soy sauce
1/2 cup apricot preserves

1. Brown sausage chunks in butter.
2. Stir in onion and brown it in the meat drippings.
3. Add tomatoes, and cook over low heat for 5 minutes.
4. Meanwhile, in a small bowl, combine cornstarch and ginger. Mix in vinegar and soy sauce, stirring until smooth. Add preserves and combine well.
5. Stir into sausage-vegetable mixture.
6. Cook covered over low heat, stirring occasionally, until sauce thickens.
7. When heated through, serve over rice.

Variations: If you want, add 1 green pepper, chunked, to Step 3, and 2 cups drained pineapple chunks to Step 6.

Jiffy Jambalaya

Carole M. Mackie
Williamsfield, IL

Makes 6 servings

Prep Time: 30 minutes
Cooking Time: 10-15 minutes

1 onion, chopped
1/2 cup chopped green pepper
2 Tbsp. oil
1 lb. cooked kielbasa *or* Polish sausage, cut into 1/4" slices
28-oz. can diced tomatoes, undrained
1/2 cup water
1 Tbsp. sugar
1 tsp. paprika
1/2 tsp. dried thyme
1/2 tsp. dried oregano
1/4 tsp. garlic powder
3 drops hot pepper sauce
1 1/2 cups uncooked minute rice

1. In skillet, sauté onion and green pepper in oil until tender.
2. Stir in sausage, tomatoes, water, sugar, and seasonings. Bring to a boil.
3. Add rice. Cover and simmer for 5 minutes, until rice is tender.

Sausage Tortellini

Christie Detamore-Hunsberger
Harrisonburg, VA

Makes 8 servings

Prep Time: 25-30 minutes
Cooking Time: 65-80 minutes

1 lb. sausage, cut into 1/2" slices
1 cup chopped onions
2 cloves garlic, minced
5 cups beef *or* chicken broth
1/2 cup water
1/2 cup red cooking wine
2 14-oz. cans diced tomatoes, undrained
1 cup thinly sliced carrots
1/2 tsp. dried basil
1/2 tsp. dried oregano
16-oz. can tomato sauce
1/2 cup sliced zucchini, *optional*
16-oz. pkg. tortellini
3 Tbsp. parsley

1. In large stockpot, brown sausage in its own drippings. When well browned, stir in onions, and garlic. Cook until browned.
2. Add next 8 ingredients (through the tomato sauce), cover, and simmer 35-40 minutes.
3. Add zucchini if you wish, and tortellini. Simmer another 20-25 minutes over low heat, or until tortellini is cooked.
4. Stir in parsley and serve.

Favorite Casserole

Laverne Nafziger
Goshen, IN

Makes 6 servings

Prep Time: 30 minutes
Cooking/Baking Time:
55-70 minutes

2 cups dry noodles, cooked
   according to package
   directions
2 Tbsp. chopped onions
1 clove garlic, minced
1 lb. bulk sausage
1 cup cottage cheese
1 cup milk
10.75-oz. can cream of
   mushroom soup
1 cup shredded cheddar
   cheese
3 eggs

1. Brown sausage, onions, and garlic in skillet. Drain off drippings.

2. In large bowl, mix all ingredients except cheddar cheese and eggs. Pour into a greased 8 x 12, or 2-qt., baking dish.

3. Beat eggs with fork. Add cheddar cheese. Pour over top of casserole.

4. Bake uncovered at 350° for 45-60 minutes, or until bubbly and browned.

Sausage and Corn Casserole

Julia Horst
Gordonville, PA

Makes 6 servings

Prep Time: 20 minutes
Cooking/Baking Time:
50 minutes

1 lb. bulk sausage
2 cups cooked corn
2 cups cooked, diced
   potatoes
4 hard-boiled eggs, diced
1/4 cup butter
1 tsp. minced onions
1/4 cup flour
1/4 tsp. salt
2 cups milk
2 Tbsp. butter
1/2 cup bread crumbs

A Tip —

When I cook hamburger or sausage to mix with other ingredients, I cook it over low heat so it will stay soft and crumble well. I stir the meat until it is done. Large, hard chunks don't flavor as well or blend as well.

1. Brown sausage in skillet, stirring to break up chunks. Drain off drippings.

2. Layer meat, corn, potatoes, and eggs in a 3-qt. greased casserole dish.

3. In a saucepan, melt 1/4 cup butter. Sauté onions in butter until just softened.

4. Stir in flour and salt. Stir over low heat for about 2 minutes until slightly browned.

5. Gradually pour in milk, stirring constantly until mixture begins to bubble. Continue stirring until sauce begins to thicken. Continue cooking another minute or 2, until sauce becomes smooth and thickened, stirring constantly.

6. Pour white sauce over casserole ingredients. Mix lightly.

7. Melt 2 Tbsp. butter in small saucepan. Stir in bread crumbs until well coated with butter. Spoon evenly over casserole.

8. Bake uncovered at 350° for 30 minutes, or until heated through.

Italian Barbecue

Pat Bishop
Bedminster, PA

Makes 8-10 servings

Prep Time: 10 minutes
Cooking Time: 80 minutes

1 lb. bulk sausage,
    uncooked
1 lb. chipped steak,
    uncooked
4 large onions, cut in rings
2 medium-sized green
    peppers, sliced
4-oz. can sliced
    mushrooms, drained
28-oz. jar spaghetti sauce
1 Tbsp. dried oregano
salt to taste
8-10 hoagie rolls

1. In a large skillet, brown
the sausage. Remove from
pan and set aside.
2. Brown chipped steak in
the sausage drippings in the
same skillet. Pull steak apart
with 2 forks. Remove from
pan and set aside.
3. Brown onions and peppers in skillet drippings. Stir
meats back in and add
remaining ingredients. Cover
and simmer 1 hour.
4. Serve on hoagie rolls.

Pork Tenderloin Sandwiches

Karen Kirstein
Schenectady, NY

Makes 4 servings

Prep Time: 15 minutes
Cooking Time: 15 minutes

1 lb. pork tenderloin
1/2 tsp. salt
1/4 tsp. pepper
1 cup flour
1 egg, beaten
1 Tbsp. vegetable oil
1/2 cup sour cream
1 tsp. horseradish
romaine lettuce
red onion, thinly sliced
4 bread rolls

1. Slice tenderloin into 4
1/4"-thick slices and pound
flat.
2. In a small bowl, mix
flour with salt and pepper.
Dip meat slices into flour and
then into beaten egg. Fry in
oil until brown. Turn and
brown other side. (Be careful
not to crowd the pan so the
meat can brown well and
cook through.) Set finished
slices aside and keep warm
while you brown the rest.
3. Meanwhile, in a small
bowl, mix sour cream with
horseradish.
4. To serve, place meat,
lettuce, and onion on rolls
and top with sour cream mixture.

Ham & Cheese Ring

Desi Rineer, Millersville, PA

Makes 6 servings

Prep Time: 20 minutes
Baking Time: 25 minutes

1 Tbsp. butter, at room
    temperature
2 Tbsp. prepared mustard
1 tsp. lemon juice
2 Tbsp. chopped onions
1/4 cup parsley
1 cup chopped broccoli,
    fresh *or* frozen (thawed)
1 cup chopped *or* shredded
    ham
1 1/2 cups shredded cheese
    (your choice of variety)
1 tube refrigerated crescent
    rolls

1. In a medium-sized mixing bowl, mix together butter,
mustard, and lemon juice.
2. Add onions, parsley,
broccoli, ham, and cheese.
Blend well.
3. In a lightly greased baking dish, arrange crescent
rolls in a circle with points
out like a star and centers
overlapping.

4. Place meat/vegetable mixture in center and fold ends of rolls into the middle.

5. Bake at 350° for 25 minutes.

Stromboli

Monica Kehr
Portland, MI

Makes 6 servings

Prep Time: 20 minutes
Rising Time: 30-40 minutes
Baking Time: 20 minutes
Standing Time: 10 minutes

1 loaf frozen bread dough,
   thawed, *or*
   3/4 **cup water**
2 Tbsp. oil
2 cups bread flour
1/2 tsp. sugar
1/2 tsp. salt
2 tsp. dry yeast
Italian seasoning
2 cups mozzarella cheese,
   grated
3 ozs. sliced pepperoni
4 ozs. chipped cooked ham
1/2 cup sliced black olives
1/3 cup sliced mushrooms,
   optional
2 Tbsp. chopped onions,
   optional
2 Tbsp. chopped green *or*
   red bell pepper, *optional*

1. Make dough in bread machine, or use 1 loaf frozen bread dough, thawed. Roll dough to 10 x 15 rectangle on lightly floured surface.

2. Sprinkle dough with Italian seasoning. Cover entire rectangle with cheese, pepperoni, ham, black olives, and any of the other ingredients you want. Press toppings down gently into dough.

3. Starting with the long side of the rectangle, roll dough up into a log shape. Seal ends by pinching dough together.

4. Carefully lift onto a lightly greased baking sheet. Cover and allow to rise 30-40 minutes.

5. Bake on sheet for 20 minutes at 400°, or until lightly browned.

6. Allow to stand for 10 minutes before slicing.

Tip: Microwave pepperoni slices between paper towels before putting in stromboli to eliminate some calories.

Lamb Main Dishes

Hoosier Lamb Chops

Willard E. Roth, Elkhart, IN

Makes 6 servings

Prep Time: 10 minutes
Cooking Time: 20 minutes

1 Tbsp. oil
6 lamb chops
1 onion, finely chopped
1 Tbsp. balsamic vinegar
1 tsp. coarsely ground
   black pepper
1/4 cup black currant *or*
   black raspberry jam
1/4 cup red wine
1 Tbsp. fresh mint,
   chopped

1. Heat oil in skillet over medium heat. Cook chops, 2 or 3 at a time, for 2 minutes per side until browned. Set aside. Reserve drippings.

2. Sauté onion for 1 minute in same skillet. Add vinegar, pepper, jam, and wine to skillet. Cook until thickened. Stir in fresh mint.

3. Return chops to skillet. Cook 2-3 minutes per side, or until just done. Adjust seasoning. Serve.

Tip: This sauce makes a good gravy for couscous. If you want to do that, double the amounts of the sauce ingredients and proceed according to the recipe.

Chicken Main Dishes

Crusty Baked Chicken Breast

Eileen Eash, Carlsbad, NM

Makes 8-10 servings

Prep Time: 20-25 minutes
Baking Time: 20 minutes

2 cups dry bread crumbs
3/4 cup grated Parmesan cheese
1 tsp. paprika
1 tsp. garlic salt
1 tsp. pepper
4 Tbsp. chopped parsley
1/2 cup buttermilk

1 tsp. Worcestershire sauce
1 tsp. dry mustard
4 whole boneless, skinless chicken breasts, cut in strips

1. In a shallow bowl, combine bread crumbs, cheese, paprika, garlic salt, pepper, and parsley.
2. In another shallow bowl, combine buttermilk, Worcestershire sauce, and mustard.
3. Dip chicken pieces in buttermilk mixture and then roll in crumbs. Place coated chicken in a greased 9 x 13 baking dish in a single layer.
4. Pour remaining buttermilk over chicken.
5. Bake at 400° for 20 minutes.

Variation:
In Step 2, use 1 stick (1/2 cup) melted butter, instead of buttermilk. Use 2 tsp. prepared mustard instead of dry mustard.
— **Erma Martin**
East Earl, PA

Baked Chicken Fingers

Lori Rohrer, Washington Boro, PA

Makes 6 servings

Prep Time: 20 minutes
Baking Time: 20 minutes

7 boneless, skinless chicken breast halves, cut into 1 1/2" slices

1 1/2 cups fine, dry bread crumbs
1/2 cup grated Parmesan cheese
1 1/2 tsp. salt
1 Tbsp. dried thyme
1 Tbsp. dried basil
1/2 cup butter, melted

1. Combine bread crumbs, cheese, salt, and herbs in a shallow bowl. Mix well.
2. Dip chicken pieces in butter, and then into crumb mixture, coating well.
3. Place coated chicken on greased baking sheet in a single layer.
4. Bake at 400° for 20 minutes.

Variations:
1. In Step 1 use 1 Tbsp. garlic powder, 1 Tbsp. chives, 2 tsp. Italian seasoning, 2 tsp. parsley, 1/2 tsp. onion salt, 1/2 tsp. pepper, and 1/4 tsp. salt (instead of 1 1/2 tsp. salt, 1 Tbsp. thyme, and 1 Tbsp. basil).
— **Ruth Miller**
Wooster, OH

2. Use boneless, skinless chicken thighs, and do not cut them into slices. Bake at 350° for 20 minutes. Turn chicken. Bake an additional 20 minutes.
— **Eleanor Larson**
Glen Lyon, PA

A Tip —

Invest in good quality knives. They make preparation much easier.

Almond Lemon Chicken

Judi Janzen
Salem, OR

Makes 6 servings

Prep Time: 35-40 minutes
Marinating Time: 1 hour
Cooking Time: 25-30 minutes

5 Tbsp. lemon juice
3 Tbsp. prepared mustard
2 cloves garlic, finely
  chopped
6 Tbsp. olive oil, *divided*
6 boneless, skinless
  chicken breast halves
1 cup sliced almonds
2 cups chicken broth
1 tsp. cornstarch dissolved
  in 1 Tbsp. water
2 Tbsp. orange *or* lemon
  marmalade
2 Tbsp. chopped fresh
  parsley
1/4 tsp. red pepper flakes

1. In a large bowl, combine first 3 ingredients. Stir in 5 tablespoons oil. Add chicken and marinate one hour at room temperature.

2. Meanwhile, in large skillet, sauté almonds in 1/2 Tbsp. oil until golden. Remove almonds from pan and set aside. Reserve drippings. Add remaining 1/2 Tbsp. oil.

3. Drain chicken, reserving marinade. Cook chicken over medium-high heat in skillet until brown on each side, about 6-10 minutes total, or until tender. Remove and keep warm.

4. Pour marinade into pan. Add chicken broth and cornstarch mixture. Cook over high heat, until it boils and is reduced by slightly more than half, about 5 minutes. Stir occasionally to loosen browned bits from skillet and to keep sauce smooth.

5. Add marmalade and stir over medium heat until melted. Stir in parsley and red pepper flakes.

6. Return chicken to pan and heat through.

7. Place chicken on serving platter. Spoon sauce over. Sprinkle with toasted almonds.

Lemon Chicken

Ruth Shank
Gridley, IL

Makes 6 servings

Prep Time: 10-15 minutes
Baking Time: 40-50 minutes

3 lbs. boneless, skinless
  chicken breasts
1/4 cup lemon juice
1/4 tsp. garlic powder
1/4 tsp. pepper
1/2 tsp. salt
2 tsp. dried oregano leaves
olive oil

1. Trim excess fat from chicken breasts and cut into serving-sized pieces.

2. Arrange chicken pieces in a greased 9 x 13 baking dish.

3. In a small mixing bowl, combine lemon juice, garlic powder, pepper, salt, and oregano. Pour over chicken.

4. Bake, uncovered, at 375° for 40-50 minutes. Brush with olive oil every 10 to 15 minutes, turning chicken pieces over occasionally.

Savory Stir-Fried Chicken Breasts

Carolyn Baer
Conrath, WI

Makes 6-8 servings

Prep Time: 10 minutes
Cooking Time: 6-8 minutes

1 cup flour
4 tsp. seasoning salt
1 tsp. paprika
1 tsp. poultry seasoning
1 tsp. ground mustard
1/2 tsp. pepper
4 whole boneless, skinless
  chicken breasts, cubed
  into 1 1/2" pieces
1/2 cup vegetable *or* olive
  oil

1. In a plastic bag, combine flour, seasoning salt, paprika, poultry seasoning, ground mustard, and pepper.

2. Add chicken breast cubes and shake bag until chicken is well coated.

3. In a large skillet, sauté coated chicken in oil for 6-8 minutes. Stir constantly while sauting.

Tip: This way of making chicken breasts keeps them moist, and it is so easy to prepare quickly. Be sure to make the breasts as you finish preparing your meal so you don't have to keep them warm. They are best when eaten immediately.

Chicken-Veggies-Peanut Stir-Fry

Becky Gehman, Bergton, VA

Makes 6-8 servings

Prep Time: 25 minutes
Cooking Time: 10-12 minutes

Chicken and Vegetables:
2 Tbsp. olive oil
1 medium-sized carrot, sliced thin
1 medium-sized green pepper, sliced thin
1 cup mushrooms, sliced thin
2 cups broccoli, cut into small pieces
1-1½ lbs. boneless, skinless, uncooked chicken breast, cut into 1" pieces
5-oz. can water chestnuts, sliced and drained
¾ cup unsalted ground peanuts

Sauce:
¼ cup cornstarch
2 Tbsp. brown sugar
½ tsp. minced gingerroot or ground ginger
1 clove garlic, minced
¼ cup soy sauce

2 Tbsp. cider vinegar
1 cup chicken or beef broth
2 Tbsp. cooking wine
2 Tbsp. water

1. Make the stir-fry sauce by mixing the first 4 ingredients in a jar with a tight lid. Add the remaining ingredients and shake until well mixed. Set aside.

2. In a large skillet or wok, heat oil. Stir-fry carrot, pepper, mushrooms, and broccoli for 3-5 minutes.

3. Add chicken and water chestnuts and continue stir-frying until the chicken is no longer pink.

4. Add stir-fry sauce to chicken and vegetables. Stir while heating over medium heat, just until the sauce has thickened.

5. Spoon onto platter and sprinkle with peanuts. Serve with rice.

Chicken Marengo

Bernadette Veenstra
Rockford, MI

Makes 4-6 servings

Prep Time: 15-20 minutes
Cooking Time: 25-35 minutes

1 Tbsp. oil
4 bone-in chicken breast halves, skin removed, or 6 bone-in thighs
1 Tbsp. flour
½ tsp. dried basil

¼ tsp. garlic powder
1 tsp. salt
⅛ tsp. pepper
½ cup white wine, or chicken broth
2 Tbsp. tomato paste
2 14.5-oz. or 16-oz. cans of stewed tomatoes
half a coarsely chopped green pepper
1 onion, cut into 8 wedges
½ cup halved or sliced olives
1 lb. cooked wide egg noodles

1. Brown all sides of chicken in oil in a large skillet.

2. In a medium-sized bowl, mix together flour, basil, garlic powder, salt, pepper, wine or broth, tomato paste and tomatoes. Pour over chicken.

3. Bring to a boil. Reduce heat, cover, and simmer 20-25 minutes. About halfway through, add green pepper, onion, and olives. Stir occasionally.

4. When finished cooking, debone chicken. Stir back into sauce.

5. Serve over noodles.

A Tip —

Slice raw chicken breast while it's still partly frozen. It's much easier to handle that way.

Chicken Parmesan

Julette Rush, Harrisonburg, VA

Makes 4 servings

Prep Time: 15 minutes
Cooking Time: 20 minutes

1/2 cup bread crumbs
1/2 cup grated Parmesan
   cheese
1 tsp. dried basil
4 boneless, skinless
   chicken breasts, cut into
   bite-sized pieces
1 Tbsp. olive oil
14.5-oz. can Italian diced
   tomatoes
6-oz. can tomato paste
5.5-oz. can tomato juice
1 1/2 Tbsp. sugar
1/3 cup water
1 cup shredded mozzarella
   cheese
8 ozs. angel-hair pasta

1. Combine bread crumbs, Parmesan cheese, and basil in a large resealable bag. Shake lightly to mix.
2. Add chicken pieces to bag, and shake until chicken is coated.
3. Pour olive oil into a non-stick pan. Cook coated chicken pieces until chicken is cooked through and browned on all sides.
4. In another skillet, combine diced tomatoes, tomato paste, tomato juice, sugar, and water. Cook over medium heat until sauce is hot.
5. Stir chicken into sauce. Sprinkle with mozzarella cheese.

6. Cover skillet and cook over low heat until cheese melts.
7. Serve over angel-hair pasta, cooked according to package directions.

Chicken Cacciatore

Linda Thomas, Sayner, WI

Makes 4-5 servings

Prep Time: 10 minutes
Coooking/Baking Time:
   70 minutes

1 whole chicken, cut up
1/2 cup oil
1/4 cup water
10.5-oz. can tomato soup
1 Tbsp. cider vinegar
2 tsp. dried oregano
1/2 tsp. salt
1/4 tsp. pepper
1 green pepper, sliced,
   optional

1. Heat oil in large skillet. Brown chicken pieces in batches, placing them in a greased 9 x 13 baking dish as they finish browning.
2. In a small mixing bowl, combine water, soup, oregano, salt, and pepper. Mix well; then spoon one-third of sauce over chicken pieces. Bake uncovered at 350° for 15 minutes.
3. Remove from oven and spoon another one-third of the sauce over the chicken. Bake uncovered for another 20 minutes.

4. Remove from oven and spoon the remaining third of the sauce over the meat. Top with green pepper slices. Bake uncovered for 20-25 minutes more.

Chipper Chicken

Kim Jensen
Thornton, CO

Makes 4-6 servings

Prep Time: 15 minutes
Baking Time: 55 minutes

2 1/2 cups crushed potato
   chips
1/4 tsp. garlic powder
1/2 tsp. paprika *or* chili
   powder
1 tsp. dried oregano *or*
   parsley
1 chicken, cut up, *or* 3 lbs.
   selected chicken pieces
1/2 cup melted butter

1. Crush potato chips in a plastic bag. Add garlic powder and your choice of spices. Shake to mix.
2. Dip chicken pieces in melted butter. Place each piece, one-by-one, in the plastic bag and shake it in the potato-chip mixture.
3. Place coated chicken pieces in a greased 9 x 13 baking dish, skin-side up.
4. When finished coating the chicken, pour any remaining chips and butter over the chicken.

5. Bake uncovered at 375° for 50-60 minutes, or until tender and browned. Do not turn chicken while baking.

Garlic Chicken Cutlets

Elaine Vigoda
Rochester, NY

Makes 6 servings

Prep Time: 10 minutes
Cooking Time: 20 minutes

4 chicken cutlets, approx.
  1½ lbs.
2 Tbsp. flour *or* matzo meal
1 Tbsp. oil
6-8 garlic cloves, peeled and very lightly crushed
½ lb. fresh mushrooms, any combination of varieties, cut into bite-sized pieces or slices
¼ cup balsamic vinegar
¾ cup chicken stock
1 bay leaf
¼ tsp. dried thyme,
  or 3 springs fresh thyme
1 tsp. apricot jam

1. Dust chicken lightly with matzo meal or flour.
2. In large skillet, heat the oil over medium-high heat and add garlic. Sauté about 3 minutes, until browned.
3. Remove with a slotted spoon and reserve.
4. Add chicken to skillet and brown on one side for 3 minutes.

5. Turn chicken and top with reserved garlic and mushrooms. Cook 3 minutes.
6. While chicken is cooking, mix together vinegar, chicken stock, bay leaf, thyme, and jam in a small bowl. Pour over chicken and vegetables.
7. Reduce heat to low, cover the skillet, and cook approximately 10 minutes, or until chicken is done.

Tips —

For thawing meat safely:

1. In the refrigerator on the bottom shelf in a platter or deep dish.
2. In the microwave.
3. As part of the cooking process.
4. In a bowl of cold water, changing the water every 20 minutes.
5. Never at room temperature.

Chicken Monterey

Sally Holzem
Schofield, WI

Makes 4 servings

Prep Time: 15 minutes
Baking Time: 30 minutes

4 boneless, skinless chicken breast halves, about 1½ lbs. total
¼ tsp. salt
⅛ tsp. pepper
⅓ cup bottled barbecue sauce
4-8 slices cooked bacon, according to your taste preference
1 cup shredded cheddar cheese
4 scallions, trimmed and sliced
1 small tomato, chopped

1. Heat oven to 350°.
2. Place chicken in a single layer in a greased baking dish.
3. Sprinkle with salt and pepper. Spoon on the barbecue sauce.
4. Bake in 350° oven for 25 minutes, or until all pink is gone.
5. Top each breast half with 1 or 2 slices of cooked bacon. Sprinkle with cheddar cheese.
6. Bake in oven 5 more minutes.
7. Top each breast half with fresh scallions and tomatoes just before serving.

Mexican Stuffed Chicken

Karen Waggoner
Joplin, MO

Makes 6 servings

Prep Time: 20 minutes
Baking Time: 25-35 minutes

6 boneless skinless chicken
  breast halves, about
  1 1/2 lbs.
6 ozs. Monterey Jack
  cheese, cut into 2"-long,
  1/2"-thick sticks
2 4-oz. cans chopped green
  chilies, drained
1/2 cup dry bread crumbs
1/4 cup grated Parmesan
  cheese
1 Tbsp. chili powder
1/2 tsp. salt
1/4 tsp. ground cumin
3/4 cup flour
1/2 cup butter, melted

1. Cover each chicken
breast with plastic wrap and,
on a cutting board, flatten
each with a mallet to 1/8"
thickness.
2. Place a cheese stick in
the middle of each and top
with a mound of chilies. Roll
up and tuck in ends. Secure
with toothpick. Set aside each
breast half on a platter.
3. In a shallow dish, mix
together bread crumbs,
Parmesan cheese, chili powder, salt, and cumin.
4. In another shallow dish,
coat chicken with flour. Dip
into melted butter. Roll in
crumb mixture.

5. Place, seam-side down,
in a greased 9 x 13 baking
dish.
6. Bake, uncovered, at
400° for 25-35 minutes, or
until chicken juices run clear.
7. Be sure to remove tooth-
picks before serving.

Chicken Angelo

Elaine Rineer
Lancaster, PA

Makes 4 servings

Prep Time: 20 minutes
Baking Time: 30-35 minutes

1/2 lb. fresh mushrooms,
  sliced, *divided*
4 boneless, skinless
  chicken breast halves
2 eggs, beaten
1 cup dried bread crumbs
2 Tbsp. butter *or*
  margarine
6 ozs. shredded mozzarella
  cheese
3/4 cup chicken broth

1. Place half of mush-
rooms in greased 9 x 13 baking pan.
2. Beat eggs in a shallow
bowl. Place bread crumbs in
another shallow bowl. Dip
chicken in egg. Then dip in
bread crumbs, spooning
bread crumbs over all sides
of the chicken.
3. Melt butter in skillet.
Brown chicken on both sides
in batches; do not crowd the
skillet. As you finish brown-

ing pieces, place them on top
of the mushrooms.
4. Arrange remaining
mushrooms over chicken. Top
with cheese. Pour broth over
top, being careful not to disturb the cheese.
5. Bake uncovered at 350°
for 30-35 minutes.
6. Serve with angel-hair
pasta. Garnish with parsley.

Brandied Peach Chicken

Shari Jensen, Fountain, CO

Makes 6 servings

Prep Time: 20 minutes
Baking Time: 45 minutes

6 boneless, skinless
  chicken breast halves
1 1/4 tsp. salt
1/2 cup finely chopped
  white onions
1/2 cup chopped cashews *or*
  pecans
1/2 tsp. ground ginger
5 fresh *or* canned peaches,
  divided
5 1/3 Tbsp. (1/3 cup) butter,
  melted
1/2 cup light brown sugar
2 tsp. prepared mustard
1 cup sour cream
1 Tbsp. brandy

1. Cut a pocket in the side
of each chicken breast, or
pound chicken breasts to 1/4"
thickness between sheets of
waxed paper. Sprinkle with
salt.

2. Prepare filling in a mixing bowl by combining onions, chopped nuts, ginger, and 3 of the peaches cut into small pieces.

3. Divide peach mixture between the six chicken breasts by stuffing it into the created pockets or by placing it on top of each flat cutlet, rolling and securing the stuffed meat with a toothpick.

4. Pour melted butter into a foil-lined 9 x 13 baking dish. Place chicken on top of butter.

5. Bake uncovered at 350° for 25 minutes. Turn chicken over and bake 20 minutes longer.

6. While chicken bakes the last 20 minutes, combine the remaining 2 peaches (sliced), brown sugar, mustard, sour cream, and brandy in a saucepan.

7. Heat for 5 minutes over medium heat, making sure it doesn't boil. Serve over chicken breasts.

Chicken Breasts with Fresh Fruit

Robin Schrock
Millersburg, OH

Makes 4 servings

Prep Time: 15-20 minutes
Cooking Time: 15 minutes

1½ Tbsp. olive oil
½ tsp. salt

½ tsp. pepper
¼ tsp. garlic powder
4 large boneless, skinless chicken breast halves
¼ cup butter
8-oz. can pineapple tidbits, drained, *or* fresh pineapple chunks
1 cup fresh, quartered strawberries
1 kiwi, peeled, quartered, and sliced
¼ cup chopped red onions
half a 4-oz. can chopped green chilies
1 tsp. cornstarch
⅓ cup orange juice

1. In a small bowl, combine oil, salt, pepper, and garlic powder. Spread over one side of each chicken breast.

2. In skillet, sauté chicken in butter, seasoned side down, 4-6 minutes. Turn and cook another 4-6 minutes, or until chicken juices run clear.

3. While chicken is sauting, cut up fruit and onions into mixing bowl. Stir in chilies.

4. In a small bowl, combine cornstarch and juice until smooth.

5. Remove cooked chicken from skillet to serving platter. Keep warm. Stir juice mixture into skillet and bring to a boil. Cook and stir for 1-2 minutes, or until thickened. Remove from heat and pour over fruit/onion/chilies mixture. Gently toss to coat.

6. Serve about ⅓ cup fruit sauce over each chicken breast.

Polynesian Chicken

Sheila Plock
Boalsburg, PA

Makes 6 servings

Prep Time: 15 minutes
Baking Time: 75 minutes

6 chicken breast halves, *or* the equivalent with other chicken pieces
1 onion, sliced in rings
16-oz. can sliced peaches, drained
16-oz. can dark sweet cherries, drained
1 cup sweet-and-sour sauce
1 cup barbecue sauce

1. Place chicken in bottom of a greased 9 x 13 baking pan.

2. Place onions over chicken. Arrange peaches over onions. Top with cherries.

3. In a small mixing bowl, mix together sweet-and-sour sauce and barbecue sauce. Spoon evenly over all other ingredients.

4. Cover. Bake at 350° for 30 minutes. Uncover and bake another 45 minutes.

Poppy Seed Chicken

Andrea Cunningham
Arlington, KS

Makes 6 servings

Prep Time: 25 minutes
Baking Time: 30 minutes

4 to 6 boneless, skinless
   chicken breast halves,
   cooked
1 cup sour cream
10.75-oz. can cream of
   chicken soup
1 sleeve butter crackers,
   enough to make about
   1½ cups crumbs
¼ cup butter
1-2 Tbsp. poppy seeds

1. Cut chicken into cubes.
Place in greased 9 x 13 baking pan.
2. Mix sour cream and
cream of chicken soup
together. Pour over chicken.
3. Crush crackers and
place in a mixing bowl.
4. Melt butter and pour
over crushed crackers. Stir
well. Mix in poppy seeds.
Spoon over chicken and
sauce.
5. Bake uncovered at 350°
for 30 minutes, or until
heated through.

Variations:
   *1. Place uncooked cubed
chicken in greased 9 x 13 baking pan. Proceed with Steps 2-
5, except bake for 1 hour.*
      — Norma Denlinger
      Strasburg, PA

Cranberry Chili Chicken

Kelly Bailey
Mechanicsburg, PA

Makes 4-6 servings

Prep Time: 5-10 minutes
Cooking Time: 20 minutes

½ cup chili sauce
2 Tbsp. orange marmalade
½ cup whole-berry
   cranberry sauce
¼ tsp. ground allspice
4-6 boneless, skinless
   chicken breast halves
2 tsp. vegetable oil

1. In a small mixing bowl,
combine chili sauce, orange
marmalade, cranberry sauce,
and allspice. Set aside.
2. In a large skillet, brown
several breast halves at a time
in oil for about 5 minutes on
each side. (Be careful not to
crowd the skillet or the
breasts won't brown as well.)
Place browned breasts on a
platter until all are finished
browning.
3. Return all breasts to
skillet. Pour chili-cranberry
mixture over chicken. Cover
and simmer 8 minutes.
Uncover and continue cooking 2 more minutes, or until
chicken is cooked and sauce
is of desired consistency.

A Tip —
   Plan your meals a week
in advance so you can prepare a grocery list.

Chicken Scallopine

Betsy Chutchian
Grand Prairie, TX

Makes 6-8 servings

Prep Time: 5-10 minutes
Cooking Time: 25-30 minutes

6-8 boneless, skinless
   chicken breast halves
½ tsp. salt
¼ tsp. pepper
¼ cup flour
7 Tbsp. butter, *divided*
¼ lb. fresh mushrooms,
   sliced
2 tsp. lemon juice
2 Tbsp. olive oil
¼ lb. ham, cut into thin
   strips
½ cup dry sherry
½ cup chicken broth

1. Place chicken breasts
between 2 sheets of plastic
wrap and pound with a mallet or rolling pin to flatten.
2. Place salt, pepper, and
flour in shallow bowl. Dip
each breast half into mixture,
coating both sides well.
3. Melt 3 tablespoons butter in skillet. Add mushrooms
and sauté about 5 minutes.
4. Remove mushrooms
and sprinkle with lemon
juice. Set aside.
5. Heat remaining butter
and oil in skillet. Add several
chicken breasts to the skillet
(do not crowd them), and
sauté until lightly browned
on both sides. Remove
chicken pieces as they brown
and keep them warm on a
platter covered with foil.

6. Add ham to skillet and brown. Remove and keep warm in a separate bowl.

7. Add sherry and broth to skillet, bringing to a boil and cooking for 2 minutes.

8. Stir up any brown particles in the skillet so that they flavor the sauce. Return chicken and mushrooms to skillet. Bring sauce to a boil again, then simmer uncovered for 3-5 minutes, until reduced by one-third.

9. Place chicken on a serving platter.

10. Spoon ham and mushrooms on top of chicken.

11. Pour sauce over chicken and serve.

Chicken in Alfredo Sauce

Joyce Clark, East Amherst, NY

Makes 4-6 servings

Prep Time: 20-30 minutes
Cooking/Baking Time:
30-35 minutes

1/2 **cup cooked spinach, stems removed,** *or* **frozen chopped spinach, thawed**
4 **boneless, skinless chicken breast halves, slightly flattened**
2 **thin slices ham, each cut in half**
1/4 **red bell pepper, cut in thin strips**
1 **Tbsp. butter**
2 **Tbsp. flour**

1 **clove garlic, minced**
3/4 **cup whipping cream**
1 1/4 **cups milk**
1 **tsp. grated lemon peel**
pinch of ground nutmeg
1/4 **tsp. salt**
1/4 **cup grated Parmesan cheese**
1 **Tbsp. chopped fresh parsley**
cooked rice *or* **pasta**

1. Squeeze spinach until dry. Divide evenly over chicken breasts. Top each breast with a half slice of ham and a few red pepper strips.

2. Roll breasts up firmly, beginning at thinnest end of breast. Secure each with a toothpick and place, seam-side down, in a single layer in a greased baking pan. Set aside.

3. In a small saucepan, melt butter. Add flour, garlic, cream, milk, lemon peel, nutmeg, salt, Parmesan cheese, and parsley. Stir and blend well. Cook over low heat, stirring occasionally until sauce begins to gently boil. Then stir continuously until smooth and thickened. Pour over chicken rolls.

4. Cover and bake at 350° for 20 minutes, turning after 10 minutes. Baste rolls with sauce.

5. Uncover and stir sauce as well as you can. Spoon up over chicken. Bake 5-7 minutes more.

6. To serve, cut meat rolls in half and serve over rice or pasta. Whisk sauce smooth and ladle over top.

Bruschetta Chicken Bake

Jennifer Yoder Sommers
Harrisonburg, VA

Makes 6 servings

Prep Time: 20 minutes
Cooking/Baking Time:
40-45 minutes

1 1/2 **lbs. boneless, skinless chicken breasts, cut into bite-sized pieces**
14.5-oz. **can diced tomatoes, undrained**
2 **cloves garlic, minced**
6-oz. **pkg. stuffing mix, chicken-flavored**
1/2 **cup water**
1 **tsp. dried basil leaves**
1 **cup shredded mozzarella cheese**

1. Place chicken pieces in a microwave-safe shallow baking dish. Sprinkle with 2 Tbsp. water. Cover with waxed paper. Microwave on high for 3 minutes. Stir. Cover and microwave on high for another 3 minutes. Allow chicken to stand for 5 minutes.

2. Meanwhile, place tomatoes with liquid in medium-sized mixing bowl. Add garlic, stuffing mix, and 1/2 cup water. Stir just until stuffing is moistened. Set aside.

3. Place cooked chicken in a greased 9 x 13 baking dish. Sprinkle with basil and cheese. Top with stuffing mixture.

4. Bake at 400°, uncovered, for 30 minutes, or until heated through.

Chicken Stuffin' Casserole

Janice Muller
Derwood, MD

Makes 6 servings

Prep Time: 20 minutes
Baking Time: 80 minutes

8-oz. pkg. bread stuffing
$1^2/3$ cups applesauce
1 Tbsp. celery flakes
1 tsp. poultry seasoning
$1/2$ tsp. sage
1 Tbsp. onion flakes
1 stick ($1/4$ lb.) butter
4 cups de-boned chicken
10.75-oz. can cream of
    chicken soup
$1/2$ soup-can of milk
pepper, black *or* lemon

1. In a large bowl, mix stuffing and applesauce together. Add celery flakes, poultry seasoning, sage, onion flakes, and enough water to make a moist stuffing mix.
2. Spread the stuffing into a greased 9 x 13 pan. Slice butter into thin pats, distributing them over the top of the stuffing. Next, distribute chicken over the stuffing.
3. In a separate bowl, mix the soup and milk together. Pour over the casserole.
4. Finally, sprinkle the seasoned pepper heavily over the entire surface of the casserole.
5. Bake covered at 350° for 1 hour. Remove cover and continue to bake until the surface has browned and has

a "crunchy" appearance, approximately 20 minutes more.

Amish Roast

Vonda Ebersole
Mt. Pleasant Mills, PA
Miriam Witmer
Lititz, PA

Makes 10-12 servings

Prep Time: 30 minutes
Baking Time: 1-$1^1/2$ hours

2 sticks ($1/2$ lb.) butter
25 slices of bread, cubed
1 cup celery, chopped
1 small onion, chopped
2-3 cups milk
5 eggs
$1/2$ tsp. pepper
$1^1/4$ tsp. garlic salt
5 cups cooked, cubed
    chicken

1. Melt butter until slightly browned.
2. In a very large bowl, pour melted butter over bread cubes. Stir thoroughly to distribute butter through the bread cubes.
3. In another mixing bowl, combine chopped celery and onion, milk, eggs, and seasonings.
4. Pour mixture over bread cubes. Add diced chicken. Mix well.
5. Place in greased roasting pans or casseroles. Cover each one.
6. Bake for 1 hour at 250°,

stirring every 15 minutes. Continue baking until heated through.

My grandmother made this for Thanksgiving and Christmas get-togethers.
   — **Vonda Ebersole**

Cordon Bleu Casserole

Denise Martin
Lancaster, PA

Makes 8-10 servings

Prep Time: 20 minutes
Baking Time: 30 minutes

6 cups cubed, fully cooked
    chicken
3 cups cubed, fully cooked
    ham
1 cup shredded cheddar
    cheese
1 cup chopped onions
$1/4$ cup butter
$1/3$ cup flour
2 cups cream
1 tsp.-1 Tbsp. dill weed,
    according to your taste
    preference
$1/8$-1 tsp. dry mustard,
    according to your taste
    preference
$1/8$-$1/2$ tsp. ground nutmeg,
    according to your taste
    preference

Topping:
1 cup dry bread crumbs
2 Tbsp. butter, melted
1/4-1 tsp. dill weed,
according to your taste
preference
1/4 cup shredded cheddar
cheese
1/4-1/2 cup chopped
walnuts, according to
your taste preference

1. In a large bowl, combine chicken, ham, and cheese. Set aside.

2. In saucepan, sauté onions in butter until tender. Add flour. Stir to form a paste.

3. Over low heat, gradually add cream, stirring constantly. Bring to a boil, and boil 1 minute or until thickened.

4. Add dill, mustard, and nutmeg and mix well. Remove from heat and pour over meat/cheese mixture. Spoon into a greased 9 x 13 baking pan.

5. In the large mixing bowl, toss together bread crumbs, butter, and dill. Stir in cheese and walnuts. Sprinkle over casserole.

6. Bake uncovered at 350° for 30 minutes, or until heated through.

Tip: This recipe can be prepared the day before through Step 4. When ready to heat, remove from the refrigerator and sprinkle on topping. Add 5-10 minutes to the baking time.

Edie's Paella

Joy Sutter
Perkasie, PA

Makes 4-6 servings

Prep Time: 15 minutes
Cooking Time: 25 minutes
Standing Time: 10 minutes

1 1/2 lbs. boneless, skinless chicken breasts, diced
1/4 cup olive oil
1 lb. Italian sausage, cut in pieces
1 large onion, chopped
3-4 tomatoes, chopped
5 cups chicken broth
15-oz. can black beans, drained and rinsed
15.5-oz. can pinto beans, drained and rinsed
15.5-oz. can Great Northern beans, drained and rinsed
1 tsp. fresh rosemary leaves
salt and pepper to taste
1 lb. small-grained rice

1. In a large stockpot, heat olive oil. Add chicken and brown.

2. Remove chicken, but reserve drippings. Brown sausage and onion in stockpot. Drain off drippings.

3. Stir in tomatoes.

4. Add chicken broth and simmer 10 minutes.

5. Add beans, rosemary, salt, and pepper. Stir well.

6. Add rice. Stir and then cook for 20-25 minutes, until rice is soft and liquid evaporates.

7. Let stand 10 minutes before serving.

Tip: This is best with fresh rosemary if you can find it!

Chicken Broccoli Lo Mein

Pamela Pierce
Annville, PA

Makes 4-6 servings

Prep Time: 10 minutes
Cooking Time: 15 minutes

1/2 lb. fettucine *or* lo mein noodles, cooked and set aside
1/4 cup peanut butter
1/4 cup soy sauce
1 1/2 Tbsp. brown sugar
1 Tbsp. lemon juice
1/3 cup hot water
2 cloves garlic, minced
2 Tbsp. oil
1 lb. uncooked boneless, skinless chicken breasts, cubed
1 medium bunch broccoli, cut in bite-sized pieces

1. In a jar with a tight lid, mix peanut butter, soy sauce, brown sugar, lemon juice, hot water, and garlic. Shake well until blended.

2. In skillet, stir-fry chicken in oil for 5-6 minutes. Add broccoli. Cook an additional 3-4 minutes.

3. Add sauce to skillet. Stir in noodles. Cook 2 more minutes and then serve.

Cheesy Chicken Tetrazzini

Andrea Yoder
Drexel, MO

Makes 16 servings

Prep Time: 20 minutes
Cooking/Baking Time:
* 60 minutes*
Standing Time: 20-30 minutes

16 boneless, skinless
  chicken breast halves
3 chicken bouillon cubes
8 ozs. uncooked spaghetti
10.75-oz. can cream of
  chicken soup
10.75-oz. can cream of
  mushroom soup
4-oz. can chopped green
  chilies, drained
2-oz. jar diced pimentos,
  drained
1/2 cup grated Parmesan
  cheese
3 cups (12 ozs.) shredded
  cheddar cheese
1 cup milk
1/8 tsp. garlic powder
4-oz. can sliced
  mushrooms
1/2 cup sliced almonds,
  optional

1. Place chicken and bouillon cubes in large stockpot. Cover with water. Cover pot and bring to a boil. Continue simmering until chicken is tender.

2. Lift chicken out of broth. Reserve broth.

3. Allow chicken to cool, and then cut into cubes. Set chicken aside.

4. While chicken is cooling, cook spaghetti in chicken broth according to package directions (adding enough water to equal one quart). Drain.

5. In a large mixing bowl, mix together soups, chilies, pimentos, cheeses, milk, garlic powder, mushrooms, and almonds.

6. Add spaghetti and chicken and mix well.

7. Bake in a greased 9 x 13 baking casserole for 30 minutes. Allow to stand for 20 or 30 minutes before serving.

Tip: Sprinkle with bread crumbs and paprika before baking, if you wish.

Chicken Vegetable Strudel

Ruth C Hancock
Earlsboro, OK

Makes 4 servings

Prep Time: 25 minutes
Baking Time: 30-35 minutes

2 cups diced cooked
  chicken
1/2 cup shredded carrots
1/2 cup finely chopped
  broccoli
1/3 cup finely chopped red
  bell pepper
1 cup shredded sharp
  cheddar cheese
1/2 cup mayonnaise
2 cloves garlic, minced
1/2 tsp. dill weed

1/4 tsp. salt
1/4 tsp. pepper
2 tubes crescent rolls
1 egg white, beaten
2 Tbsp. slivered almonds

1. In a large bowl, combine chicken, carrots, broccoli, bell pepper, cheese, mayonnaise, garlic, dill weed, salt, and pepper. Mix well.

2. Unroll crescent rolls, placing squares against each other in a greased 10 x 15 jelly-roll pan. Dough will hang over the sides of the pan. Pinch the center seam together.

3. Place chicken mixture down the center of the dough.

4. Cut dough in 1 1/2" wide strips, cutting in 3 1/2" toward the center.

5. Starting at one end, pick up alternate strips from each side, twist each one twice, and then lay each at an angle across the filling. Seal the ends against the dough when attaching them.

6. In a small mixing bowl, beat the egg white until foamy. Brush over dough. Sprinkle with almonds.

7. Bake at 375° for 30-35 minutes.

A Tip —

Don't be afraid to experiment! Some of my best dishes were made from leftovers or whatever I had on hand. The only problem . . . these dishes are rarely duplicated!

108

Chicken Pie

Pat Bishop
Bedminster, PA

Makes 6 servings

Prep Time: 30-45 minutes
Baking Time: 35-40 minutes

4 Tbsp. butter or margarine
4 Tbsp. flour
1/2 tsp. salt
1/4 tsp. thyme
1 cup chicken broth
3/4 cup milk
2 cups cooked chicken
2 cups assorted cooked
   vegetables (potatoes,
   corn, peas, carrots, etc.)
1 unbaked double pie
   crust (see "2-Crust Pie"
   recipe, opposite)

1. Melt butter in a medium saucepan. Add flour, salt, and thyme. Cook until bubbly.
2. Add broth and milk. Heat to boiling, stirring constantly. Boil 1 minute.
3. Stir in chicken and vegetables. Pour into pie crust.
4. Place dough over top. Flute edges. Prick top of dough.
5. Bake at 425 for 35-40 minutes.

I like to use leftover turkey from holiday meals for this recipe.

When I need to take a meal to help another family, this is my first choice to make.

Variations:
   1. Add 1/2 cup onion to Step 1, just after melting the butter.
   2. Use 13/4 cups chicken broth, instead of 1 cup broth and 3/4 cup milk.
   — Ruth Ann Bender
   Cochranville, PA

2-Crust Pie

Pat Bishop
Bedminster, PA

2 cups flour
1 tsp. salt
2/3 cup, plus 2 Tbsp.
   shortening
4-5 Tbsp. cold water

1. In a large mixing bowl, stir together flour and salt.
2. Cut in shortening with a pastry cutter till crumbly.
3. Stir in water with a fork. Mix until dough holds together.
4. Roll out half the dough on a lightly floured surface. Fold dough in half, and then in half again. Lift into 9" pie plate, unfold, and push gently into place.
5. Roll out the other half of the dough. Fold in half and place carefully over pie filling. Unfold—and follow directions in Step 4 of Chicken Pie (opposite).

Garden Chicken Casserole

Virginia Bender, Dover, DE

Makes 6 servings

Prep Time: 10 minutes
Baking Time: 60 minutes

2 20-oz. cans cream of
   chicken soup
11/2 cups mayonnaise
1/4 cup chopped onions
2 cups chopped celery
8-oz. can sliced water
   chestnuts, drained
4 cups diced, cooked
   chicken
2 cups cooked rice
1/2 cup sliced almonds
1 sleeve butter snack
   crackers, crushed
1/4 cup melted butter

1. In a large mixing bowl, combine soup, mayonnaise, onions, celery, water chestnuts, chicken, rice, and almonds. Pour into a greased 9 x 13 baking pan.
2. Sprinkle with crackers.
3. Pour butter over top.
4. Bake at 350° for 60 minutes.

Variations:
   1. In place of water chestnuts, stir in 4 hard-cooked chopped eggs.
   2. Replace cracker/butter topping with a layer of 3 cups crushed potato chips, followed by a layer of 2 cups shredded cheddar cheese.
   — Violette Harris Denney
   Carrollton, GA

Turkey or Chicken Curry

Angie Clemens
Dayton, VA

Makes 8-10 servings

Prep Time: 30 minutes
Cooking Time: 75 minutes

2/3 cup minced onions
1 cup chopped apples
1/4 cup vegetable oil
1/4 cup flour
1 Tbsp. curry powder
hot sauce to taste
1 qt. chicken broth
2 cloves garlic, crushed
2 pieces dried gingerroot,
  or 1/2 tsp. powdered
  ginger
1 sliced large tomato, *or* 1
  qt. stewed tomatoes,
  drained, *optional*
2 cups diced cooked turkey
  or chicken

1. In a large skillet, heat onions and apples in oil. Cook, covered, until clear, stirring several times.
2. Add flour and curry.
3. Slowly stir in hot sauce, if you wish, and the broth until well blended. Add garlic, ginger, and tomato, if you wish.
4. Bring to a boil. Cover and simmer 1 hour, stirring occasionally.
5. Add meat and cook long enough to heat through.
6. Serve over rice along with serving dishes of chutney, sliced green onions, shredded coconut, peanuts, pineapple chunks, and raisins or craisins.

Tip: Bake the rice while preparing the curry. We prefer the texture of baked rice, and I don't have to worry about it cooking over or burning on the stove.

Honey Chicken

Lisa Cutler
Willow Street, PA
Christie Detamore-Hunsberger
Harrisonburg, VA

Makes 6-8 servings

Prep Time: 15-20 minutes
Baking Time: 50-60 minutes

6-8 boneless, skinless
  chicken breast halves
4 Tbsp. butter
1/2 cup honey
1/4 cup prepared mustard
1/2 tsp. salt
1 tsp. curry
1 Tbsp. dry *or* minced
  onion, *optional*

1. Wash and pat chicken dry. Arrange in a greased 9 x 13 baking pan.
2. Melt butter in a medium-sized saucepan and then add remaining ingredients. Mix well and pour over chicken.
3. Bake uncovered, basting every 15 minutes, at 350° for 50-60 minutes, or until chicken is cooked through but not burned.

Hot Chicken Salad

Margaret Moffitt, Bartlett, TN

Makes 4 servings

Prep Time: 10 minutes
Baking Time: 10 minutes

2 cups chicken, cooked
  and diced
2 cups diced celery
1/2 cup chopped cashews
1/2 tsp. salt, *optional*
2 tsp. finely grated onions
2 Tbsp. lemon juice
2/3 cup mayonnaise

Topping:
1/2 cup grated American
  cheese
1/2 cup crushed potato chips

1. Mix all ingredients together in a bowl, excluding topping ingredients.
2. Place into a greased casserole dish. Sprinkle with topping.
3. Bake uncovered at 425° for 10 minutes.

Tip: If you'd like the celery to be less crunchy, sauté it briefly it in a nonstick pan before adding to the mixture.

Variations: Reduce the celery to 1/4 cup. Drop the cashews. Add 1/4 cup golden raisins, 1/4 cup dried cranberries, and 1/4 cup sliced almonds. Drop the Topping. Spread mixture on 6 regular-sized croissants, or on 9-12 mini-croissants (which are perfect for potlucks or picnics).
— **Rosalie Duerksen**
Canton, KS

Drop the cashews. Increase chopped onions to 2 Tbsp. Add 1/2 cup chopped green pepper and a 10.75-oz. can cream of mushroom soup. Place in a greased 11/2-qt. baking dish. For Topping, increase potato chips to 2 cups. Sprinkle chips and grated cheese over top and bake uncovered at 350° for 25 minutes.

— **Sherri Mayer**
Menomonce Falls, WI

Easy Chicken Fajitas

Jessica Hontz
Coatesville, PA

Makes 4-6 servings

Prep Time: 20 minutes
Marinating Time: 4-8 hours, or overnight
Cooking Time: 10 minutes

1 lb. boneless, skinless chicken breasts
1 pkg. dry Italian salad dressing mix
8-oz. bottle Italian salad dressing
1 cup salsa
1 green pepper, sliced
half a medium-sized onion, sliced
1 pkg. of 10 10"-flour tortillas
Optional Toppings:
shredded Monterey Jack cheese
shredded lettuce
sour cream
chopped tomatoes

salsa
hot pepper sauce

1. Cut chicken into thin strips. Place in large mixing bowl.
2. Add dry salad dressing mix and salad dressing. Mix well. Cover and marinade 4-8 hours in the fridge.
3. In a large skillet, combine drained chicken strips, salsa, and pepper and onion slices. Stir-fry until chicken is cooked and peppers and onions are soft.
4. Place chicken mix in tortillas with your choice of toppings.

Variation: The cooked chicken can also be used on salads.

A Tip —

Cook chicken breasts, or fry ground beef with onion, and then freeze them in freezer bags. When a recipe calls for shredded chicken or ground beef, you can easily and quickly pull out the frozen packages and have a headstart on your meal.

Mexican Chicken Bake

Gretchen H. Maust
Keezletown, VA

Makes 8 servings

Prep Time: 20 minutes
Baking Time: 1 hour

2 cups cooked brown rice
1 lb. cooked chicken breast, cubed
2 14.5-oz. cans diced tomatoes, undrained
15-oz. can black beans, drained
1 cup corn
1 cup red bell pepper, diced
1 cup green pepper, diced
1 Tbsp. cumin
1 Tbsp. chili powder
1/2 tsp. salt
1/4 tsp. pepper
4 garlic cloves, minced
2 cups shredded cheddar cheese

1. Spread rice on bottom of greased 3-4-qt. casserole dish.
2. In a large mixing bowl, combine remaining ingredients, except cheese. Pour over rice. Cover.
3. Bake at 375° for 45 minutes. Remove from oven. Top with cheese. Reduce heat to 300°. Bake, uncovered, for an additional 15 minutes, or until bubbly.

Variation: For a vegetarian version of this dish, leave out the chicken.

Stuffed Quesadillas

Stacy Schmucker Stoltzfus
Enola, PA

Makes 2-4 servings

Prep Time: 20-25 minutes
Cooking Time: 6-10 minutes

8 6" corn tortillas
2 cups shredded Monterey
 Jack cheese
1 cup canned black beans,
 drained
1/4 cup diced onions
1/2 cup chopped cilantro
2 plum tomatoes, chopped
1 red *or* green bell pepper,
 chopped
2 cups shredded, cooked
 chicken
1 lime, cut into wedges
sour cream and salsa

1. Place 4 tortillas onto workspace. Sprinkle 1/4 cup cheese over each tortilla.
2. Dividing each ingredient into 4 parts, continue layering on each tortilla in this order: black beans, onions, cilantro, tomatoes, pepper, and chicken. Top each with 1/4 cup cheese.
3. Squeeze lime juice over all. Cover with remaining tortillas.
4. Heat large skillet on medium-high heat. Place 2 tortilla stacks in hot skillet and cook 3-5 minutes, or until tortilla is browned.
5. Carefully flip onto other side and cook until cheese is melted.

6. Remove from pan and cut with a pizza cutter into fourths. Keep warm.
7. Continue with the remaining 2 tortilla stacks, browning and flipping until done. Cut into fourths, also.
8. Serve with sour cream and salsa on the side.

Tip: The ingredient amounts for filling are approximate. Use what you like.

Curried Chicken Pitas

Sharon Eshleman
Ephrata, PA

Makes 4 servings

Prep Time: 15 minutes

1/2 cup light mayonnaise
 or salad dressing
1 Tbsp. honey
1 Tbsp. pickle relish
3/4-1 tsp. curry powder,
 according to your taste
 preference
2 cups cubed cooked
 chicken
1 cup halved grapes *or*
 chopped apples
1/2 cup chopped pecans
4 pita breads, halved
8 lettuce leaves

1. In a bowl, combine salad dressing, honey, pickle relish, and curry powder.
2. Stir in chicken, grapes, and pecans.

3. Line pita halves with lettuce. Spoon 1/2 cup chicken mixture into each pita.

Chicken and Broccoli Pita Sandwiches

Vonnie Oyer, Hubbard, OR

Makes 4-6 servings

Prep Time: 15 minutes

2 cups chopped cooked
 chicken
2 tomatoes, chopped
1 1/2 cups chopped raw
 broccoli
1 hard-cooked egg,
 chopped
1/3 cup cooked rice
1/2 cup grated cheese
1 avocado, chopped,
 optional
4 pita breads

Dressing:
2 Tbsp. honey
2 Tbsp. prepared mustard
3/4 cup mayonnaise

1. Mix chicken, tomatoes, broccoli, egg, rice, cheese, and avocado together in a large bowl.
2. Mix dressing ingredients in a small bowl.
3. Pour dressing over chicken mixture and stir gently.
4. Cut pita breads in half. Fill with chicken mixture.

I first had this at the home of an older woman in our church. I had hung wallpaper for her, and then enjoyed her company and these pocket sandwiches for lunch.

Variations: If you'd like a zestier flavor, add salt, pepper, and curry powder, to taste, to the dressing.

Chicken Salad Sandwiches

Rosalie Duerksen
Canton, KS

Makes 6 servings

Prep Time: 15 minutes

12.5-oz can cooked
  chicken, drained
1/4 cup diced celery
1/4 cup golden raisins
1/4 cup dried cranberries
1/4 cup sliced almonds
1/4 tsp. salt
1/8 tsp. pepper
3/4 cup mayonnaise
6 croissants, sliced

1. In a bowl, place drained chicken. Add celery, raisins, cranberries, almonds, salt, and pepper.
2 Stir in mayonnaise until well blended.
3. Spread onto croissants.

Tip: Instead of buying the regular-sized croissants, I buy the mini-size to take to potlucks or picnics. Just the perfect size!

Turkey Main Dishes

Turkey Stir-Fry

Arianne Hochstetler
Goshen, IN

Makes 6 servings

Prep Time: 15-20 minutes
Cooking Time: 20 minutes

1 1/2 lbs. boneless turkey,
  cut into strips
1 Tbsp. cooking oil
1 large onion, chopped
1 carrot, julienned
half a green pepper, sliced
2 cups fresh, sliced
  mushrooms
1 cup chicken broth
3 Tbsp. cornstarch
3 Tbsp. soy sauce
1/2 tsp. ginger
1 tsp. curry powder
2 cups pea pods, trimmed,
  or 2 cups frozen stir-fry
  vegetables
1/3 cup cashews, *optional*

1. In a large skillet or wok, stir-fry turkey in oil over medium-high heat until no longer pink, about 5-6 minutes. Remove turkey from pan and keep warm.
2. Stir-fry the onion, carrot, green pepper, and mushrooms until crisp-tender, about 5 minutes.
3. In a small bowl, combine chicken broth, cornstarch, soy sauce, ginger, and curry powder until smooth.
4. Add to the skillet. Cook and stir until thickened and bubbly.
5. Return turkey to skillet with pea pods. Cook and stir until heated through.
6. Serve over cooked rice. Top with cashews, if desired.

Variation: You can use sliced beef, pork, or chicken instead of turkey.

Tips:
1. Chop all the vegetables before you cut the turkey into strips. Then all ingredients are ready to go as you need them.
2. Cook the rice at the same time as you are preparing and cooking the stir-fry.

A Tip —

I like to roast a turkey in advance of needing it. I slice the roasted breast meat into serving pieces and freeze it. And I chop all the rest of the meat and freeze it in 3-cup batches. The chopped turkey is ready for any recipe calling for cooked turkey or chicken, such as turkey or chicken salad, turkey pot pie, and so on.

Orange-Glazed Turkey Cutlets

Rosemarie Fitzgerald
Gibsonia, PA

Makes 4 servings

Prep Time: 10 minutes
Cooking Time: 10 minutes

1 lb. turkey breast cutlets
   or slices
salt and pepper to taste
ground cinnamon to taste
2 tsp. oil
1/3 cup orange marmalade
1/8 tsp. ground cinnamon
1/8 tsp. ground nutmeg
1/8 tsp. ground ginger

1. Lightly sprinkle one side of cutlets with salt, pepper, and cinnamon.
2. In large non-stick skillet, over medium-high heat, sauté turkey cutlets in oil for 1-2 minutes per side, or until turkey is no longer pink in the center. Do in batches if your skillet isn't large enough to hold the cutlets all at once with space around each one.
3. Remove turkey as it finishes browning to platter and keep warm.
4. In small saucepan, over medium heat, combine marmalade, cinnamon, nutmeg, and ginger. Cook 1-2 minutes or until marmalade melts and mixture is heated through.
5. To serve, spoon marmalade sauce over cutlets.

Savory Turkey

Clara Newswanger
Gordonville, PA

Makes 12 servings

Prep Time: 15 minutes
Baking Time: 35-45 minutes

1/2 cup onions, chopped
1 stick (1/2 cup) butter
2 9-oz. cans mushrooms, drained
4 Tbsp. flour
2 beef bouillon cubes
1 cup water
2 Tbsp. soy sauce
2 lbs. boneless skinless turkey thighs, cut in 2" chunks

1. In medium-sized saucepan, sauté onions in butter.
2. Add mushrooms and flour. Stir until well mixed.
3. Add bouillon cubes, water, and soy sauce, Mix well and bring to a boil.
4. Meanwhile, place turkey thighs in a greased baking dish. Pour sauce over thighs.
5. Bake uncovered at 350° for 35-45 minutes, or until tender.

> **A Tip —**
>
> Always preheat the oven before preparing a recipe.

Seafood Main Dishes

Shrimp with Ginger and Lime

Joy Uhler
Richardson, TX

Makes 2-4 servings

Prep Time: 15-20 minutes
Cooking Time: 10 minutes

3 Tbsp. lime juice
4 Tbsp. olive oil, *divided*
1 Tbsp. minced gingerroot
1 Tbsp. brown sugar
1 tsp. grated lime zest
1 tsp. sesame seed oil
1 large garlic clove, minced
1 lb. cooked shrimp, peeled and deveined
cooked rice
2 Tbsp. cilantro, chopped

1. In a large mixing bowl, stir together lime juice, 3 Tbsp. olive oil, gingerroot, brown sugar, lime zest,

sesame seed oil, and garlic clove.

2. Stir in shrimp and mix well so that they're covered with the marinade. Allow shrimp to marinate for 15 minutes.

3. Pour 1 Tbsp. olive oil into large skillet or wok. Spoon in shrimp mixture and stir-fry until heated through.

4. Serve over prepared rice. Sprinkle with chopped cilantro.

Cajun Shrimp

Mary Ann Potenta
Bridgewater, NJ

Makes 4-5 servings

Prep Time: just minutes!
Cooking Time: 10-12 minutes

1 1/2 sticks (12 Tbsp.) butter, *divided*
1/2 cup chopped green onions
1 tsp. minced garlic
1 tsp. cayenne pepper
1/2 tsp. white pepper
1/2 tsp. black pepper
1/4 tsp. dry mustard
1/2 tsp. salt
1 tsp. Tabasco sauce
2 lbs. shrimp, peeled and cleaned
cooked rice

1. Melt 1 stick of butter in large skillet. Add onions and garlic and sauté till clear, but not brown, about 1 minute.

2. Add peppers, mustard, and salt. Cook and stir for 3 minutes.

3. Mix in half-stick of butter and Tabasco sauce until blended.

4. Add shrimp. Cook just until pink. Do not overcook.

5. Serve over cooked rice

Note: This is hot! You can tone things down by reducing the amounts of the 3 peppers and the Tabasco sauce.

Sesame Shrimp and Asparagus

Karen Kay Tucker
Manteca, CA

Makes 6 servings

Prep Time: 30 minutes
Cooking Time: 10 minutes

1 1/2 lbs. fresh asparagus
1 Tbsp. sesame seeds
1/3 cup vegetable oil *or* olive oil
2 small red onions, sliced in rings
1 1/2 lbs. large shrimp, peeled and deveined
4 tsp. soy sauce
1 1/4 tsp. salt

1. About 30 minutes before serving, prepare asparagus. Hold base of each stalk firmly and bend. The end will break off at the spot where it becomes too tough to eat. Discard ends or freeze and use when making stock.

2. Wash and trim asparagus. Then cut into 2" pieces and steam in 1/2" water in saucepan until crisp-tender. Plunge asparagus into cold water to stop cooking. Set aside.

3. In a large skillet or wok, over medium heat, toast sesame seeds until golden brown, stirring seeds and shaking skillet often. Remove seeds to small bowl.

4. In same skillet or wok, over medium-high heat, heat oil until hot. Add onions and shrimp. Cook until shrimp are pink, about 5 minutes.

5. Drain asparagus. Add to skillet with shrimp. Stir in sesame seeds, soy sauce, and salt. Heat until asparagus is warm.

A Tip —

Don't measure ingredients over the bowl in which you are mixing or baking the recipe, in case more than you need comes tumbling out.

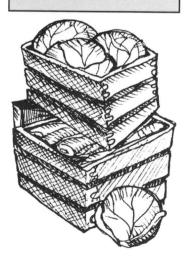

Shrimp Primavera

Elaine Rineer
Lancaster, PA

Makes 4 servings

Prep Time: 20 minutes
Cooking Time: 10 minutes

1 Tbsp., plus 1 tsp.,
  vegetable *or* olive oil
1½ cups chopped broccoli
½ cup thinly sliced carrots
1 cup sliced mushrooms
2 garlic cloves, minced
1 cup chicken broth
1 Tbsp. cornstarch
1 lb. shrimp, peeled and
  deveined
2 Tbsp. grated Parmesan
  cheese
2 Tbsp. parsley

1. In large skillet or wok, sauté broccoli and carrots in oil. Stir-fry until carrots are crisp-tender.

2. Stir in mushrooms and garlic. Stir-fry 1 minute.

3. In a small bowl, whisk together broth and cornstarch. Pour over vegetables.

4. Add shrimp. Cook until shrimp turns pink and sauce thickens.

5. Stir in remaining ingredients.

Baked Scallops

Rosemarie Fitzgerald
Gibsonia, PA

Makes 4 servings

Prep Time: 10 minutes
Baking Time: 15 minutes

1 lb. scallops
½ cup bread crumbs
1 Tbsp. butter
½ cup white wine
¼ cup grated Parmesan
  cheese
salt and pepper to taste
¼ cup chopped fresh
  parsley

1. Rinse scallops and pat dry. Place in large mixing bowl and sprinkle with bread crumbs. Toss to coat.

2. Place in a greased baking dish, large enough to hold the scallops in one layer.

3. Cut butter into bits and divide over the scallops. Pour wine into bottom of baking dish, being careful not to disturb the bread-crumb coating on the scallops.

4. Bake, uncovered, at 350° for 15 minutes. Remove from oven and turn on broiler.

5. Sprinkle scallops with Parmesan cheese. Place under broiler for 5-10 seconds, until cheese has browned slightly. Watch carefully to keep from burning.

6. Season with salt and freshly ground pepper. Sprinkle with chopped parsley.

Scallops Au Gratin

Anne Jones
Ballston Lake, NY

Makes 4 servings

Prep Time: 15 minutes
Baking Time: 20-30 minutes

16 butter-flavored crackers
½ tsp. paprika
½ tsp. garlic powder
1 lb. bay scallops
1 stick (½ cup) butter
2 Tbsp. sherry
1-1½ cups shredded Swiss
  cheese

1. Crush crackers in plastic bag. Add paprika and garlic powder and mix.

2. Add scallops to bag and shake to coat.

3. Place scallops in a greased 8 x 8 baking pan, or 4 greased individual baking dishes.

4. In a small saucepan, melt butter and add sherry. Stir to mix. Pour over scallops, dividing if using small baking dishes.

5. Bake at 375° for 15 minutes. Cover with Swiss cheese and continue baking until bubbly.

A Tip —

If you mistakenly add too much salt to a dish you're preparing, drop in a potato and continue cooking. The potato will help to absorb the extra salt.

Crab-Topped Catfish

Vicki Hill
Memphis, TN

Makes 6 serving

Prep Time: 5-10 minutes
Baking Time: 27 minutes

6 catfish fillets (totaling
   1-2 lbs.)
6-oz. can white crabmeat,
   drained and flaked
1/2 cup grated Parmesan
   cheese
1/2 cup mayonnaise
1 tsp. lemon juice
paprika
1/3 cup sliced almonds

1. Place fish on greased cookie sheet.

2. Bake, uncovered, at 350° for 22 minutes, or until fish flakes easily with a fork. Drain.

3. Meanwhile, combine crab, cheese, mayonnaise, and lemon juice in a bowl.

4. After fish has baked for 22 minutes, spoon crab mix evenly over fish. Sprinkle with paprika and sliced almonds.

5. Return to oven and bake uncovered at 350° for 5 minutes more.

Oven-Fried Catfish

Karen Waggoner
Joplin, MO

Makes 4 servings

Prep Time: 15 minutes
Baking Time: 25-30 minutes

4 catfish fillets (6 ozs.
   each)
1 cup cornflake crumbs
1/4 tsp. celery salt
1/2 tsp. onion powder
1/4 tsp. paprika
1/8 tsp. pepper
1 egg white
2 Tbsp. milk

1. Pat fish dry with paper towels. Set aside.

2. In glass pie plate, combine crumbs, celery salt, onion powder, paprika, and pepper.

3. In a shallow bowl, beat egg white. Add milk.

4. Dip fillets in egg white mixture, then dip into crumb mixture, coating well.

5. Place in greased 9 x 13 baking dish.

6. Bake, uncovered, at 350° for 25-30 minutes, or until fish flakes easily with a fork.

Seafood Enchiladas

Joleen Albrecht
Gladstone, MI

Makes 4-6 servings

Prep Time: 15 minutes
Baking Time: 30 minutes

1 onion, chopped
1 Tbsp. butter
3/4-1 lb. crabmeat, flaked
8 ozs. Colby cheese,
   shredded, *divided*
1 cup milk
1/2 cup sour cream
half a stick (1/4 cup) butter
11/2 tsp. parsley
1/2 tsp. garlic salt
6-8 10" flour tortillas

1. In a medium-sized saucepan, sauté onions in 1 Tbsp. butter. Remove from heat and stir in crabmeat and 1 cup cheese.

2. Place desired amount of mixture into each tortilla. Roll up tortillas and place seam-side down in a greased 9 x 13 baking pan.

3. Combine milk, sour cream, the half-stick of butter, parsley, and garlic salt in the saucepan. Heat until blended and warmed through.

4. Pour sauce over enchiladas and sprinkle with remaining cheese.

5. Bake uncovered at 350° for 30 minutes.

Home-Baked Fish Fingers

Andrea Cunningham
Arlington, KS

Makes 4 servings

Prep Time: 15 minutes
Baking Time: 20 minutes

1 lb. codfish, whiting, *or*
    orange roughy fillets
3/4 cup dry bread crumbs
1/4-1/2 tsp. salt
2 eggs, beaten
2 Tbsp. butter, melted

Tartar Sauce:
1 pickle, chopped
1/2 cup mayonnaise
1 lemon

1. Wash the fillets, then pat them dry with paper towels. Cut into long pieces.
2. Mix bread crumbs and salt together in a shallow bowl. Put eggs in another shallow bowl.
3. Dip each strip of fish into the eggs; then roll in bread crumbs until coated.
4. Lay fish in a greased 9 x 13 baking pan. Drizzle melted butter over fish fingers.
5. Bake at 400° for 20 minutes, or until golden brown, turning once.
6. Meanwhile, combine ingredients for tartar sauce. Serve with fish fingers.

Salmon Croquettes

Margaret Moffitt, Bartlett, TN

Makes 5-6 servings

Prep Time: 25 minutes
Cooking Time: 6-8 minutes

14.75-oz. can of salmon,
    drained and deboned
2 eggs, beaten
1/2 cup bread crumbs *or*
    finely crushed crackers
1 Tbsp. flour
1/2 tsp. salt
1/4 tsp. black pepper
1/4 cup grated onions
1/4 cup chopped celery
2 Tbsp. vegetable oil,
    divided

1. Mix all ingredients together except vegetable oil. Form into 5 or 6 croquettes.
2. Pour 1 Tbsp. oil into skillet and heat. Sauté croquettes in hot skillet without crowding them. (Do in batches if necessary.)
3. When croquettes brown on one side, turn them over and continue cooking until both sides are brown. Add second Tbsp. of oil if needed.

Variations:
    Use only 1 egg. Instead of salt, pepper, onions, and celery, mix in 2 Tbsp. ketchup and 1 tsp. paprika.
    —**Barbara W. Glueck**
    Jenks, OK

Add the following to the full recipe above: 1/4 cup finely chopped red bell pepper, 1/4 cup
finely chopped green pepper, 1 Tbsp. Worcestershire sauce. Shape into patties. Beat 1 egg in a shallow bowl; place 1 cup bread crumbs in another shallow bowl. Dip each patty into the beaten egg, and then into the bread crumbs. Proceed with Steps 2 and 3. Serve finished patties with 1/2 Tbsp. medium or hot salsa on top.
    — **Kathy Novy**
    Pueblo, CO

Instead of the celery, use 1/4 cup shredded carrots. Add 1 Tbsp. Worcestershire sauce and 1/4 tsp. dried basil or dried oregano to the full recipe above.
    — **Esther J. Yoder**
    Hartville, OH

Replace the onion and celery with 2 Tbsp. Dijon mustard and 1 Tbsp. dried onion flakes in the full recipe above.
    — **Shirley Hinh**
    Wayland, IA

A Tip —

When sautéing or frying, turn a metal colander or strainer upside down over the skillet. This allows steam to escape and keeps fat from spattering.

Baked Salmon

Erma Brubaker
Harrisonburg, VA

Makes 4 servings

Prep Time: 5 minutes
Baking Time: 30-45 minutes

1 lb. fresh salmon, cut into
    4 pieces
nonfat cooking spray
seasoning salt
1/4 cup mayonnaise
parsley

1. Spray baking dish with cooking spray. Spray salmon with cooking spray and arrange in baking dish.
2. Sprinkle with seasoning salt, spread with mayonnaise, and top with parsley.
3. Bake, uncovered, at 350° for 30-45 minutes.

Tip: Mayonnaise keeps the salmon moist. For quick clean-up, bake on an open piece of tin foil.

Oyster Sage Dressing

J.B. Miller, Indianapolis, IN

Makes 8 servings

Prep Time: 40 minutes
Baking Time: 40 minutes

1-lb. loaf whole wheat
    bread, cut into 1" cubes
1 stick (8 Tbsp.) butter
1 large onion, chopped
4 ribs celery, chopped
1 Tbsp. dried sage
2 Tbsp. fresh parsley,
    chopped
1-1 1/2 cups chicken stock
1 pint freshly shucked
    oysters with liquor,
    chopped if they're large
1/2 tsp. black pepper
2 tsp. salt, *or less*, to taste

1. If the bread you plan to use is very fresh, cube it and place it in a large uncovered bowl overnight.
2. Melt butter in a very large skillet or stockpot. Sauté onions and celery in butter until just tender.
3. Stir into bread in large bowl. Add sage and parsley. Toss gently to combine.
4. Fold in chicken stock, just enough to moisten bread.
5. Fold in oysters and oyster liquor. Season with pepper and salt.
6. Transfer to a greased 9 x 13 baking dish. Cover with foil.
7. Bake at 375° for 30 minutes.
8. Remove foil and continue baking until top is lightly browned, about 10 more minutes.

Scalloped Corn and Oysters

Evelyn Page, Lance Creek, WY

Makes 4-6 servings

Prep Time: 5-7 minutes
Baking Time: 60 minutes

2 15.25-oz. cans whole-
    kernel corn, drained
1 15.25-oz. can creamed
    corn
1 cup oysters, drained
1/4-1/2 tsp. salt
1/8-1/4 tsp. pepper
2-oz. jar pimentos, drained
8 soda crackers, crumbled
4 Tbsp. butter
1/4 cup light cream, *or half-
    and-half*

1. Place a layer of half the corns, followed by a layer of half the oysters in a greased 8 x 10 baking dish. Sprinkle with half the salt and pepper.
2. Spoon half the pimentos over top, and half the cracker crumbs.
3. Melt the butter in a small pan. Spoon half of it over the cracker crumbs.
4. Repeat the layers.
5. Pour cream over top. Drizzle with remaining butter.
6. Bake uncovered at 350° for 1 hour.

Meatless Main Dishes

Vegetarian Black Bean Burritos

Maricarol Magill
Freehold, NJ

Makes 8 burritos

Prep Time: 10 minutes
Cooking/ Baking time:
40 minutes

1¼ cup water
1 Tbsp. butter
½ cup long-grain rice
½ tsp. salt
8 10" flour tortillas
10-oz. package frozen corn
15-oz. can spicy black-bean
    chili
8-oz. can tomato sauce
shredded cheddar,
    Monterey Jack, *or*
    pepper Jack cheese

1. In a medium-sized saucepan, bring water and butter to a boil.

2. Stir in rice and salt. Cover. Simmer over low heat until rice is cooked, about 20 minutes.

3. Meanwhile, wrap tortillas in foil. Heat oven to 350° and then heat tortillas until warm, about 15 minutes.

4. When rice is done, stir in corn, black-bean chili, and tomato sauce. Heat to boiling over medium-high heat. Boil one minute.

5. Assemble burritos by spooning rice mixture onto tortillas. Top with cheese of your choice. Fold in tops of tortillas and roll up.

Black Bean and Butternut Burritos

Janelle Myers-Benner
Harrisonburg, VA

Makes 8 burritos

Prep Time: 45 minutes
Baking Time: 15-20 minutes

1 Tbsp. oil
1 small *or* medium-sized
    onion, chopped
3-4 cups butternut squash,
    cut into ½" cubes
½ tsp. cumin
¼ tsp. cinnamon
½ tsp. salt
2 cups cooked, *or* a 15-oz.
    can, black beans, drained
8 tortillas
1½ cups grated cheese
sour cream
cilantro, if you wish
salsa

1. In a large skillet or saucepan, heat oil. Sauté onions until tender.

2. Add butternut. Cover and cook over medium heat until tender.

3. Add cumin, cinnamon, and salt. Add beans. Cover, and heat through.

4. Put ⅛ of mixture in each tortilla, top with 3 Tbsp. cheese, and roll up. Place seam-side down in a greased 9 x 13 baking pan.

5. Bake uncovered in 350° oven for about 15-20 minutes, until heated through.

6. Serve with sour cream and salsa, and cilantro if you wish.

Tips: Tortillas freeze well with the mixture inside so I often make a double or triple batch. You can also freeze just the filling.

Black Bean and Kale *or* Spinach Tostada

Peg Zannotti, Tulsa, OK

Makes 4-6 servings

Prep Time: 15 minutes
Baking Time: 25 minutes

1 bunch green onions,
    chopped
3 garlic cloves, minced
1½ tsp. cumin
1½ tsp. coriander
1 Tbsp. poblano pepper,
    minced

3 Tbsp. olive oil
15-oz. can black beans,
    drained and rinsed
1/2 cup orange juice
1 bunch kale, *or* 3 cups
    fresh spinach, chopped
salt to taste
8 6" corn tortillas
1/3-1/2 cup grated cheese of
    your choice
1/3-1/2 cup sour cream,
    optional

1. In a large skillet, sauté onions, garlic, cumin, coriander, and poblano in olive oil for 8 minutes. (Wear gloves when you deseed the pepper, and do not allow the pepper to touch your eyes or skin.)

2. Add black beans and cook for 3 minutes, stirring and mashing the beans with the back of a spoon.

3. Add orange juice and kale or spinach. Cover and simmer for about 10 minutes, stirring frequently.

4. Add salt to taste.

5. Heat tortillas by lightly frying them, microwaving them, or heating them in the oven for several minutes.

6. For each serving, start with a heated tortilla, cover it generously with the black bean mixture, 1-2 Tbsp. cheese, and 1-2 Tbsp. sour cream if you wish.

Tip: The filling in this recipe also works well as a dip for chips.

Taco-Ritto

Marlene Fonken
Upland, CA

Makes 4 servings

Prep Time: 20-25 minutes
Cooking Time: 5 minutes

1 Tbsp., plus 1 tsp.,
    vegetable oil
1 1/2 cups broccoli florets
1 cup sliced fresh
    mushrooms
1/2 cup chopped green
    peppers
1/2 cup sliced onions
1/2 cup diced tomatoes
4 ozs. shredded cheddar,
    or pepper, cheese
4 1-oz. flour tortillas,
    warmed

1. In a skillet, heat oil over medium-high heat. Add broccoli, mushrooms, green peppers, and onions. Stir-fry until tender-crisp, about 2-5 minutes.

2. Remove from heat and stir in tomatoes and cheese. Stir until cheese is partially melted.

3. Divide among the 4 tortillas. Roll up to eat!

Tip: Add some taco sauce to Step 2 if you wish.

Double Corn
Tortilla Casserole

Kathy Keener Shantz
Lancaster, PA

Makes 4-6 servings

Prep Time: 15-20 minutes
Baking Time: 30 minutes

8 corn tortillas
1 1/2 cups shredded
    Monterey Jack cheese
1 cup frozen corn
4 green onions sliced,
    about 1/2 cup
2 eggs, beaten
1 cup buttermilk
4-oz. can diced green
    chilies

1. Tear 4 tortillas into bite-sized pieces. Arrange in greased 2-qt. baking dish.

2. Top with half the cheese, half the corn, and half the green onions. Repeat layers.

3. In a mixing bowl, stir together eggs, buttermilk, and chilies. Gently pour over tortilla mixture.

4. Bake at 325° for 30 minutes, or until knife inserted in center comes out clean.

A Tip —

Always taste the food you've prepared before serving it, so you can correct the seasonings, if necessary.

Exceptional Eggplant Casserole

Lisa Good
Harrisonburg, VA

Makes 6-8 servings

Prep Time: 15-20 minutes
Baking Time: 45-50 minutes

½ cup chopped onions
½ cup chopped green peppers
½ cup chopped celery
1 tsp. oil
2 8-oz. cans tomato sauce
⅓ cup brown sugar
1½ tsp. dried oregano
½ tsp. minced garlic
1 medium-sized eggplant, peeled or unpeeled, sliced in ⅛"-thick slices
1½ cups mozzarella cheese

1. In a large skillet or saucepan, sauté the onions, green peppers, and celery in the oil.
2. Add the tomato sauce, brown sugar, oregano, and garlic to the sautéed vegetables. Mix well.
3. Layer one-third of the sauce mixture, one-third of the eggplant, and one-third of the cheese into a greased 2-qt. baking dish. Repeat the layers twice.
4. Bake uncovered at 350° for 45-50 minutes.

Eggplant Pita

Donna Conto
Saylorsburg, PA

Makes filling for 4 pita sandwiches

Prep Time: 10 minutes
Standing Time: 2 hours
Cooking Time: 5 minutes

1 large eggplant, peeled and diced
3 Tbsp. salt
½ cup oil
½ tsp. garlic salt
½ tsp. pepper
½ tsp. salt
15-oz. can diced tomatoes, drained
1 small onion, chopped
2 Tbsp. parsley
4 pita breads

1. Cover diced eggplant with water. Stir in 3 Tbsp. salt. Let stand for 2 hours. Drain.
2. Heat oil in skillet. Add eggplant, garlic salt, pepper, and ½ tsp. salt. Sauté for 5 minutes until soft. Drain off excess oil.
3. Put seasoned eggplant in mixing bowl. Add tomatoes, onion, and parsley.
4. Mix well, stuff in pita bread halves, and serve immediately.

Baked Southwest Grits

Jane Steele
Moore, OK

Makes 8-10 servings

Prep Time: 25 minutes
Baking Time: 45 minutes

4 cups water
1½ tsp. salt
1 cup uncooked grits
2 eggs
½ stick (4 Tbsp.) butter
minced garlic to taste
4-oz. can chopped green chilies
2 cups grated Mexican cheese, *or* Monterey Jack/cheddar combined, *divided*

1. Place water in large saucepan, add salt, and cover. Bring to boil.
2. Add grits and stir for 1 minute.
3. Cover and cook until thick and creamy, about 5-7 minutes. Stir occasionally.
4. Beat eggs in a small bowl. Stir in ¼ cup cooked grits and blend together. Add mixture to saucepan of grits.
5. Melt butter in a medium-sized pan. Stir in garlic, chilies, and 1½ cups cheese. Add to the grits mixture and stir well.
6. Spoon into a greased 2-qt. casserole. Top with remaining ½ cup cheese.
7. Bake uncovered at 350° for 45 minutes.

Lentils and Rice with Tomato Cucumber Salad

Mary Longenecker
Bethel, PA

Makes 4-6 servings

Prep Time: 20 minutes
Cooking Time: 45 minutes

3/4 **cup brown lentils, rinsed**
3 1/2 **cups water**
1 **cup long-grain rice**
2 **tsp. salt**
1/2-1 **tsp. cumin, according to your taste preference**
3 **Tbsp. oil**
1-2 **sliced onions, whichever you prefer**

Salad:
2 **small cucumbers, diced**
2 **medium-sized tomatoes, diced**
1/2-1 **small onion, diced**
2 **Tbsp. lemon juice**
2 **Tbsp. oil**
1 **garlic clove, minced** *or* **crushed**
2 **tsp. salt**

1. In a large saucepan, combine lentils and water. Cover and bring to a boil. Cook on medium heat for 10 minutes.
2. Add rice, salt, and cumin. Cover and bring to a boil. Cook on low for 20-25 minutes, or until rice is cooked.

3. While rice and lentils cook, place oil in skillet. Sauté sliced onions in 3 Tbsp. oil until brown and limp. Set sautéed onions aside until time to serve.
4. In a mixing bowl, combine cucumbers, tomatoes, and diced onions.
5. In a small bowl, stir together lemon juice, 2 Tbsp. oil, garlic, and salt. Pour over cucumber mixture. Stir gently together.
6. To serve, press lentil/rice mixture into a cup or small bowl. Unmold in center of a large plate or platter. Top with sautéed onions. Place spoonfuls of salad around the lentil mixture. Sprinkle extra juice from salad over all.

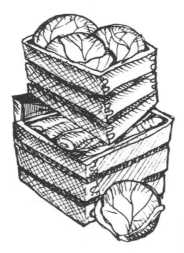

Jamaican Rice and Beans

Lorraine Pflederer
Goshen, IN

Makes 4 servings

Prep Time: 10 minutes
Cooking Time: 30 minutes
Standing Time: 5 minutes

14-oz. **can light coconut milk**
1/2 **cup water**
scant 1/2 **tsp. allspice**
1/2 **tsp. salt**
3 **fresh thyme sprigs,** *or* 1 **tsp. dried thyme**
1 **garlic clove, crushed**
1 **cup long-grain white rice**
15-oz. **can dark red kidney beans, drained and rinsed**

1. Combine first 6 ingredients (through garlic) in a medium-sized saucepan over medium-high heat. Cover and bring to a boil.
2. Stir in rice. Reduce the heat to low. Cover and cook 20 minutes, or until all the liquid is absorbed. Check periodically to make sure the rice isn't sticking.
3. Remove pan from heat. Remove the thyme sprigs and discard.
4. Gently stir in the beans. Cover and let stand 5 minutes before serving.

Spinach Souffle

Kaye Taylor
Florissant, MO

Makes 6-8 servings

Prep Time: 5-10 minutes
Baking Time: 60-75 minutes

4 Tbsp. flour
1/4 lb. Colby cheese, grated
1/4 lb. cheddar cheese, grated
1/2 stick (1/4 cup) butter, melted
1-lb. carton small-curd cottage cheese
3 eggs, beaten
1/4-1/2 tsp. salt
1/8 tsp. pepper
10-oz. pkg. chopped spinach, thawed and squeezed dry

1. Blend together flour, cheeses, and butter in a large mixing bowl.
2. Stir in remaining ingredients.
3. Pour into a greased 2-qt. baking casserole.
4. Bake uncovered at 325° for 60-75 minutes, or until knife inserted in center comes out clean.

A Tip —

Look for spices in whole foods markets where they are likely to be sold in bulk. Then you can buy only what you need, and usually for much less than in a grocery store.

Apple-Stuffed Acorn Squash

Susan Guarneri
Three Lakes, WI

Makes 4 servings

Prep Time: 20 minutes
Baking Time: 50 minutes

2 acorn squash
3 tart apples, *divided*
1 Tbsp. fresh lemon juice, taken from half a lemon (reserve the other half)
1 1/2 tsp. grated lemon rind, taken from half a lemon (reserve the other half)
1/4 cup melted butter, *divided*
1/3 cup brown sugar
1/2 tsp. salt
1 tsp. cinnamon

1. Cut squash in half. Scoop out seeds. Place in baking dish, cut-side down, and add 1/2" boiling water. Bake, covered with aluminum foil, at 400° for 20 minutes.
2. Pare, core, and dice 2 apples. In small bowl, mix with lemon juice, rind, 2 Tbsp. butter, and brown sugar.
3. Remove squash halves from oven. Brush cut halves with remaining 2 Tbsp. butter. Sprinkle with salt and cinnamon.
4. Fill squash halves with apple mixture.
5. Place squash halves cut-side up in baking dish. Add 1/2" boiling water. Cover with foil and bake 30 minutes longer.
6. Before serving, pour pan juices over squash. Garnish each half with slices from the reserved apple and the reserved lemon half.

Quick Squash

Shirley Taylor, Yuba City, CA

Makes 4 servings

Prep Time: 10 minutes
Cooking Time: 4-6 minutes

1 lb. mix of yellow squash and zucchini
1 onion, thinly sliced
1 red bell pepper, chopped
1/4 tsp. dried basil
dash of pepper
salt to taste, if you wish
1/4 cup grated Parmesan cheese

1. Slice squash and zucchini into microwave-safe casserole dish. Top with onions and red peppers.
2. Cover and microwave on high for 2-4 minutes, or until vegetables are crisp-tender. (If you want the vegetables to be softer, cook another 2-4 minutes and then test to see if they're done to your liking. Continue cooking for a few minutes if you wish.)
3. Stir in basil, pepper, and salt if you wish. Sprinkle top with grated Parmesan cheese. Cover and let stand 2 minutes before serving.

Tomato-Artichoke Scallop

Clara Earle Baskin
Quinton, NJ

Makes 6-8 servings

Prep Time: 20 minutes
Baking Time: 10-15 minutes

½ cup butter
½ cup finely chopped onions
2 Tbsp. finely chopped scallions
14-oz. can artichoke hearts, drained
35-oz. can whole plum tomatoes, drained
½ tsp. fresh, *or* pinch of dried, basil
1-2 tsp. sugar, your preference
salt and pepper to taste
¼ cup grated Parmesan cheese

1. In a large skillet or saucepan, melt butter. Sauté onions and scallions until tender.
2. Rinse artichokes and cut into quarters. Add to skillet.
3. Stir in tomatoes and basil. Heat 2 to 3 minutes, stirring occasionally.
4. Season with sugar, salt, and pepper. Turn into greased shallow baking dish. Sprinkle with Parmesan cheese.
5. Bake at 325° for 10-15 minutes, or until vegetables are tender.

Sun-Dried Tomato Casserole

Barbara Jean Fabel
Wausau, WI

Makes 12 servings

Prep Time: 15-20 minutes
Standing Time: 8 hours or overnight, plus 10 minutes
Baking Time: 40 minutes

2 9-oz. pkgs. cheese ravioli (look for them in the dairy case)
half an 8-oz. jar sun-dried tomatoes in oil, drained and chopped
1½ cups shredded cheddar cheese
1½ cups shredded Monterey Jack cheese
8 eggs, beaten
2½ cups milk
1-2 Tbsp. fresh basil, snipped, *or* 1-2 tsp. dried basil

1. Grease a 3-qt. baking dish. Place uncooked ravioli evenly in bottom.
2. Sprinkle ravioli with tomatoes. Top evenly with cheeses. Set aside.
3. In a mixing bowl, whisk eggs and milk until well combined. Pour over layers in casserole dish.
4. Cover and chill for 8 hours or overnight.
5. Bake, uncovered, at 350° for 40 minutes, until center is set and knife inserted in center comes out clean.

6. Let stand 10 minutes before serving. Just before serving, sprinkle with basil.

Tip: If you don't like sun-dried tomatoes, replace them with something you do like, such as sliced black olives or artichokes.

Veggie Burgers

Esther Becker, Gordonville, PA

Makes 12-14 servings

Prep Time: 20 minutes (after soaking and cooking)
Cooking Time: 8-10 minutes

1 cup dry oat bran
1 cup dry oats
1 cup cooked brown rice
½ cup dry lentils, soaked and cooked
½ cup dry black beans, soaked and cooked
½ cup dry black-eyed peas, soaked and cooked
½ cup salsa
½ cup chopped onions
half a green pepper, chopped
half-square of tofu, at room temperature
4-oz. pkg. cream cheese, softened
cooking oil

1. Mix all ingredients together and shape into 12-14 patties.
2. Brown on both sides in a skillet in enough oil to cover the bottom of the pan.

Double Cheese Zucchini Bake

Janet Schaeffer
Lansing, IL

Makes 12-15 servings

Prep Time: *15-20 minutes*
Baking Time: *35-40 minutes*

1/2 cup butter
1 clove garlic, chopped
8 medium-sized, peeled *or*
   unpeeled, zucchini,
   sliced
1 cup Italian-seasoned
   bread crumbs, *divided*
3 cups shredded Monterey
   Jack cheese, *divided*
2 cups grated Parmesan
   cheese, *divided*
1 Tbsp. Italian seasoning
3 eggs
2 cups half-and-half, *or*
   2 cups whipping cream

1. In large saucepan, melt butter. Add garlic and cook about 3 minutes.
2. Add zucchini to garlic and butter. Sauté until soft, about 10 minutes.
3. Stir in 1/2 cup bread crumbs, 2 cups Monterey Jack cheese, 1 cup Parmesan cheese, and Italian seasoning. Blend well.
4. Spoon mixture into a greased 9 x 13, or larger, baking dish.
5. In a mixing bowl, beat eggs. Mix in half-and-half. Pour over baking dish contents and let it settle into the zucchini mixture.

6. Top with remaining 1 cup Monterey Jack cheese, 1 cup Parmesan cheese, and 1/2 cup bread crumbs.
7. Bake at 350°, uncovered, for 35-40 minutes, or until knife inserted in center comes out clean.

Tip: You can make the dish the day before serving it and refrigerate it unbaked. If you put it in the oven cold, increase the baking time to 50-60 minutes.

Zucchini Babka

Esther J. Mast
Lancaster, PA

Makes 6-8 servings

Prep Time: *20 minutes*
Baking Time: *30-45 minutes*

3 eggs
1/2 cup vegetable oil
4 cups diced zucchini,
   peeled *or* unpeeled
1 medium-sized onion,
   chopped
1 cup all-purpose baking
   mix
1/2 cup grated cheddar
   cheese
1 tsp. salt
1 tsp. dried oregano
dash of pepper
Parmesan cheese

1. In a large mixing bowl, beat eggs. Blend in oil.
2. Add zucchini, onions, baking mix, cheese, salt, oregano, and pepper. Mix well.

3. Pour into greased 1 1/2-2-qt. baking dish. Sprinkle with Parmesan cheese.
4. Bake at 350° for 30-45 minutes, or until nicely browned.

Variations:
1. Use 3 cups zucchini and 1 cup cheese in the batter.
2. Use 1 clove minced garlic instead of onions.
   — **Evie Hershey**
   Atglen, PA

3. Use 3 cups zucchini and 4 eggs.
4. Use 2 Tbsp. parsley, 1/2 tsp. salt, and 1/2 tsp. dried oregano.
   — **Joyce Kreiser**
   Manheim, PA
   — **Virginia Martin**,
   Harrisonburg, VA
   — **Joanne Kennedy**
   Plattsburgh, NY

5. Use 4 eggs.
6. Add 1/2 cup shredded Swiss cheese to the batter, and sprinkle the Parmesan cheese on top.
   — **Becky Frey**
   Lebanon, PA

A Tip —

Before leaving for work in the morning, assemble and measure all ingredients for your evening meal that don't require refrigeration. When you return home, dinner preparation will be easier, plus you'll know that you have all the ingredients you need.

Pastas and Pizzas

Macaronis and Cheese

Elaine Rineer
Lancaster, PA

Makes 4-6 servings

Prep Time: 20 minutes
Baking Time: 20-25 minutes

8 ozs. shell macaronis
3 Tbsp. butter, *divided*
2 Tbsp. flour
1 tsp. salt
1 tsp. dry mustard
2½ cups milk
2 cups (8 ozs.) shredded
**   Cooper sharp,** *or a*
**   sharp cheddar, cheese,**
**   divided**
¼ cup bread crumbs
paprika

1. Cook shells according to package directions. Drain and set aside.
2. While shells are cooking, melt 2 Tbsp. butter in a large saucepan.
3. Blend in flour, salt, and dry mustard.
4. Add milk. Heat, stirring constantly until sauce thickens and is smooth.
5. Add 1½ cups cheese. Heat until melted, continuing to stir.
6. Combine sauce and cooked macaronis. Pour into a greased 2-qt. casserole.
7. Melt 1 Tbsp. butter. Stir in bread crumbs.
8. Top macaronis and cheese with remaining cheese, buttered bread crumbs, and paprika.
9. Bake uncovered at 375° for 20-25 minutes.

Variation: Use evaporated milk instead of regular milk. Use 2 Tbsp. Parmesan cheese instead of buttered bread crumbs as topping.

— Andrea Cunningham
Arlington, KS

A Tip —

To keep pasta from boiling over, bring the cooking water to a boil, and then add salt and the pasta. Turn off the heat, cover the pan, and let it sit on the burner for 10 minutes. Drain. (Thinner pasta takes less time; thicker pasta takes more time.)

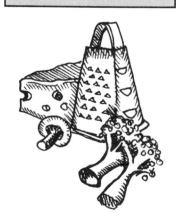

Tomato-y Penne Pasta

Joy Sutter
Perkasie, PA

Makes 4 servings

Prep Time: 15 minutes
Cooking Time: 25 minutes

1 Tbsp. butter
1 Tbsp. olive oil
1 small onion, chopped
28-oz. can Italian plum
　tomatoes, drained,
　seeded, and chopped
1 cup whipping cream
1/4 cup vodka
1/4 tsp. dried crushed red
　pepper flakes
salt and pepper to taste
1 lb. penne pasta
1/4 cup, *or more,* freshly
　grated Parmesan cheese
2 Tbsp., *or* more, minced
　fresh chives

1. In a large heavy saucepan, melt butter with oil over medium heat.
2. Add onions and sauté until translucent. Add tomatoes and cook uncovered until almost no liquid remains.
3. Stir in cream, vodka, and red pepper flakes, and boil until the mixture reaches a sauce consistency, about 2 minutes. Add salt and pepper to taste.
4. Meanwhile, cook pasta according to package directions. Drain.

5. Pour hot sauce over cooked pasta.
6. Toss and sprinkle with Parmesan cheese and chives.

Tip: You can prepare this sauce a day ahead of when you want to use it. Just cover and refrigerate until you need it.

Easy Fettucine Alfredo

Trish Propst
Tinton Falls, NJ

Makes 4 servings

Preparation time: 5-10 minutes
Cooking time: 15 minutes

8 ozs. fettucine noodles
1/2 cup whipping cream
1 stick (1/2 cup) butter
3/4 cup grated Parmesan
　cheese
1/2 tsp. salt
dash of pepper
2 tsp. parsley

1. Cook noodles according to package. Drain and keep warm.
2. In a medium-sized saucepan, heat butter and whipping cream over low heat, just until melted. Stir to blend.
3. Stir in cheese, salt, and pepper.
4. Pour sauce over hot noodles. Sprinkle with parsley. Serve.

Spinach Pesto

Vic and Christina Buckwalter
Keezletown, VA

Makes 1 1/2 cups Pesto

Prep Time: 15 minutes
Cooking Time: 12 minutes

Pesto:
4 packed cups fresh
　spinach leaves
3 garlic cloves
2 Tbsp. pine nuts
1/4 packed cup fresh basil,
　or 1 1/2 Tbsp. dried basil
1/2 cup extra-virgin olive oil
1/8 tsp. salt

Pasta for 4-5 servings:
1 lb. linguine, *or* pasta of
　your choice
1/4-1/2 cup pesto
2 Tbsp. Parmesan cheese,
　freshly grated
2 Tbsp. pasta water

1. Process Pesto ingredients in blender until smooth. Store in refrigerator or freeze for later use.
2. When ready to use, cook 1 lb. linguine according to package directions. Drain, saving 2 Tbsp. of pasta water.
3. Mix together 1/4-1/2 cup of pesto, Parmesan cheese, and reserved pasta water. Stir mixture into pasta.

Variations:
　1. Sometimes we toss chopped fresh tomatoes from the garden into Step 3.
　2. This pesto makes an excellent pizza topping, along with your favorite cheeses.

Southwestern Pesto Pasta

Carrie Wood
Paxton, MA

Makes 4-6 servings

Prep Time: 10 minutes
Cooking Time: 10-12 minutes

1 cup loosely packed
  cilantro leaves
1 cup loosely packed flat
  parsley
1/3 cup toasted pepitas
  (pumpkin seeds)
1 clove garlic, peeled
1/2 cup crumbled feta
  cheese
1/2 cup extra-virgin olive oil
salt to taste
1 lb. spaghetti *or* linguine

1. Process all ingredients except pasta in a food processor until a rough paste is formed, adding additional olive oil if the paste seems too dry.
2. Cook spaghetti or linguine according to package directions. Drain.
3. Toss pesto thoroughly with hot pasta and then serve.

Spaghetti! Quick!

Helen E. Shenk
Quarryville, PA

Makes 8-10 servings

Prep Time: 10-15 minutes
Baking Time: 10-45 minutes

9-10 ozs. dry spaghetti
1/4 cup butter, melted
3-4 cups shredded cheese,
  your choice of flavors
2 10-oz. pkgs. frozen
  spinach, thawed and
  squeezed dry
1/2 lb. sliced fresh
  mushrooms
1 1/2 cups sour cream
dash of oregano
1/2 cup chopped onions
salt to taste
pepper to taste

1. Cook spaghetti in large stockpot according to package directions. Drain.
2. Return spaghetti to stockpot and stir in butter.
3. Add cheese. Stir until well mixed and partially melted.
4. Add remaining ingredients. Mix well.
5. Pour into greased 3-qt. baking dish.
6. Bake at 350° for 10-15 minutes if spaghetti is still warm; 30-45 minutes if not.

Variation: Use fresh spinach instead of frozen. Use spaghetti squash instead of the pasta.
— **Tina Hartman**
Lancaster, PA

Sausage Ziti Bake

Margaret Morris
Middle Village, NY

Makes 8 servings

Prep Time: 15 minutes
Baking Time: 45 minutes

1 1/2 lbs. sweet Italian bulk
  sausage
1 lb. uncooked ziti
2 cups sliced fresh
  mushrooms
1 large onion, chopped
32-oz. jar spaghetti sauce
salt to taste
pepper to taste
4-8 ozs. shredded
  mozzarella cheese,
  according to your
  preference

1. Brown sausage in large stockpot.
2. Meanwhile, cook the ziti according to the package directions. Drain.
3. After sausage is browned remove it to a bowl and drain off all but 1 Tbsp. drippings. Add mushrooms and onions to stockpot. Cook gently until tender.
4. Stir in sauce, sausage, cooked and drained ziti, salt, and pepper. Spoon into a greased 9 x 13 baking dish. Cover.
5. Bake at 350° for 30-40 minutes, or until heated the whole way through.
6. Sprinkle with cheese. Bake uncovered an additional 5 minutes.

Pasta Venesa

Barry Coggin
Jacksonville, FL

Makes 6 servings

Prep Time: 30 minutes
Cooking Time: 1 hour
and 45 minutes

2 medium-sized onions,
  chopped
1 yellow bell pepper,
  chopped
1 orange bell pepper,
  chopped
3 cloves garlic, thinly sliced
10.75-oz. can tomato puree
3 8-oz. cans tomato sauce
6-oz. can tomato paste
1 pkg. (5 links) sweet
  Italian sausage, chopped
3 links hot Italian sausage,
  chopped
salt to taste
pepper to taste
1½ tsp. Italian seasoning
2 large Tbsp. honey
1 cup water
1 cup whipping cream
1 lb. spaghetti, uncooked
4 Tbsp. fresh parsley,
  chopped

1. In a large nonstick skillet, sauté onions, bell peppers, and garlic until just tender.
2. Add tomato puree, sauce, and paste. Blend well. Simmer covered for 1 hour.
3. Meanwhile, in a separate skillet, brown sausages. Add to tomato mixture.
4. Season with salt, pepper, and Italian seasoning. Then stir in honey and water.
5. Simmer covered for 30 minutes.
6. Just before serving, add whipping cream to tomato mixture. Cook until heated through, but do not boil.
7. As you begin Step 5, begin to cook the spaghetti according to the package directions. Drain.
8. Serve tomato sauce over cooked spaghetti. Sprinkle with fresh parsley.

Tip: You can prepare the sauce ahead of time—all but the whipping cream—and warm it when you are ready to serve. Add the whipping cream when the sauce is fully heated, and do not allow the sauce to boil after you've stirred in the whipping cream.

Chicken Manicotti

Lori Showalter, New Hope, VA

Makes 4 servings

Prep Time: 30 minutes
Baking Time: 65-70 minutes

¾ lb. boneless skinless
  chicken breasts
1½ tsp. garlic powder
7 uncooked manicotti
  shells
26-oz. jar spaghetti sauce,
  divided
½ lb. bulk sausage, cooked
  and drained
¼ lb. fresh mushrooms,
  sliced, *or* canned
  mushrooms, drained
2 cups (8 ozs.) shredded
  mozzarella cheese
⅓ cup water

1. Cut chicken into small chunks. In large bowl, toss chicken with garlic powder.
2. Stuff chicken into manicotti shells.
3. Spread 1 cup spaghetti sauce in the bottom of a greased 7 x 11 baking dish. Arrange stuffed shells on top of sauce.
4. Sprinkle with sausage and mushrooms. Pour remaining spaghetti sauce over top.
5. Sprinkle with cheese.
6. Spoon water around the edge of the dish. Cover and bake at 375° for 65-70 minutes, or until chicken juices run clear and pasta is tender.

Tip: I like to double the recipe and freeze the second dish for another meal. The dish can be frozen for up to one month. When ready to use, thaw it in the refrigerator; then let it stand at room temperature for 30 minutes before baking as directed.

Pork Tenderloin with Pasta in Tomato & Red Pepper Sauce

Joyce Clark, East Amherst, NY

Makes 4-6 servings

Prep Time: 15 minutes
Cooking Time: 30 minutes

1 Tbsp. butter
1 Tbsp. vegetable oil
2 cups sliced mushrooms
2 onions, chopped
2 garlic cloves, crushed
1 red bell pepper, chopped
1 tsp. dried oregano
1 lb. pork tenderloin, cut into 1"-cubes
2 Tbsp. flour
1 tsp. chili powder
1/2 tsp. salt
1/2 tsp. black pepper
3 cups milk
9 ozs. dry penne pasta
14-oz. can tomato sauce

1. Melt butter in a large skillet. Add vegetable oil, mushrooms, onions, garlic, red pepper, and oregano. Cook over medium heat until onion is softened.

2. Place flour, chili powder, salt, and pepper in a ziplock plastic bag. Add pork pieces and shake to coat.

3. Add floured pork and any remaining flour mixture to skillet. Cook, stirring occasionally, until pork is browned on all sides.

4. Add milk, pasta, and tomato sauce. Bring mixture to a boil, stirring constantly.

5. Reduce heat, cover, and simmer 15 minutes until pasta is tender.

Baked Spaghetti

Amber Veenstra
Lake Odessa, MI
Lynette Nisly
Lancaster, PA

Makes 12 servings

Prep Time: 40 minutes
Baking Time: 30-35 minutes

1 lb. ground beef
2 Tbsp. butter
1 cup chopped onions
1 cup chopped green peppers
28-oz. can diced tomatoes, undrained
4-oz. can mushroom slices, drained
2.25-oz. can sliced black olives, drained
2 tsp. dried oregano
1 tsp. garlic salt
1 tsp. onion salt
1 lb. spaghetti *or* angel-hair pasta
2 cups (8 ozs.) shredded cheddar cheese, *divided*
10.75-oz. can cream of mushroom soup
1/4 cup water
1/4 cup grated Parmesan cheese

1. In a large skillet, brown ground beef in 2 Tbsp. butter. Drain off all but 1 Tbsp. drippings. Add onions and peppers to beef and reserved drippings and cook until softened.

2. Add tomatoes, mushrooms, olives, oregano, garlic salt, and onion salt. Simmer uncovered for 10 minutes.

3. Meanwhile, cook spaghetti in a large stockpot according to package directions. When cooked, drain well, and return to pot.

4. Place half of spaghetti in a greased 9 x 13 baking pan. Spread half of meat mixture over pasta. Sprinkle with 1 cup cheddar cheese. Repeat layers.

5. In a small bowl, combine soup and water until smooth. Pour over casserole contents. Sprinkle with Parmesan cheese.

6. Bake, uncovered, at 350° for 30-35 minutes.

A Tip —

Do not add salt to cold water in a cooking pan. Wait until the water boils. Otherwise, the salt can pit the pan.

Southwestern Shells

Elaine Rineer, Lancaster, PA

Makes 6 servings

Prep Time: 30-35 minutes
Baking Time: 25-35 minutes

1-1½ lbs. ground beef
1 medium-sized onion,
 chopped
16-oz. jar picante sauce
8-oz. can tomato sauce
½ cup water
1 tsp. chili powder
4-oz. can chopped green
 chilies, drained
1 cup grated Monterey
 Jack cheese, *divided*
24 jumbo shells, cooked

1. In large nonstick skillet, brown ground beef and onion together.
2. Meanwhile, mix together in a mixing bowl the picante sauce, tomato sauce, and water.
3. When meat and onions are brown, stir chili powder, chilies, ½ cup cheese, and ½ cup picante sauce mix into the meat. Mix well.
4. Pour half of remaining picante sauce mixture into a greased 9 x 13 baking pan.
5. Fill each shell with 1-2 Tbsp. meat mixture. Place in baking dish.
6. Pour remaining sauce over shells. Cover with foil.
7. Bake at 350° for 20-30 minutes. Uncover. Sprinkle with remaining cheese. Bake 5 minutes, or until cheese melts.

Lasagne Roll-Ups

Dorothy Van Deest
Memphis, TN

Makes 6 servings

Prep Time: 20 minutes
Baking Time: 35-40 minutes
Standing Time: 10 minutes

8-oz. pkg. lasagna noodles
1 pint creamy cottage
 cheese
2 cups shredded
 mozzarella cheese
1 egg, beaten
½ cup chopped parsley,
 optional
pepper to taste
3 cups spaghetti sauce,
 with or without meat,
 divided

1. In a large stockpot, bring 4-5 qts. water to a boil. Cook lasagna noodles for 10 minutes, uncovered. Rinse cooked noodles in cool water. Drain.
2. In a mixing bowl, combine cottage cheese, mozzarella cheese, egg, parsley if you wish, and pepper.
3. Pour 1 cup spaghetti sauce in bottom of a greased 9 x 13 baking dish.
4. Spread ¼-⅓ cup cheese mixture on each lasagna noodle and roll up jelly-roll fashion. Place seam-side down in the sauce.
5. Cover with remaining sauce. Cover dish with aluminum foil.
6. Bake at 350° for 35-40 minutes until hot and bubbly.

7. Allow to stand 10 minutes before serving.

Mexican Lasagna

Diane Eby
Holtwood, PA

Makes 12 servings

Prep Time: 20-30 minutes
Baking Time: 1 hour, plus
 5 minutes
Standing Time: 15 minutes

2 lbs. ground beef
16-oz. can refried beans
4-oz. can chopped green
 chilies
1 envelope dry taco
 seasoning
2 Tbsp. hot salsa
12 ozs. uncooked lasagna
 noodles
4 cups (16 ozs.) shredded
 Monterey Jack cheese,
 divided
16-oz. jar mild salsa
2 cups water
2 cups (16 ozs.) sour cream
2¼-oz. can sliced ripe
 olives, drained
3 green onions, chopped

1. In a large nonstick skillet, cook beef over medium heat until no longer pink. Drain off drippings.
2. Add the beans, chilies, taco seasoning, and hot salsa to the beef. Mix well.
3. In a deep greased 9 x 13 baking dish or lasagna pan, layer one-third of the uncooked noodles topped by one-third of the meat mix-

ture. Sprinkle with 1 cup cheese. Repeat layers twice.

4. Combine mild salsa and water; pour over top.

5. Cover and bake at 350° for 1 hour or until heated through.

6. Uncover. Top with sour cream, olives, onions, and remaining cheese. Bake 5 minutes longer uncovered. Let stand 10-15 minutes before serving.

Tip: You can prepare this up to 24 hours in advance. Cover it and keep it chilled. Remove from the refrigerator 30 minutes before baking. You may need to bake it 15 minutes longer (covered, and before adding toppings in Step 6) if it's still quite cold when you put it in the oven.

Vegetable Alfredo Lasagna

Judy Buller
Bluffton, OH

Makes 10-12 servings

Prep Time: 30-45 minutes
Baking Time: 55-60 minutes
Standing Time: 15 minutes

9 lasagna noodles
1/2 cup chopped onions
1 clove garlic, minced
1 Tbsp. olive oil
1 carrot, shredded
4 cups fresh, chopped
  spinach, or 10-oz. pkg.
  chopped frozen spinach,
  thawed and squeezed dry

1 cup chopped broccoli
1/4 tsp. salt
1/4 tsp. pepper
17-oz. jar Alfredo sauce,
  divided
15-oz. carton ricotta cheese
1/2 cup Parmesan cheese
1 egg
2 cups shredded Colby, *or*
  Monterey Jack, cheese
1 cup shredded mozzarella
  cheese

1. Soak noodles in hot water for 15 minutes. Rinse, drain, and set aside.

2. In large skillet, cook onion and garlic in 1 Tbsp. oil until crisp-tender. Add carrot, spinach, broccoli, salt, and pepper.

3. Remove 1/2 cup Alfredo sauce and set aside.

4. Stir remaining Alfredo sauce into skillet. Mix well and heat thoroughly. Set aside.

5. Combine ricotta and Parmesan cheeses, egg, and Colby or Monterey Jack cheese in a large bowl. Mix well.

6. In a greased 9 x 13 baking pan, spread 1/2 cup Alfredo sauce on bottom. Layer in this order: 3 noodles, one-third of the cheese mixture, one-third of the Alfredo sauce mixture.

7. Repeat layers two more times. Top with mozzarella cheese.

8. Cover and bake at 350° for 45 minutes. Uncover and bake 10-15 minutes more.

9. Let stand 15 minutes before serving.

Creamy Chicken Lasagna

Joanne E. Martin
Stevens, PA

Makes 8-10 servings

Prep Time: 30 minutes
Baking Time: 40-45 minutes
Standing Time: 15 minutes

8 ozs. lasagna noodles
10.75-oz. can cream of
  mushroom soup
10.75-oz. can cream of
  chicken soup
1/2 cup grated Parmesan
  cheese
1 cup sour cream
3 cups diced cooked
  chicken
2 cups grated mozzarella
  cheese, *divided*

1. Cook noodles as directed on package. Drain.

2. In a large mixing bowl, blend soups, Parmesan cheese, and sour cream. Stir in diced chicken.

3. Put one-fourth of creamy chicken mixture in the bottom of a greased 9 x 13 baking pan.

4. Alternate layers of 1/3 noodles, 1/3 chicken mixture, and 1/3 mozzarella cheese, repeating the layers 2 more times.

5. Bake uncovered at 350° for 40-45 minutes.

6. Allow to stand for 15 minutes before serving.

Cheesy Chicken Casserole

Miriam Christophel
Goshen, IN

Makes 6 servings

Prep Time: 20-30 minutes
Baking Time: 30 minutes in the oven, or 8-10 minutes in the microwave

1/2 cup mayonnaise, salad dressing, *or* 10.75-oz. can cream of mushroom soup
1 1/2 cups shredded cheddar cheese, *divided*
1 1/2 cups chopped, cooked chicken
1 1/2 cups dry (4 ozs.) rotini, cooked and drained
2 cups mixed frozen vegetables
1/4 cup milk
1/2 tsp. dried basil leaves

1. In a large mixing bowl, combine all ingredients except 1/2 cup cheese.

2. Spoon into a greased 1 1/2-qt. casserole. Sprinkle with reserved 1/2 cup cheese.

3. Bake uncovered at 350° for 40 minutes, or until heated through.

Variation: To make this in the microwave, be sure to use a microwave-safe casserole. Heat on high 8-10 minutes, or until thoroughly heated.

Pastitsio

Sheila Soldner, Lititz, PA

Makes 12 servings

Prep Time: 30-45 minutes
Baking Time: 35 minutes

1 large onion, grated
2 lbs. ground beef
1/2 cup tomato sauce
1/2 tsp. sugar
1/2 tsp. nutmeg
1/4 tsp. pepper
1 tsp. salt
1 lb. ziti
10 Tbsp. butter, *divided*
1/2 cup grated Romano cheese
4 eggs, *divided*
5 1/2 Tbsp. flour, *divided*
3 cups milk, *divided*
1/2 cup grated cheddar cheese
dash of nutmeg
dash of salt
dash of pepper

1. Brown onion and ground beef in large nonstick skillet until moisture is absorbed.

2. Add tomato sauce, sugar, nutmeg, pepper, and salt and simmer for 15 minutes.

3. Meanwhile, boil ziti in salted water in a large stockpot for 10 minutes. Drain and rinse with cold water. Place in large bowl.

4. Melt 2 Tbsp. butter. Then pour the melted butter, Romano cheese and 2 slightly beaten eggs over ziti. Mix gently.

5. Grease a 9 x 13 baking pan, or a deep lasagna pan. Place half the ziti in the bottom of the pan. Pour meat/tomato mixture on top of ziti. Cover with remaining ziti.

6. In a small mixing bowl, whisk together 1/2 Tbsp. flour and 1 cup milk. Pour over the baking dish contents.

7. Make the cream sauce by melting 1 stick (8 Tbsp.) butter in a medium-sized saucepan. Add 5 Tbsp. flour and blend well. Add 2 cups milk slowly. Cook over medium heat, stirring constantly until thickened and smooth.

8. Remove pan from heat. Add 2 beaten eggs to mixture and stir until smooth.

9. Spoon sauce over ziti. Top with grated cheddar cheese. Sprinkle with nutmeg, salt, and pepper.

10. Bake uncovered at 350° for 35 minutes.

Tip:

For a creamier effect, you can increase the amount of each sauce ingredient by half, or double all of their amounts (Step 4).

I have found this to be a great dish to serve at Christmas or other get-togethers when I have a large crowd to feed.

A Tip —

Do not overcook pasta!

Quick Shrimp Pasta

Sandra Chang, Derwood, MD

Makes 4-6 servings

Prep Time: 30 minutes
Cooking Time: 20 minutes

1 lb. spaghetti
1 Tbsp. vegetable oil
1 lb. raw shrimp, peeled
    and deveined
kosher salt
ground black pepper
1 medium-sized zucchini,
    unpeeled and cut into
    1/2" pieces
3 cloves garlic, minced
1/2 cup extra-virgin olive oil
1/3 cup fresh flat-leaf
    parsley
1/2 tsp. cracked black
    pepper
1 cup grated Parmesan
    cheese, *divided*

1. Cook spaghetti according to package directions. When finished cooking, drain, return to cooking pot, and keep warm.
2. Meanwhile, in a large skillet, heat 1 Tbsp. vegetable oil over high heat until smoking hot.
3. Place shrimp in pan and sear for 1 to 2 minutes per side, or until just cooked through. Stir in a dash of kosher salt and a dash of pepper. Remove seasoned shrimp to a large serving bowl and keep warm.
4. Sauté zucchini pieces and minced garlic briefly in skillet until crisp-tender.

5. Add zucchini and garlic to shrimp.
6. Mix in olive oil, garlic, parsley, pepper, and 1/2 cup Parmesan cheese.
7. Add cooked pasta and remaining cheese. Toss well and serve.

Variation: Substitute 1 1/2 lbs. scallops for the shrimp for a different quick meal.

Low-Fat Fettucine Alfredo with Veggies and Shrimp

Norma Grieser, Clarksville, MI

Makes 4-6 servings

Prep Time: 15 minutes
Cooking Time: 30 minutes

2 Tbsp. onions, chopped
2 Tbsp. oil, *divided*
2 cups sliced asparagus
    or broccoli
1/2 cup nonfat dry milk
1 1/2 cups skim milk
1 1/2 Tbsp. flour
2 Tbsp. low-fat cream
    cheese, at room
    temperature
2/3 cup grated Parmesan,
    or mozzarella, cheese
9 ozs. fettucine
1 tsp. minced garlic
1/2 lb. raw shrimp, peeled
    and deveined, *or* 1/2 lb.
    fresh scallops

1. In a large skillet, sauté onions in 1 Tbsp. oil. Add asparagus or broccoli and stir-fry until just crisp-tender.
2. Combine milks and flour in a saucepan and whisk together until smooth. Cook until thickened.
3. In a small bowl, mix cream cheese with a small amount of white sauce until the cheese softens. Stir into rest of white sauce.
4. In a large stockpot, cook pasta according to directions on box. Drain and keep warm. Pour stir-fried vegetables into cooked pasta.
5. Pour remaining Tbsp. of oil into large skillet and sauté seafood and garlic. Add to pasta.
6. Pour sauce over pasta and toss.

A Tip —

When cooking rice or macaronis, add 1 Tbsp. butter to keep the pot from boiling over.

Simple Shrimp Scampi

Anne Jones
Ballston Lake, NY

Makes 4 servings

Prep Time: 5 minutes
Cooking Time: 5 minutes for the Scampi; 30 minutes for the pasta

1 stick (1/2 cup) butter
2 cloves garlic, crushed
1 Tbsp. lemon juice
1 Tbsp. dried parsley
1 lb. shrimp, shelled and deveined
shredded Parmesan cheese, *divided*
1 lb. cooked pasta of your choice

1. In a large skillet or wok, over low heat, melt butter.
2. Add garlic, lemon juice, and parsley. Cook until garlic is tender.
3. Add shrimp and 1 Tablespoon Parmesan cheese. Cook over low heat until shrimp becomes opaque, stirring frequently, about 3 minutes.
4. Serve over pasta. Sprinkle with Parmesan cheese.

Shrimp and Mushroom Linguine

Cyndie Marrara
Port Matilda, PA

Makes 4 servings

Preparation Time: 10 minutes
Cooking Time: 30 minutes

2 cups fresh mushroom slices
1 stick (1/2 cup) butter
1/4 cup flour
1/8 tsp. pepper
3 cups milk
2 cups peeled and cooked shrimp
1/4 cup Parmesan cheese
8 ozs. linguine
Parmesan cheese

1. In a large skillet, sauté mushrooms in butter. Blend in flour and pepper.
2. Add milk, and stir constantly until thickened.
3. Add shrimp and Parmesan cheese. Heat thoroughly.
4. Meanwhile, cook linguine according to package directions. Drain.
5. Combine shrimp sauce with linguine. Toss lightly and sprinkle with additional Parmesan cheese.

Tip: I've doubled and tripled this recipe with no problem. The sauce is not really thick, so don't think you did something wrong. The pasta thickens the dish when you mix the sauce and cooked pasta together.

Scallop Linguine ala York

Shirley Hedman
Schenectady, NY

Makes 12-15 servings

Prep Time: 7-10 minutes
Cooking Time: 15-20 minutes

1 Tbsp. oil
1 green pepper, chopped
2 garlic cloves, minced
1 cup diced onions
8-oz. can mushrooms, sliced, undrained
1/2 tsp. salt
1/4 tsp. pepper
1 tsp. dried basil
1 tsp. dried oregano
2 25.5-oz. jars marinara sauce
2 lbs. scallops
1 lb. cooked linguine

1. Heat oil in large skillet. Cook pepper, garlic, and onions until crisp-tender.
2. Add mushrooms. Cook 2 minutes.
3. Stir in salt, pepper, basil, and oregano.
4. Stir in marinara sauce. Cover and cook until bubbly.
5. Add scallops and cook 5 minutes.
6. Serve over linguine.

Spaghetti with Red Clam Sauce

Kate Good
Lancaster, PA
Rebecca Fennimore
Harrisonburg, VA

Makes 6 servings

Prep Time: 10-15 minutes
Cooking Time: 15-25 minutes

1 lb. spaghetti
1 Tbsp. olive oil
1 large onion, chopped
2 6.5-oz cans chopped
   clams, with their juice
1/4 cup dry white wine
1 cup crushed tomatoes
pinch of red pepper flakes
1/4 tsp. salt
pinch of ground pepper
1/4 cup fresh parsley
Parmesan cheese

1. Cook pasta according to package directions in large stockpot. Drain pasta, reserving 1/2 cup of cooking liquid. Keep pasta warm.
2. While pasta is cooking, heat oil in a skillet. Add onion and brown.
3. Stir in clams with juice, wine, tomatoes, red pepper flakes, salt, and pepper.
4. Reduce heat and simmer uncovered until sauce is thickened slightly, about 5 minutes.
5. Stir sauce, parsley, and reserved pasta cooking liquid into cooked pasta in stockpot. Cover and cook 1 minute.
6. Serve immediately with Parmesan cheese for individual servings.

A Tip —

If you use lots of eggs, stack the cartons of eggs in your fridge with the freshest carton of eggs on the bottom. Then you'll be sure to use up the older eggs first because they'll be in the carton on top. That also makes it more likely that you'll hard-boil the easiest-to-peel eggs, because older eggs are best for this.

Lazy Linguine with White Clam Sauce

Anne Jones
Ballston Lake, NY

Makes 4 servings

Prep Time: 20 minutes
Cooking Time: 20 minutes

half a stick (4 Tbsp.) of
   butter
4 cloves garlic, crushed
1/2 cup diced onions
2 Tbsp. flour
2 6-oz. cans chopped clams
1 cup milk
3/4 tsp. salt
1/4-1/2 tsp. pepper
1 Tbsp. parsley
1 lb. linguine
shredded Parmesan cheese

1. In a medium-sized saucepan, melt butter. Sauté garlic and onions until tender.
2. Add flour and stir until smooth.
3. Drain clams, reserving liquid.
4. Stir milk and reserved clam juice into flour mixture. Continue heating over medium heat, stirring constantly until thickened.
5. Add salt, pepper, parsley, and clams. Warm through.
6. Meanwhile, prepare linguine according to package directions.
7. Drain linguine. Place in large serving bowl. Stir clam sauce into it. Sprinkle with shredded Parmesan cheese.

Creamy Crab-Stuffed Shells

James R. Johnston
Pahrump, NV

Makes 6-8 servings

Prep Time: 45 minutes
Baking Time: 30 minutes

24-30 jumbo pasta shells
1 Tbsp. chopped green
   pepper
1 Tbsp. chopped red
   onions
3 Tbsp. butter, *divided*
12 ozs. crabmeat
1/2 tsp. pepper
1 tsp. Old Bay Seasoning
1 egg, beaten
2 Tbsp., plus 1 1/2 cups
   milk, *divided*
1/2 cup mayonnaise
2 Tbsp. flour
1 1/2 cups skim milk
1/2 cup grated Parmesan
   cheese

1. Cook pasta according to package directions. Drain and set aside.
2. Sauté green pepper and onions in 1 Tbsp. butter in skillet until tender. Remove from heat.
3. Combine crabmeat, pepper, Old Bay, egg, 2 Tbsp. milk, and mayonnaise with sautéed vegetables.
4. Spoon mixture into shells.
5. Place a single layer of shells in a greased 9 x 13 baking pan.
6. Melt 2 Tbsp .butter in the skillet. Gradually whisk

in flour. Then slowly add 1 1/2 cups milk, stirring continuously until mixture thickens.
7. When white sauce is thickened and smooth, stir in Parmesan cheese.
8. Drizzle sauce over shells. Sprinkle with Old Bay Seasoning.
9. Bake uncovered for 30 minutes.

Creamy Salmon Casserole

Mary Jane Ebersole
Millmont, PA

Makes 4-6 servings

Prep Time: 25 minutes
Baking Time: 35 minutes

2 cups dry macaronis
half a stick (1/4 cup) of
   butter
1/4 cup chopped onions
2 Tbsp. parsley
1/3 cup flour
1/2 tsp. salt
1/4 tsp. pepper
1/4 tsp. Old Bay Seasoning,
   optional
3 cups milk
1 cup shredded cheddar
   cheese
14.75-oz. can salmon,
   drained and de-boned
2 Tbsp. butter
1/2 cup bread crumbs

1. Cook macaronis according to package directions. Drain and set aside.

2. Meanwhile, melt half stick of butter in a large saucepan. Add onions and parsley. Cook 5 minutes, stirring occasionally.
3. Stir in flour, salt, pepper, and Old Bay Seasoning if you wish.
4. Gradually add milk, stirring constantly.
5. Blend in cheese and salmon.
6. Add cooked macaronis. Mix well.
7. Pour into a greased 2-qt. casserole.
8. Melt 2 Tbsp. butter in a small pan. Stir in crumbs. Sprinkle buttered crumbs over casserole contents.
9. Bake uncovered at 350° for 35 minutes.

Personal Pizza

Ruth Shank, Gridley, IL

Makes 6 servings

Prep Time: 10-20 minutes
Resting Time: 10 minutes
Baking Time: 9-12 minutes,
   per baking sheet

3 cups flour
1 1/2 cups whole wheat
   flour
2 Tbsp., *or* 2 envelopes,
   rapid-rise yeast
1 1/2 tsp. salt
1 1/2 tsp. sugar
1 1/2 cups hot (120-130°)
   water
cornmeal
pizza *or* spaghetti sauce,
   toppings, and cheese

1. Stir flours, yeast, salt, and sugar together in a large bowl.

2. Stir in hot water until dough pulls away from sides of the bowl.

3. Turn out onto floured surface and knead 5 minutes, until smooth.

4. Place dough on a floured surface, cover with plastic wrap, and let rest 10 minutes. (Dough will just start to rise.)

5. Divide dough into 6 pieces. Shape each piece into a disk.

6. Put oven rack in lowest position. Preheat oven to 500°.

7. Sprinkle a cookie sheet with cornmeal and place individual dough crusts on the sheet. (You'll be able to fit more than one dough crust on a sheet.)

8. Top each dough crust with pizza sauce, your favorite toppings, and cheese.

9. Bake on the oven's lowest rack position at 500° for 9-12 minutes.

With individual-sized pizzas, each person may choose the toppings s/he likes best.

A Tip —

When cooking pasta, make sure you use a pan large enough to allow the pasta to circulate freely while cooking and to expand. Salt the boiling water generously.

Crazy Crust Pizza
Pamela Metzler
Gilman, WI

Makes 8 serving

Prep Time: 20 minutes
Baking Time: 20 minutes
Standing Time: 5 minutes

---

2 cups flour
4 eggs
2 tsp. salt
1 1/2 cups milk
1 lb. ground beef *or* sausage
1/2-1 cup chopped onions, according to your taste preference
2 tsp. dried oregano
1/2 tsp. salt
pepper to taste
26-oz. can tomato sauce
1/2-1 cup shredded mozzarella cheese
1/2-1 cup shredded cheddar cheese

1. In a mixing bowl, mix together flour, eggs, 2 tsp. salt, and milk until smooth. Pour onto a greased and floured jelly-roll pan.

2. In a large skillet, brown ground beef and onions. Season with oregano, 1/2 tsp. salt, and pepper. Stir in tomato sauce. Pour over crust.

3. Sprinkle cheeses evenly over top.

4. Bake at 475° for 20 minutes. Let stand 5 minutes before cutting.

Pillow Pizza
Sharon Miller
Holmesville, OH

Makes 8 servings

Prep Time: 20 minutes
Baking Time: 20 minutes

---

2 tubes refrigerated biscuits (10 biscuits per tube)
1 1/2 lbs. ground beef
16-oz. can pizza sauce
optional ingredients:
    chopped onions
    chopped peppers
    canned mushrooms
    pepperoni
1 lb. mozzarella cheese

1. Cut each biscuit into quarters and place in the bottom of a greased 9 x 13 baking dish.

2. In a skillet, brown beef. Drain off drippings. Add sauce to beef in skillet and stir together.

3. Pour over biscuit quarters.

4. Top with any optional ingredients as you would a pizza. Sprinkle cheese over top.

5. Bake at 400° for 20 minutes.

Pizza Roll-Ups

Vonnie Oyer
Hubbard, OR

Makes 10 servings

Prep Time: 30 minutes
Standing and Rising Times:
1¹/₂ hours
Baking Time: 20-25 minutes

1¹/₂ Tbsp. yeast
³/₈ cup warm (110-115°)
    water
¹/₂ tsp. sugar
1¹/₂ Tbsp. sugar
1¹/₂ Tbsp. shortening
1¹/₃ tsp. salt
1¹/₂ cups hot (120-130°)
    water
5-6 cups flour
2 cups shredded
    mozzarella cheese
¹/₂ tsp. salt
¹/₂ tsp. parsley
1 tsp. Italian seasoning
¹/₄ tsp. pepper
2 cups tomato sauce
1¹/₂ tsp. sugar
1¹/₂ tsp. Italian seasoning
1¹/₂ tsp. parsley
1¹/₂ tsp. dried basil
¹/₂ tsp. garlic powder
¹/₄ tsp. pepper

A Tip —

Always check twice
that you have the right
ingredients—and the right
amount—before you toss
them into the mix. It can
be hard to fix an "oops."

1. In a small bowl dissolve
yeast and ¹/₂ tsp. sugar in
³/₈ cup water.
2. In a large bowl, com-
bine 1¹/₂ Tbsp. sugar, shortening, salt and hot water. Add
yeast mixture.
3. Stir in flour. Knead for
10 minutes, or until smooth
and elastic. Place in greased
bowl, turning once.
4. Let rise to double.
Punch down and let rest
10 minutes.
5. Roll dough into a
14"-wide strip, ¹/₄" thick.
6. In a small bowl, mix
cheese with salt, parsley,
Italian seasoning, and ¹/₄ tsp.
pepper. Sprinkle over dough.
Press slightly into dough.
7. Roll up dough beginning
with a narrow end, like a
jelly roll. Cut roll into 1"-
thick slices.
8. Grease 2 baking sheets,
or line with bakers paper.
Place roll-ups on baking
sheets, cut-side up, and let
stand 10-20 minutes.
9. Bake at 400° for 20-25
minutes.
10. Mix tomato sauce and
the seasonings and herbs in a
saucepan. Heat. Serve roll-
ups with small bowls of
sauce for dunking.

Tips: You can add chopped
pepperoni with the cheese and
seasonings (Step 6) if you wish.

Mexican Pizza

Erma Martin
East Earl, PA
Ruth Ann Bender
Cochranville, PA

Makes 12-16 servings

Preparation Time: 30 minutes
Baking Time: 10 minutes

2 8-oz. tubes refrigerated
    crescent rolls
8-oz. package cream
    cheese, softened
1 cup sour cream
1 lb. ground beef
1 envelope dry taco
    seasoning mix
2.25-oz. can sliced ripe
    olives, drained
1 medium tomato,
    chopped
³/₄ cup shredded cheddar
    cheese
³/₄ cup shredded
    mozzarella cheese
1 cup shredded lettuce

1. Flatten crescent rolls
onto an ungreased 10 x 15
baking pan. Seal the seams.
2. Bake at 375° for 8-10
minutes. Cool.
3. Meanwhile, combine
cream cheese and sour
cream. Spread on cooled
crust.
4. Brown beef in a skillet.
Drain off drippings. Stir in
taco seasoning. Add water
according to seasoning package directions. Simmer for
5 minutes.
5. Spread meat over cream
cheese layer.

6. Layer olives, tomato, cheeses, and lettuce, over top.

7. Cut into serving size pieces. Refrigerate or serve immediately.

Variations:

1. Add 1/4 cup chopped onions and 1/2 cup chopped green pepper to the toppings in Step 6.

2. Replace taco seasoning and water in Step 4 with 1 minced garlic clove, 1/4 cup chopped green chilies, 1/4 tsp. dried oregano, 1/2 tsp. salt, and a scant 1/2 tsp. cumin powder. Simmer for 5 minutes; then proceed with rest of the recipe.

— Bonita Ensenberger
Albuquerque, NM

Pizza Muffins
Jean Johnson
Dallas, OR

Makes 2 quarts of pizza mix

Prep Time: 30 minutes
Baking Time: 5-10 minutes

1 lb. salami, ground
10 ozs. mild Colby cheese, grated
10 ozs. sharp cheddar cheese, grated
2 4-oz. cans mushrooms, stems and pieces, drained
4.5-oz. can chopped black olives, drained
2 8-oz. cans tomato sauce
2 Tbsp. dried oregano
English muffins

1. Combine all ingredients except English muffins in a large bowl.

2. When ready to serve, split English muffins and spread about 3 Tbsp. on each half. Broil until bubbly and cheese is melted.

Tips:

1. This refrigerates well and is great to have on hand for hungry kids or drop-in guests.

2. Other meat, like fully cooked ham or pepperoni, can be substituted for the salami.

Chicken Fajita Pizza
Ann Henderson
Cincinnati, OH

Makes 6-8 servings

Prep Time: 20-30 minutes
Baking Time: 15-20 minutes

1 Tbsp. oil
1 small boneless skinless chicken breast, about 3/4 lb., cut into 2" x 1/2" strips
1 clove garlic, pressed, *or* 1/2 tsp. garlic powder
1-2 tsp. chili powder, according to your taste preference
1/2 tsp. salt
1 cup onions, thinly sliced
1 cup combination of green, red, and orange pepper slices
10-oz. pkg. refrigerated pizza crust
cornmeal
1/2 cup salsa *or* picante sauce
2 cups shredded Monterey Jack cheese

1. Heat oil in skillet. Add chicken strips and stir-fry just until lightly browned.

2. Stir in garlic, chili powder, and salt. Add onions and peppers and cook for 1 minute until tender-crisp.

3. Unroll dough and roll onto cornmeal-covered pizza stone. Par-bake dough at 425° for 8-10 minutes.

4. Spoon chicken and vegetable mixture onto crust. Cover with salsa and cheese.

5. Bake at 425° for about more 5 minutes, or until crust is browning.

Pasta Pizza Pronto

Shari Jensen
Fountain, CO

Makes 6 servings

Prep Time: 20 minutes
Baking Time: 37-40 minutes

Crust:
2 cups uncooked
macaronis
3 eggs
1/3 cup finely chopped
onions
1 cup shredded cheddar
cheese

Topping:
1 1/2 cups prepared pizza *or*
pasta sauce
3-oz. pkg. sliced pepperoni
2.25-oz. can sliced olives,
drained
1 cup toppings: mix or
match sliced
mushrooms, diced
cooked ham or chicken,
diced bell peppers
1 1/2 cups shredded
mozzarella cheese

1. In a saucepan, cook macaronis according to package directions. Drain well.

2. In a large bowl, beat eggs. Stir in onions, cheddar cheese, and cooked macaronis.

3. Spread pasta mixture evenly on generously greased 14-16" pizza pan.

4. Bake at 375° for 25 minutes on lower oven rack. Remove from oven.

5. Top with your favorite pizza or pasta sauce. Spread to within 1/2" of edge, using the back of a spoon.

6. Top evenly with pepperoni, olives, and 1 cup of the other toppings.

7. Finish by sprinkling with mozzarella cheese.

8. Return to oven and bake 12-15 minutes longer, until cheese is bubbly.

9. Remove from oven and slice with pizza cutter into 6-8 slices. Serve warm.

Tips:

1. Don't overload with toppings. Stay within the 1-cup suggestion.

2. Using the lower shelf of oven will crisp the crust. If not available in your oven, the middle shelf is okay.

3. Keep pasta pieces touching each other. No gaps.

A Tip —

Sprinkle cornmeal on a pizza pan before rolling out the pizza crust. It gives the crust a bit of a pan-pizza taste.

Grilling

Flank steaks benefit by marinating for 2-24 hours (or overnight) in a flavorful sauce before being put on the grill. Their flavor is enhanced; their texture is improved.

Here are 5 **marinade** recipes, each to serve with 2 lbs. flank steak, enough for 6-8 servings. Choose the one that suits your fancy and that matches the ingredients you have on hand.

The procedure is the same for each: Mix the marinade ingredients thoroughly in a long shallow container. Add the meat and submerge it as well as you can in the marinade. Cover the container and refrigerate it for 2-24 hours (or overnight). If you're home and available to do so, flip the meat several times as it marinates to allow the whole piece to have contact with the sauce.

When you're ready to grill, remove the steak from the sauce and grill over hot coals, from 5-10 minutes on each side, depending on how well done you like the meat. Baste frequently while the meat is cooking.

When finished grilling, allow to stand for 10 minutes. Then slice as thin as possible—across the grain.

Teriyaki Flank Steak Marinade
Marsha Sabus
Fallbrook, CA

3/4 cup oil
2 Tbsp. chopped green onions
1/4 cup soy sauce
1/4 cup honey
1 clove garlic, chopped
2 Tbsp. cider vinegar
1 1/2 tsp. ground ginger

Carne Asada
Judy Gonzalez
Fishers, IN

1/2 cup olive oil
1/2 cup red wine vinegar
1/2 cup lemon juice
1 Tbsp. salt
1 tsp. cumin
1 tsp. garlic salt
1 tsp. chili powder
1 tsp. dried oregano

Marinated Flank Steak
Dorothy Reise
Severna Park, MD

1/4 cup soy sauce
1/4 cup dry sherry
1/4 cup olive oil
2 tsp. ground ginger
1 clove garlic, crushed
1 tsp. sugar

Grilled Flank Steak

Joyce Parker
North Plainfield, NJ

1 tsp. **salt**
half an onion chopped or
    grated
1/2 tsp. **pepper**
2 Tbsp. **wine vinegar**
1 tsp. **dried basil**
3 Tbsp. **olive oil**
1 tsp. **dried rosemary**
1 tsp. **minced garlic**

Steak, Pork, or Venison Marinade

Dawn Ranck, Lansdale, PA

2 tsp. **onion salt**
2 tsp. **celery salt**
2 tsp. **garlic salt**
1 tsp. **dry mustard**
1 tsp. **pepper**
3/8 cup **cider vinegar**
3/4 cup **olive oil**

Tips:

1. You can use this marinade for chicken, too, but then marinate the meat for only 1-2 hours.

2. This is one of the most flavorful marinades I've ever eaten. I use it to marinate shish kabobs that include any or all of these: beef, pork, chicken, onion, squash, zucchini, pepper, fresh pineapple, and mushrooms.

Grilled Tenderloin of Pork

Joyce Parker
North Plainfield, NJ

Makes 6-8 servings

Prep Time: 15 minutes
Marinating Time: 3-8 hours,
    or overnight
Grilling Time: 20-30 minutes

1-2 lbs. **pork tenderloin**

Marinade:
3/4 cup **soy sauce**
1/4 cup **olive oil**
1/4 cup **sherry** *or* **cooking
    wine**
3/4 cup **orange juice**
1-2 Tbsp. **minced garlic**
1 Tbsp. **fresh ginger,
    grated,** *or* 1/4 tsp. **ground
    ginger**
1 bunch **scallions, sliced,**
    or **green onions, grated**

1. In a bowl, mix all marinade ingredients together.

2. Marinate pork for at least 3-8 hours or overnight.

3. Grill 10-15 minutes on each side.

4. Slice thin and serve.

Tip: Many grocery stores sell minced or grated fresh ginger. If you want to buy fresh ginger-root in the produce department, grate what you need and freeze the rest until you need it again.

Zesty Grilled Ham

Pat Bechtel
Dillsburg, PA
Jenelle Miller
Marion, SD

Makes 6-8 servings

Prep Time: 10 minutes
Grilling Time: 20 minutes

2 1"-thick, fully cooked
    center-cut **ham slices**
    (about 3 1/2 lbs. total)
1 cup **brown sugar, packed**
1/3 cup **horseradish**
1/4 cup **lemon juice**

1. Score both sides of ham slices 1/4" deep in diamond pattern.

2. In small saucepan, combine remaining ingredients. Heat to boiling, stir, and continue to boil for 1 minute.

3. Grill ham over medium heat for about 10 minutes on each side, basting frequently with sugar-horseradish mixture.

Tip: When bringing a sugar mixture to a boil, watch it carefully. It will tend to boil over quickly, resulting in a very messy stove!

144

Grilled Ham Sauce

Yvonne Kauffman Boettger
Harrisonburg, VA

Makes about ⅓ cup sauce

Prep Time: 5 minutes
Grilling Time: 15-20 minutes

2 Tbsp. butter
1 Tbsp. ketchup
2 Tbsp. brown sugar
½ tsp. Worcestershire
  sauce
1 tsp. vinegar
1 tsp. prepared mustard
1½-2 lbs. ham steak

1. In a microwave-safe mixing bowl, melt butter in microwave.
2. Add ketchup, brown sugar, Worcestershire sauce, vinegar, and mustard. Mix well.
3. Spread onto a thick ham steak and grill over indirect heat 15-20 minutes.

Marinated Grilled Chicken

Stephanie O'Conner, Cheshire, CT

Makes 6 servings

Prep Time: 15 minutes
Marinating Time: 4-8 hours
Cooking Time: 10 minutes

6 boneless, skinless
  chicken breast halves

½ cup orange juice
¼ cup olive oil
4-6 medium-sized garlic
  cloves, finely chopped
6-8 branches fresh
  rosemary, washed,
  or 1 Tbsp. dried
  rosemary, *or* less if you
  don't like a strong
  rosemary flavor
10-12 stems fresh thyme,
  washed, *or* 2 tsp. dried
  thyme
salt and pepper to taste

1. Wash and pat dry chicken. Pound to ½" thickness.
2. Combine juice, oil, garlic, rosemary, thyme, salt, and pepper in a shallow glass (non-reactive) or plastic container.
3. Marinate chicken in mixture for 4-8 hours.
4. Grill over low, indirect heat for about 4 minutes on each side. Baste occasionally.

Tips: This recipe is quite versatile. You can serve the chicken as a dinner entree with rice and vegetables.
  Or slice it over salads, especially a Caesar.
  My family's favorite is to serve it on fresh Portuguese rolls with yummy spreads such as roasted red pepper, pesto, or basil mayonnaise. Be sure to include delicious toppings such as cheddar cheese, tomatoes, lettuce, or more.

Barbecued Chicken

Dawn Ranck, Lansdale, PA

Makes 8 servings

Prep Time: 10 minutes
Grilling Time: 25-30 minutes

8 legs and thighs,
  or 8 whole breasts
½ cup vinegar
½ Tbsp. salt
1 stick (½ cup) butter

Topping:
¼ cup lemon juice
1 Tbsp. brown sugar
1 Tbsp. Worcestershire
  sauce
1 tsp. salt
½ tsp. dry mustard
1 stick (½ cup) butter
¾ cup ketchup
2 Tbsp. fresh parsley,
  chopped
2 Tbsp. fresh, *or* ¾ tsp.
  dried, lemon thyme
2 Tbsp. chives, chopped

1. In a small saucepan, combine vinegar, salt, and 1 stick butter. Heat until butter is melted.
2. Grill chicken, brushing frequently with vinegar mixture, until chicken is almost fully cooked.
3. In another saucepan, combine all topping ingredients. Heat until butter is melted. Stir to blend well.
4. Brush topping on chicken. Grill 5 minutes. Turn chicken over. Brush topping on other side and grill an additional 5 minutes.

Barbecued Marinated Chicken Breasts

Janelle Reitz
Lancaster, PA

Makes 8 servings

Prep Time: 20 minutes
Marinating Time:
  3-8 hours, or overnight
Grilling Time: 10 minutes

8 boneless, skinless
  chicken breast halves
2 cloves garlic, minced *or*
  pressed
2 tsp. grated fresh
  gingerroot, *or* 1 tsp.
  ground ginger
1 tsp. pepper
1 tsp. cumin
2 tsp. curry powder
1 tsp. dried oregano
1/4 cup soy sauce
1/4 cup olive oil
1 Tbsp. lemon juice
8 tsp. butter, *optional*

1. Place chicken breasts in a single layer in a glass or ceramic pan.

2. In a mixing bowl, combine garlic, ginger, pepper, cumin, curry powder, and oregano. Blend in soy sauce, oil, and lemon juice.

3. Spread mixture over chicken breasts, coating each piece well.

4. Cover and refrigerate 3-8 hours, or overnight.

5. Drain meat; then grill 5 minutes on each side, basting frequently. When nearly done, top each piece of meat with a teaspoon of butter.

Tips:
  1. This marinade also dresses up inexpensive cuts of steak.
  2. This is a long list of ingredients, but it is really easy to prepare.
  3. Pepper does not need to be freshly ground.

Marinated Chicken Breasts

Mary Longenecker, Bethel, PA

Makes 3/4-1 cup marinade, enough for 4-12 servings of chicken

Prep Time: 10 minutes
Marinating Time: 3-8 hours
Grilling Time: 10-12 minutes
Standing Time: 10 minutes

1-3 lbs. boneless, skinless,
  chicken breast halves
2 Tbsp. olive oil
3 Tbsp. red wine vinegar
1/4 cup honey
1/4 cup soy sauce
1 garlic clove, crushed
2 Tbsp. chopped fresh
  parsley
1/2 tsp. pepper

1. Pound chicken between sheets of plastic wrap until it is 1/2" thick. Place flattened chicken in a shallow glass or plastic bowl(s) in a single layer.

2. In a small bowl, combine oil, vinegar, honey, soy sauce, garlic, parsley, and pepper.

3. Pour over chicken. Marinade for 3-8 hours.

4. Grill until tender, about 5 minutes per side.

5. After removing from grill, allow to stand for 10 minutes before slicing.

6. Serve with hot vegetables, or to top a salad, or as sandwich filling.

Sizzlin' Chicken Skewers

Cheryl Lapp, Parkesburg, PA

Makes 6 servings

Prep Time: 30 minutes
Marinating Time: 1 1/2 hours
Grilling or Broiling Time:
  12 minutes

1/3 cup hot water
1/4 cup barbecue sauce
1/4 cup creamy peanut
  butter
1/4 cup soy sauce
2 Tbsp. honey Dijon
  mustard
1 lb. boneless, skinless
  chicken breasts, cut into
  small pieces
1 red pepper, cut into
  chunks
1 yellow pepper, cut into
  chunks
2 15-oz. cans whole
  potatoes
20-oz. can pineapple
  chunks
1 small zucchini, cut into
  chunks

1. In a small mixing bowl, combine first 5 ingredients. Brush small amount onto chicken pieces, enough to cover. Let stand for 1½ hours.

2. Alternate chicken and vegetables on skewers and brush with remaining sauce.

3. Place skewers on the grill or under the broiler for approximately 6 minutes. Turn and grill or broil another 6 minutes.

Curried Coconut Chicken

Dawn Ranck, Lansdale, PA

Makes 4 servings

Prep Time: 10 minutes
Marinating Time: 30 minutes-
  6 hours
Grilling Time: 10 minutes

8 boneless, skinless chicken
  thighs *or* breast halves
4 garlic cloves, crushed
1 Tbsp. grated fresh ginger
1 onion, chopped
1 handful cilantro,
  chopped
3 Tbsp. fish sauce
1 Tbsp. garam masala mix
  (below)
⅓ cup coconut milk
salt to taste
pepper to taste

bamboo skewers

1. Spread chicken thighs or breasts flat. Thread 2 skewers diagonally through each thigh or breast to form a cross. Place in baking pan with sides.

2. In blender, combine garlic, ginger, onion, cilantro, fish sauce, masala mix, and coconut milk. Pulse until smooth. Pour over chicken. Cover and refrigerate for 30 minutes-6 hours.

3. Grill over medium-hot coals for 5 minutes per side, or until chicken is cooked (opaque with no trace of pink). Or do the chicken in the broiler for 5 minutes per side.

Garam Masala Mix

Makes ½ cup

3 Tbsp. cardamom pods
2½ Tbsp. cumin seeds
2 Tbsp. coriander seeds
1½ Tbsp. black
  peppercorns
1 Tbsp. whole cloves
2 tsp. ground cinnamon
1 tsp. ground nutmeg

1. Lightly crush cardamom pods. Discard skins and reserve seeds.

2. Place a dry cast iron skillet over medium heat for 2 minutes. Add cardamom seeds, cumin, coriander, peppercorns, and cloves. Toast by shaking the pan until the spices are dark and aromatic, about 5 minutes. Remove spices from pan. Cool.

3. Crush toasted spices to a powder. Add cinnamon and nutmeg.

4. Use to make Curried Coconut Chicken (above) or rub on pork chops 8 hours before grilling, on chicken breasts 4 hours before grilling, on shrimp 2 hours before grilling, or on fish 30 minutes before grilling.

A Tip —

When camping, always prepare extra food. You'll likely need six servings to feed four ravenous campers!

Zesty Grilled Fish
Julie McKenzie
Punxsutawney, PA

Makes 6 servings

Prep Time: 5 minutes
Marinating Time: 1-2 hours
Grilling Time: 10-11 minutes

2 lbs. fresh fish steaks *or* thick fillets
1/4 cup soy sauce
1/4 cup orange juice
2 Tbsp. ketchup
2 Tbsp. vegetable oil
1 Tbsp. lemon juice
1/2 tsp. dried oregano
1/2 tsp. pepper
1 garlic clove, finely chopped

1. Arrange fish in a single layer in a glass or plastic dish. In a small bowl, combine remaining ingredients and pour over fish. Marinate 1-2 hours.

2. Grill fish over a hot fire, using foil with holes punched in it, or a fish basket. Cook approximately 6 minutes on first side; then turn over and cook another 4-5 minutes, checking to see if fish flakes easily. Do not overcook!

Note: You can baste the fish with the marinade while grilling the first side, if you wish.

Grilled Barbecued Shrimp
Denise Martin
Lancaster, PA

Makes 6 servings

Prep Time: 10 minutes
Marinating Time: 1-2 hours
Grilling Time: 6 minutes

1 Tbsp. Worcestershire sauce
1/2 cup olive oil
1 tsp. seasoning salt
1/2 tsp. Tabasco sauce
2 cloves garlic, minced
2 Tbsp. lemon juice
1 tsp. dried oregano
1/4 cup ketchup
2 lbs. large raw shrimp, peeled and deveined

1. Combine all ingredients except raw shrimp. Blend well.

2. Add shrimp to marinade. Cover and let stand 1-2 hours in the refrigerator.

3. To grill, place shrimp on a screen or grate with small holes. Grill about 3 minutes per side over medium heat, or until shrimp are bright pink, basting often.

Tip: You can also broil the shrimp, following the directions above.

A Tip —

Be sure to preheat the grill.

Sweet Bourbon Salmon
Barbara Walker
Sturgis, SD

Makes 2 large servings

Prep Time: 10 minutes
Marinating Time: 1-3 hours
Grilling Time: 10-14 minutes

1/4 cup pineapple juice
2 Tbsp. soy sauce
2 Tbsp. brown sugar
1 tsp. bourbon
1/4 tsp. cracked black pepper
1/8 tsp. garlic powder
1/2 cup vegetable oil
2 8-oz. fresh salmon fillets
2 tsp. snipped fresh chives

1. In a small bowl, combine pineapple juice, soy sauce, brown sugar, bourbon, pepper, and garlic powder. Stir until sugar is dissolved. Stir in oil.

2. Remove skin from salmon. Place in shallow dish. Pour marinade over salmon. Cover. Refrigerate for 1-3 hours.

3. Grill 5-7 minutes per side, or until salmon flakes easily. Brush with marinade as you grill the salmon.

4. Sprinkle with chives before serving.

Grilled Onions
Cricket Turley
Dodge City, KS

Makes 1 onion per serving

Prep Time: 5-10 minutes
Grilling Time: 45 minutes

medium-sized onions
seasoning salt
butter, *optional*

1. Soak whole onions in water for 5-10 minutes. Do not peel.
2. Place on lower rack of grill while it is warming up. Move onions to top rack when you're ready to grill the meat. Onions are done when they are soft when squeezed.
3. Cut off the root end of each and squeeze the onion out into a serving bowl.
4. Cut onions into quarters and sprinkle with seasoning salt.
5. If you wish, add a small amount of butter, to the onions and stir to melt.

Grilled Veggies
Tim Smith
Rutledge, PA

Makes 4-6 servings

Prep Time: 10-20 minutes
Grilling Time: 20-40 minutes

2 large potatoes
1 medium zucchini
1 medium yellow squash
1 small red onion
1 small white onion
2 Tbsp. crushed garlic
1 tsp. pepper
1/2 tsp. white pepper
1 Tbsp. fresh basil leaves
3 Tbsp. oil

1. Slice potatoes paper-thin.
2. Slice zucchini and squash 1/4" thick.
3. Slice onions.
4. Combine all ingredients in a large mixing bowl.
5. Cut a piece of heavy-duty foil large enough to hold all ingredients. Spoon vegetables into center of foil. Close tightly.
6. Place on preheated grill. Grill over medium heat for 20-40 minutes, turning every 5 minutes. Open and jag potatoes after 20 minutes to see if the vegetables are done to your liking. Close up and continue grilling if you want them more tender, checking again after 10 minutes. Continue until they are as tender as you want them.

Grilled Apple Crisp
Charlotte Shaffer
East Earl, PA

Makes 6-8 servings

Prep Time: 30 minutes
Grilling Time: 20-25 minutes

10 cups thinly sliced apples (about 8 medium-sized)
1 cup dry old-fashioned oats
1 cup packed brown sugar
1/4 cup flour
3 tsp. cinnamon
1 tsp. nutmeg
half a stick (1/4 cup) butter, cold

1. Spread apple slices over a double thickness of heavy duty foil, approximately 12 x 24" in size.
2. In small bowl, combine oats, brown sugar, flour, cinnamon, and nutmeg. Cut in butter until mixture is crumbly. Sprinkle over apples.
3. Fold foil around apple mixture and seal tightly.
4. Grill over medium heat for 20-25 minutes, or until apples are tender.

Tip: Put this package of apples on the grill after you've finished grilling your meat. The apples will bake while you eat your main course and be ready in time for dessert.

Grilled Peach Melba

Stacy Schmucker Stoltzfus
Enola, PA

Makes 4 servings

Prep Time: 10 minutes
Grilling Time: 5-10 minutes

4 large, unpeeled peaches
  or nectarines
2 tsp. sugar
2 cups red raspberries,
  fresh *or* frozen
sugar, *optional*
vanilla ice cream

1. Halve and pit peaches or nectarines.
2. Press fresh or thawed raspberries through sieve. Save juice and discard seeds. Sweeten to taste with sugar, if needed.
3. Grill unpeeled peaches cut-side down for approximately 2 minutes. Turn peaches over. With cut-side up, fill each cavity with 1/2 tsp. sugar, and continue grilling until grill marks appear on skins.
4. Serve immediately with a scoop of vanilla ice cream and drizzle with the raspberry sauce.

Grilled Pizza

Robin Schrock
Millersburg, OH

Makes 4 12" pizzas

Prep Time: 30 minutes
Rising/Resting Time: 2 1/2 hours
Grilling Time: 10 minutes

1 cup warm water
  (110-115°)
1 Tbsp. sugar
1 pkg. (1/4 oz.) active dry
  yeast, *or* 2 1/4 tsp.
  granular yeast
3 1/4 cups flour
1 Tbsp. salt
2 Tbsp. olive oil
pizza sauce
grated cheese
toppings of your choice

1. In a medium-sized bowl, mix water, sugar, and yeast together. Let stand until foamy, about 5 minutes.
2. In large mixing bowl, combine flour and salt. Add oil to yeast mixture; then add yeast mixture to flour mixture.
3. Mix until stiff. Turn onto floured surface and knead about 10 minutes.
4. Place dough in lightly oiled bowl and let rise in a warm place until doubled, about 2 hours.
5. Punch down and let rest 30 minutes.
6. Meanwhile, prepare the grill with a hot fire.
7. Divide dough into 4 balls and roll each into a 12"-wide circle.
8. Transfer dough circles to the hottest part of the grill. Close lid and cook 2-3 minutes.
9. Use tongs to flip crusts over and move to the coolest side of the grill. Brush crusts with olive oil. Close grill lid until crust is done, about 2-3 minutes.
10. Remove crusts and top with pizza sauce and your choice of toppings—cheese, raw vegetable pieces, sliced sausage or pepperoni, etc.
11. Return pizzas to grill. Place over medium heat and close lid on grill. Heat through until cheese melts.
12. Serve hot from the grill.

A Tip —

When you try a new recipe, write on the recipe the date on which you tried it. Note if you liked it, how you would change it, and whether it's worth repeating.

Vegetables

Beloved recipes not only endure, they also often prove to be amazingly adaptable. One such is a **Vegetable Au Gratin** recipe.

At its sturdy heart are the ingredients and variations listed below.

Following the base recipe are several vegetables which many cooks love and often make as au gratin dishes. Try one of these proven combinations, or find your own favorite way of departing from them!

A Tip —

To cook spinach or Swiss chard, heat 2 Tbsp. butter or olive oil in a large skillet or stockpot. Sauté 2 Tbsp. onions in the butter. Fill the pan with washed leaves with a lot of water hanging on them. Cover with a tight-fitting lid. Steam slowly for only a few minutes. The ready-to-eat vegetables will stay green and have no excess water.

Vegetable Au Gratin Base

3 Tbsp. butter
1/2 cup chopped onions
10.75-oz. can cream of mushroom, celery, *or* chicken soup*
1/2 lb. cheddar cheese, grated

1. Melt butter in medium-sized saucepan. Stir in onions and sauté until just softened. Remove from heat.
2. Blend in soup.
3. Stir in cheese.
4. Stir in vegetable of your choice and seasonings.

Instead of using a canned cream soup, you can make your own cream base. Melt 4 1/2 Tbsp. butter in a medium-sized saucepan. Blend in 4 1/2 Tbsp. flour. Over medium heat, whisk in 1 1/2 cups milk. Stir continually until sauce becomes smooth and thickens. (Use this in place of Step 2 above.)

Vegetable Au Gratin Toppings— choose one!

1. 2 cups butter crackers, crushed, mixed with 4 Tbsp. melted butter
2. 3 cups stuffing mix, mixed with 1/3 cup melted butter
3. 2 cups bread crumbs, fresh or dry, mixed with 4 Tbsp. melted butter

Asparagus Au Gratin Bake

Dorothy Shank
Sterling, IL

Makes 6 servings

Prep Time: 15 minutes
Baking Time: 35 minutes

2 cups fresh asparagus, chopped, *or* a 16-oz. can of asparagus, drained
2 hard-cooked eggs, chopped
1/2 cup slivered almonds
au gratin base (page 151)
au gratin topping, your choice (page 151)

1. Combine asparagus, eggs, almonds, and au gratin base in a greased 8 x 8 baking dish.
2. Sprinkle with your choice of topping.
3. Bake uncovered at 350° for 35 minutes.

Carrot Casserole

Orpha Herr
Andover, NY

Makes 8 servings

Prep Time: 40 minutes
Baking Time: 20 minutes

4 cups sliced carrots
au gratin base (page 151)
1/2 tsp. salt

1/8 tsp. pepper
au gratin topping, your choice (page 151)

1. In medium-sized saucepan, cook carrots and onions until crispy soft.
2. Add au gratin base and seasonings to vegetables.
3. Pour into a greased 3-qt. casserole dish.
4. Spread your choice of toppings over vegetables.
5. Bake, uncovered, at 350° for 20 minutes.

Broccoli Stuffing

Christine Heuser
Farmingdale, NJ

Makes 5-6 servings

Prep Time: 15 minutes
Baking Time: 25-30 minutes

16-oz. pkg. frozen chopped broccoli
3 Tbsp. chicken bouillon granules
au gratin base (page 151)
au gratin topping, variation #2 (page 151)
1/2 cup water

1. Cook broccoli until just tender. Drain and set aside.
2. In mixing bowl, stir bouillon granules into au gratin base.
3. Spoon broccoli into bowl and mix base and broccoli together.
4. Pour into a greased 1 1/2-2-qt. casserole dish.

5. Place topping in the mixing bowl. Stir in water. Mix well and spoon over broccoli.
6. Bake at 350° for 25-30 minutes.

Zucchini Casserole

Clara Yoder Byler
Hartville, OH

Makes 10 servings

Prep Time: 15 minutes
Baking Time: 30 minutes

5-6 cups grated zucchini
1/2 cup chopped onions
1 1/2 Tbsp. butter
10.75-oz. can cream of chicken soup
1 cup sour cream
1 cup shredded carrots
au gratin topping, variation #2 (page 151)

1. In large skillet, sauté zucchini and onions in 1 1/2 Tbsp. butter until just tender. Drain.
2. In a mixing bowl, combine soup, sour cream, and carrots. Fold in zucchini.
3. Prepare au gratin topping, variation #2.
4. Place half of au gratin topping in a greased 9 x 13 baking pan. Pour in zucchini mixture. Top with remaining au gratin topping.
5. Bake, uncovered, at 350° for 30 minutes.

Surfside Summer Squash

Ginny Cutler, Westminster, MD

Makes 6-8 servings

Prep Time: 25-30 minutes
Baking Time: 30 minutes

5 medium-sized summer
  squash
2 eggs, beaten
1/2 cup milk
1 medium onion, chopped
1/2 lb. cheddar *or* Monterey
  Jack, cheese, grated
1 tomato, chopped
1/2 stick (4 Tbsp.) butter,
  cut in pieces
Parmesan cheese
Italian bread crumbs

1. Cut up or slice squash.
Steam or microwave until just
tender. Drain and set aside.
2. In a mixing bowl, beat
together eggs and milk. Add
onion, cheese, and tomato.
3. Add squash to egg/
cheese mixture.
4. Pour into a greased
9 x 13 baking dish. Add cut-
up butter and stir.
5. Sprinkle with Parmesan
cheese and bread crumbs
until well covered.
6. Bake uncovered at 400°
for 30 minutes.

A Tip —

Leftover corn from a
previous meal makes a
great addition to a
Mexican dish or salsa.

Cheesy Spinach or Broccoli Casserole

Christie Detamore-
Hunsberger
Harrisonburg, VA

Makes 4-6 servings

Prep Time: 20 minutes
Baking Time: 30 minutes
Standing Time: 10 minutes

3 eggs
2 Tbsp. flour
10-oz. pkg. chopped
  spinach *or* broccoli,
  thawed
4 ozs. cottage cheese
1 1/2 cups (6 ozs.) cheddar
  cheese, grated
1-1 1/2 tsp. dried oregano,
  according to your taste
  preference
3/4 tsp. dried basil
1/8 tsp. pepper
2 Tbsp. butter
bread crumbs
Parmesan cheese

1. In a large mixing bowl,
beat eggs and flour until
smooth.
2. If you're using spinach,
squeeze it dry. Then add it
and the cottage and cheddar
cheeses, oregano, basil, and
pepper to the egg mixture.
Stir.
3. Melt butter in a 9 x 9
glass baking dish. Pour mixture into dish. Sprinkle with
bread crumbs and Parmesan
cheese.
4. Bake uncovered at 375°
for 30 minutes. Let stand 10
minutes before serving.

Spinach Quiche

Mary Jane Hoober
Shipshewana, IN

Makes 6-8 servings

Prep Time: 20 minutes
Baking Time: 30-35 minutes

1/2 lb. bacon
1 cup (8 ozs.) sour cream
3 eggs, separated
2 Tbsp. flour
1/8 tsp. pepper
10-oz. pkg. frozen chopped
  spinach, thawed and
  squeezed dry
1/2 cup shredded sharp
  cheddar cheese
1/2 cup dry bread crumbs
1 Tbsp. butter, melted

1. Fry bacon. When crisp,
drain. Then crumble and set
aside.
2. In a large mixing bowl,
combine sour cream, egg
yolks, flour, and pepper.
3. In a separate bowl, beat
egg whites until stiff peaks
form. Gently stir one-fourth
of egg whites into sour cream
mixture. When well blended,
fold in remaining egg whites.
4. In a greased round 2-qt.
baking dish, layer spinach,
sour-cream mixture, cheese,
and bacon in casserole dish.
6. Combine bread crumbs
and butter. Sprinkle over
bacon.
7. Bake, uncovered, at
350° for 30-35 minutes, or
until a knife inserted in the
center comes out clean.

Stir-Fried Broccoli

Vicki Dinkel
Sharon Springs, KS

Makes 4 servings

Prep Time: 15 minutes
Cooking Time: 5 minutes

1 onion, diced
1 Tbsp. oil
1 lb. broccoli, cut in pieces,
   fresh *or* frozen
1/2 cup chicken broth
1 tsp. cornstarch
2 Tbsp. soy sauce
1 tsp. sugar

1. Brown onion in oil in a
large skillet. Add broccoli.
Stir-fry 3 minutes.

2. In a small bowl, com-
bine chicken broth, corn-
starch, soy sauce, and sugar.
Add to broccoli. Cook 1-2
minutes until sauce clears.

3. Serve over cooked rice.

Variations:
1. Replace half of broccoli
with cauliflower or any other
vegetable of your choice.
2. Add strips of boneless skin-
less chicken breasts to Step 1.

Baked Cabbage

Karen Gingrich
New Holland, PA

Makes 6 servings

Prep Time: 20 minutes
Cooking/Baking Time:
   45 minutes

1 medium-sized head of
   cabbage
water
1/2 tsp. salt
1 1/2 cups hot milk
1 Tbsp. flour
1 tsp. salt
1/2 tsp. pepper
2 Tbsp. butter
1/2–1 cup grated sharp
   cheddar cheese

1. Cut cabbage in wedges
3/4" thick. Cook, covered, in a
saucepan in 1/2" water, sprinkled with 1/2 tsp. salt, for 10
minutes. Drain and place cabbage in a greased 2-qt. baking
casserole.

2. While cabbage is cook-
ing (Step 1), warm milk in a
small saucepan until it forms
a skin but does not boil.

3. Sprinkle cabbage with
flour, 1 tsp. salt, and pepper.

4. Pour hot milk over,
being careful not to wash off
the flour and seasonings. Dot
with butter. Top with grated
cheese.

5. Bake, uncovered, at
350° for 35 minutes.

Cheesy Cauliflower

Joan Erwin
Sparks, NV

Makes 4-5 servings

Prep Time: 5-10 minutes
Baking Time: 11 minutes

1 head of cauliflower
1 Tbsp. water
1 cup mayonnaise
1 Tbsp. prepared mustard
1/2 cup chopped green *or*
   red onions
1 cup shredded Monterey
   Jack and cheddar
   cheeses, combined, *or*
   one of the two

1. Place whole cauliflower
head in microwavable glass
baking dish. Add water.
Cover. Microwave on high for
9 minutes, until crisp-cooked.

2. Meanwhile, combine
mayonnaise, mustard, and
onions in a small bowl.
Spread over cooked cauli-
flower. Sprinkle with cheese.

3. Cover and microwave
on high for 1 minute, or until
cheese is melted.

Variation: You may break the
cauliflower into florets and pro-
ceed with Step 1.

A Tip —

When choosing cab-
bage, select a bright green
head that is firm and
solid.

Carrots with Sausage and Rosemary

J.B. Miller
Indianapolis, IN

Makes 12 servings

Preparation Time: 15 minutes
Cooking Time: 20 minutes

3 lbs. carrots, sliced
  crosswise, about 1/4"
  thick
2 Tbsp. extra-virgin olive
  oil
3/4 lb. sweet Italian
  sausage, removed from
  casing
1 medium-sized onion,
  finely chopped
1 Tbsp., plus 1 tsp.,
  chopped fresh rosemary,
  or 2 tsp. dried rosemary
1 Tbsp. tomato paste
1/2 cup water
salt and pepper
1/4 cup chopped parsley

1. In a large pot, boil carrots in salt water over moderately high heat until tender, about 7 minutes. Do not overcook. Drain carrots.

2. In a large, deep skillet, heat olive oil. Add sausage and cook over moderate heat, breaking up the meat with a wooden spoon until no pink remains.

3. Add onions and rosemary to sausage. Cook over moderately low heat, stirring occasionally until onions are softened, about 6 minutes.

4. Stir in carrots and cook until heated through.

5. In a small bowl, blend tomato paste with water. Add to carrots. Season with salt and pepper.

6. Remove from heat and stir in parsley just before serving.

We often serve this at Thanksgiving. It's a great alternative to more traditional vegetables at holiday-times.

Stewed Tomatoes

Esther J. Mast, Lancaster, PA

Makes 4-5 servings

Prep Time: 5 minutes
Cooking Time: 10 minutes

2 Tbsp. chopped onions
2 Tbsp. freshly chopped
  celery leaves
2 Tbsp. butter
2 cups canned diced
  tomatoes, undrained
2 Tbsp. cornstarch
4 Tbsp. sugar
1/2 tsp. salt
1/8 tsp. cinnamon

1. In a large skillet or saucepan, sauté onions and celery leaves in butter until soft but not brown.

2. Add tomatoes and stir in well.

3. In a small bowl, combine cornstarch, sugar, salt, and cinnamon. Pour just enough tomato mixture into

dry mixture to moisten. Immediately stir into remaining tomato mixture. Continue cooking and stirring until thickened.

Tip: If the mixture gets too thick, add water until the tomatoes reach the consistency you want.

Variations:

1. Stir 1 1/2 tsp. prepared mustard into Step 2.

2. Butter and toast 3 slices of bread. Then cut them into cubes and place them on top of the casserole at the end of Step 3. Slide under broiler to brown.
— **Dorothy Hartley**
Carmichaels, PA

3. Stir 1 Tbsp. fresh basil, chopped, or 3/4 tsp. dried basil, into Step 2.

4. If you add #2 Variation (just above), sprinkle the buttered toast with a dusting of dried oregano before cutting the toast into cubes.
— **Colleen Heatwole**
Burton, MI

I got this recipe from the school cafeteria where I worked when our sons were in junior high school. It became a family favorite—served as a side dish to macaroni and cheese.
— **Esther J. Mast**
Lancaster, PA

A Tip —

A teaspoon or two of brown sugar in tomato dishes enhances the flavor and helps to smooth out the acid.

Marge's Cauliflower

Pat Taylor
Paw Paw, WV

Makes 4 servings

Prep Time: 30 minutes
Cooking/Baking Time:
25 minutes

1 fresh head of cauliflower
water
1/2 cup butter, melted
1 cup dry bread crumbs
1 tsp. Italian seasoning
1 cup shredded cheddar
 cheese

1. Separate cauliflower into florets. Place in microwavable dish. Sprinkle with 1 Tbsp. water. Cover and cook on high for 3-4 minutes.

2. Drain florets and allow to cool until you can handle them.

3. Place melted butter in a shallow dish. Mix the bread crumbs and seasoning together in another shallow dish.

4. Dip each floret into melted butter, and then into the seasoned bread crumbs, rolling to cover well.

5. Place in greased 9 x 13 baking dish. Bake, uncovered, at 375° for 20 minutes. Turn off oven. Sprinkle with shredded cheese and return to oven to melt.

Garden Vegetable Medley

Ruth Fisher, Leicester, NY

Makes 4 servings

Prep Time: 10 minutes
Cooking Time: 20 minutes

1 Tbsp. olive oil
4 cups zucchini, chopped
 into 1/2" pieces
1 cup chopped onions
1 red *or* green pepper,
 chopped
2 medium-sized tomatoes,
 chopped
1/4 tsp. garlic powder
1/2 tsp. salt
4 slices of your favorite
 cheese

1. Heat oil in stir-fry pan over medium heat. Add zucchini and onions. Heat until tender, about 10 minutes.

2. Add peppers and tomatoes and stir-fry until just tender.

3. Stir in garlic powder and salt.

4. Lay cheese over top. Turn off heat and let stand until cheese is melted.

Variations:

1. Use only 3 cups zucchini and add 1 baby eggplant, cut up into 1/2" pieces.

2. Substitute 1-2 tsp. dried Italian seasoning for garlic powder and salt.

3. Instead of slices of cheese, sprinkle liberally with Parmesan cheese.

— **Stephanie O'Conner**
Cheshire, CN

Oven Roasted Vegetables & Herbs

Bonnie Goering
Bridgewater, VA

Makes 4-5 servings

Prep Time: 10 minutes
Baking Time: 45-60 minutes

3 potatoes, cut in 1" pieces
3 carrots, cut in 1" pieces
2 onions, cut in wedges
1/4 cup olive oil
2 Tbsp. minced fresh, *or*
 3/4 tsp. dried, rosemary
2 Tbsp. minced fresh, *or*
 3/4 tsp. dried, thyme
1 Tbsp. fresh, *or* 1 tsp.
 dried parsley
3/4 tsp. salt
1/4 tsp. freshly ground
 black pepper
1/2 lb. freshly mushrooms,
 cut into halves or
 quarters

1. Combine potatoes, carrots, and onions in a large mixing bowl.

2. Drizzle olive oil over vegetables.

3. In a small bowl, combine rosemary, thyme, parsley, salt, and pepper. Sprinkle over vegetables.

4. Arrange vegetables in a single layer on a large greased baking sheet.

5. Bake at 400° for 30 minutes.

6. Remove from oven and stir in mushrooms. Return to oven and continue baking for

another 15-30 minutes, or until potatoes and carrots are tender.

Peas with Bacon & Crispy Leeks

J.B.Miller
Indianapolis, IN

Makes 12 servings

Prep Time: 15 minutes
Cooking Time: 45 minutes

3 large leeks, *divided*
vegetable oil
salt and pepper to taste
6 thick slices of bacon
4 fresh thyme springs, *or*
  1/2 tsp. ground thyme
1 cup chicken broth,
  divided
3/4 cup light cream *or* half-
  and-half
30 ozs. frozen baby peas,
  thawed
salt and pepper
1 tsp. cornstarch
1 Tbsp. water

1. Using only the white and tender green part of the leeks, slice the leeks cross-wise into 1/4" thick pieces. Separate into rings. Wash and pat dry.

2. Heat 1/4" of oil in a large saucepan until shimmering. Add all but 1/2 cup of leeks. Cook over moderate heat, stirring until golden brown.

3. Using a slotted spoon, transfer leeks to a paper-towel-lined plate to drain. Discard oil. Season leeks with salt and pepper.

4. In the same saucepan, cook bacon until brown and crispy. Remove bacon, but reserve its drippings. Place bacon on paper towels. When drained, crumble.

5. Add remaining 1/2 cup leeks and the thyme to the skillet. Cook until soft.

6. Add 1/2 cup chicken broth and cook uncovered until broth is reduced by half.

7. Add cream. Cook until the creamy broth is reduced by half.

8. Stir in peas, crumbled bacon, and the remaining 1/2 cup broth. Bring to a boil.

9. If using fresh thyme sprigs, discard. Season cooked mixture with salt and pepper.

10. In a small bowl, stir cornstarch into water until smooth. Stir into hot sauce. Continue stirring until it thickens slightly.

11. Spoon the peas into a serving dish and top with the reserved crispy leeks just before serving.

A Tip —

To save peeling time when using fresh toma-toes, dip the tomatoes into boiling water until their skins begin to crack. Then the skins will peel off eas-ily.

Stuffed Peppers

Stacy Schmucker Stoltzfus
Enola, PA

Makes 4 servings

Prep Time: 15-20 minutes
Baking Time: 25 minutes

4 large bell peppers of any
  color
1/2 lb. ground beef
half or a whole onion,
  diced
1/2–1 cup cooked rice *or*
  corn
1/4 cup crushed soda
  crackers
3/4 cup chopped tomatoes
salt and pepper to taste
1/4 cup grated cheese of
  your choice

1. Cut peppers in half through their stem ends. Seed and de-vein. In covered pan, par-boil for 5 minutes in 1 inch of water. Drain and cool.

2. In a skillet, brown meat and onion. Drain.

3. In a mixing bowl, stir together meat and onion, rice, crackers, tomatoes, salt, and pepper.

4. Place peppers in a greased 9 x 13 pan and divide the meat mixture among the halves.

5. Bake, uncovered, at 350° for 20 minutes. Remove from oven and top with cheese.

6. Turn oven to 400°. Return pan to oven and heat stuffed peppers for 5 more minutes.

Aunt Mary's Baked Corn

Becky Frey
Lebanon, PA
Doris Beachy
Stevens, PA
Cynthia Morris
Grottoes, VA
Susie Nisley
Millersburg, OH

Makes 4-5 servings
Makes 1½-2-quart casserole

Prep Time: 15 minutes
Standing Time: 1 hour
Baking Time: 1 hour

1½ cups milk
3 Tbsp. butter
3 cups creamed corn,
   fresh, frozen, *or* canned
3 Tbsp. cornstarch
3 eggs, beaten
2 Tbsp. sugar
1 tsp. salt
⅛ tsp. pepper

1. In a small saucepan, heat milk until it forms a skin but does not boil. Stir in butter.
2. While butter melts, mix corn and cornstarch in a good-sized mixing bowl until cornstarch is dissolved. Add beaten eggs, sugar, and seasonings. Mix in milk and butter.
3. Put in a greased 1½-2-qt. baking dish.
4. Let stand for 1 hour.
5. Bake, uncovered, at 350° for 1 hour, or until set in the middle.

When my mom's cousins had their annual Christmas dinner at a local firehall, we always had ham, candied sweet potatoes, and baked corn, among other things. (The second cousins brought cookies, and we had many varieties to choose from after the main course!)

Becky Frey
Lebanon, PA

Squash Apple Bake

Lavina Hochstedler
Grand Blanc, MI

Makes 8 servings

Prep Time: 20 minutes
Baking Time: 45-50 minutes

3 Tbsp. brown sugar
⅓ cup orange juice, *or*
   apple juice, *or* apple
   cider
4 cups cubed butternut *or*
   buttercup squash
salt
2 apples, cored and thinly
   sliced
¼ cup raisins
cinnamon
1 Tbsp. butter

1. Combine brown sugar and juice in a small mixing bowl. Set aside.
2. Place half the cubed squash in a greased 2-qt. baking dish. Sprinkle with salt.
3. Follow with a layer of half the apples and raisins.

Sprinkle generously with cinnamon.
4. Repeat the layers.
5. Pour juice mixture over all. Dot with butter.
6. Cover and bake at 350° for 45-50 minutes, or until tender.

Variation: Stir 1 Tbsp. orange rind into Step 1.
   — **Christie Detamore-Hunsberger**
Harrisonburg, VA

Baked Sweet Potatoes

Mable Hershey
Marietta, PA

Makes 16-20 servings

Prep Time: 30 minutes
Baking Time: 1-1½ hours

16-20 medium-sized raw
   orange yams, *or* sweet
   potatoes
3-4 Tbsp. butter
1½ Tbsp. flour
1 tsp. salt
1 cup light brown sugar
½ cup dark corn syrup
½ cup water

1. In a large stockpot, boil sweet potatoes for 10 minutes, or until they slightly soften.
2. Peel and arrange in a greased 9 x 13 baking dish.
3. In a saucepan, melt butter. Add flour, salt, brown

sugar, syrup, and water. Stir until well blended.

4. Cook until slightly thickened.

5. Pour over sweet potatoes. Bake, uncovered, at 350° for 1-1½ hours, or until sauce carmelizes over potatoes. Baste potatoes every 10-15 minutes with the sauce during the baking time.

Variations:

1. Substitute 1 cup apricot nectar for the water and 3 Tbsp. cornstarch for 1½ Tbsp. flour.

— **Mable Hershey**
Marietta, PA

2. After pouring sauce over potatoes, top them with 8 marshmallows cut into pieces and ½ cup chopped nuts. Pour 1 cup light cream over all.

— **Emma Oberholtzer**
Bamberg, SC

Harvest Sweet Potato Bake

Ellie Oberholtzer
Smoketown, PA

Makes 8 servings

Prep Time: 15 minutes
Cooking/Baking Time:
1½-2 hours

6 cups mashed sweet potatoes (3-4 lbs. uncooked sweet potatoes)
6 Tbsp. melted butter
6 eggs, beaten

2 tsp. salt
1 can evaporated milk
peeled apple slices

Crumb mixture:
6 Tbsp. butter
6 Tbsp. flour
3/4-1 cup brown sugar
1½ tsp. cardamom
2/3 cup pecans, chopped

1. Place whole, unpeeled sweet potatoes in a large stockpot. Add several inches of water, cover, and cook over medium heat until very soft.

2. Cool the cooked potatoes until you can handle them. Peel. Place in mixer or food processor and mash until creamy.

3. Add butter, eggs, salt, and evaporated milk. Mix until thoroughly blended. Place in large greased baking dish.

4. Arrange apple slices over top to cover.

5. While the potatoes are cooking, melt 6 Tbsp. butter in saucepan. Stir in remaining crumb mixture ingredients. Sprinkle over apples in baking dish.

6. Cover baking dish and bake at 350° for 1 hour.

Variations: To prepare a dish with fewer calories, substitute egg beaters for the 6 eggs, use low-fat or fat-free evaporated milk, and reduce the butter blended into the potatoes to 3 Tbsp.

Spiced Sweet Potatoes

J.B. Miller
Indianapolis, IN

Makes 4 servings

Prep Time: 10-15 minutes
Baking Time: 30-40 minutes

1 tsp. coriander seeds
1/2 tsp. fennel seeds
1/2 tsp. dried oregano
1/2 tsp. dried hot red pepper flakes
1 tsp. salt
1 lb. medium-sized sweet potatoes
3 Tbsp. vegetable oil

1. Coarsely grind all spices in coffee/spice grinder. (This yields a potent flavor, releasing the oils just before they're added to the other ingredients.) Add salt.

2. Cut potatoes lengthwise into 1"-wide wedges. Place them in a large mixing bowl. Toss them with the vegetable oil and spice mixture.

3. When well coated, place them in a single layer on a greased baking sheet.

4. Bake at 425° for 15 minutes. Turn them over and bake another 15 minutes, or until soft. Check the potatoes ever 5 minutes after you've turned them over to be sure they don't burn.

Yam Fries

Kathy Keener Shantz
Lancaster, PA

Makes 6 servings

Prep Time: 10 minutes
Baking Time: 20 minutes

2 Tbsp. olive oil
1 tsp. salt
1 tsp. pepper
1 tsp. curry
1/2 tsp. hot sauce
4 medium-sized yams,
    sliced like French fries

1. In a large mixing bowl, combine oil, salt, pepper, curry, and hot sauce.
2. Stir in sliced yams.
3. When thoroughly coated, spread on lightly greased baking sheet.
4. Bake at 375° for 20 minutes, or until tender.

A Tip —

Yams and sweet potatoes are not the same. Yams are much drier. Likewise, there are many varieties of apples, from very tart to very sweet, firm texture to soft. Experiment with different kinds to discover your favorite for a recipe.

Baked Beans

Linda E. Wilcox
Blythewood, SC

Makes 5 servings

Prep Time: 5-10 minutes
Cooking Time: 20 minutes
    in microwave

6 slices bacon
1/2 cup chopped onions
3 11-oz. cans pork and
    beans, drained
1/2 cup brown sugar
1 apple, chopped
1 Tbsp. prepared mustard
1 1/2 tsp. Worcestershire
    sauce
1/2 cup ketchup
1/2 cup raisins

1. Sauté bacon in skillet until brown. Remove bacon from skillet. Drain and crumble. (Reserve 1 Tbsp. drippings.)
2. Sauté onions in bacon drippings.
3. Combine all ingredients in a large bowl. Pour into a greased 2-qt. microwavable baking dish.
4. Cook on high in microwave for 10 minutes. Stir. Place a piece of waxed paper on top of dish and microwave an additional 10 minutes.

Baked Lima Beans

Jean Butzer, Batavia, NY

Makes 8-10 servings

Prep Time: 5-10 minutes
Soaking Time: 8 hours,
    or overnight
Cooking Time: 1 hour,
    plus 2 hours

1 lb. dried lima beans
3/4 cup brown sugar
1/2 cup butter, at room
    temperature
2 tsp. salt
1 Tbsp. dried mustard
2 Tbsp. light corn syrup
1 cup sour cream

1. Place beans in a large soup pot and cover with water. Allow to soak for 8 hours, or overnight.
2. Cook in soaking water, covered, until almost tender. Drain and rinse.
3. In a large mixing bowl, combine cooked beans, brown sugar, butter, salt, mustard, corn syrup, and sour cream. Pour into a greased 2 1/2-qt. casserole and cover.
4. Bake at 300° for 2 hours, stirring several times.
5. Mixture will be thin when taken from the oven, but it thickens as it cools.

Many Beans Casserole

Donna Neiter, Wausau, WI

Makes 8 servings

Prep Time: 20 minutes
Baking Time: 45 minutes

1/2 lb. bacon, diced
1/2 lb. ground beef
1 cup chopped onions
28-oz. can pork and beans
15-oz. can lima beans,
    drained and rinsed
15-oz. can kidney beans,
    drained and rinsed
15-oz. can butter beans,
    drained and rinsed
1/2 cup barbecue sauce
1/2 cup ketchup
1/2 cup sugar
1/2 cup brown sugar
2 Tbsp. prepared mustard
2 Tbsp. molasses
1 tsp. salt
1/2 tsp. chili powder

1. In a large skillet, brown bacon and beef. Drain, retaining 1 Tbsp. drippings. Cook onions in drippings until just tender.

2. Transfer to a greased 2½-quart baking dish. Add beans and mix well.

3. In a small bowl, combine barbecue sauce, ketchup, sugar, brown sugar, mustard, molasses, salt, and chili powder. Stir combination into beef and bean mixture.

4. Cover and bake at 350° for 30 minutes. Uncover and bake for 15 minutes.

Variations:
1. Use 1 lb. bulk sausage of your preference instead of the bacon and ground beef.
— **Karen Denney**
Roswell, GA

2. Stir 1 or 2 6.5-oz. cans mushroom stems and pieces, drained, into Step 2.
— **Ruth Shank**
Gridley, IL

Spicy Green Beans

Miriam Kauffman
Harrisonburg, VA

Makes 8 servings

Prep Time: 25 minutes
Cooking and Baking Time:
    75 minutes

3 cups canned tomatoes
2 Tbsp. minced onions
2 Tbsp. diced celery
1/2-1 tsp. dried oregano,
    according to your taste
    preference
1/2-1 tsp. chili powder,
    according to your taste
    preference
1 Tbsp. sugar
1 bay leaf
dash of red pepper
1/2 tsp. garlic salt
1/8 tsp. ground cloves
1/8 tsp. pepper
2 Tbsp. flour
1 qt. canned green beans
1/2 cup buttered bread
    crumbs *or* grated cheese

1. In a large saucepan, combine all ingredients except flour, beans, and bread crumbs. Simmer, covered, for 15 minutes.

2. Meanwhile, drain the beans, reserving 2 Tbsp. liquid. Place the beans in a large mixing bowl.

3. Pour the reserved bean liquid into a small bowl. Mix in flour to form a paste.

4. Add the paste to the tomato mixture. Cook until thickened. Pour thickened sauce over beans. Stir well.

5. Place mixture in a greased 3-qt. baking dish. Bake, covered, at 350° for 45 minutes.

6. Top with buttered crumbs or grated cheese. Bake, uncovered, an additional 15 minutes.

A Tip —

Broccoli stems are usable if you peel them and cut them into bite-sized pieces.

Sweet and Sour Beets

Shirley Taylor
Yuba City, CA

Makes 6 servings

Prep Time: 10 minutes
Cooking Time: 30 minutes

1/2 cup sugar
1 Tbsp. cornstarch
1/2 tsp. salt
2 whole cloves
1/2 cup vinegar
3 15-oz. cans sliced beets, drained
3 Tbsp. orange marmalade
2 Tbsp. butter *or* margarine

1. Combine sugar, cornstarch, salt, and cloves in a large heavy saucepan. Stir in vinegar. Cook over medium heat, stirring constantly, until thickened and bubbly.

2. Add beets to sauce. Cover and cook 15 minutes.

3. Stir in marmalade and butter until both melt.

Amish Onion Pie

Kathi Rogge, Alexandria, IN

Makes 6-8 servings

Prep Time: 30 minutes
Cooking/Baking Time:
75 minutes

4 thick slices of bacon, diced
2 cups chopped onions
1 cup sour cream
2 eggs, lightly beaten
1 Tbsp. flour
1/2 tsp. salt
1/4 tsp. pepper
9" pie shell, unbaked
caraway seeds, *optional*

1. Sauté bacon in a large skillet until evenly browned. Drain, but reserve 2 Tbsp. drippings. Crumble bacon and set aside.

2. Sauté onions in reserved bacon drippings until clear. Return crumbled bacon to skillet.

3. Stir in sour cream, eggs, flour, salt, and pepper. Mix well.

4. Pour filling into pie crust.

5. Sprinkle with caraway seeds, if you wish.

6. Bake at 425° for 1 hour, or until onions are golden brown.

A Tip —

A few drops of lemon juice added to simmering rice will keep the grains separated.

Up-Town Rice

Judy Buller
Bluffton, OH

Makes 8 servings

Prep Time: 15-20 minutes
Cooking/Baking Time:
55 minutes

1 1/2 cups uncooked white rice
1/2 lb. sliced fresh, *or* 4-oz. can sliced, mushrooms
1/2 cup slivered almonds
2 Tbsp. chopped onions
1 stick (1/2 cup) butter
3 cups chicken broth
1 Tbsp. parsley

1. Sauté rice, mushrooms, almonds, and onions in butter for 10-15 minutes on medium heat, stirring constantly. When almonds look slightly toasted and rice has a yellow cast, remove from heat.

2. Add broth and parsley and mix well. Pour into a greased 3-qt. casserole dish.

3. Cover and bake at 325° for 40 minutes.

4. Stir before serving.

Variations:

1. Add 1/2 cup chopped celery to Step 1.

2. Instead of 3 cups chicken broth, use 14-oz. can chicken broth, 1/3 cup water, and 1-2 Tbsp. soy sauce.

— **Amber Swarey**
Honea Path, SC

Green Chili Rice

John D. Allen
Rye, CO

Makes 6 servings

Prep Time: 20 minutes
Baking Time: 35 minutes

3/4-lb. block Monterey Jack cheese
3 cups sour cream
2 4-oz. cans chopped green chilies, drained
3 cups cooked white rice
salt to taste
pepper to taste
1/2 cup grated cheddar cheese

1. Cut Monterey Jack cheese into strips.
2. In a small bowl, combine sour cream and chilies.
3. Season rice with salt and pepper.
4. Layer one-third of the rice, half the sour cream mixture, and half the cheese strips into a greased casserole dish. Repeat the layers, ending with a layer of rice on top.
5. Bake, covered, at 350° for 25 minutes. Remove cover and top dish with grated cheddar cheese. Bake an additional 10 minutes, uncovered.

Variation: Replace rice with cooked macaronis or hominy.

Spinach Potatoes

Janet Derstine
Telford, PA

Makes 6-8 servings

Prep Time: 25 minutes
Baking Time: 25 minutes

6 medium-sized potatoes, cooked soft
2 tsp. chives
1 cup sour cream
1 stick (1/4 lb.) butter, at room temperature
1 cup grated cheese of your choice
1/4 tsp. dill weed
1-2 tsp. salt, according to your taste preference
1/4 tsp. pepper
10-oz. box frozen chopped spinach, thawed and squeezed dry

1. Mash all ingredients together except spinach.
2. When thoroughly blended, stir in spinach until well distributed.
3. Place in greased casserole dish and bake for 25 minutes, uncovered, at 350°.

Variation: Instead of 1 cup grated cheese, use 8-oz. pkg. cream cheese at room temperature.

— **Doyle Rounds**
Bridgewater, VA

Potatoes and Onions

Christie Anne Detamore-Hunsberger
Harrisonburg, VA

Makes 8-10 servings

Prep Time: 15-20 minutes
Baking Time: 1 hour

6 large potatoes, thickly sliced
4 to 6 medium-sized onions, thinly sliced
1/4-1/2 cup butter
1 large garlic clove, minced
1/4 tsp. pepper
1/4 tsp. celery seed
paprika

1. Cover bottom of a greased 9 x 13 glass baking dish with half the potato slices. Top with half the onion slices. Create a second layer of potatoes followed by a second layer of onion slices.
2. Melt butter in a small saucepan. Stir in garlic, pepper, and celery seed. Pour over potatoes and onions.
3. Bake at 400° for 40 minutes, covered with foil.
4. Remove from oven and sprinkle with paprika.
5. Bake for an additional 20 minutes, uncovered.

A Tip —

Pricking potatoes all over with a fork before baking prevents the potato from exploding.

Potato Casserole

Marilyn Wanner
New Holland, PA

Makes 6-8 servings

Prep Time: 30-40 minutes
Baking Time: 40-45 minutes

6-8 medium red potatoes,
  cooked and diced
1/2 cup sour cream
1/2 cup Ranch dressing
1/4 cup fried bacon,
  crumbled
2 Tbsp. chopped parsley
1 cup shredded cheddar
  cheese
2 cups cornflakes, crushed
1/4 cup butter, melted

1. Layer potatoes in a
greased 9 x 13 baking pan.
2. In a small bowl, mix
together sour cream and
Ranch dressing. Spread over
potatoes.
3. Sprinkle with bacon,
parsley, and cheese.
4. In the small bowl, mix
together cornflakes and butter. Top casserole with mixture.
5. Bake, uncovered, at
350° for 40-45 minutes.

*Tips: Crush the cornflakes in a
plastic bag for less mess.*
  *Don't peel the potatoes if
you want to retain their beauti-
ful color.*

Cottage Potatoes

Janice Yoskovich
Carmichaels, PA

Makes 6 servings

Prep Time: 30 minutes
Baking Time: 45-60 minutes

6 large potatoes, cooked
  and diced
half an onion, diced
half a green pepper, diced
3 slices of bread, broken
  into pieces
1/2 lb. cheddar cheese,
  cubed
3/4 tsp. salt
1/4 tsp. pepper
1 stick (8 Tbsp.) butter

1. In a large mixing bowl,
combine potatoes, onions,
green pepper, bread, cheese,
salt, and pepper.
2. Melt butter in a small
saucepan and pour over all.
3. Spoon into a 2-qt. baking dish.
4. Bake, covered, at 350°
for 45-60 minutes.

A Tip —

As you dice, slice, or
shred raw potatoes, put
them in cold water to keep
them from turning
brown/gray. Drain them
when you are ready to use
them.

Crusty Twice-Baked Potatoes

Amy Jensen, Fountain, CO

Makes 4 servings

Prep Time: 10 minutes
Baking Time: 60-65 minutes

4 large baking potatoes
1/2 cup melted butter
3/4 cup cornflake crumbs
2 Tbsp. sesame seeds
1 tsp. salt
1/4 tsp. pepper
1/2 tsp. garlic powder

1. Scrub potatoes. Prick
with a fork and bake at 425°
for 45 minutes, or until tender
but not mushy.
2. Remove from oven and
cool. Peel, keeping the potatoes whole.
3. Cut deep gashes, 1/4"
apart, crosswise across the top
and almost through to the bottom of each potato. Brush surface and inside each gash with
melted butter.
4. Combine crumbs, seeds,
salt, pepper, and garlic powder in a mixing bowl.
5. Spoon crumb mixture
over potatoes, spreading each
one slightly so the crumbs fall
between the gashes.
6. Place potatoes cut-side
up in a 9 x 13, or other shallow, baking dish. Bake at 375°
for 15-20 minutes, or until
heated through and browned.

*Variation: Crumble bleu
cheese over the crumb-topped
potatoes, just before Step 6.*

Golden Potato Casserole

Andrea Igoe
Poughkeepsie, NY

Makes 8 servings

Prep Time: 20 minutes
Cooking/Baking Time:
1 1/2-2 hours
Chilling Time: 3-4 hours, or
overnight

8 large potatoes
8 ozs. cheddar cheese,
grated
1 bunch of scallions,
chopped fine
1 tsp. salt
1/8 tsp. pepper
2 cups (1 pt.) sour cream
3-4 Tbsp. milk
3/4 cup bread crumbs
4 Tbsp. butter, melted

1. Boil potatoes until tender but firm. Chill thoroughly 3-4 hours or overnight. Peel and grate.
2. In a large mixing bowl, stir cheese and grated potatoes together.
3. Fold in scallions, salt, pepper, sour cream, and milk. Mix well.
4. Spread in a greased 9 x 13 baking dish.
5. Combine bread crumbs and butter. Sprinkle over potatoes.
6. Bake at 350° for 60 minutes.

Potluck Potatoes

Mattie Yoder,
Millersburg, OH

Makes 15 servings

Prep Time: 45-50 minutes
Chilling Time: 3 hours
Cooking/ Baking Time:
1 hour and 45 minutes

2 lbs. potatoes
1 1/2 sticks (3/4 cup) butter,
divided
1 pint sour cream
2 cups Velveeta cheese,
cubed
1 tsp. salt
1 tsp. pepper
10.75-oz. can cream of
chicken soup
2 cups crushed cornflakes

1. Peel potatoes. Cook in large stockpot until soft. Cool in refrigerator.
2. When potatoes are fully chilled, shred or put through ricer into a large mixing bowl.
3. Melt 1 stick (1/2 cup) butter in a large saucepan. Stir in sour cream, Velveeta, salt, pepper, and soup. Heat over low heat until cheese is melted.
4. Pour over shredded potatoes and mix gently but well. Spoon into a 5-quart greased casscrole.
5. In a saucepan, melt remaining half stick of butter. Stir in crushed cornflakes. Top casserole with mixture.
6. Bake, uncovered, at 350° for 45 minutes.

Variation: Use cream of celery soup instead of cream of chicken soup.
— Jere Zimmerman
Reinholds, PA

Crusty Baked Potatoes

Anna Stoltzfus, Honey Brook, PA

Makes 6 servings

Prep Time: 15 minutes
Baking Time: 60 minutes

1 cup cracker crumbs
1/2 tsp. salt
1 tsp. dried oregano
1 tsp. seasoning salt
1 tsp. parsley flakes
4 Tbsp. butter, melted
4 medium-sized potatoes,
sliced

1. In a shallow bowl, add seasonings to cracker crumbs.
2. Place melted butter in another shallow bowl.
3. Dip potato slices in butter. Then dredge in cracker crumbs.
4. When coated, place slices in a greased baking dish.
5. Bake, uncovered, at 375° for 60 minutes.

A Tip —

Add 1/2 tsp. baking powder to every 2 cups of potatoes to mash. Sprinkle it into the potatoes before adding milk. This helps to keep them white and not stiffen up.

Oven-Fried Potatoes

Robin Schrock, Millersburg, OH

Makes 8 servings

Prep Time: 10 minutes
Baking Time: 1 hour

4 large baking potatoes,
    unpeeled
1/3 cup vegetable oil
2 Tbsp. Parmesan cheese
1/2 tsp. salt
1/4 tsp. garlic powder
1/4 tsp. paprika
1/8 tsp. pepper

1. Cut each potato lengthwise into 6 wedges.
2. Place wedges skin-side down in a greased 9 x 13 baking dish.
3. In a mixing bowl, combine oil, cheese, salt, garlic powder, paprika, and pepper. Brush over potatoes.

Or, mix all ingredients except the potatoes in a large mixing bowl. When thoroughly blended, stir in potato wedges. Stir until they're well covered. Then place in a single layer in the baking dish.
4. Bake at 375° for 1 hour.

Variation: To create a crustier finish on the potatoes, add 3 Tbsp. flour to Step 3. And increase the Parmesan cheese to 1/3 cup.

— **Jere Zimmerman**
    Reinholds, PA
— **Jena Hammond**
    Traverse City, MI
— **Sara Wilson**
    Blairstown, MO

Corn Bread Stuffing

Janice Muller
Derwood, MD

Makes 4 servings

Prep Time: 15 minutes
Baking Time: 30 minutes

1 cup chopped onions
1 cup chopped celery
1 stick (1/2 cup) butter
8-oz. pkg. corn bread
    stuffing
16-oz. jar applesauce
1/2 tsp. dried thyme
1/2 tsp. dried marjoram
1/2 tsp. poultry seasoning
1/4 tsp. lemon-pepper
1/3 cup boiling water

1. In a large skillet, sauté onions and celery in butter until soft.
2. Add stuffing mix, applesauce, herbs, and seasoning, and boiling water. Toss until evenly moist.
3. Stuff turkey, or if baking separately, spoon into a buttered 1-qt. baking dish.
4. Cover with foil. Put in a 325° oven during the last 30 minutes that your turkey is baking. Or bake at 325° for 30 minutes on its own.

Potato Filling

Joanne E. Martin
Stevens, PA

Makes 6-8 servings

Prep Time: 30-40 minutes
Cooking/Baking Time:
    1 1/2-2 hours

2 lbs. potatoes
1/2 cup finely chopped
    onions
1/2 cup finely chopped
    celery
1 1/2 sticks (3/4 cup) butter
4 cups bread cubes
2 tsp. salt
1/2 tsp. pepper
1 Tbsp. parsley
2 eggs, beaten
1 cup milk

1. Peel potatoes and cut into quarters. Cook in several inches of water, covered. When very soft, mash potatoes. (You'll need 4 cups mashed for this dish. If you've got more, save them for another dish!)
2. Meanwhile, in a skillet, sauté onions and celery in butter till soft.
3. In a large mixing bowl, mix bread cubes, salt, pepper, parsley, eggs, milk, sautéed vegetables, and mashed potatoes together until well blended.
4. Pour into a greased baking dish. Bake, uncovered, at 350° for 1 hour.

Salads

Festive Tossed Salad

Cheryl A. Lapp
Parkesburg, PA
Yvonne Kauffman Boettger
Harrisonburg, VA
Sally Holzem
Schofield, WI

Makes 8-10 servings

Prep Time: 30 minutes

1/2 cup sugar
1/3 cup cider *or* red wine
   vinegar
2 Tbsp. lemon juice
2 Tbsp. finely chopped
   onions
1/2 tsp. salt
2/3 cup olive oil
2 tsp. poppy seeds
10 cups torn romaine
   lettuce
1 cup shredded Swiss
   cheese

1 medium-sized apple,
   cored and cubed
1 medium-sized pear,
   cored and cubed
1/4 cup dried cranberries
1/2 cup chopped cashews

1. In a blender, combine first 5 ingredients until well blended.
2. With a blender running, gradually add oil. Add poppy seeds and blend.
3. In salad bowl, combine lettuce, cheese, apple, pear, and cranberries.
4. Just before serving, drizzle salad with desired amount of dressing. (You'll have more dressing than you need, so save what's left for a future salad.) Add cashews and toss to coat.

Variation: Add 1 tsp. Dijon mustard to the dressing in Step 1.

— **Jennifer Eberly**
Harrisonburg, VA

A Tip —

If you're delayed in tossing a salad, you can keep the greens fresh under a drape of paper towels, wrung out of ice water.

Dried Cherry Salad

Stacy Schmucker Stoltzfus
Enola, PA

Makes 12 servings

Prep Time: 20 minutes
Cooking Time: 10 minutes

half a head of romaine
    lettuce, chopped
half a head of red leaf
    lettuce, chopped
half a large red onion,
    sliced
1 cup dried cherries
1 cup feta cheese
1/3 cup sugar
1 cup pecan halves

Raspberry Dressing:
4 Tbsp. raspberry vinegar
1/2 tsp. Tabasco sauce
1/2 tsp. salt
4 Tbsp. sugar
pepper to taste
1 Tbsp. chopped parsley
1/2 cup vegetable oil

1. Place lettuces in a large salad bowl. Sprinkle with onion slices, dried cherries, and feta cheese.

2. In skillet, over medium heat, combine 1/3 cup sugar and pecans. Stir constantly until sugar melts and pecans are coated. Immediately pour pecans onto waxed paper to cool.

3. Sprinkle cooled nuts over salad.

4. To make dressing, combine vinegar, Tabasco sauce, salt, 4 Tbsp. sugar, pepper, and parsley in a small mixing bowl.

While whisking, slowly pour in oil until emulsified. Just before serving, pour over salad.

Caesar Salad

Colleen Heatwole
Burton, MI

Makes 8 servings

Prep Time: 15-20 minutes

8-12 cups romaine lettuce,
    or spring mix, torn into
    bite-sized pieces
1/3 cup oil
3 Tbsp. red wine vinegar
1 tsp. Worcestershire sauce
1/2 tsp. salt
3/4 tsp. dry mustard
    powder
1 large garlic clove, minced
11/2–2 Tbsp. fresh lemon
    juice
dash of pepper
1/4-1/2 cup grated Parmesan
    cheese
2 cups Caesar-flavored,
    or garlic, croutons

1. Place lettuce in a large bowl.

2. Combine next 6 ingredients in a blender or food processor.

3. Add fresh lemon juice and process until smooth.

4. Just before serving, toss with lettuce.

5. Sprinkle with pepper. Add Parmesan cheese and toss well. Serve croutons separately.

Tips:

1. *I have made this on more Sundays than I can count. I prepare the lettuce, blend the 6 ingredients, and get the hard cheese ready for my son to grate. I always use fresh lemon or fresh lime.*

2. *My family prefers a tart dressing. My friend adds 1 Tbsp. sugar.*

Greek Salad

Ruth Feister
Narvon, PA

Makes 8 servings

Prep Time: 20 minutes

head of torn romaine
    lettuce
1 medium-sized cucumber
    sliced thin
2 medium-sized tomatoes,
    cut in pieces
half a red onion, finely
    chopped
parsley
4-oz. can sliced black
    olives, drained
3-4 ozs. crumbled feta
    cheese
several artichoke hearts,
    quartered

Dressing:
1/4 cup chicken stock
2 Tbsp. red wine vinegar
2 tsp. lemon juice
1 tsp. sugar
1/2 tsp. dried basil
1/2 tsp. dried oregano

1. Combine dressing ingredients in a jar with a tightly fitting lid. Shake until mixed well.

2. Place lettuce, cucumber, tomatoes, onions, and parsley in a large serving bowl.

3. Just before serving, drizzle with dressing and toss.

4. Top with olives, cheese, and artichoke hearts.

Bibb Lettuce with Pecans and Oranges

Betty K. Drescher
Quakertown, PA

Makes 8 servings

Prep Time: 10-15 minutes

4 heads Bibb lettuce
3/4 cup pecan halves, toasted
2 oranges, peeled and sliced

Dressing:
1/3 cup vinegar
1/2 cup sugar
1 cup vegetable oil
1/2 tsp. salt
half a small onion, chopped
1 tsp. dry mustard
2 Tbsp. water

1. Place lettuce, pecans, and oranges in a salad bowl.

2. Combine dressing ingredients in blender. (You can make this ahead of time and refrigerate it.)

3. Toss dressing with salad ingredients just before serving.

Grand Tossed Salad

Kathy Hertzler
Lancaster, PA
Carol Stroh
Akron, NY

Makes 8 servings

Prep Time: 45-60 minutes
Cooking Time: 10 minutes

1/2 cup sliced almonds
8 tsp. sugar
medium-sized head of romaine lettuce
medium-sized head of red *or* green leaf lettuce
2 green onions, sliced
2 ribs of celery, sliced
11-oz. can mandarin oranges, drained
1/4 cup oil
2 Tbsp. sugar
2 Tbsp. white wine vinegar
1 Tbsp. snipped parsley
1/4 tsp. salt
Tabasco sauce to taste

1. Cook almonds and sugar over low heat, stirring constantly until sugar is melted and almonds are coated. Cool and break apart.

2. Toss together lettuces, onions, celery, oranges, and sugared almonds.

3. Blend together oil, sugar, vinegar, parsley, salt, and Tabasco sauce. Just before serving, pour over salad. Toss to mix.

Blueberry Spinach Salad

Judi Robb
Manhattan, KS

Makes 6-8 servings

Prep Time: 15-20 minutes

1/2 cup vegetable oil
1/4 cup raspberry vinegar
2 tsp. Dijon mustard
1 tsp.-1 Tbsp. sugar, according to your taste preference
1/2 tsp. salt
10-oz. pkg. fresh torn spinach
4-oz. pkg. bleu cheese, crumbled
1 cup fresh blueberries
1/2 cup chopped pecans, tasted

1. In a jar with a tight-fitting lid, combine oil, vinegar, mustard, sugar, and salt. Shake well.

2. In a large salad bowl, toss spinach, bleu cheese, blueberries, and pecans.

3. Just before serving, add dressing and toss gently.

Spinach Salad with Walnut Dressing

Dolores Metzler
Lewistown, PA

Makes 8 servings

Prep Time: 15 minutes
Standing Time: 30 minutes

Dressing:
1/4 cup vegetable oil
1 Tbsp. honey
1/4 tsp. salt
2 Tbsp. lemon juice
2 tsp. Dijon mustard
dash of pepper
2/3 cup walnuts, chopped
2 Tbsp. sliced green onions

Salad:
4-6 cups spinach and/*or*
other greens
1 cup diced Swiss cheese
1 cup diced fresh fruit
(apples, peaches, and
pears are all good,
dipped in lemon juice to
keep from discoloring)

1. Mix oil, honey, salt,
lemon juice, mustard, pepper,
walnuts, and onions in a jar
with a tight-fitting lid.

2. Cover and shake until
well mixed. Then let stand
for 30 minutes to enhance flavor.

3. Mix spinach, Swiss
cheese, and diced fruit in a
large mixing bowl.

4. Just before serving, add
dressing to salad and toss
together.

Spinach-Strawberry Salad

Pat Bechtel
Dillsburg, PA
Sarah M. Balmer
Manheim, PA

Makes 6-8 servings

Prep Time: 20 minutes

12 ozs. fresh spinach
1 qt. fresh strawberries,
sliced
2 Tbsp. sesame seeds
1 Tbsp. poppy seeds

Dressing:
1/2 cup vegetable oil
1/2 cup sugar
1 1/2 tsp. grated onion
1/4 tsp. Worcestershire
sauce
1/4 tsp. paprika
1/4 cup cider vinegar

1. Layer spinach, strawberries, sesame seeds, and poppy
seeds in a large salad bowl.

2. Combine the dressing
ingredients in a blender.
Blend for 2 minutes.

3. Just before serving pour
the dressing over the spinach
and toss lightly to coat the
spinach and berries.

*This is one of our favorite
salads. I make the dressing and
store it in the refrigerator. Then
I make the amount of salad I
want and just add as much
dressing as it needs.*

Variations:

*1. For the dressing, use 1/4
cup honey, heated until thin,
instead of the 1/2 cup sugar.*
— **Ellie Oberholtzer**
Smoketown, PA

*2. To the salad itself, add 1
cup shredded Monterey Jack
cheese and 1/2 cup chopped walnuts.*

— **Tina Snyder**
Manheim, PA

Salad with Hot Bacon Dressing

Joanne E. Martin
Stevens, PA

*Makes 8-10 servings
(2 cups dressing)*

Prep Time: 15 minutes
Cooking Time: 7 minutes

6-8 strips of bacon
1 1/2 cups sugar
2 eggs, beaten
1/3 cup vinegar
2/3 cup water

salad greens
grated carrots
hard-cooked eggs

1. In a skillet, brown
bacon. Drain off drippings.
Crumble and set aside.

2. In the same skillet, mix
sugar, beaten eggs, vinegar,
and water. Bring to boil, stirring up browned bacon drippings. Stir dressing until
slightly thickened.

3. Stir in bacon.

4. Just before serving, toss warm salad dressing with mixture of salad greens, grated carrots, and hard-cooked eggs.

Black Bean Taco Salad with Lime Vinaigrette

Joy Sutter
Perkasie, PA

Makes 4-6 servings

Prep Time: 15-20 minutes (if the chicken is already cooked)

Vinaigrette:
1/4 cup chopped, seeded tomatoes
1/4 cup chopped fresh cilantro
2 Tbsp. olive oil
1 Tbsp. cider vinegar
1 tsp. grated lime rind
1 Tbsp. fresh lime juice
1/4 tsp. salt
1/4 tsp. ground cumin
1/4 tsp. chili powder
1/4 tsp. black pepper
1 garlic clove, peeled

Salad:
8 cups thinly sliced lettuce
1 1/2 cups roasted, boneless chicken breast pieces
1 cup chopped tomatoes
1 cup diced onions

1/2 cup sharp cheddar cheese, grated
15-oz. can black beans, drained and rinsed
4 cups tortilla chips

1. Combine vinaigrette ingredients in a blender or food processor until smooth.

2. Combine lettuce, chicken, tomatoes, onions, cheese, and black beans in a large bowl.

3. Add vinaigrette and toss well to coat. Serve with chips.

Broccoli Slaw

Bonnie Heatwole
Springs, PA

Makes 8 servings

Prep Time: 15 minutes

16-oz. pkg. broccoli slaw
1 cup sunflower seeds
1 cup slivered almonds
2 3-oz. pkgs. chicken-flavored Ramen noodles
1 cup diced green onions

Dressing:
1/2 cup oil
1/3 cup white vinegar
1/2 cup sugar
2 seasoning packets from Ramen noodles

1. Combine salad ingredients in a large bowl.

2. Shake the dressing ingredients together in a jar with a tight-fitting lid. (The dressing is probably more

than needed for the amount of salad, so begin by adding only half of what you've made. Add more if you need it.) Add the dressing right before serving. Toss to mix.

Variations:

1. Instead of broccoli slaw, use 10-oz. pkg. cole slaw mix, 6-oz. pkg. fresh spinach, and 2 cups shredded lettuce. Add 3 Tbsp. sesame seeds, lightly toasted to the salad.

— **Sharon Eshleman**
Ephrata, PA

2. Instead of broccoli slaw, use 6-oz. pkg. fresh spinach and half a head of torn romaine lettuce. Substitute walnuts or pecans for the almonds, if you wish.

— **Elena Yoder**
Carlsbad, NM
— **Colleen Heatwole**
Burton, MI
— **Betty Moore**
Plano, IL
— **Clara Newswanger**
Gordonville, PA
— **LuAnna Hochstedler**
East Earl, PA

A Tip —

For the best flavor, toast nuts before using them in a salad. But watch them carefully so they don't burn.

Broccoli Salad

Sherlyn Hess, Millersville, PA
Ruth Zendt, Mifflintown, PA

Makes 6-8 servings

Prep Time: 20 minutes
Chilling Time: 2 hours

1 cup raisins
2 cups boiling water
6 cups chopped broccoli
 tops
2/3 cup chopped red onions
10 strips of bacon, cooked
 and crumbled
1/4 cup shredded carrots
1/2 cup salad dressing
1/2 cup mayonnaise
2 Tbsp. vinegar
1/2 cup sugar

1. Soak raisins for a few minutes in boiling water. Drain.
2. Combine plumped raisins, broccoli, onions, bacon, and carrots.
3. Whisk together remaining ingredients in a separate bowl. Pour over broccoli mixture. Toss to mix.
4. Refrigerate at least 2 hours before serving.

Variations:
1. Add 1 cup grated cheese and/or 1/2 cup chopped peanuts to Step 2.
 — Ruth Zendt
 Mifflintown, PA

2. Add 1 cup chopped celery and 1/2 cup hulled sunflower seeds to Step 2.
 — Jean Butzer
 Batavia, NY

Trees & Seeds Salad

Nanci Keatley
Salem, OR

Makes 8-10 servings

Prep Time: 10-20 minutes
Chilling Time: 30 minutes

4 cups cauliflower florets
3 cups cut-up broccoli
1 cup diced red onions
2 pts. cherry tomatoes,
 halved
1/2-1 lb. bacon, cooked and
 diced, according to your
 preference
3 Tbsp. sesame seeds
1/4 cup sunflower seeds
1/4 cup slivered almonds

Dressing:
1 cup mayonnaise
1/2 cup sugar *or* sugar
 substitute
3 Tbsp. cider vinegar
1/2 tsp. salt
1/2 tsp. pepper

1. In a large serving bowl, combine cauliflower, broccoli, onions, tomatoes, bacon, seeds, and nuts.
2. In a separate bowl, mix together mayonnaise, sugar, vinegar, salt, and pepper. Pour over vegetables.
3. Refrigerate at least 30 minutes to blend flavors.

Tip: This is great to make ahead. Mix all ingredients together except the dressing. Chill, then add the dressing half an hour before serving. Refrigerate until serving time.

Variations:
 1. Change the "green" base of this salad to: 3 cups shredded cabbage or coleslaw mix; 2 cups broken cauliflower; 2 cups chopped broccoli.
 — Teresa Martin
 Gordonville, PA

 2. Add 1/3 cup grated Parmesan cheese to the Dressing in Step 2.
 — Phyllis Smith
 Goshen, IN

 3. Add 8 sliced radishes to Step 1.
 — Sara Wilson
 Blairstown, MO

Spring Pea Salad

Dottie Schmidt, Kansas City, MO

Makes 4 servings

Prep Time: 20 minutes
Chilling Time: 30 minutes

10-oz. pkg. frozen peas
1 cup diced celery
1 cup chopped fresh
 cauliflower florets
1/4 cup diced green onions
1 cup chopped cashews
1/4 cup crisp-cooked and
 crumbled bacon
1/4 cup sour cream
1/2 cup Ranch salad
 dressing

1/4 tsp. Dijon mustard
1 small clove garlic, minced

1. Thaw peas. Drain.
2. In a large mixing bowl, combine peas, celery, cauliflower, onion, cashews, and bacon with sour cream.
3. In a small bowl, mix together Ranch dressing, mustard, and minced garlic. Begin by pouring only half the dressing over salad mixture. Toss gently. Add more if needed. (The dressing amount is generous.) Chill before serving.

Creamy Coleslaw
Tammy Yoder
Belleville, PA

Makes 6 servings

Prep Time: 10 minutes
Chilling Time: 30 minutes

half a head of cabbage
1/2 cup mayonnaise
2 Tbsp. vinegar
1/3 cup sugar
pinch of salt
pinch of pepper
1 Tbsp. celery seed, *or* to taste
1/4 cup grated carrots

1. Shred cabbage. Place in a large mixing bowl.
2. Mix all remaining ingredients together in another bowl.
3. Stir dressing into shredded cabbage, mixing well.

4. Chill for 30 minutes before serving.

Variations:
1. If you're short on time, use a bag of prepared shredded cabbage with carrots.
2. For added zest, stir 1/2 tsp. dry mustard into the dressing in Step 2.
— **Maricarol Magill**
Freehold, NJ

Cabbage Slaw with Vinegar Dressing
Betty Hostetler
Allensville, PA

Makes 10-12 servings

Prep Time: 30-45 minutes
Chilling Time: 3-4 hours

8 cups grated cabbage
1/4 cup grated carrots
1/4 cup diced celery
1/4 cup chopped red pepper
1/4 cup chopped yellow pepper
1/8 cup chopped green pepper
1 Tbsp. celery seed
3/4-1 cup sugar
1 tsp. salt
1/2 cup white vinegar
1/4 cup, plus 2 Tbsp., oil

1. Combine vegetables, celery seed, sugar, and salt in a large mixing bowl. Mix well.
2. In a small saucepan, bring vinegar to a boil. Add oil. Pour over vegetables. Mix well.

3. Refrigerate for 3-4 hours before serving.

Variations:
1. Add 1 medium-sized onion, chopped to the vegetables in Step 1.
2. Reduce celery seed to 1 tsp. and add 1 1/2 tsp. mustard seed and 1/2 tsp. turmeric.
— **Emilie Kimpel**
Arcadia, MI

Cranberry Coleslaw
Carolyn Baer, Conrath, WI

Makes 6-7 servings

Prep Time: 15 minutes
Chilling Time: 45 minutes

1/2 cup mayonnaise
2 Tbsp. honey
2 Tbsp. vinegar
1/4 cup fresh cranberries, chopped, *or* snipped dried cranberries
5 cups shredded cabbage (1 small head)

1. Combine mayonnaise, honey, and vinegar. Stir in cranberries.
2. Place shredded cabbage in a large bowl.
3. Pour dressing over cabbage. Toss to coat.
4. Cover and chill for 45 minutes.

This salad is very pretty for holiday parties, but it is delicious anytime.

Crispy, Crunchy Cabbage Salad

Jolyn Nolt, Leola, PA
Karen Stoltzfus, Alto, MI
Andrea O'Neil, Fairfield, CT

Makes 4-5 servings

Prep Time: 10-15 minutes

1 whole chicken breast,
  cooked and diced,
  or 2 5-oz. cans cooked
  chicken
2 Tbsp. toasted sesame
  seeds
2 ozs. slivered toasted
  almonds
half a head of cabbage,
  shredded fine
2 green onions, sliced
30-oz. pkg. chicken-
  flavored dry Ramen
  noodles

Dressing:
1 pkg. Ramen noodle
  seasoning mix
3 Tbsp. sugar
1/2 cup vegetable oil
3 Tbsp. red wine vinegar
1/2 tsp. salt
1/2 tsp. pepper

1. In a large bowl, com-
bine chicken with sesame
seeds, almonds, cabbage,
onions, and uncooked noo-
dles, broken apart.
2. In a separate bowl, mix
dressing ingredients together,
stirring until dry ingredients
are dissolved. Add to salad
ingredients. Toss together
gently.

3. Cover and refrigerate
until serving time.

*Tip: This salad is also tasty
without the chicken.*

*Variation: Add 1-2 grated car-
rots and 1/2 cup sunflower seeds
to Step 1.*
— Tabitha Schmidt
Baltic, OH

Greek Cabbage Salad

Colleen Heatwole
Burton, MI

Makes 8-10 servings

Prep Time: 30 minutes
Chilling Time: 1 hour

6-8 cups thinly sliced
  cabbage
1/2 cup sliced black olives
1/2 cup thinly sliced red
  onions
3/4 cup feta cheese, diced or
  crumbled

Dressing:
1 cup apple cider vinegar
6 Tbsp. oil
1 tsp. dry mustard
1/2 tsp. celery seed

1. Combine first 4 salad
ingredients in a large bowl.
2. Combine dressing ingredients in a blender or food
processor, or beat well with a
whisk.
3. Add salad dressing to cabbage mixture. Chill in refrigera-

tor at least 1 hour before serving to combine flavors.

Potato Salad

Gladys Shank, Harrisonburg, VA
Sheila Soldner, Lititz, PA
Sue Suter, Millersville, PA

Makes 8-10 servings

Prep Time: 20-30 minutes
Cooking Time: 45 minutes
Cooling Time: 3-4 hours

8 medium-sized potatoes,
  diced, peeled or
  unpeeled
1 1/2 tsp. salt
water
4 hard-boiled eggs, diced
1/2-1 cup celery, chopped
1/4-1 cup onions, chopped

Dressing:
2 eggs, beaten
3/4 cup sugar
1 tsp. cornstarch
1/3 cup vinegar
1/3 cup milk
3 Tbsp. butter
1 tsp. prepared mustard
1 cup mayonnaise

1. Cooked diced potatoes
in salt water to a firm soft-
ness (don't let them get
mushy). Cool.
2. Cook eggs. Cool, peel,
and dice.
3. Mix cooled potatoes and
eggs with celery and onions.
4. Mix eggs, sugar, corn-
starch, vinegar and milk in a
saucepan and cook until

thickened. Add butter, mustard, and mayonnaise. Cool.

5. Pour cooled dressing over potatoes, eggs, celery, and onions.

6. Refrigerate and chill for several hours before serving.

Variations:

1. Stir 1 tsp. celery seed into the dressing (Step 4), or substitute celery seed for the celery if you wish.

— **Ruth Schrock**
Shipshewana, IN

2. Shred the potatoes after they're cooked, instead of cubing them before they're cooked. And substitute 1/3 cup sour cream for the milk in the dressing.

— **Martha Belle Burkholder**
Waynesboro, VA

Easy Red Potato Salad

Becky Harder,
Monument, CO

Makes 6 servings

Prep Time: 20 minutes
Cooking Time: 20 minutes
Standing Time: 30 minutes

2 lbs. red potatoes
1/3 cup cider vinegar
2 medium-sized ribs of
　celery, chopped
1/3 cup sliced green onions,
　including some green
　tops

1/2 cup mayonnaise
1/2 cup sour cream
1 1/2 tsp. salt
1/2 tsp. pepper
sprinkle of paprika

1. Place potatoes in pot and cover with water. Cover and bring to a boil over high heat. Reduce heat to medium-low. Cover and simmer 10 minutes, or until potatoes are tender in the center. Drain and cool.

2. Cut potatoes into quarters, or eighths if they're large. Place in large mixing bowl. Pour vinegar over them and stir.

3. Let the potatoes stand for 30 minutes while you prepare the celery and onions. Stir the potatoes occasionally.

4. Mix mayonnaise, sour cream, salt, and pepper together in a small bowl.

5. Add the celery and onions to the potatoes. Toss gently.

6. Stir in dressing and mix together gently. Sprinkle with a dash of paprika. Chill until ready to serve.

Variations:
1. Add 3 hard-cooked eggs, chopped, to Step 5.
2. Use 3/4 tsp. celery seed instead of the chopped celery.
— **Lori Newswanger,**
Lancaster, PA

A Tip —

　Marinate carrot sticks in dill pickle juice for a surprising snack.

Sweet Potato Salad

Jean Johnson, Dallas, OR

Makes 6 servings

Prep Time: 10 minutes
Cooking Time: 20 minutes
Chilling Time: 3 hours

4 medium-sized sweet
　potatoes
1/2 cup mayonnaise
1/2 cup plain yogurt
1-1 1/2 tsp. curry powder
salt to taste
2 medium-sized Granny
　Smith apples, chopped
2 medium-sized oranges,
　peeled and chopped, *or*
　2 11-oz. cans mandarin
　oranges, drained
1/2 cup raisins
1/2 cup chopped dates
20-oz. can pineapple
　chunks, drained
1 cup sliced celery

1. Place whole, unpeeled sweet potatoes in a saucepan. Add 2 inches of water. Cover and cook over medium-high heat until tender in the middle, but not mushy.

2. Meanwhile, combine mayonnaise, yogurt, curry powder, and salt in a large bowl. Mix well.

3. When the cooked sweet potatoes are cool enough to handle, peel them. Then cut into chunks about the size of the pineapple chunks. Add to mayonnaise mixture.

4. Add remaining ingredients. Toss well.

5. Refrigerate at least 3 hours before serving.

Creamy Dill Pasta Salad

Jan Mast
Lancaster, PA

Makes 10 servings

Prep Time: 15 minutes
Cooking Time: 12-15 minutes

3 cups uncooked tri-color
  spiral pasta
6-oz. can black olives,
  halved and drained
1/2 cup red pepper,
  chopped
1/2 cup green pepper,
  chopped
1/2 cup onions, chopped
2 tomatoes, chopped
1 Tbsp. dill weed

Dressing:
3/4 cup mayonnaise
2 Tbsp. prepared mustard
1/4 cup vinegar
1/3 cup sugar

1. Cook pasta according to
package directions, being
careful not to overcook. Rinse
in cool water. Drain well.
Place in large mixing bowl.
2. Add vegetables and dill
weed and toss.
3. In a mixing bowl, com-
bine mayonnaise, mustard,
vinegar, and sugar.
4. Pour over pasta and vegetables and stir to coat.
5. Chill and serve.

Greek Orzo Salad

Lavina Hochstedler
Grand Blanc, MI

Makes 8 servings

Prep Time: 20 minutes
Cooking Time: 12 minutes
Chilling Time: 2-24 hours

1 cup uncooked orzo pasta
6 tsp. olive oil, *divided*
1 medium-sized red onion,
  finely chopped
1/2 cup minced fresh
  parsley
1/3 cup cider vinegar
1 1/2 tsp. dried oregano
1 tsp. salt
1 tsp. sugar
1/8 tsp. pepper
1 large tomato, chopped
1 large red pepper,
  chopped
1 medium-sized cucumber,
  peeled, seeded, and
  chopped
1/2 cup black olives, sliced
  and drained, *optional*
1/2 cup crumbled feta
  cheese

1. Cook pasta according to
directions. Drain.
2. In a large mixing bowl,
toss cooked orzo with 2 tsp.
olive oil.
3. In a separate bowl, combine the onion, parsley, vinegar, oregano, salt, sugar, pepper, and remaining oil. Pour
over orzo and toss to coat.
4. Cover and refrigerate 2-
24 hours.
5. Just before serving, gently stir in tomato, red pepper,
cucumber, olives, and cheese.

Summer Pasta Salad

Judy Govotsos
Frederick, MD

Makes 15-18 servings

Prep Time: 8-10 minutes
Cooking Time: 15 minutes

1 lb. uncooked penne *or*
  corkscrew pasta
1 yellow pepper, sliced
1 green pepper, sliced
1 red pepper, sliced
1 red onion, sliced
8 ozs. crumbled feta
  cheese, *optional*
1/2 lb. pitted Kalamata
  olives, *optional*
cherry tomatoes, *optional*
16-oz. bottle Caesar salad
  dressing
10-oz. pkg. chicken strips,
  cooked, *optional*

1. Cook pasta according to
package directions. Drain.
2. In a large mixing bowl,
combine all ingredients
except salad dressing and
chicken.
3. Pour dressing over pasta
mixture. Toss.
4. Add chicken immedi-
ately before serving.

Variations:
*1. Instead of yellow and red
peppers, substitute 2 cups cut-
up broccoli florets in Step 2.*
*2. Instead of feta cheese, use
1 cup shredded cheddar cheese.*

3. Instead of Caesar salad dressing, use Three-Cheese Ranch dressing.

— Lois Smith
Millersville, PA

Italian Tuna Campanelle

Bonita Ensenberger
Albuquerque, NM

Makes 3-4 servings

Prep Time: 20 minutes
Cooking Time: 10 minutes

Vinaigrette:
1/4 cup white wine vinegar
1 tsp. Dijon mustard
1/2 tsp. sugar
1/4 tsp. salt
1/8 tsp. pepper
1/4 tsp. dried marjoram
1/4 tsp. dried basil
1/8 tsp. dried oregano
1/4 cup olive oil

Salad:
2 cups dry rotini
14-oz. can canellini beans, rinsed and drained
6-oz. can solid white tuna, drained and flaked
1/2 cup onions, chopped
3 Tbsp. sliced black olives, drained
1/2 cup green pepper, chopped
1 cup fresh tomato, diced
6 ozs. fresh spinach
1/2 cup Parmesan cheese, grated

1. Cook rotini according to package directions. Drain.
2. While the rotini is cooking, whisk together in a mixing bowl the vinegar, mustard, sugar salt, pepper, and herbs.
3. Then whisk in the oil thoroughly. Set aside.
4. In a large mixing bowl, combine the cooked pasta, beans, tuna, onions, black olives, and bell pepper.
5. Gently mix in the vinaigrette.
6. Stir in the diced tomatoes.
7. To serve, place a thin bed of spinach on each salad plate. Spoon pasta salad on top.
8. Garnish with grated Parmesan cheese.

Tip: You can make the vinaigrette a day ahead and refrigerate it until you make the salad.

A Tip —

To remove onion odor from your fingers, rub a metal spoon between your finger and thumb under running water.

Pasta Salad with Tuna

Sheila Soldner
Lititz, PA

Makes 6-8 servings

Prep Time: 15 minutes
Cooking Time: 15 minutes

1/2 lb. uncooked rotini pasta
12.5-oz. can solid white tuna, drained and flaked
2 cups thinly sliced cucumber
1 large tomato, seeded and sliced, *or* 1/2 pint cherry *or* grape tomatoes
1/2 cup sliced celery
1/4 cup chopped green pepper
1/4 cup sliced green onions
1 cup bottled Italian dressing
1/4 cup mayonnaise
1 Tbsp. prepared mustard
1 tsp. dill weed
1 tsp. salt
1/8 tsp. pepper

1. Prepare rotini according to package directions. Drain.
2. In a large bowl, combine rotini, tuna, cucumbers, tomato, celery, green pepper, and onions.
3. In a small bowl, blend together Italian dressing, mayonnaise, mustard, and seasonings. Add to salad mixture. Toss to coat.
4. Cover and chill. Toss gently before serving.

Crab Pasta Salad

April Swartz
Lake Cadessa, MI

Makes 16 servings

Prep Time: 20 minutes
Cooking Time: 8-10 minutes

16-oz. box uncooked pasta
   of your choice
1/2-1 lb. imitation crab,
   your choice of amount
4-oz. jar sliced pimentos,
   drained
4-oz. can sliced black
   olives, drained
1 small onion, diced
16-oz. bottle Ranch
   dressing

1. Cook pasta according to package directions, until firm-soft. Drain and cool in a large mixing bowl.

2. Cut up crab into bite-sized pieces. Add to pasta.

3. Stir in pimentos, olives, and onions.

4. Pour dressing over top. Toss until well coated.

A Tip —

   Onions won't sting your eyes as much if they've been stored in the refrigerator.

Linguine Salad with Peanut Sauce

Gretchen H. Maust
Keezletown, VA

Makes 6 servings

Prep Time: 15 minutes
Cooking Time: 15 minutes

8-oz. box dry linguine
1/2-1 cup chopped scallions
1 diced cucumber
1/4 cup peanut butter
1/3 cup cider *or* rice vinegar
1/4 cup soy sauce
1/4 cup warm water
1/3 cup sesame oil
2 cloves minced garlic
1/2 tsp. 5-spice powder
hot sauce to taste
dark green lettuce leaves
toasted sesame seeds and
   tomato wedges for
   garnish

1. Cook linguine as directed on box, but under-cook slightly. Drain. Rinse with cool water.

2. In a large bowl, combine linguini, scallions, and cucumber.

3. In a separate bowl, whisk together peanut butter, vinegar, soy sauce, water, oil, garlic, 5-spice powder, and hot sauce.

4. Arrange lettuce on platter. Spoon linguine mixture into the middle. Drizzle dressing over top. Garnish with sesame seeds and tomato wedges.

Variations:
   1. For a heartier dish, add cubed cooked chicken or turkey.
   2. Serve hot, replacing the cucumbers with cooked zucchini.

Tip: *I like to triple the peanut sauce and keep it in the refrigerator to use as a salad dressing or dipping sauce for grilled chicken.*

Orzo and Corn Off the Cob

Karen Kay Tucker
Manteca, CA

Makes 6-8 servings

Prep Time: 30 minutes
Cooking Time: 8-9 minutes

4 fresh ears of corn, *or*
   2 cups canned *or* frozen
   (thawed)
1 1/4 cups uncooked orzo
1 cup black olives, pitted
   and halved
1 medium-sized red sweet
   pepper, chopped
1/4 cup thinly sliced green
   onions
1/4 cup finely snipped
   fresh, *or* 1 Tbsp. and
   1 tsp. dried basil
1/4 cup finely snipped fresh
   parsley, *or* 1 Tbsp. and
   1 tsp. dried parsley
1/4 cup olive oil
2 Tbsp. white wine vinegar
1/4 tsp. salt
1/4 tsp. pepper

1. Cut corn off the cob, about 2 cups-worth. Set aside.

2. Bring a large pot of lightly salted water to a boil. Add orzo and cook, stirring occasionally for 8 to 9 minutes, or until tender, adding corn during the last 3 minutes of cooking time. Drain and place in a large serving bowl.

3. Stir in the olives, sweet pepper, green onion, basil, and parsley.

4. In a small bowl, combine the olive oil, vinegar, salt, and pepper. Whisk together.

5. Pour dressing over orzo mixture. Toss gently to combine.

Noodle Mushroom Salad

D. Fern Ruth, Chalfont, PA

Makes 4-6 servings:

Prep Time: 30 minutes
Cooking Time: 7 minutes
Chilling Time: 1 hour

Sesame Ginger Dressing:
3/4 cup vegetable oil
1/2 cup, plus 1 Tbsp., white vinegar
1/3 cup water
2-3 tsp. fresh ginger, grated *or* thinly shaved, packed lightly
3 cloves garlic, minced
1 Tbsp. white sugar
1/4 tsp. salt
1/4 tsp. hot pepper sauce, *optional*

Salad:
8 ozs. dry fine egg noodles
1/2 lb. fresh mushrooms, thickly sliced
6 scallions with tops sliced thin diagonally
medium-sized red bell pepper, cut into strips
1/3 cup parsley, coarsely chopped
3 Tbsp. toasted sesame seeds

1. In blender, mix oil, vinegar, water, ginger, garlic, sugar, salt, and pepper sauce. Puree until smooth. Set aside.

2. In saucepan, bring 2 qts. water to boil. Add noodles and cook until tender (it takes only a few minutes). Immediately rinse with cold water and drain thoroughly.

3. In a large mixing bowl, mix together noodles, mushrooms, scallions, red pepper strips, and parsley.

4. Pour sesame ginger dressing over salad mixture and toss well.

5. Refrigerate 1 hour to blend flavors before serving.

6. To serve, top with sesame seeds and more parsley.

Tips:

1. To toast sesame seeds, place in dry skillet over medium heat. Shake/stir till golden, approximately 5 minutes.

2. This salad can be made ahead. But wait to add mushrooms, red pepper strips, and parsley until 1 hour before serving.

3. Increase or decrease amount of fresh ginger to your taste.

4. This has a pleasing, light oriental flavor.

Tuna Salad

Frances Schrag
Newton, KS

Makes 4 servings

Prep Time: 15 minutes

6-oz. can tuna, drained
2 Tbsp. onion, chopped
3 Tbsp. pickle, chopped
1/2 cup chopped celery
3 hard-cooked eggs, diced
1/4 tsp. salt
1/8 tsp. pepper
2 Tbsp. Ranch dressing *or* mayonnaise
lettuce leaves, *or*
4 sandwich rolls
***or* English muffins**

1. Combine all ingredients except the lettuce or rolls in a good-sized mixing bowl.

2. Serve as a salad on lettuce leaves, or use to fill sandwiches. Or spread the salad on split English muffins, top with cheese, and broil until the cheese melts.

Variations:
1. Mix 1 1/2 tsp. prepared mustard into the salad in Step 1.
2. Instead of the salt and pepper, use 1/2 tsp. Mrs. Dash seasoning.

— **Lauren Eberhard**
Seneca, IL

Albacore Tuna Stuffed Tomato

Joe Barker
Carlsbad, NM

Makes 6-8 servings

Prep Time: 1 hour

6-8 Roma tomatoes
2 6-oz. cans albacore tuna, drained
1 Tbsp. mayonnaise
1/2 tsp. prepared mustard
1 1/2 tsp. blue cheese dressing
2 tsp. green onion, thinly sliced
1 1/2 tsp. chives, chopped
1 1/2 tsp. black olives, chopped
1 1/2 tsp. cucumber, chopped
1 1/2 tsp. red bell pepper, chopped
1 1/2 tsp. yellow bell pepper, chopped
celery leaves
paprika
6-8 mint leaves

1. Cut tomatoes in half and remove seeds and veins. Keep for another use. Keep the tomato shells cool.
2. Mix remaining ingredients together in a bowl.
3. Stuff tomato halves with tuna mixture.
4. Sprinkle paprika lightly over top.
5. Garnish each tomato with a mint leaf.
6. Keep cold until ready to serve.

Exotic Chicken Salad

Mable Hershey, Marietta, PA

Makes 6 servings

Prep Time: 30 minutes
Cooking Time: 15-20 minutes, if cooking the chicken
Chilling Time: 2-3 hours

1 lb. green seedless grapes, halved
1-1 1/2 cups slivered, toasted almonds, *divided*
4 cups cooked chicken, cut in pieces, *or* 2 5-oz. cans cooked chicken
4-oz. can sliced water chestnuts, drained
1 cup celery, sliced
1 1/2 cups mayonnaise
1 1/2 tsp. curry powder
1 Tbsp. soy sauce
1 Tbsp. lemon juice
lettuce leaves

1. Cut grapes in half.
2. Toast almonds by spreading them into a large dry skillet. Place over medium-high heat, stirring them frequently so they brown on both sides and don't burn.
3. Combine grapes, 1 cup almonds, chicken, water chestnuts, and celery in a large mixing bowl.
4. In a smaller bowl, mix together mayonnaise, curry powder, soy sauce, and lemon juice. Add to chicken mixture.
5. Chill several hours.
6. Sprinkle with remaining almonds.

7. Serve over lettuce leaves.

Variations:
1. Add 1/3 cup minced onions to Step 3.
2. Replace mayonnaise, curry powder, and lemon juice with 1 1/2 cups peach or lemon yogurt. Increase the soy sauce to 2 Tbsp.
3. In Step 7, garnish prepared plates with melon wedges before serving.
— Donna Treloar
Hartford City, IN

Peachy Chicken Salad

Pat Unternahrer
Wayland, IA

Makes 4-6 servings

Prep Time: 10-15 minutes

1/3 cup mayonnaise
2 Tbsp. milk
1/4 tsp. pepper
1/2 tsp. salt
1/4 tsp. dried tarragon, *or* 1 tsp. chopped fresh tarragon
2 1/2 cups cubed cooked chicken, *or* 1 5-oz. can cooked chicken
1 cup seedless red grapes, halved
1 cup frozen peas, thawed
2 large peaches, peeled and chopped
1 cup pecan halves, toasted
lettuce leaves, *optional*

1. In a large bowl, stir the mayonnaise, milk, pepper, salt, and tarragon together until smooth.

2. Add chicken and toss to coat.

3. Stir in grapes, peas, peaches, and pecans.

4. Serve in a lettuce-lined bowl if you wish.

Asparagus, Apple, and Chicken Salad

Betty Salch
Bloomington, IL
Wilma Stoltzfus
Honey Brook, PA

Makes 3-4 servings

Prep Time: 20 minutes
Cooking Time: 3-4 minutes,
    if using pre-cooked chicken

1 cup fresh asparagus, cut
    into 1"-long pieces
2 Tbsp. cider vinegar
2 Tbsp. vegetable oil
2 tsp. honey
2 tsp. minced fresh parsley
1/2 tsp. salt
1/4 tsp. pepper
1 cup cubed cooked
    chicken, *or* 5-oz. can
    cooked chicken
1/2 cup diced red apples,
    unpeeled
2 cups torn mixed greens
alfalfa sprouts, *optional*

1. In a small saucepan, cook asparagus in a small amount of water until crisp-tender, about 3-4 minutes. Drain and cool.

2. In a good-sized mixing bowl, combine the next 6 ingredients.

3. Stir in the chicken, apples, and asparagus. Toss.

4. Serve over greens. Garnish with alfalfa sprouts if you wish.

Asparagus Bean Salad

Carol Coggin
Jacksonville, FL

Makes 6 servings

Prep Time: 20 minutes
Cooking Time: 10 minutes
Chilling Time: 1 hour

1 lb. fresh asparagus, cut
    in 1" pieces
6 dried tomatoes
2 cloves garlic, minced
1 1/2 Tbsp. brown sugar
4 Tbsp. olive oil
4 Tbsp. rice vinegar
2 Tbsp. water
1 1/2 tsp. Dijon mustard
1/4 tsp. sage
1/4 tsp. salt
1/4 tsp. pepper
15-oz. can white navy
    beans, rinsed and
    drained
1/4 cup chopped onions
3 tsp. capers, drained
3 Tbsp. grated Parmesan
    cheese

1. Place cut-up asparagus in a saucepan. Add 1" water. Cover and cook just until crisp-tender. Drain and chill.

2. Place dried tomatoes in a saucepan with 1" water. Cover and place over medium heat for about 4 minutes, or until they plump up. Drain. Then chop into small chunks and chill.

3. In a small bowl, whisk together garlic, brown sugar, oil, vinegar, water, mustard, sage, salt, and pepper.

4. In a large mixing bowl, toss together the asparagus, tomatoes, beans, onions, and capers.

5. Pour the dressing over all. Mix well and chill for an hour before serving.

6. Sprinkle with Parmesan cheese to serve.

A Tip —

Grate ends of cheese blocks (cheddar, Swiss, Monterey Jack, etc.) together into a Ziploc bag and keep the grated cheese on hand for sprinkling over salads, casseroles, and toasted cheese bread.

Black Bean Fiesta Salad

Lorraine Pflederer
Goshen, IN

Makes 6 servings

Prep Time: 30 minutes
Chilling Time: 2-8 hours,
  or overnight

15-oz. can black beans,
  rinsed and drained
1 cup frozen corn, thawed
1 green pepper, diced
1 sweet red pepper, diced
1 cup diced red onions
2 celery ribs, chopped
3/4 cup cubed Monterey
  Jack cheese
3 Tbsp. lemon juice
3 Tbsp. red wine, *or* cider,
  vinegar
2 Tbsp. olive oil
2 garlic cloves, minced
1 Tbsp. Italian seasoning
1 tsp. pepper
1/2 tsp. ground cumin

1. In a large bowl, combine beans, corn, peppers, onions, celery, and cheese.
2. In a jar with a tight-fitting lid, combine the remaining ingredients. Shake well.
3. Pour over vegetable mixture and toss gently.
4. Cover and chill for 2 hours or overnight.

Boston Bean Salad

Joyce Shackelford
Green Bay, WI

Makes 10 servings

Prep Time: 30 minutes
Chilling Time: 4-8 hours,
  or overnight

14-oz. can navy beans,
  rinsed and drained
15-oz. can red kidney
  beans, rinsed and
  drained
15-oz. can black beans,
  rinsed and drained
1 cup (2 ribs) celery, sliced
1/2 cup green onions, sliced
1/2 cup vinegar
1/4 cup molasses
1/4 cup oil
1 Tbsp. Dijon mustard
1/4 tsp. pepper
lettuce leaves to line the
  salad bowl
2 cups curly endive lettuce
  leaves, torn
2 slices bacon, crisp-
  cooked and crumbled

1. In a large bowl, combine all the beans, celery, and green onions.
2. In a jar with a tight-fitting lid, combine vinegar, molasses, oil, mustard, and pepper. Shake well.
3. Pour dressing over bean mixture. Chill 4-24 hours.
4. Line a large bowl with lettuce leaves.
5. Stir endive and bacon into bean mixture. Spoon bean mixture into salad bowl.

Green Bean Salad

Jean H. Robinson
Cinnaminson, NJ

Makes 6-8 servings

Prep Time: 20 minutes
Cooking Time: 10 minutes
Chilling Time: 2 hours

4 cups water
1 Tbsp. salt
2 lbs. fresh green beans,
  cut into 2" pieces
1 rib celery, chopped fine
1/2 cup chopped green
  onions
2 cups cherry tomatoes,
  halved
1/2 cup feta cheese

Dressing:
1/2 cup oil
2 Tbsp. rice vinegar
1 tsp. Dijon mustard
salt to taste
pepper to taste

1. Bring water and salt to a boil in a large stockpot. Place beans into boiling water and cook for 6 minutes. Remove from stove and drain. Plunge beans immediately into ice water. Drain.
2. In a large mixing bowl, combine beans, celery, onions, tomatoes, and cheese.
3. In a jar with a tight-fitting lid, combine oil, vinegar, mustard, salt, and pepper. Shake well.
4. Pour dressing over bean mixture. Toss.
5. Chill for at least 2 hours before serving.

Colorful Bean Salad

Patricia Eckard
Singers Glen, VA
Betty B. Dennison
Grove City, PA

Makes 6 servings

Prep Time: 30 minutes
Cooking Time: 5 minutes
Chilling Time: 2-8 hours,
  or overnight

15-oz. can green beans,
  drained
15-oz. can peas, drained
15-oz. can shoepeg corn,
  drained
15-oz. can baby lima
  beans, drained
1 medium-sized red onion,
  chopped
4-oz. jar pimentos, drained
1/2 cup chopped celery
1/2 cup chopped red bell
  pepper

Dressing:
3/4 cup apple cider vinegar
1 cup sugar

1. Mix all vegetables
together in a large bowl.
2. Combine vinegar and
sugar in a small saucepan.
Bring to a boil. Boil for 3
minutes, stirring occasionally.
3. Pour over vegetables.
Cover and refrigerate 2-8
hours, or overnight.

Variations:
1. Add a 4-oz. can sliced mush-
rooms, drained; a 15-oz. can of
kidney beans, rinsed and

drained; and a 15-oz. can of
yellow wax beans, rinsed and
drained, to Step 1.
2. Add 1/2 cup oil, 1 tsp. celery
salt, and 1/4 tsp. pepper to the
dressing, and whisk together—
without cooking the mixture.
Proceed with Step 3.
  *— **Mary Lynn Miller***
  Reinholds, PA

Marinated Mushrooms

Lisa Harnish
Christiana, PA

Makes 12 servings

Prep Time: 10 minutes
Cooking Time: 20 minutes

2 lbs. (50-60) medium-
  sized fresh mushrooms
2 cloves garlic
1 cup red wine vinegar
1 cup water
1/2 cup olive oil
1/2 cup vegetable oil
1 bay leaf
1 tsp. salt
1/2 tsp. dried thyme leaves
12 whole black
  peppercorns
fresh parsley

1. Clean mushrooms and
set aside.
2. Flatten garlic or use garlic press.
3. In Dutch oven, combine
all ingredients except mushrooms and parsley.
4. Bring to a boil. Reduce
heat and simmer 5 minutes.

5. Add mushrooms and
simmer uncovered 10 min-
utes.
6. Remove from heat and
let stand until cooled slightly.
7. Transfer mushrooms
and marinade to a storage
container. Cover and refrigerate until ready to serve.
8. To serve, remove mush-
rooms from marinade and
place in serving dish. Garnish
with fresh parsley.

Lime Cucumbers

Norma I. Gehman
Ephrata, PA

Makes 4 servings

Prep Time: 10 minutes

1/2 tsp. grated lime rind
1 Tbsp. lime juice
2 Tbsp. olive oil
1/4 tsp. salt
1/8 tsp. pepper
1 large burpless, seedless
  cucumber, thinly sliced

1. Whisk together first 5
ingredients in a bowl.
2. Add cucumber and mix
well.

Refreshing Cucumber Salad

Kathy Alderfer
Broadway, VA

Makes 4 servings

Prep Time: 15 minutes
Chilling Time: 1 hour

1/4 cup mayonnaise
1/4 cup sour cream
1 Tbsp. sugar
1 Tbsp. vinegar
1 tsp. dill weed
salt and pepper to taste
3 cups thinly sliced
   cucumbers (about
   3 medium-sized ones)
1 cup grape tomatoes,
   halved
2-4 small green onions,
   sliced into rings, amount
   according to your
   preference

1. In a medium-sized mixing bowl, mix mayonnaise, sour cream, sugar, vinegar, dill, salt, and pepper. Blend thoroughly.
2. Add cucumbers, tomatoes, and green onions to creamy mixture and stir together.
3. Allow to marinate in refrigerator for at least 1 hour before serving.

Chinese Cucumber with Peanut Sauce

Sharleen Nichols
State College, PA

Makes 4 servings

Prep Time: 15 minutes

1 seedless cucumber
1/4 cup peanut butter
sesame seeds, toasted
sesame oil
3-4 drops chili oil

1. Peel cucumber, cut into 1/2" slices, and then quarter. Set aside in a serving dish.
2. Make peanut sauce in a small bowl by adding sesame oil to the peanut butter until it flows. Add chili oil to suit your taste.
3. Sprinkle sesame seeds over top of sauce.
4. Dip cucumbers into sauce.

Tip: This sauce is also good for dipping other vegetables.

My husband and I saw this dish being served at the next table at a restaurant in China. Our command of the Chinese language was very limited so we pointed and said we'd like to have that recipe!

Mozzarella / Tomato / Basil Salad

Makes 6 servings

Prep Time: 8 minutes

1 pint buffalo mozzarella
   cheese balls, *or* 1/4-1/2 lb.
   buffalo mozzarella
   cheese, sliced
2 large tomatoes, sliced
   and quartered
1/2 cup black olives, sliced
1/2 cup basil leaves, torn
1 Tbsp. olive oil
1 Tbsp. red wine vinegar
1/4 tsp. salt
1/8 tsp. pepper

1. If the mozzarella balls are in liquid, rinse and drain them. Place in a mixing bowl.
2. Add tomatoes, black olives, and basil leaves. Mix together gently.
3. Mix olive oil, vinegar, salt, and pepper together. Pour over salad ingredients and and mix gently.

Variations:
1. Add 1 sweet Vidalia onion, sliced, to Step 2.
2. Serve the dressed salad on a bed of arugula leaves.
— **Bonita Ensenberger**
Albuquerque, NM

Marinated Garden Tomatoes

Bonnie Goering
Bridgewater, VA

Makes 10 servings

Prep Time: 10 minutes
Chilling Time: 1 hour or more

6 large firm tomatoes,
   cut in wedges
1/2 cup sliced onions
1/2 cup sliced green bell
   pepper
1/4 cup olive oil
2 Tbsp. red wine vinegar
1/4 tsp. garlic powder
1/2 tsp. salt
1/4 tsp. pepper
2 Tbsp. sugar
2 Tbsp. minced fresh, *or*
   2 tsp., parsley flakes
1 Tbsp. snipped fresh, *or*
   1 tsp. dried, thyme

1. Arrange tomatoes, onions, and peppers in a flat dish.
2. In a jar with a tight-fitting lid, mix together oil, vinegar, garlic powder, salt, pepper, and sugar. Pour over vegetables.
3. In a small bowl, combine parsley and thyme and sprinkle on top.
4. Refrigerate for one hour or more before serving.

Summer Vegetable Cheese Salad

Jan Mast, Lancaster, PA

Makes 8 servings

Prep Time: 15 minutes
Chilling Time: 1 hour

3 cups cheese, shredded
   (cheddar, Monterey
   Jack, *or* mozzarella, *or* a
   combination of them)
1 medium-sized cucumber,
   chopped
1 medium-sized tomato,
   seeded and chopped
1 onion, thinly sliced
1 cup green and red
   pepper, chopped
lettuce leaves

Dressing:
1/2 cup sour cream
1/4 cup mayonnaise
1 Tbsp. lemon juice
1 garlic clove, minced
1/2 tsp. Dijon mustard
1/2 tsp. dried basil
1/2 tsp. paprika
1 tsp. sugar

1. In a large mixing bowl, combine cheese, cucumber, tomato, onion, and green and red peppers.
2. In a separate bowl, combine sour cream, mayonnaise, lemon juice, garlic, mustard, basil, paprika, and sugar.
3. Pour dressing over cheese and vegetables. Toss to coat.
4. Chill for 1 hour.
5. Serve in a lettuce-lined bowl.

Beet Salad

Dorothy Lingerfelt
Stonyford, CA

Makes 6 servings

Prep Time: 10 minutes
Cooking Time: 5 minutes
Chilling Time: 4 hours

16-oz. can diced beets,
   drained, juice reserved
3-oz. pkg. lemon gelatin
2/3 cup orange juice
1 tsp. grated onion
2-3 tsp. grated horseradish,
   depending upon how
   much zip you like
1 tsp. vinegar
1 tsp. salt
2/3 cup chopped celery

1. Drain beets, reserving juice.
2. Pour beet juice into a 1-cup measure. Fill to the top with water. Pour into a small saucepan. Bring to a boil.
3. Dissolve gelatin in boiling beet juice. Stir in orange juice, onion, horseradish, vinegar, and salt. Mix well.
4. Chill beet-gelatin mixture until slightly thickened.
5. Stir in beets and celery. Pour into mold.
6. Chill until firm. Unmold on a serving plate.

A Tip —

   Have one or two "company specials" you can make when friends show up unexpectedly.

Pickled Beet and Eggs

Beverly Flatt-Getz
Warriors Mark, PA

Makes 10-12 servings

Prep Time: 15 minutes
Cooking Time: 15 minutes
Chilling Time: 1-2 days

12 eggs
3/4 cup vinegar
1 cup sugar
2 16-oz. cans whole red
  beets

1. Hard-cook eggs. Peel and prick whites slightly with fork.
2. In saucepan, heat vinegar.
3. Add sugar and stir over heat until dissolved.
4. Stir in beet juice and heat through.
5. Put eggs in a large jar with a lid. Pour juice over eggs. Add beets on top. Refrigerate for 1-2 days.
6. To serve, cut eggs in half lengthwise. Place on a serving dish, along with the red beets.

Tip: In order to have the eggs be uniformly colored, stir them every few hours. And the longer the eggs are in the beet juice, the more they absorb its flavor.

Deviled Eggs

Leona Yoder
Hartville, OH

Makes 8 servings

Cooking Time: 15-20 minutes
Prep Time: 10 minutes

4 eggs
1/8 tsp. salt
2 tsp. vinegar
1 Tbsp. mayonnaise
1/8 tsp. pepper
1/4 tsp. prepared mustard
1 Tbsp. cream *or* milk
1/4 cup finely chopped red
  onions
paprika *or* fresh parsley
  leaves

1. Place eggs in a saucepan. Cover with water. Cover pan and bring water to boil.
2. Remove pan with eggs from heat. Keep covered and allow eggs to sit in hot water for 15 minutes. Remove eggs from pan and allow to cool. Peel carefully.
3. Cut eggs in half lengthwise. Remove yolks and place in a small bowl. Mash until smooth.
4. Add other ingredients to mashed yolks and mix well.
5. Refill the whites and garnish with paprika or parsley just before serving.

Tip: You can use this recipe as the filling for egg salad sandwiches. Simply cut up the hardcooked eggs (whites and yolks) and mix gently with the other ingredients.

Zippy Fruit Salad

Violette Harris Denney
Carrollton, GA

Makes 8 servings

Prep Time: 20 minutes
Cooking Time: 10 minutes
Chilling Time: 4 hours

1/2 cup water
21-oz. can cherry pie filling
6-oz. pkg. cherry gelatin
15-oz. can crushed
  pineapple
half a 12-oz. can of Coke
1 cup chopped nuts
2 apples, chopped

1. In a saucepan, combine water and pie filling. Bring to a boil, stirring frequently.
2. Reduce heat and cook for 5 minutes, stirring frequently. Remove from heat.
3. Add gelatin. Mix until dissolved. Cool until the mixture starts to congeal.
4. Fold in pineapple, Coke, nuts, and apples. Pour into serving bowl. Chill until firm.

Frozen Waldorf Salad

Bonita Ensenberger
Albuquerque, NM

Makes 6-9 servings

Prep Time: 20 minutes
Freezing Time: 8 hours,
or overnight

8 ozs. cream cheese,
softened
1/2 cup mayonnaise
2 cups frozen whipped
topping, slightly thawed
1 cup apples, unpeeled
and chopped
1/2 cup celery, sliced
1 cup seedless grapes,
halved
3/4 cup crushed pineapple,
drained
3/4 cup English walnuts,
toasted and chopped

1. In a large mixing bowl,
whip together cream cheese
and mayonnaise, either by
hand or with a mixer or food
processor. Fold in whipped
topping.
2. Fold in apples, celery,
grapes, and pineapple.
3. Pour into a greased
8 x 8 baking dish. Cover and
freeze for 8 hours or
overnight.
4. Remove from freezer 10-
15 minute before serving. Cut
into squares. Top each serving with toasted walnuts.

Strawberry Gelatin Salad

Vonda Ebersole
Mt. Pleasant Mills, PA

Makes 12 servings

Prep Time: 15 minutes
Chilling Time: 3-4 hours

2 cups water
6-oz. box strawberry
gelatin
4 cups fresh *or* frozen
strawberries
15-oz. can crushed
pineapples, undrained
3 large bananas, sliced

1. Bring water to a boil in
a saucepan. Stir gelatin into
boiling water until dissolved.
2. Stir in additional ingredients.
3. Refrigerate until gelatin
is firm.

Tip: If you're in a hurry, use
frozen strawberries. They'll
speed up the gelling process.

A Tip —

Never add fresh kiwi to
a salad using gelatin. It
will "un-gell" the whole
thing!

Favorite Blueberry Salad

Vicki Hill
Memphis, TN

Makes 10-12 servings

Prep Time: 10-20 minutes
Chilling Time: 4 hours

6-oz. pkg. raspberry gelatin
1 1/2 cups boiling water
16 1/2-oz. can blueberries,
undrained
20-oz. can crushed
pineapple, undrained
8-oz. pkg. cream cheese,
softened
1 cup sour cream
1/4 cup sugar
1/2 cup chopped nuts

1. In a large saucepan or
mixing bowl, dissolve gelatin
in water.
2. Stir in blueberries and
pineapple. Pour into a 9 x 13
pan. Chill until set, about 4
hours.
3. Meanwhile, cream
together cream cheese, sour
cream, and sugar, either by
hand, or with an electric
mixer or food processor.
Spread on top of congealed
salad.
4. Sprinkle with nuts.

Holiday Cranberry Mousse

Rhoda Atzeff
Harrisburg, PA

Makes 8-10 servings

Prep Time: 30 minutes
Chilling Time: 4-5 hours

20-oz. can crushed
    pineapple, juice reserved
6-oz. pkg. strawberry
    gelatin
1 cup water
1-lb. can whole-berry
    cranberry sauce
3 Tbsp. fresh lemon juice
1 tsp. grated lemon peel
1/4 tsp. ground nutmeg
2 cups sour cream
1/2 cup chopped pecans

1. Drain pineapple well,
reserving all juice.
2. Add juice to gelatin in a
2-qt. saucepan. Stir in water.
Bring to a boil, stirring to dissolve gelatin. Remove from
heat.
3. Blend in cranberry
sauce, lemon juice, lemon
peel, and nutmeg.
4. Chill until mixture
thickens slightly, about 1-2
hours.
5. Blend sour cream into
gelatin mixture. Fold in
drained pineapple and
pecans.
6. Pour into a 1-qt. mold,
or into a 9 x 13 pan.
7. Chill until firm, about 2-
3 hours. Unmold onto a plate
or cut into squares and serve.

Red Raspberry Cranberry Salad

Phyllis Attig
Reynolds, IL

Makes 10-12 servings

Prep Time: 10-15 minutes
Chilling Time: 4 hours

1 1/2 cups water
6-oz. package raspberry
    gelatin
3-oz. package raspberry
    gelatin
1-lb. can whole-berry
    cranberry sauce
15-oz. can jellied cranberry
    sauce
1 cup applesauce
1 bag frozen red
    raspberries
8-oz. can crushed
    pineapple, drained

1. Bring water to a boil in
a saucepan. Stir in both packages of gelatin until dissolved.
2. Add the 2 cranberry
sauces, applesauce, red raspberries, and drained pineapple. Mix well.
3. Refrigerate until firm,
about 4 hours.

Cranberry Salad

Mary Lynn Miller
Reinholds, PA

Makes 6-8 servings

Prep Time: 30-40 minutes
*Chilling Time: 6-8 hours,
    or overnight*

4 cups fresh cranberries,
    rinsed and drained
4 oranges (2 peeled,
    2 unpeeled)
4 apples, peeled and cut
    into quarters
2 cups sugar

1. Grind cranberries,
oranges, and apples. Mix
well.
2. Pour sugar over fruit
and mix well.
3. Refrigerate for 6-8 hours
before serving.

Lemon Cream Salad

Helen J. Myers
Silver Spring, MD

Makes 8-10 servings

Prep Time: 20 minutes
Chilling Time: 4 hours

10 ozs. lemon-lime soda
1 cup miniature
    marshmallows
2 3-oz. pkgs. cream cheese,
    cubed

6-oz. pkg. lemon-flavored
gelatin
20-oz. can crushed
pineapple with juice
3/4 cup chopped pecans,
optional
8-oz. carton whipped
topping

1. In a heavy saucepan, combine soda, marshmallows, and cream cheese. Bring to boil over low heat. Remove from heat.
2. Add gelatin, stirring until dissolved.
3. Stir in pineapple and pecans. Chill until the consistency of unbeaten egg whites, about an hour.
4. Fold in whipped topping. Pour into lightly oiled mold. Chill until firm, about 3 hours.

Orange Sherbet Salad

Marlys Martins
Waukon, IA

Makes 6 servings

Prep Time: 15-20 minutes
Chilling Time: 3-4 hours

1 cup water
6-oz. pkg. orange gelatin
1 cup orange juice
1 pint orange sherbet
11-oz. can mandarin
oranges, drained

1. Bring water to a boil in a saucepan. Stir in gelatin until dissolved. Pour into an electric mixer bowl.
2. Add orange juice and sherbet. Beat with mixer at low speed until smooth.
3. Fold in oranges.
4. Pour into serving bowl. Refrigerate until firm, about 3-4 hours.

Sea Foam Pear Salad

Esther J. Mast
Lancaster, PA

Makes 12 servings

Prep Time: 15 minutes
Chilling Time: 4 hours

29-oz. can pears, drained,
with juice reserved
1 cup reserved pear juice
3-oz. pkg. lime gelatin
8-oz. pkg. cream cheese,
softened
2 Tbsp. light cream *or* milk
2 cups frozen whipped
topping, thawed

1. Mash drained pears and set aside.
2. In a saucepan, heat pear juice to the boiling point and add lime gelatin. Stir until dissolved.
3. With an electric mixer, beat softened cream cheese until smooth and creamy. Gradually add gelatin mixture. Continue beating with electric mixer until blended.
4. Chill until thickened but not until stiff, about 1 hour.

5. Fold in mashed pears and whipped topping.
6. Pour into mold or glass serving dish to set fully, about 3 hours.

Saucy Fruit Salad

Tracey Hanson Schramel
Windom, MN

Makes 6-8 servings

Prep Time: 10-15 minutes
Chilling Time: 1-2 hours

2 11-oz. cans mandarin
oranges, drained
2 20-oz. cans pineapple
chunks, drained
4 bananas, sliced
2 red apples, sliced,
optional

Fruit sauce:
3.4-oz. box instant vanilla
pudding
1 cup milk
1/3 cup orange juice
concentrate
6-oz. carton banana, *or*
French vanilla, yogurt

1. Mix all fruit in a large bowl and set aside.
2. In a small mixing bowl, combine dry pudding with milk, orange juice, and yogurt. Beat with wire whisk until smooth.
3. Pour sauce over fruit and fold together. Chill for 1-2 hours.

Easy Fruit Salad

Shirley Sears
Tiskilwa, IL

Makes 12 servings

Prep Time: 20-25 minutes
Chilling Time: 3-4 hours

20-oz. can pineapple
    chunks, drained and
    halved
11-oz. can mandarin
    oranges, drained
15-oz. can apricot halves,
    drained and quartered
15-oz. can peach slices,
    drained and quartered
2 cups fresh green grapes,
    halved
3 bananas, sliced
20-oz. can peach pie filling
1/2 cup pecan halves,
    optional

1. In a large mixing bowl,
stir all drained, canned fruit
together.
2. Add grapes and sliced
bananas.
3. Mix in peach pie filling.
4. Refrigerate several
hours before serving.
5. Garnish with pecan
halves just before serving, if
you wish.

Tips:
1. Drain the fruit well.
*2. If you need a larger salad
just use larger cans or more
cans of fruit. You could add
marshmallows or apples, too, if
you want.*

*This is quick to make. I
keep these canned ingredients
on hand all the time for last-
minute preparation. I only need
to purchase fresh grapes and
bananas. My mom introduced
me to this recipe in 1968, and
I've given it to others many
times.*

Grandma's Special Fruit Salad

Jan Moore
Wellsville, KS

Makes 6 servings

Prep Time: 15 minutes
Cooking Time: 5 minutes
Chilling Time: 1-2 hours

1 apple
1 orange, peeled
1/2 cup strawberries
1 kiwi
1 peach
2 apricots
1 banana
15-oz. can sliced pineapple,
    drained, with juice
    reserved
1/2 cup orange juice
1/4 cup reserved pineapple
    juice
2 tsp. cornstarch
1 egg, beaten
1/2 cup grated coconut
1/2 cup pecans, chopped

1. Cut all fruit into bite-
sized pieces and place in a
large bowl.
2. In a small saucepan,
heat orange juice over

medium heat.
3. Mix cornstarch and
pineapple juice together in a
small bowl. Add to heated
orange juice.
4. Add egg, stirring until
sauce thickens.
5. Pour over fruit. Add
coconut and pecans and mix
well.
6. Chill 1-2 hours and then
serve.

Honey Apple Salad

Esther Becker
Gordonville, PA

Makes 6 servings

Prep Time: 15-20 minutes

3 1/2 cups diced red apples,
    unpeeled
2 Tbsp. lemon juice
2 cups green grapes, halved
1 cup thinly sliced celery
1/2 cup raisins *or* craisins
2 Tbsp. sour cream
1/2 cup mayonnaise
1/2 tsp. salt
1/4 cup honey
1/2 cup chopped walnuts *or*
    pecans

1. In a large bowl, toss
apples with lemon juice. Add
grapes, celery, and raisins.
2. In a small bowl, com-
bine sour cream, mayonnaise,
salt, and honey. Mix well.
Pour over apple mixture and
stir to coat.
3. Stir in nuts just before
serving.

Apple Salad
Vera Campbell
Dayton, VA

Makes 6-8 servings

Prep Time: 15 minutes

4 large apples of your
favorite kind, diced
1 large banana, diced
1/4 cup raisins
1/3 cup peanuts

Dressing:
1/3 cup mayonnaise *or*
salad dressing
1/3 cup peanut butter
1/4 tsp. vanilla
1 tsp. lemon juice
1/4 cup half-and-half
1/2 cup brown sugar

1. Combine apples,
banana, raisins, and peanuts
in a large bowl.
2. In a small bowl, mix
together mayonnaise, peanut
butter, vanilla, lemon juice,
half-and-half, and sugar until
smooth.
3. Just before serving, toss
the dressing with the fruit.

*Tip: You can use this either as
a salad or as a light dessert.*

*Variation: For a more
caramel-like dressing, eliminate
the mayonnaise or salad dressing.*

Double Apple Salad
Anne Nolt
Thompsontown, PA

Makes 10-12 servings

Prep Time: 20 minutes
Chilling Time: 1 hour

1 large golden delicious
apple, unpeeled and
diced
1 large red delicious apple,
unpeeled and diced
1 tsp. lemon juice
20-oz. can pineapple
chunks, drained
1 cup miniature
marshmallows
2/3 cup flaked coconut
1/2 cup chopped walnuts
1/4 cup raisins
1/4 cup mayonnaise
2 Tbsp. thinly sliced celery

1. In a large mixing bowl,
toss apples with lemon juice
until coated.
2. pineapple, marshmal-
lows, coconut, walnuts,
raisins, mayonnaise, and celery.
3. Mix well and transfer to
a serving bowl. Cover and
chill for 1 hour before serving.

Southwest Salad
Sue Hamilton
Minooka, IL

Makes 6-7 servings

Prep Time: 5 minutes
*Cooking Time: 10 minutes, if
cooking the Quick Barley*
Chilling Time: 1 hour

2 cups cooked barley
15-oz. can black beans,
rinsed and drained
15-oz. can kidney beans,
rinsed and drained
12-oz. can Mexican corn,
drained
1 green onion, diced
1 cup minced cilantro
1/2 cup vinegar
4 Tbsp. olive oil
1 pkg. dry chili seasoning
mix

1. Combine all ingredients
in a large bowl. Mix well.
2. Chill for an hour before
serving.

*Tip: Use "Quick Barley," which
only takes 10 minutes to cook.*

A Tip —

When you're making
an evening meal, make a
little extra for the next
day's lunch. You'll save
money and probably eat
more nutritionally.

Wheat Berry Salad

Sara Harter Fredette
Goshen, MA

Makes 6 servings

Prep Time: 5 minutes
Cooking Time: 1 hour
Chilling Time: 2-4 hours

1¹/3 cups dry wheat berries
1 qt. water
¹/3 cup raspberry vinegar
2¹/2 Tbsp. olive oil
¹/4 cup fresh parsley,
    chopped
3 scallions, sliced
¹/2 cup dried cranberries
Tabasco to taste
1 Tbsp. lemon juice
¹/4 tsp. salt
1 Tbsp. sesame oil

1. In a medium-sized saucepan, simmer wheat berries in 1 qt. water for 1 hour, or until tender. (You can also soak the berries overnight and then simmer them for 40 minutes.) Rinse and cool to room temperature.
2. In a large mixing bowl, mix wheat berries with the remaining ingredients.
3. Chill for 2-3 hours.
4. Taste and add more of any of the last 4 ingredients for additional flavor.

Mandarin Couscous Salad

Lourene G. Bender
Harrisonburg, VA

Makes 6-7 servings

Prep Time: 25 minutes

1¹/3 cups water
1 cup uncooked couscous
1 cup frozen peas
11-oz. can mandarin
    oranges, drained
¹/2 cup slivered almonds,
    toasted
¹/3 cup red onions,
    chopped
¹/4 cup red wine vinegar
2 Tbsp. olive oil
4 tsp. sugar
¹/4 tsp. salt
¹/4 tsp. hot pepper sauce,
    *or slightly more, if you
    wish*

1. Bring water to a boil in a saucepan. Stir in couscous, cover, and remove from heat. Let stand 5 minutes.
2. Fluff with fork and add frozen peas.
3. In a mixing bowl, combine oranges, almonds, and onions. Stir into couscous/peas mixture.
4. Combine vinegar, oil, sugar, salt, and hot pepper sauce in a jar with a lid. Shake well.
5. Pour dressing over couscous mixture and toss to coat.
6. Serve at room temperature or chilled.

Variations:
    1. Use fresh oranges instead of mandarin oranges.
    2. Instead of peas use diced cucumbers or cut-up blanched green beans.

Lotsa-Tomatoes Salsa

Wafi Brandt
Manheim, PA

Makes 2¹/2 cups

Prep Time: 30 minutes
Cooking Time: 30 minutes
Chilling Time: 2 hours

3 cups cubed tomatoes
³/4 cup chopped onions
¹/4 cup (3 medium-sized)
    seeded, chopped
    jalapeno peppers
³/4 tsp. salt
¹/4 tsp. pepper
2 Tbsp. vinegar
¹/2 cup chopped green
    peppers
¹/4 tsp. garlic powder
1 Tbsp. lemon juice

1. Combine all ingredients in a medium-sized saucepan.
2. Cover and cook over medium heat for 30 minutes.
3. Chill for 2 hours before serving.

Tofu Salad

Sara Harter Fredette
Goshen, MA

Makes 4-6 servings

Prep Time: 10 minutes
Cooking Time: 10 minutes
Chilling Time: 2-3 hours

1 pkg. extra-firm tofu,
  cubed
1 carrot, grated
1 scallion, sliced
1 clove garlic, minced
1/3-1/2 cup sunflower seeds
1 Tbsp. soy sauce
2 Tbsp. lemon juice and
  rind
2 Tbsp. olive oil
1/4 tsp. salt
1/8 tsp. pepper

1. In a saucepan, steam tofu in 1" of water for 10 minutes.
2. Drain, and cool. Crumble with fork.
3. Place crumbled tofu, carrot, scallion, garlic, and seeds in a large mixing bowl. Combine gently.
4. In a jar with a tight-fitting lid, combine all remaining ingredients.
5. Pour dressing over the tofu/veggies mixture. Combine well.
6. Cover and chill for 1-2 hours.

Fresh Corn Salsa

J.B. Miller, Indianapolis, IN

Makes about 3½-4 cups

Prep Time: 20 minutes
Cooking Time: 15 minutes
Marinating Time: 3-4 hours,
  or overnight

Dressing:
1 tsp. chili powder
1/4 tsp. garlic granules, *or*
  1 clove garlic
black pepper to taste
1 Tbsp. water
2 Tbsp. fresh lime juice
5 Tbsp. corn *or* vegetable
  oil
1 tsp. sugar
1/2 tsp. salt, *divided*

Salsa:
3 ears sweet corn
1 bell pepper
1 jalapeno pepper, cored,
  seeded, and minced
1/2 cup chopped tomatoes
1/4 cup (about 3-4) green
  onions, sliced
cilantro to taste, *optional*

1. To make dressing, mix chili powder, garlic, and black pepper with 1 Tbsp. water in a small bowl. Let stand 5 minutes.
2. Add lime juice, oil, sugar, and 1/4 tsp. salt.
3. Whisk to combine and set aside.
4. Place husked corn in a large pot of rapidly boiling water and cook 10 minutes. Rinse with cold water and drain.

5. While corn is boiling, roast the bell pepper; then chop.
6. Cut off cooked corn kernels, cutting as deeply as possible without getting cob.
7. Place kernels in a large bowl, along with the chopped roasted bell pepper. Add jalapeno, tomatoes, and onions.
8. Pour the mixed dressing over the salsa and toss gently to combine. Refrigerate 3-4 hours or overnight.
9. Just before serving, toss again, taste, and adjust seasoning to your liking. Add 1/4 tsp. salt and cilantro, if you wish.
10. Serve with white and yellow corn chips.

Raspberry Vinaigrette

Colleen Heatwole
Burton, MI

Makes 1-1½ cups dressing

Prep Time: 5-10 minutes

1 cup raspberries, fresh *or*
  frozen and thawed
1/4 cup raspberry vinegar
2 Tbsp. olive oil
1 Tbsp. honey
1/4 tsp. dry mustard

1. Blend all ingredients in food processor or blender.
2. Refrigerate.

Zesty French Dressing
Erma Rutt
Newmanstown, PA

Makes about 2 cups dressing

Prep Time: 5-10 minutes

1 small onion, chopped
2/3 cup vegetable oil
1/2 cup white sugar
1/3 cup vinegar
2 Tbsp. ketchup
1 1/2 tsp. Worcestershire sauce
1 tsp. salt
1 tsp. prepared mustard
1 tsp. paprika
1/2 tsp. garlic powder
1/2 tsp. celery seed

1. Combine all ingredients in blender.
2. Blend until smooth.
3. Store in refrigerator.

Favorite Balsamic Dressing
Ann Bender
Fort Defiance, VA

Makes about 1/2 cup dressing

Prep Time: 5 minutes

1/4 cup olive oil
2 Tbsp. balsamic vinegar
1 tsp. prepared mustard
1 clove garlic

2 Tbsp. sugar
1/8 tsp. salt
1/8 tsp. pepper

1. Combine olive oil, vinegar, mustard, garlic, sugar, salt, and pepper in blender.
2. Blend until smooth.
3. Store in refrigerator.

Country Sweet-and-Sour Dressing
Annabelle Unternahrer
Shipshewana, IN

Makes about 3 1/4 cups

Prep Time: 5 minutes
Chilling Time: 1 hour

1 1/2 cups sugar
1/2 cup light mayonnaise
1 1/2 cups olive oil
1/2 tsp. pepper
1 1/2 tsp. celery seed
3/4 cup cider vinegar
2 Tbsp. dry mustard
2 Tbsp. chopped onions

1. In a blender, combine all ingredients.
2. Blend on high for 2 minutes.
3. Refrigerate 1 hour before serving. Refrigerate any leftover dressing.

Ranch Dressing
Pat Unternahrer
Wayland, IA

Makes 3/4 cup dressing

Prep Time: 5 minutes

2/3 cup cottage cheese
2 Tbsp. milk
1 Tbsp. tarragon vinegar
1 garlic clove, minced
1 Tbsp. sliced green onions

1. Blend cottage cheese, milk, vinegar, and garlic in blender or food processor.
2. Add green onions and blend just to combine.
3. Store in refrigerator.

Desserts

Crisps, Cobblers, & Puddings

Ultimate Apple Crisp
Judi Manos, West Islip, NY

Makes 6-8 servings

Prep Time: 15 minutes
Cooking/Baking Time:
25 minutes

6-8 apples (use baking apples if you can find them)

1 cup brown sugar
1 cup dry oats, quick *or* rolled (both work, but rolled have more texture)
1 cup flour
1 Tbsp. cinnamon
1½ sticks (¾ cup) butter, melted
half a stick (¼ cup) butter, cut in pieces

1. Core, peel if you want, and slice apples. Place in microwave and oven-safe baking dish (a Pyrex-type pie plate works well).
2. In a separate bowl, mix together brown sugar, oats, flour, and cinnamon. Add melted butter and mix with a fork until thoroughly mixed.
3. Place mixture on top of the apples. Microwave on high, uncovered, for 10 minutes. Let stand for 2 minutes.
4. Cut up the half stick of butter, and place on top of heated apple mixture.
5. Place in oven and bake at 350° for 15 minutes.

Cherry Berry Cobbler
Carol DiNuzzo, Latham, NY

Makes 6 servings

Prep Time: 10 minutes
Baking Time: 30 minutes

21-oz. can cherry pie filling
10-oz. pkg. frozen red raspberries, thawed and drained
1 tsp. lemon juice
½ cup flour
¼ cup sugar
⅛ tsp. salt
half a stick (¼ cup) butter

1. In a saucepan, combine pie filling, raspberries, and lemon juice. Bring to a boil over medium heat.
2. Turn into a greased 1-qt. casserole.
3. In a bowl, mix together flour, sugar, and salt. Cut in butter until crumbly. Sprinkle over fruit.
4. Serve warm (not hot) alone, or over ice cream.

Apple Pear Crisp

Christie Detamore-Hunsberger
Harrisonburg, VA

Makes 6-8 servings

Prep Time: 20 minutes
Baking Time: 45 minutes

3 to 4 large apples, peeled and sliced (use baking apples if you can find them)
3 to 4 large pears, peeled and sliced
1/2 cup sugar
1 Tbsp. lemon juice
1 Tbsp. flour

Topping:
1 cup flour
1 cup brown sugar
2/3 cup dry oats, quick *or* rolled (rolled have more texture)
1/2 tsp. cinnamon
6 Tbsp. cold butter

1. In a large bowl, mix together apples, pears, sugar, lemon juice, and flour. Place in a greased 9 x 13 baking dish.
2. In the same bowl, mix dry topping ingredients.
3. Cut butter into chunks. Cut into dry topping ingredients with a pastry cutter or two knives. When topping resembles small peas, sprinkle over fruit mixture.
4. Bake uncovered at 375° for 45 minutes.

Cranberry Pudding

Barbara Jean Fabel
Wausau, WI

Makes 9 servings

Prep Time: 10 minutes
Baking Time: 30 minutes

Pudding:
2 cups flour
1 cup sugar
1/4 tsp. salt
4 tsp. baking powder
1 cup milk, *or more*
3 Tbsp. butter, melted
2 cups raw cranberries, cut in half

Sauce:
2 cups half-and-half
2/3 cup sugar
2 Tbsp. cornstarch
1/8 tsp. salt
2-4 Tbsp. butter

1. To make pudding, mix ingredients together in order named.
2. Bake in a greased 9 x 9 baking pan at 400° for 30 minutes.
3. While the pudding is baking, make the sauce by scalding the half-and-half.
4. In a small bowl, combine the sugar, cornstarch, and salt. When thoroughly mixed add to the hot half-and-half in the saucepan.
5. Bring to a boil, stirring constantly until mixture thickens. Stir in butter.
6. Serve hot over hot pudding.

This has been our family's Christmas dessert for 3 generations!

Fruit Cobbler

Abbie Christie
Berkeley Heights, NJ

Makes 6-8 servings

Prep Time: 10 minutes
Baking Time: 30-45 minutes

1 stick (1/2 cup) butter
1 cup flour
1 cup milk
1 cup sugar
2 tsp. baking powder
dash of salt
3-4 cups fresh fruit

1. Preheat oven to 350°.
2. Melt butter in a greased 9 x 9 baking dish.
3. Add all other ingredients except fruit. Stir well.
4. Arrange fruit on top of dough.
5. Bake 40-55 minutes, or until lightly browned and fruit is tender.
6. Serve warm with ice cream or milk.

Tip: Use fruit that is in season. The more fruit the better!

In the summer, we would pick blackberries at my sister-in-law's farm, and she would make this for dessert. I always think of her when I make it.

Rhubarb Crisp

Carolyn Lehman Henry
Clinton, NY

Makes 12 servings

Prep Time: 30 minutes
Baking Time: 35 minutes

2 qts. rhubarb cut in
   1″ pieces
1 cup sugar
1/3 cup flour

Topping:
1 cup flour
1/2 cup sugar
1/2 cup brown sugar
1/2 cup dry rolled oats
1/2 cup butter, melted

1. Combine first 3 ingredients and pour into a greased 9 x 13 baking pan.
2. Combine the topping ingredients in a mixing bowl. Sprinkle over rhubarb mixture.
3. Bake uncovered at 375° for 35 minutes.

Variation: Speed things up by preparing this in a microwave. Place the first 3 ingredients in a greased glass 9 x 13 baking pan. Cover with plastic and microwave on high for 3 minutes.

After placing the topping ingredients over the rhubarb, microwave the dish uncovered on high for 8-10 minutes, or until the rhubarb is tender.
   — Wendy Nice
   Goshen, IN

Rhubarb Delight

Donna Lantgen
Rapid City, SD
Dorla Verhey
Mitchell, SD

Makes 12 servings

Prep Time: 15 minutes
Cooking/Baking Time:
60-75 minutes

1 cup flour
2 tsp. sugar
1 stick (1/2 cup) buttter,
   melted
11/4 cups sugar
3 egg yolks, beaten
1/3 cup sour cream, *or*
   light cream, *or*
   condensed milk
2 Tbsp. flour
3 cups rhubarb

Meringue:
3 egg whites, whipped
1/4 cup sugar

1. Combine 1 cup flour, 2 tsp. sugar, and butter. Press into a greased 9 x 9 baking pan.
2. Bake uncovered at 325° for 20 minutes.
3. In a saucepan, combine 11/4 cups sugar, egg yolks, sour cream (or light cream or condensed milk), 2 Tbsp. flour, and rhubarb. Cook over medium heat until the rhubarb is tender and starts to thicken and bubble, about 1/2 hour. Pour into crust.
4. Make the meringue by whipping egg whites in a large bowl until stiff. Add sugar one tablespoon at a time.
5. Spoon meringue over top of rhubarb filling. Bake uncovered at 325° for 10-15 minutes, or until meringue is brown.

Rhubarb-Strawberry Dessert

Betty K. Drescher
Quakertown, PA

Makes: 6-8 servings

Prep Time: 10 minutes
Cooking Time: 15-20 minutes
Chilling Time: 3 hours

3/4 cup sugar
3 Tbsp. instant tapioca
2 cups boiling water
2 cups sliced rhubarb
3-oz. box strawberry
   gelatin
1 cup water
3/4 cup fresh strawberries

1. In a medium-sized saucepan, combine sugar, tapioca, and boiling water. Let stand 5 minutes. Then bring to a boil, stirring frequently.
2. Add rhubarb and simmer for 5 minutes. Remove from heat.
3. Stir in gelatin and water.
4. When cooled and slightly thickened, add fresh strawberries.
5. Spoon into a serving dish and chill until set, about 3 hours.

Frozen Fruit Slush

Ida Stoltzfus
Free Union, VA

Makes 15-20 servings

Prep Time: 20 minutes
Freezing Time: 4-8 hours,
or overnight

1 cup sugar
pinch of salt
2 cups warm water
6-oz. can orange juice
concentrate
20-oz. can pineapple
tidbits, undrained
8 bananas, sliced
1 pt. frozen peaches,
partially thawed
1-2 cups red *or* green
grapes

1. In a large mixing bowl, dissolve sugar and salt in water.
2. Add orange juice concentrate and pineapple. Mix well.
3. Fold in bananas, peaches, and grapes. Mix well.
4. Pour into a 9 x 13 pan. Freeze.
5. Before serving, put slush in refrigerator for 1-2 hours.

Tips:
   1. You can substitute mandarin oranges or canned peaches for frozen peaches.
   2. I sometimes put the slush into 4- or 6-oz. containers to freeze. Individual cups make excellent lunch-box ingredients

or appetizers for a brunch.

Variation:
1. Reduce the number of bananas to 2. Substitute 2 cups sliced fresh or frozen strawberries for the grapes.
— **Janet Oberholtzer**
Ephrata, PA

Award-Winning Ice Cream

Monica Leaman Kehr
Portland, MI

Makes 6 servings

Prep Time: 10 minutes
Chilling Time: 1-2 hours
Churning and freezing time
(in an electric ice-cream
maker): 30-40 minutes

12-oz. can evaporated milk
14-oz. can sweetened
condensed milk
1½ cups milk (2% works
well)
1½ cups heavy whipping
cream
2 Tbsp. vanilla
1 cup sugar

1. Mix all ingredients very well. Chill.
2. Mix again before pouring into your ice cream freezer.
3. Follow your ice-cream freezer's directions for churning and freezing.

Ice Cream-in-a-Bag

Annabelle Unternahrer
Shipshewana, IN

Makes 2+ cups

Prep Time: 10 minutes
Shaking Time: 10-15 minutes

2 cups skim milk
⅓ cup sugar
1 tsp. vanilla
5 cups ice
¾ cup rock salt
¼ cup water

1. In a 1-qt. resealable bag, combine milk, sugar, and vanilla.
2. In a 1-gallon resealable bag, combine ice, salt, and water. Then add bag with ice cream mix in it.
3. Close gallon bag very securely. Wrap with a heavy towel.
4. Shake 10-15 minutes, or until ice cream is frozen.

Kids ages 3-90 love to make this recipe.

A Tip —

   When working with large amounts of sugar in a recipe, measure it all out ahead of time, and set it aside. That way you won't forget how much you have already put in.

198

Chocolate Mocha Sauce

Lorraine Arnold
Rhinebeck, NY
Jane S. Lippincott
Wynnewood, PA

Makes 2 cups

Prep Time: 5 minutes
Cooking Time: 15 minutes

3/4 **cup unsweetened cocoa powder**
1/2 **cup cream**
1/2 **cup milk**
1 **Tbsp. butter**
1 **Tbsp. dry instant coffee**
1/8 **tsp. salt**
1 **cup light brown sugar**
1/2 **cup sugar**
1 **tsp. vanilla**

1. Mix all ingredients except vanilla in a heavy saucepan. Bring to a boil over medium-high heat.
2. Turn heat down and simmer 5 minutes. When cool, stir in vanilla.
3. Serve with brownies or vanilla ice cream.

My grandmother made this sauce when I was a child. She will soon be 100 years old, and she no longer cooks. But my sister and I still make her recipes.

Variation:
Substitute fat-free half-and-half for the cream. It works!
— Cassandra Ly
Carlisle, PA

Chocolate Ice Cream Syrup

Christine Weaver
Reinholds, PA

Makes 2 1/2-3 cups

Prep Time: 5 minutes
Cooking Time: 30 minutes

3/4 **cup semi-sweet chocolate chips,** *or* **6 squares unsweetened chocolate**
3 **Tbsp. butter (no substitutes)**
2 **cups sugar**
12-oz. **can evaporated milk**

1. Microwave the chocolate and butter in a microwave-safe dish, stirring a few times, for approximately 3-4 minutes.
2. Transfer chocolate to a heavy saucepan. Add sugar and milk alternately, stirring until blended.
3. Cook 15 minutes over low heat, stirring frequently.
4. Serve warm over ice cream. Refrigerate leftovers.

Hot Fudge Sauce

Doris Bachman
Putnam, IL

Makes 1 1/2-2 cups

Prep Time: 12 minutes
Cooking Time: 12 minutes

1 **cup sugar**
1/3 **cup unsweetened cocoa powder**
2 **Tbsp., + 1 tsp., flour**
pinch of salt
1 **cup water**
1 **Tbsp. butter**

1. In a saucepan, mix all dry ingredients together well.
2. Pour in water, stirring until well mixed. Add butter and bring to a boil.
3. Cook slowly for 8 minutes, stirring often.

A Tip —

When having a group for a meal, do as much as possible in advance—set the table, peel the potatoes and cover them with cold water, and so on. Do it the evening before if you can.

Blueberry Sauce

Jeannine Dougherty
Tyler, TX

Makes 2½ cups

Prep Time: 5 minutes
Cooking Time: 15-20 minutes

¼-½ cup sugar, according
    to your taste preference
2 tsp. cornstarch
pinch of salt
½ cup water
2 cups fresh *or* frozen
    blueberries
2 tsp. lemon juice

1. In a medium-sized
saucepan, combine sugar,
cornstarch, and salt. Mix
well.
2. Add water and blueberries. Mix well.
3. Bring mixture to a boil,
stirring constantly. Cook until
thick and translucent.
4. Remove from heat and
stir in lemon juice.

*Here's a great dessert—or
quick meal: place a waffle or a
couple of thin pancakes on a
plate. Add a scoop of good ice
cream and cover with warm
blueberry sauce.*

*When cold, this sauce is also
very good over plain ice cream,
yogurt, or cottage cheese. Or
serve it as a topping for pound
cake or angel food cake.*

Raspberry Sauce

Jennifer Kuh
Bay Village, OH

Makes 2 cups sauce

Prep Time: 5 minutes

12-oz. bag frozen
    raspberries
½ cup confectioners sugar
¼ tsp. lemon juice
¼ cup amaretto

1. Blend all ingredients in
a blender until smooth.
2. Pour/drain through a
strainer to separate seeds.
3. Serve over pound cake,
ice cream, frozen yogurt,
yogurt, chocolate mousse,
pancakes, or waffles.
4. Refrigerate unused portion.

A Tip —

If you're using a recipe
that calls for beaten eggs
and shortening, break the
eggs into a measuring cup
before you use the cup to
measure the shortening.
Then, when you use the
cup for the shortening, it
will slip right out.

Lemon Butter

Lois Niebauer
Pedricktown, NJ

Makes 3½ cups

Prep Time: 20 minutes
Baking Time: 15-20 minutes

3 large lemons
4 large eggs
1 cup sugar
2 cups water
2-3 Tbsp. butter
3 heaping Tbsp. cornstarch

1. Wash lemons. Finely
grate the yellow part of the
skins. Set aside.
2. Squeeze juice of lemons.
Get rid of seeds.
3. In a small bowl, beat
eggs to break up the egg
whites.
4. In a saucepan, combine
all ingredients. Bring to a low
boil, stirring constantly.
5. When mixture thickens,
remove from heat. Pour into
a bowl and chill.
6. Serve as a side dish like
applesauce, or over cake or
gingerbread.

Oreo Ice Cream Dessert

Wanda Marshall
Massillon, OH

Makes 12-15 servings

Prep Time: 20 minutes
Freezing Time: 8 hours,
  or overnight

30 Oreo cookies
¼ cup melted butter
2 Tbsp. instant coffee
  powder
½ gallon vanilla ice cream,
  partially softened
⅔ cup chocolate syrup
salted pecans

1. Crush Oreo cookies and mix with melted butter. Cover bottom of 9 x 13 pan with the mixture.
2. Blend coffee into softened ice cream using mixer. Drop spoonfuls of ice cream over the crust. Carefully spread the mixture over the cookie crust, being careful not to disturb the crust.
3. Pour chocolate syrup over ice cream. Swirl chocolate syrup through ice cream using a table knife.
4. Sprinkle salted pecans over top and place in freezer.
5. Freeze for 8 hours, or overnight, before cutting into pieces to serve.

Variations:
  1. Use hot fudge sauce instead of chocolate sauce.
  2. Use peanuts instead of pecans.

3. After freezing (Step 5), spread an 8-oz. container of thawed whipped topping over the nuts. Then top with a cup of cookie crumbs. Freeze again for 4 hours before cutting to serve.

— **Pam Hochstedler**
Kalona, IA

Frozen Heath Bar Mocha Mousse

Ida Stoltzfus
Free Union, VA

Makes 15-18 servings

Prep Time: 20-30 minutes
Chilling Time: 30-60 minutes
Freezing Time: 6 hours,
  or overnight
Thawing Time: 1 hour

1½ cups crushed Oreo
  cookies
¼ cup butter, melted
2¾ cups cold milk
2 3.9-oz. pkgs. instant
  chocolate pudding
3 tsp. instant coffee
  powder
2 Tbsp. hot water
1 ice cube
8 ozs. frozen whipped
  topping, thawed
1 cup, plus 2 Tbsp.,
  crushed Heath Bars,
  divided

1. Mix crushed Oreos and butter. Press into a 9 x 13 pan. Put into freezer until pudding is made.
2. In a mixing bowl, stir together pudding and milk. Chill until of soft-set consistency.
3. Mix coffee powder with hot water in a mug until dissolved. Add ice cube until mixture cools. Remove any remaining cube.
4. Fold cooled coffee and whipped topping into soft-set pudding until blended.
5. Add 1 cup crushed Heath Bars.
6. Spoon into cookie crust in pan, being careful not to disturb the crust crumbs.
7. Garnish with 2 tablespoons crushed Heath Bars.
8. Freeze for 6 hours, or overnight.
9. Thaw in refrigerator for 1 hour prior to serving.

Caramel Pudding

Esther S. Martin
Ephrata, PA

Makes 16 servings

Prep Time: 10 minutes
Cooking Time: 15-20 minutes
Chilling Time: 2-3 hours

1 stick (8 Tbsp.) butter
2 cups brown sugar
1/2 cup water
2 qts. milk
pinch of salt
6 eggs
5 rounded Tbsp.
    cornstarch
5 rounded Tbsp. flour
1 Tbsp. vanilla
whipped topping *or*
    whipped cream

1. In heavy saucepan, melt butter. Add brown sugar. Bring to a boil and continue simmering until mixture browns. Stir occasionally so it doesn't stick and burn.

2. Remove from heat and add water. Stir in milk and salt. Return pan to stove over low heat.

3. In a blender, mix eggs, cornstarch, and flour.

4. Add to caramel-milk mixture and heat until boiling, stirring constantly or whisking as mixture thickens.

5. Remove from stove and add vanilla.

6. Pour into two serving dishes.

7. Chill. Top with whipped topping or whipped cream just before serving.

Rice Pudding

Judy Koczo
Plano, IL

Makes 6 servings

Prep Time: 30 minutes
Cooking Time: 25-30 minutes
Chilling Time: 2-3 hours

1 1/3 cups uncooked,
    converted rice
1/2 cup sugar
pinch of salt
1/2 tsp. nutmeg
2 Tbsp. butter
1 tsp. vanilla
5 cups milk
5-oz. can evaporated milk
2 egg yolks
3 Tbsp. milk
whipped topping, *optional*
cinnamon, *optional*

1. Combine all ingredients—except egg yolks and 3 Tbsp. milk—in a pan. Cover and cook over low heat. After it comes to a slow boil, cook for 20 minutes.

2. While rice is cooking, beat 2 egg yolks with 3 tablespoons milk in a small bowl.

3. When rice is cooked, remove rice from heat. Add egg-yolk mixture immediately.

4. Refrigerate until chilled and then serve. Garnish with whipped topping and sprinkles of cinnamon, if you wish.

Tapioca Pudding

Miriam Christophel
Goshen, IN

Makes 5 servings

Prep Time: 10 minutes
Cooking Time: 15 minutes
Cooling Time:
    20 minutes-2 hours

3 Tbsp. dry instant tapioca
1/3 cup sugar
1/8 tsp. salt
1 egg, beaten
3 cups milk
3/4 tsp. vanilla

1. In a 2-quart saucepan, combine all ingredients except vanilla. Let stand 5 minutes.

2. Bring ingredients to a boil, stirring constantly. Boil for 1 minute.

3. Remove from heat. Stir in vanilla.

4. Stir once after cooling for 20 minutes.

5. Serve warm or cold.

This is good just as it is, or with a sliced banana and some whipped cream stirred in. It is our kids' favorite dessert. I like it because it isn't as sweet as some puddings are.

Strawberr-i-oca

Pauline Hindal
Grandin, MI

Makes 12 servings

Prep Time: 15 minutes
Cooking Time: 20 minutes
Chilling Time: 4 hours

4 cups water
1 cup sugar
3/4 cup dry minute tapioca
1/4 tsp. salt
2 3-oz. pkgs. strawberry
  gelatin
1 qt. partially frozen
  strawberries
2 bananas, *optional*
1-2 cups whipped topping
  or whipped cream

1. In a 4-quart saucepan mix together water, sugar, tapioca, and salt. Cook on high, stirring until sugar is dissolved and mixture comes to a boil. Turn to medium-low and continue cooking for 10 minutes, stirring frequently.

2. Remove from heat. Add gelatin and stir until dissolved.

3. Add partially frozen strawberries and sliced bananas, if you wish.

4. Pour into a serving bowl and refrigerate until soft-set.

5. Fold in whipped topping and refrigerate until fully set.

Bread Pudding

Betty Moore
Plano, IL

Makes 15 servings

Prep Time: 20 minutes
Cooking/Baking Time:
  70 minutes

4 cups milk
1/4 tsp. salt
1 cup sugar
2 Tbsp. butter
4 eggs, beaten
4 cups cubed bread
1 tsp. vanilla
1/2 cup raisins, *optional*

Vanilla Sauce:
1/2 cup sugar
1 Tbsp. cornstarch
1/8 tsp. salt
1/4 tsp. nutmeg
1 cup water
1 tsp. vanilla
2 Tbsp. butter

1. In a medium-sized saucepan, scald milk. When it has formed a skin, stir in salt, sugar, and butter.

2. Beat eggs in a large mixing bowl. Pour the scalded milk mixture slowly over the beaten eggs. Mix well.

3. Fold in bread cubes and vanilla.

4. Stir in raisins, if you wish.

5. Spoon into a greased 9 x 13 baking pan. Bake uncovered at 350° for 1 hour.

6. While the bread is baking, make the vanilla sauce by combining in the saucepan, the sugar, cornstarch, salt, and nutmeg. Stir in water and vanilla.

7. Cook over medium heat, stirring continuously, until sauce is thick and clear.

8. Stir in butter. Spread sauce over top of bread pudding as soon as it comes out of the oven.

9. Serve warm or cold.

Variation: Instead of the Vanilla Sauce, blend 2 cups fresh or frozen strawberries in a food processor. Stir in 1/4 cup sugar. Serve over warm bread pudding.

— Eleanor J. Ferreira
North Chelmsford, MA

A Tip —

When buying bakeware and kitchen tools, spend the extra money for good quality.

Fruity Bread Pudding with Brandy Sauce

Sonya Reimer
Salisbury Mills, NY

Makes 10-12 servings

Prep Time: 20 minutes
Cooking Time: 70 minutes
Cooling/Standing Time:
25 minutes

15 slices of bread, *or* 1 loaf
of French bread
13-oz. can evaporated milk
2½ cups milk
1 stick (½ cup) butter, cut
into pieces
5 eggs, well beaten
2 cups sugar
1 Granny Smith apple,
peeled and diced, *or*
another firm, tart apple
10-oz. pkg. frozen peaches,
chopped and drained
½ cup raisins
1 tsp. allspice
1 tsp. nutmeg
1½ tsp. cinnamon
1 Tbsp. vanilla

Brandy Sauce, *optional:*
2 cups sugar
1 Tbsp. lemon juice
1 stick (½ cup) butter
2 large eggs, lightly beaten
2 large egg yolks
1 tsp. vanilla
⅓ cup brandy

1. Tear bread into pieces
and place in a large glass bowl.
2. In a saucepan, over low
heat, combine evaporated
milk, milk, and butter. Heat
until butter is melted and milk
is hot.
3. Pour over bread, mix
well, and let stand for 10 minutes.
4. Combine beaten eggs,
sugar, apple, peaches, and
raisins. Stir into bread.
5. Combine allspice, nut-
meg, cinnamon, and vanilla.
Stir into bread.
6. Pour into a lightly
greased 9 x 13 baking pan. Set
baking pan into a larger baking
pan with 1 inch of water in it.
7. Bake at 350° for 1 hour.
Cool 15 minutes.
8. Serve hot or cold, with or
without brandy sauce.
9. If you want to include
the sauce, make it while the
bread is baking. Heat sugar
and lemon juice in a saucepan
over medium heat. Stir often
until mixture turns light
brown.
10. In another pan, over
low heat, melt butter. Remove
from heat. Whip eggs and egg
yolks with butter until
blended.
11. Add vanilla and brandy
to sugar/lemon juice mixture.
Mix well.
12. Slowly beat
brandy/sugar mixture into egg
mixture.
13. Return to stove and heat
over low heat until sauce
thickens.
14. Spoon warm sauce over
bread pudding just before serving.

Tips:
1. The bread pudding is best
served warm.
2. Keep any leftover sauce in
the fridge. Reheat it in the
microwave when you're ready
to use it.
3. Freezing the bread pud-
ding may affect its texture.
4. This is a great dish for
breakfast or dessert.

Pumpkin Ginger Squares

Margaret Culbert, Lebanon, PA
Gina Hargitt, Quinter, KS

Makes 16-20 servings

Prep Time: 20 minutes
Baking Time: 50-55 minutes
Chilling Time: 2 hours

1 cup flour
½ cup dry quick oats
½ cup brown sugar
1 stick (½ cup) butter,
softened
2 cups pumpkin
12-oz. can evaporated milk
2 eggs
¾ cup sugar
½ tsp. salt
1 tsp. cinnamon
½ tsp ginger
½ cup chopped pecans *or*
walnuts
½ cup brown sugar
2 Tbsp. butter, melted

1. In a large mixing bowl, mix together flour, quick oats, and 1/2 cup brown sugar. When well blended, cut in 1/2 cup butter with a pastry cutter until mixture is crumbly.

2. Press into the bottom of a lightly greased 9 x 13 baking pan. Bake at 350° for 15 minutes.

3. In the same mixing bowl, combine pumpkin, evaporated milk, eggs, sugar, salt, cinnamon, and ginger. Mix well.

4. Spoon pumpkin mixture over baked crust, being careful not to disturb the crumbs. Return to oven and bake another 20 minutes at 350°.

5. Meanwhile, combine pecans or walnuts, 1/2 cup brown sugar and 2 Tbsp. melted butter. Sprinkle over baked pumpkin.

6. Return to oven and bake 15-20 minutes more at 350°.

7. Allow to cool completely before cutting into squares to serve.

A Tip —

When a recipe calls for eggs, break them into a separate bowl or cup. You can remove any loose shells before adding the eggs to the recipe you're preparing.

Pumpkin Cream
Esther J. Mast
Lancaster, PA

Makes 8-10 servings

Prep Time: 5 minutes
Cooking Time: 15-20 minutes
Chilling Time: 1-2 hours

2 cups pumpkin, canned or freshly sieved
2 cups milk
4 Tbsp. cornstarch
1 cup sugar
1 tsp. salt
1 tsp. cinnamon
1/2 tsp. nutmeg
2 eggs, beaten
1 tsp. cold water
8-oz. container whipped topping

1. Combine pumpkin and milk in a microwavable dish. Microwave on high for 10-15 minutes, or until liquid reaches boiling point.

2. In a mixing bowl, mix together cornstarch, sugar, salt, cinnamon, and nutmeg. Beat in the eggs and water.

3. Stir into the pumpkin/milk mixture and microwave on high an additional 5 minutes, or until thickened.

4. Chill in refrigerator.

5. Reserve some of the whipped topping as a garnish and mix the remainder into the cooled, thickened pumpkin.

This is a creamy alternative to pumpkin pie, with much less work.

Mother's Pumpkin Pudding
Dawn Ranck, Lansdale, PA

Makes 6 servings

Prep Time: 15 minutes
Baking Time: 1 hour

2 eggs, beaten
2 cups mashed pumpkin
1/2 cup sugar
1 Tbsp. flour
1/4 tsp. salt
1/2 cup grated coconut
dash of cinnamon
dash of nutmeg
1 cup milk
8 full-sized marshmallows

1. Combine all ingredients except marshmallows in a large mixing bowl.

2. Pour into a greased 9 x 13 baking dish.

3. Bake at 350° for 30 minutes.

4. Top with marshmallows. Bake an additional 30 minutes.

5. Serve warm or chilled.

Lemon Almond Torte

Kathy Hertzler
Lancaster, PA

Makes 10 servings

Prep Time: 15-20 minutes
Baking Time: 50 minutes
Cooling Time: 15 minutes

2 sticks (1 cup) butter,
 softened
1 cup sugar
1½ cups finely ground
 almonds, *divided*
4 large eggs
1 tsp. vanilla
1 tsp. lemon extract
1 tsp. almond extract
1 Tbsp. grated lemon rind
1 cup flour
1 tsp. baking powder
¼ tsp. salt
¼ cup fresh lemon juice

Glaze:
¼ cup fresh lemon juice
1½-2 cups confectioners
 sugar
10 whole almonds,
 optional

1. In a large electric mix-ing bowl, cream together but-ter, sugar, and 1 cup finely ground almonds until fluffy.

2. Add eggs, one at a time, beating well after each addi-tion.

3. Add 3 extracts and lemon rind. Beat again to incorporate.

4. In a separate mixing bowl, stir together flour, bak-ing powder, and salt. Add to creamed mixture alternately with lemon juice.

5. Spoon batter into a greased and floured 8" spring-form pan.

6. Bake at 350° for 50 min-utes. Cool for 15 minutes. Release springform pan.

7. While cake is still warm, and with the pan sides removed, whisk together lemon juice and confectioners sugar to make the glaze.

8. Spread glaze generously over top and sides of cake. Sprinkle remaining ground almonds over glaze while it is still wet. Garnish with whole almonds if you wish.

Coconut Almond Crunch

Sarah Miller
Harrisonburg, VA
Sherri Grindle
Goshen, IN

Makes 9 servings

Prep Time: 20 minutes
Baking Time: 25-30 minutes
Chilling Time: 1-2 hours

1 stick (½ cup) butter,
 softened
¼ cup brown sugar
½ cup slivered almonds
1 cup grated coconut
1 cup flour
3-oz. box instant vanilla
 pudding
3-oz. box instant coconut
 pudding
2⅔ cups milk
8-oz. container frozen
 whipped topping,
 thawed

1. In a large mixing bowl, combine butter, brown sugar, almonds, coconut, and flour until mixture becomes crumbly.

2. Spread crumbs out on a large baking sheet.

3. Bake at 350° for 25-30 minutes, stirring about every 10 minutes.

4. Meanwhile, beat pud-dings and milk in an electric mixer at low speed 1-2 min-utes. Slowly fold in whipped topping.

5. Layer half the baked crumbs in the bottom of a glass serving bowl. Spoon all the pudding over the crumbs. Top with the remaining crumbs.

6. Chill 1-2 hours.

Variations:
1. Use 2 boxes instant vanilla pudding and drop the coconut pudding, if you prefer.
 — Dolores Metzler
 Lewistown, PA

2. Instead of 2 boxes pud-ding and 2⅔ cups milk, use 1 box instant French vanilla pud-ding and 1⅓ cups milk. Prepare according to Step 4 above.

In Step 5, after spooning pudding into the serving bowl, slice 2 or 3 bananas over the pudding. Then top with crumbs.
 — Kathy Bless
 Fayetteville, PA

Colossal Caramel Apple Trifle

Jane Hindal
Grandin, MI

Makes 35-40 servings

Prep Time: 35 minutes
Baking Time: 30 minutes
Cooling Time: 50-60 minutes

1 pkg. yellow cake mix
6 cups cold milk
3 3.4-oz. pkgs. instant
  vanilla pudding
1 tsp. cinnamon
12.25-oz. container of
  caramel ice cream
  topping
1 1/2 cups chopped pecans,
  divided
2 21-oz. cans apple pie
  filling
2 16-oz. cartons frozen
  whipped topping,
  thawed

1. Make cake according to package directions. Bake in two greased 9" round cake pans.
2. Cool 10 minutes in pans before removing to wire racks to cool completely.
3. In a large bowl, whisk milk, dry pudding mix, and cinnamon for 2 minutes. Let stand 2 minutes or until soft-set.
4. Cut (if necessary) one cake layer to fit evenly in a clear 8-qt. punch bowl. Poke holes in cake with a long wooden skewer. Gradually pour 1/3 of the caramel topping over the cake.

5. Sprinkle with 1/2 cup pecans and spread with half the pudding mixture.
6. Spoon one can pie filling over pudding.
7. Spread one carton whipped topping over pie filling.
8. Top with remaining cake and repeat layers.
9. Drizzle with remaining caramel topping and sprinkle with remaining pecans.

Tips for building this Colossus:

1. If your punch bowl is larger in the middle than at the bottom and top, use the cut-off pieces of cake from the first layer to fill in around the edges of the cake on the second layer.

2. Again, if your bowl is larger in the middle than at the bottom and top, you'll need a scant third of the caramel topping on the first layer, and more than a third on the second layer.

3. When spreading the top layer of whipped topping, use the back of a large spoon to even it out. Then touch the spoon here-and-there to the topping and lift to form peaks.

A Tip —

Buy an oven thermometer so you can check your oven's true heat and temperature.

Apple Bake

Barbara Sparks, Glen Burnie, MD

Makes 6-8 servings

Prep Time: 10-15 minutes
Baking Time: 20-30 minutes

2/3 cup sugar
3/4 cup flour
pinch of salt
1 1/2 tsp. baking powder
1/2 tsp. cinnamon, *or to
  taste*
2 eggs
3/4 tsp. vanilla
3/4 cup chopped nuts
1 1/2 cups Gala apples,
  chopped, *or other
  baking apple, peeled or
  unpeeled*
a little water to thin

1. Lightly grease an 8" or 9" pie plate.
2. Thoroughly mix all ingredients and spread in pie plate.
3. Bake at 350° for 20-30 minutes, until top is browned. (The mix will puff up to fit the pie plate.)

Variation: Cut the cake into wedges and spoon the following warm sauce over top:

1 cup sugar
1 stick (1/2 cup) butter, cut
  in pieces
1/2 cup heavy cream
1 tsp. vanilla

Place all ingredients in a saucepan. Stir. Bring to a boil over medium-high heat. Cook 3 minutes, stirring frequently.
— **Christine Heuser**
Farmingdale, NJ

Gooey Apple Dumplings

Kathy Deal, Noblesville, IN

Makes 8 servings

Prep Time: 15-25 minutes
Cooking/Baking Time:
50-70 minutes

2 8" pie crusts, unbaked
3-4 firm baking apples
   (Granny Smith are good)
8 tsp. brown sugar
8 tsp. butter
8 dashes of cinnamon

Syrup:
1 cup sugar
2 cups water
3 Tbsp. butter
1/4 tsp. cinnamon

1. In a medium-sized saucepan, mix the syrup ingredients together. Boil 3 minutes, watching carefully that the mixture doesn't boil over.

2. Meanwhile, cut the pie crusts into quarters.

3. Divide sliced, pared apples over the crust quarters. Top each with 1 teaspoon brown sugar, 1 teaspoon butter, and a dash of cinnamon.

4. Wrap up each dumpling. Seal the seam with a dab of water.

5. Place in a greased 9 x 13 baking pan. Pour syrup over top.

6. Bake at 350° for 40-60 minutes, or until nicely browned.

Apple Custard Dessert

Barbara Smith
Bedford, PA

Makes 12 servings

Prep Time: 15 minutes
Baking Time: 35-45 minutes

1 pkg. butter recipe golden
   cake mix
1 cup shredded *or* flaked
   coconut
1 stick (1/2 cup) butter, at
   room temperature
6 cups sliced firm baking
   apples, approximately
   6 apples
1 cup water
1/4 cup lemon juice
whipped topping *or* ice
   cream

1. Combine dry cake mix and coconut in a large bowl. Cut in butter with a pastry cutter.

2. Place sliced apples in a greased 9 x 13 baking dish. Sprinkle crumb mixture over apples.

3. In a small bowl, combine water and lemon juice. Pour over apples and crumbs.

4. Bake at 350° for 35-45 minutes, or until lightly browned and set.

5. Cool slightly and serve with whipped topping or ice cream.

Apple Dandy

Eileen Eash
Carlsbad, NM

Makes 12 servings

Prep Time: 20 minutes
Baking Time: 30-40 minutes

2 cups flour
1/2 tsp. baking powder
1 1/2 cups, plus 1 Tbsp.,
   sugar, *divided*
1/2 tsp. salt
3/4 cup shortening
6 Tbsp. milk
6 cups sliced firm apples,
   peeled *or* unpeeled
1 tsp. cinnamon, *divided*
1/2 cup butter
1 3/4 cups boiling water

1. In a large mixing bowl, stir together flour, baking powder, 1 Tbsp. sugar, and salt.

2. Cut in shortening until crumbly. Stir in milk and blend well.

3. Divide dough in half. Roll each piece into a 10 x 14 rectangle.

4. Place one piece in the bottom of a 9 x 13 baking pan. (Reserve the other piece.)

5. In the large mixing bowl, combine apples, 1/2 cup sugar, and 1/2 tsp. cinnamon. Pour into pastry crust.

6. Place second pastry crust on top of apples. When you've evenly covered the apples, cut the unbaked Dandy into 12 pieces, cutting through all layers.

7. In the large mixing bowl, combine the remaining 1 cup sugar, 1/2 tsp. cinnamon, butter, and water. Stir until butter is melted and sugar is dissolved. Pour over dough and apples.

8. Bake at 400° until apples are tender and top is lightly browned, about 30-40 minutes.

Almond Bake

Jeanne Allen
Rye, CO

Makes 10-12 servings

Prep Time: 25 minutes
Baking Time: 30 minutes

2 1/2 cups white *or* yellow cake mix
1 egg, beaten
1/4 cup butter, melted
1 tsp. almond extract
2 3-oz. pkgs. cream cheese, softened
2 eggs
2 1/2 cups, plus 2-4 Tbsp., confectioners sugar
1/2 cup sliced almonds

1. In a large mixing bowl, combine cake mix, egg, butter, and extract. Spread in a greased 9 x 13 baking pan.

2. In the same mixing bowl, blend cheese and eggs. Add confectioners sugar. Mix well.

3. Spoon over bottom layer, spreading carefully. Sprinkle almonds over top.

4. Bake at 350° for 30 minutes, or until golden brown. Sprinkle with confectioners sugar. Serve warm with whipped cream or ice cream.

Butter Rum Bananas

Shari Jensen
Fountain, CO

Makes 4 servings

Prep Time: 5 minutes
Cooking Time: 10 minutes

2 Tbsp. butter
1/2 cup sugar
2 Tbsp. water
2 Tbsp. light rum
1/2 Tbsp. lemon juice
grated rind of half a lemon
1/2 tsp. vanilla *or* rum flavoring
4 small bananas, peeled and halved
whipping cream *or* ice cream

1. Melt butter in a large skillet. Add sugar and water. Stir well. Cook until reduced to heavy syrup, stirring occasionally so the mixture doesn't stick to the bottom of the pan.

2. Add rum, lemon juice, rind, and your choice of flavoring. Cook 2 minutes, or until golden in color.

3. Remove from stove and add banana pieces. Plunge them into the syrup, covering them as well as possible.

4. Serve warm, not hot, topped with a dollop of whipped cream or alongside scoops of ice cream.

Blueberry Crinkle

Makes 6-8 servings

Prep Time: 15-20 minutes
Baking Time: 20 minutes

1/2 cup brown sugar
3/4 cup dry quick oats
1/2 cup flour, white *or* whole wheat
1/2 tsp. cinnamon
dash of salt
6 Tbsp. butter, at room temperature
4 cups blueberries, fresh *or* frozen
2 Tbsp. sugar
2 Tbsp. instant tapioca
2 Tbsp. lemon juice
1/2 tsp. grated lemon peel

1. In a large bowl, combine brown sugar, oats, flour, cinnamon, and salt. Cut in butter to make crumbs. Set aside.

2. In a separate bowl, stir together blueberries, sugar, tapioca, lemon juice, and lemon peel.

3. Spoon into a greased 8" square baking pan. Sprinkle crumbs over blueberries.

4. Bake at 375° for 20 minutes.

Blueberry Tart

Susan Kasting
Jenks, OK

Makes 6-8 servings

Prep Time: 20 minutes
Cooking and Baking Time:
  25 minutes
Chilling Time: 1-2 hours

1 pkg. frozen puff pastry,
  thawed
1 egg
3 Tbsp. water, *divided*
1/2 cup, plus 2 Tbsp.,
  sugar, *divided*
31/2 cups blueberries, fresh
  or frozen
2 Tbsp. instant tapioca
2 tsp. finely grated lemon
  peel
1 Tbsp. lemon juice

1. Roll dough into a 12"
square. Fit into 10" tart or pie
pan. Cut off excess dough.
2. Roll out scraps and cut
into small shapes with cookie
cutters.
3. In a small bowl, beat
together egg and 1 Tbsp.
water. With a pastry brush,
brush sides of tart and small
cut-outs with egg wash.
Sprinkle tart shell and cut-
outs with 2 Tbsp. sugar.
4. Lay cut-outs in a cake
pan. Place in oven, along
with the tart shell. Bake at
400° for 12-15 minutes, until
golden brown.
5. While the pastry is baking combine in a saucepan,
the blueberries, 1/2 cup sugar,
2 Tbsp. water, tapioca, lemon

peel, and lemon juice. Bring
to a boil until berries burst.
6. Lower temperature and
simmer until tapioca dis-
solves (about 10 minutes) and
mixture has thickened. Stir
occasionally.
7. Pour berry mixture into
shell. Lay pastry cut-outs over
top.
8. Chill for 1-2 hours
before serving.

Mom's Cherry Pudding Cake

Willard E. Roth
Elkhart, IN

Makes 6 servings

Prep Time: 10-15 minutes
Baking Time: 25 minutes

1 cup sugar
1 Tbsp. butter, at room
  temperature
1 egg, beaten
1 tsp. baking soda
1 cup flour
15-oz. can pitted red sour
  cherries, *divided, juice*
  reserved
1 Tbsp. cornstarch

1. In a large mixing bowl,
cream butter and sugar. Stir
in egg.
2. In a separate bowl, mix
together baking soda and
flour. Stir into the creamed
mixture until well blended.
3. Fold in 1 cup cherries
(reserve the juice and any
remaining cherries).

4. Spread into an 8" round
cake pan.
5. Bake at 350° for 25 minutes.
6. While the cake is baking
make the glaze. Pour the
reserved juice from the cherries into a saucepan. Stir in
cornstarch. Cook over
medium heat until thickened,
stirring constantly. Stir in
remaining cherries. Serve
warm over warm pudding
cake.

This is a family favorite, pre-
pared for generations without a
formal recipe.

Berry Berry Good Dessert

Katrina Eberly, Stevens, PA

Makes 6 servings

Prep Time: 15 minutes
Chilling Time: 1 hour

8 ozs. cream cheese,
  softened
2 3.4-oz. pkgs. instant
  vanilla pudding
3 cups milk
1 qt. fresh berries of your
  choice—blueberries,
  strawberries, *or*
  raspberries
1 cup whipped topping
1 cup miniature
  marshmallows

1. In a large mixing bowl, beat cream cheese until soft and creamy. Stir in dry pudding mix and milk. Blend well until smooth and soft.

2. Fold in fruit until well blended. Then fold in whipped topping and marshmallows.

3. Chill and serve.

Tips:

1. Bananas or fresh peaches also work well in this recipe.

2. I make this with all fat-free ingredients and it is delicious.

3. Beware: leftovers of this dessert can get watery.

Chocolate Raspberry Torte
Pam McAllister
Wooster, OH

Makes 10-12 servings

Prep Time: 35 minutes
Baking Time: 25-30 minutes
Cooling Time: 1 hour

18.25-oz. pkg. chocolate cake mix
3-oz. pkg. cream cheese, softened
3/4 cup cold milk
3.4-oz. pkg. instant vanilla pudding
8-oz. container frozen whipped topping, thawed
2 cups fresh raspberries
confectioners sugar
fresh mint and additional raspberries, *optional*

1. Prepare the cake according to package directions, using 3 greased and floured 9" round cake pans.

2. Bake at 350° for 25-30 minutes, or until toothpick inserted in center comes out clean.

3. Cool for 10 minutes in pan. Remove from pans to wire racks to cool completely.

4. While the cake is baking, beat the cream cheese in a mixing bowl until fluffy.

5. In a separate bowl, combine milk and pudding. Add to cream cheese mixture and mix well.

6. Fold whipped topping and raspberries into creamy mixture.

7. Place one cake layer on a serving plate. Spread with half the creamy fruit filling. Repeat layers, ending with a cake layer.

8. Just before serving, dust with confectioners sugar. Garnish with mint leaves and raspberries if you wish. Store in the refrigerator until the moment you're ready to serve.

Tip: You can substitute sliced fresh strawberries for raspberries.

A Tip —

Use light brown sugar for a caramel flavor. Use dark brown sugar when you prefer a molasses flavor and color.

Graham Cracker Pudding Cake
Sandi Degan, Kintnersville, PA

Makes 18-24 servings

Prep Time: 20-30 minutes
Chilling Time: 12-24 hours

Cake:
2 5.1-oz. boxes instant vanilla pudding
3 cups milk
8 ozs. frozen whipped topping, thawed
14-oz. box graham crackers

Frosting:
2 ozs. chocolate
1 1/2 cups confectioners sugar
3 Tbsp. milk
1 tsp. vanilla
1 tsp. light corn syrup
3 Tbsp. melted butter

1. In a large mixing bowl, mix pudding and milk until thickened. Fold in whipped topping.

2. Layer bottom of 9 x 13 dish with whole graham crackers. Top with one-third of the pudding.

3. Repeat layers, ending with a layer of crackers.

4. Melt the chocolate either in the microwave or in a double boiler.

5. Mix melted chocolate, confectioners sugar, milk, vanilla, corn syrup, and melted butter together.

6. Cover top cracker layer with frosting.

7. Refrigerate 12-24 hours.

Chocolate Chip Date Cake

Shari Jensen
Fountain, CO
Rebecca Meyerkorth
Wamego, KS

Makes 9 servings

Prep Time: 20 minutes
Baking Time: 30-35 minutes

1 cup chopped dates
1½ cups boiling water
1¾ tsp. baking soda, *divided*
½ cup butter, at room temperature
1 cup sugar
1½ cups flour
2 eggs
1 tsp. vanilla

Topping:
½ cup sugar
½ cup chopped walnuts
6-oz. pkg. chocolate chips

1. Combine dates, boiling water, and 1 tsp. baking soda in a small bowl. Let cool.
2. In a large mixing bowl, cream together butter and sugar.
3. In a separate bowl, combine flour and ¾ tsp. baking soda. Stir into creamed mixture.
4. Add eggs and vanilla. Stir well.
5. Stir in cooled dates.
6. Pour into a lightly greased 9" square baking dish.
7. Make topping by combining sugar, walnuts, and chocolate chips. Sprinkle over cake batter.
8. Bake at 375° for 30-35 minutes. (Warning: The cake will likely sink in the middle. Despite that, it's ready to serve when a toothpick inserted in the center comes out clean.) Serve warm or cold.

A Tip —

Try baking with glass pans and metal pans to see which you prefer. You may have to lower the oven temperature by 25-50 degrees when cooking in glass pans to prevent burning.

Variation: Bake the cake according to Step 8 after completing Step 6 above. In other words, eliminate the topping. Instead, make the following sauce, cube the finished cake, and layer the cake and sauce together in a serving bowl.

Sauce:
3-4 Tbsp. flour
½ cup cold water
1 cup brown sugar
1½ cups hot water
1 Tbsp. butter
1 tsp. vanilla
pinch of salt
whipped cream

1. Combine flour and cold water in a jar with a tight-fitting lid. Shake until well mixed and without lumps. Set aside.
2. Combine the brown sugar, hot water, butter, vanilla, and salt in a saucepan. Bring to a gently boil.
3. Shake flour-water mixture again. Then pour slowly into boiling syrup mixture in saucepan. Stir constantly until mixture thickens and becomes smooth.
4. Cool sauce to room temperature.
5. To serve, break the cake into small pieces. In a serving bowl, place a layer of cake cubes. Top with sauce. Continue layering until all cake and all sauce are used. Top with whipped cream.

Lemon Fluff

Helen J. Myers
Silver Spring, MD
Arleta Petersheim
Haven, KS

Makes 15-20 servings

Prep Time: 20 minutes
Baking Time: 15 minutes
Cooling Time: 30-45 minutes

1 stick (1/2 cup) butter,
   softened
1 1/2 cups flour
1 cup chopped nuts, *divided*
8-oz. pkg. cream cheese,
   softened
1 cup confectioners sugar
2 3-oz. pkgs. instant lemon
   pudding
3 1/2 cups cold milk
9-oz. container frozen
   whipped topping, thawed

1. Beat soft butter and flour
together. Spread in a greased 9
x 13 baking pan.
2. Sprinkle 1/2 cup nuts over
top, pushing slightly into
dough.
3. Bake at 350° for 12-15
minutes. Remove from oven.
Cool.
4. Beat cream cheese until
fluffy. Stir in sugar until well
mixed. Spread mixture carefully over crust, being sure not
to pull up the crust as you go.
5. In a mixing bowl, mix
pudding with milk. When
thickened, spread over cream
cheese layer.
6. Top with whipped top-
ping. Garnish with remaining
nuts.

*Variation: Replace lemon pud-
ding and nuts with vanilla pudding and coconut, or with
chocolate pudding and nuts.*

Peanut Butter
and Hot Fudge
Pudding Cake

Bernadette Veenstra
Rockford, MI

Makes 8 servings

Prep Time: 15 minutes
Baking Time: 30 minutes

1 cup flour
1 1/2 cups sugar, *divided*
1 1/2 tsp. baking powder
2/3 cup milk
2 Tbsp. oil
1 tsp. vanilla
1/2 cup peanut butter
6 Tbsp. cocoa powder
2 cups hot water

1. In a large mixing bowl,
mix together flour, 1/2 cup
sugar, and baking powder.
2. Add milk, oil, and
vanilla. Stir until smooth.
3. Stir in peanut butter.
4. Place mixture in a
greased 9 x 13 baking pan.
5. In a small bowl, com-
bine 1 cup sugar and cocoa
powder. Sprinkle on top.
6. Pour water over every-
thing.
7. Bake at 400° for 30 minutes.

Hot Fudge
Sundae Cake

Cricket Turley, Dodge City, KS

Makes 9 servings

Prep Time: 15 minutes
Baking Time: 40 minutes
Standing Time: 15 minutes

1 cup flour
3/4 cup sugar
2 Tbsp., plus 1/4 cup, dry
   cocoa powder, *divided*
2 tsp. baking powder
1/4 tsp. salt
1/2 cup milk
2 Tbsp. oil
1 tsp. vanilla
1 cup chopped nuts
1 cup brown sugar
1 3/4 cups hottest tap water
ice cream

1. In an ungreased 9 x 9
baking pan, stir together
flour, sugar, 2 tablespoons
cocoa powder, baking pow-
der, and salt.
2. Mix in milk, oil, and
vanilla with a fork until
smooth. Stir in nuts.
3. Spread mixture evenly
in pan. Sprinkle with brown
sugar and 1/4 cup cocoa powder.
4. Pour hot water over batter.
5. Bake at 350° for 40 minutes. Let stand 15 minutes;
cut into squares.
6. Invert each square onto
a dessert plate or bowl. Top
with ice cream and spoon
sauce from pan over each
serving.

213

Butterscotch Pie Dessert

Karen Stoltzfus
Alto, MI

Makes 12 servings

Prep Time: *15-20 minutes*
Baking Time: *20-25 minutes*
Cooling Time: *30-45 minutes*

1½ cups flour
1 cup butter, melted
½ cup chopped walnuts
8-oz. pkg. cream cheese
1 cup confectioners sugar
2 3.4-oz. pkgs. instant
    butterscotch pudding
3 cups milk
1 tsp. vanilla
8-oz. container frozen
    whipped topping,
    thawed
½ cup butterscotch chips

1. Combine flour, butter, and nuts in a mixing bowl. Press into a greased 9 x 13 baking pan. Bake at 350° for 20 minutes. Cool.

2. In a mixing bowl, beat cream cheese until fluffy. Beat in powdered sugar until creamy. Spread over crust, being careful not to pull the crust up.

3. In the same mixing bowl, beat pudding, milk, and vanilla until thickened. Spread over top of cream cheese layer.

4. Spread whipped topping over pudding. Sprinkle with butterscotch chips.

Variations:
1. Replace butterscotch pudding and butterscotch chips with chocolate pudding and chocolate chips.
2. Replace butterscotch pudding and butterscotch chips with pistachio pudding and chopped walnuts.

Pineapple Cheese Torte

Diane Eby, Holtwood, PA

Makes 12-16 servings

Prep Time: *15-20 minutes*
Cooking/Baking Time:
   45 minutes
Chilling Time: *8 hours, or*
   overnight

Pat-in-the-Pan Crust:
1 cup flour
1¼ cups confectioners
    sugar
¼ cup finely chopped
    almonds
⅓ cup butter, softened

Filling:
2 8-oz. pkgs. cream cheese,
    softened
½ cup sugar
2 eggs
⅔ cup unsweetened
    pineapple juice

Pineapple Topping:
¼ cup flour
¼ cup sugar
20-oz. can crushed
    pineapple, *juice drained*
    and reserved
½ cup whipping cream
fresh strawberries, *optional*

1. Combine crust ingredients in a mixing bowl. Pat into the bottom of an 8 x 12 baking dish.

2. Bake at 350° for 20 minutes.

3. Meanwhile, beat cream cheese in a mixing bowl until fluffy. Beat in sugar and eggs until fluffy. Stir in juice. Pour filling over hot crust.

4. Return pan to oven and bake at 350° for 20 minutes, or until center is set. Cool.

5. To make topping, combine flour and sugar in a saucepan. Stir in 1 cup reserved pineapple juice. Bring to a boil, stirring constantly. Boil and stir 1 minute. Remove from heat.

6. Fold in drained pineapple. Cool.

7. Whip cream until stiff peaks form. Fold into cooled pineapple topping. Spread carefully over dessert.

8. Refrigerate 6 hours or overnight. Garnish with strawberries, if you wish, just before serving.

Fresh Plum Kuchen

Scarlett von Bernuth
Canon City, CO

Makes 9 servings

Prep Time: 10-15 minutes
Baking Time: 50-60 minutes

1/4 cup butter, softened
3/4 cup sugar
2 eggs
1 tsp. grated lemon peel
1 cup flour
1 tsp. baking powder
1/4 cup milk
2 cups fresh plums (about 4 medium-sized ones)
1 Tbsp. cinnamon
1/2 cup brown sugar

1. In a mixing bowl, cream butter and sugar together.
2. Beat in the eggs and lemon peel.
3. In a separate bowl, combine the flour and baking powder.
4. Stir the flour mixture into the creamed ingredients. Add the milk, mixing well.
5. Grease a 9 x 9 baking pan. Sprinkle greased bottom and sides lightly with sugar. Spoon in batter.
6. Slice the plums and arrange on top of dough.
7. In a small bowl, stir together the cinnamon and brown sugar. Sprinkle over the plums.
8. Bake at 350° for 50-60 minutes. Let cool and serve with whipped topping or ice cream.

Fresh Raspberry Soup

Esther Nafziger
Bluffton, OH

Makes 6 servings

Prep Time: 10 minutes
Cooking Time: 10 minutes
Cooling Time: 6 hours, or overnight

---

7 cups (2 lbs.) fresh raspberries
1/4 cup, plus 2 Tbsp., sugar
2 Tbsp. cornstarch
2 cups fresh orange juice
1/2 tsp. grated orange rind
2/3 cup water
2/3 cup, plus 2 Tbsp., vanilla yogurt, *divided*
6 fresh mint leaves *or* sprigs

1. Place raspberries in an electric blender or food processor. Cover and process until smooth. Drain and discard seeds.
2. In a medium-sized, non-aluminum saucepan, combine raspberry puree, sugar, cornstarch, orange juice, orange rind, and water. Stir well.
3. Cook over medium heat, stirring constantly, until mixture comes to a boil. Reduce heat and simmer 1 minute, stirring constantly. Remove from heat. Cool to room temperature.
4. Pour into a large bowl, cover, and chill thoroughly. Allow 4 hours, or overnight.
5. Add 2/3 cup yogurt to cooled raspberry mixture, stirring well.
6. Ladle into individual bowls and garnish each serving with 1 tsp. yogurt and a mint leaf or sprig.

A Tip —

Have eggs at room temperature before using them in baking.

Cookies & Bars

Chocolate-Almond Biscotti

Beth Maurer
Columbus Grove, OH

Makes 48 biscotti slices

Prep Time: 30-40 minutes
Baking Time: 40-47 minutes
per sheet
Cooling Time: 2 hours

1½ **cups sliced almonds,
    toasted,** *divided*
2 **sticks (1 cup) butter,
    softened**
2 **cups sugar**
⅔ **cup unsweetened cocoa
    powder**
1 **tsp. baking powder**
1 **tsp. baking soda**
½ **tsp. salt**
3 **eggs**
1 **tsp. almond extract**
3½ **cups flour**
4 **blocks white almond
    bark, melted**

1. Preheat the oven to 350°. Lightly grease a cookie sheet and set it aside.

2. Place ¾ cup almonds in a food processor and pulse until ground.

3. In a large electric mixer bowl, beat butter with mixer. Add sugar and beat until well mixed.

4. Add cocoa powder, baking powder, baking soda, and salt to mixer bowl. Beat until combined.

5. Beat in eggs and almond extract.

6. Add flour by cupfuls, mixing well after each addition. Batter will be quite stiff, and you may need to add the last cup of flour by hand.

7. Remove from mixer, and by hand stir in remaining ¾ cup sliced almonds.

8. Divide dough in half. On waxed paper, and with floured hands, shape dough into two 14"-long rolls.

9. Place rolls on greased and floured cookie sheet, at least 5" apart. Flatten slightly.

10. Bake 25-30 minutes, or until wooden pick inserted near center comes out clean.

11. Cool on cookie sheet for 1 hour. On a cutting board, cut each roll diagonally into ½" thick slices, about 24 slices from each roll.

12. Place slices cut-side down on the same cookie sheets you used for the first baking. Bake at 350° for 8 minutes.

13. Turn cookies over and bake 7-9 more minutes, or until cookies are dry and beginning to get crisp.

14. Remove from cookie sheets to wire racks. Cool completely.

15. With a spoon, drizzle melted almond bark over tops of biscotti.

16. Store in an airtight container.

These are great in the morning with coffee or in the evening as dessert. They are perfect for dipping in your favorite hot beverage.

I made these for my mother as part of her Christmas gift. They disappeared very quickly, and she keeps asking me to make more!

A Tip —

I have several "half-sheet" commercial baking pans. They are a little heavier than regular cookie sheets and I never have trouble with burned cookies. They are wonderful. Mine came from a big-box store, but they are likely available at restaurant supply stores, as well.

Chocolate Chip Toffee Cookies

Luanne Berkey, Canby, OR

Makes 5-8 dozen cookies, depending on their size

Prep Time: *15 minutes*
Baking Time: *10 minutes per sheet*

1 cup butter, at room
　temperature
1 cup brown sugar
1 cup sugar
2 eggs
1 tsp. vanilla
2 cups flour
1 tsp. baking soda
1 tsp. baking powder
1/4 tsp. salt
2 cups dry quick oats
1 cup grated coconut
1 cup chocolate chips
1/2 cup toffee bits

1. In a large electric mixing bowl, or by hand, cream butter and sugars thoroughly.

2. Add eggs and vanilla and mix until fluffy.

3. In a separate bowl, sift together flour, baking soda, baking powder, and salt. Add to creamed mixture alternately with the dry oatmeal.

4. Mix in coconut, chocolate chips, and toffee bits by hand.

5. Drop onto greased cookie sheet. Bake at 375° for approximately 10 minutes.

Variations: *Substitute raisins, cut-up gumdrops, or white chocolate chips for the chocolate chips and toffee bits.*

Chocolate Chip Cookies

Mary Martins
Fairbank, IA

Makes 3 dozen big cookies

Prep Time: *15 minutes*
Baking Time: *9 minutes per sheet*
Chilling Time: *1 hour*

1 cup butter, at room
　temperature
1 cup brown sugar
1 cup sugar
3 eggs, beaten
3 1/2 cups flour
2 tsp. cream of tartar
2 tsp. baking soda
1/2 tsp. salt
1 tsp. vanilla
12-oz. pkg. chocolate chips
1 cup chopped nuts,
　optional

1. In a large mixing bowl, combine butter, sugars, and eggs.

2. In a separate mixing bowl, sift together flour, cream of tartar, baking soda, and salt.

3. Add about one-third of the dry ingredients to the creamed mixture. Mix well. Add half of the remaining dry ingredients and mix well. Add the remaining dry ingredients and mix until thoroughly blended.

4. Stir in vanilla, chocolate chips, and nuts. Chill in the fridge for 60 minutes.

5. Drop by spoonfuls onto a greased cookie sheet.

6. Bake at 400° for about 9 minutes, or until lightly browned

Tips:

1. If you like smaller cookies, make the spoonfuls in Step 5 about the size of a level teaspoon.

2. I usually bake a cookie-sheet full and then cover the rest of the dough and keep it in the refrigerator for a day or so so that I can have freshly baked cookies.

3. Use macadamia nuts in Step 4 for a real treat.
　— Barb Yoder
　Angola, IN

A Tip —

A gadget that works well for decorating sugar cookies is an empty, clean, plastic thread spool. Simply dip the spool in sugar and press it into the dough, imprinting a flower design.

Quick Chocolate Sandwich Cookies

Connie Miller, Shipshewana, IN

Makes 6 dozen cookies

Prep Time: 30 minutes
Baking Time: 10 minutes
per sheet

2 18¼-oz. pkgs. chocolate
  cake mix
1 cup vegetable oil
4 large eggs

Filling:
8-oz. pkg. cream cheese,
  softened
¼ cup butter, at room
  temperature
2½ cups confectioners
  sugar
1 tsp. vanilla

1. In a mixing bowl, combine the cake mixes, oil, and eggs. Mix well.
2. Dust your hands with cocoa powder, if you have some nearby, and then roll the dough into 1" balls.
3. Place balls 2 inches apart on ungreased baking sheets. Do not flatten.
4. Bake at 350° for 8-10 minutes. Take out after 10 minutes, even if they don't look like they're done.
5. Cool 5 minutes before removing to wire racks. (Cookies will flatten as they cool.)
6. In a mixing bowl, beat cream cheese and butter together.

7. Add confectioners sugar and vanilla. Beat until smooth.
8. Spread on half the cookies and top with remaining cookies.
9. Store in the refrigerator.

Peanut Butter Chocolate Chip Cookies

Wendy B. Martzall
New Holland, PA

Makes 100 small cookies

Prep Time: 10 minutes
Baking Time: 8-10 minutes
per sheet

1 cup peanut butter
¾ cup butter, at room
  temperature
¾ cup sugar
¾ cup packed brown sugar
1 tsp. vanilla
2 large eggs
2 cups flour
1 tsp. baking soda
2 cups semi-sweet
  chocolate chips

1. Preheat oven to 375°.
2. Beat together peanut butter, butter, sugars, and vanilla with an electric mixer.
3. Beat in eggs. Gradually beat in flour and baking soda.
4. Stir in chocolate chips by hand.
5. Drop by rounded teaspoons, 2 inches apart, on ungreased cookie sheets.

6. Bake 8-10 minutes, or until lightly browned.
7. Cool on cookie sheets for 1 minute before removing. Cool completely on wire racks.

Variations:

1. Use the same dough, but get a different result! After Step 3, refrigerate the dough for half an hour or so, so that it's easy to handle.

Using a 7-oz. pkg. of miniature peanut butter cups, wrap a ball of cookie dough around each little peanut butter cup. Place the wrapped balls in the fridge for 1 hour.

When ready to bake, place balls 2 inches apart on ungreased cookie sheets. Bake at 350° for 12-14 minutes, or until the bottom edges of the balls are golden.

After the baked balls have cooled, drizzle them with melted chocolate chips.

— Stacy Schmucker
  Stoltzfus, Enola, PA

2. After Step 3, chill the dough for half an hour in the fridge. Then roll into small walnut-sized balls and place each ball in a cup in a mini-muffin tin.

Bake at 375° for 8-9 minutes. Remove from oven. Gently press 1 miniature peanut butter cup into each cookie.

Cool in pan 10 minutes. Remove from pan and finish cooling on a wire rack.

— Carol Sherwood
  Batavia, NY

Ginger Snaps

Joan Brown, Warriors Mark, PA

Makes 3 dozen cookies

Prep Time: 30 minutes
Baking Time: 15 minutes per sheet

3/4 cup solid shortening
1 cup sugar
1 egg
1/4 cup molasses
2 cups flour
1 1/2 tsp. baking soda
3/4 tsp. allspice
1 tsp. cinnamon
1 tsp. ginger
sugar

1. In an electric mixing bowl, cream shortening and sugar together. Add unbeaten egg and molasses. Beat until smooth.

2. In a separate bowl, sift together flour, baking soda, allspice, cinnamon, and ginger. Gradually add to creamed mixture. Mix well.

3. Roll into 1" balls. Roll in sugar. Place on ungreased cookie sheets.

4. Bake at 350° for 15 minutes.

Variation: Instead of allspice, use 3/4-1 tsp. ground cloves.
— **Cova Rexroad**
Kingsville, MD

Soft, Chewy Molasses Cookies

Martha Ann Auker
Landisburg, PA

Makes 3 dozen cookies

Prep Time: 10 minutes
Baking Time: 8-10 minutes per cookie sheet

1 stick (1/2 cup) butter, at room temperature
1 cup brown sugar
1 egg
2 cups flour
2 tsp. baking soda
2 tsp. ginger
2 tsp. cinnamon
4 Tbsp. black strap molasses
sugar

1. In an electric mixing bowl, cream together butter and sugar. Add egg. Mix well.

2. In a separate bowl, mix together flour, baking soda, ginger, and cinnamon. Add to creamed mixture, alternately with the molasses, until well blended.

3. Shape batter into 1" balls. Roll each in sugar. Place 2" apart on a greased cookie sheet.

4. Bake at 350° for 8-10 minutes.

5. Let stand on cookie sheet about 2 minutes before removing to wire rack to cool.

Variation: Add 1/2 tsp. ground cloves to Step 2, if you wish.
— **Marjora Miller**
Archbold, OH

Mom's Sugar Cookies

Marie Skelly, Babylon, NY

Makes 36 cookies

Prep Time: 15-20 minutes
Baking Time: 8-12 minutes per sheet

1 cup sugar
1/2 cup solid shortening
1 egg
2 Tbsp. milk
1/2 tsp. vanilla
2 cups flour
2 tsp. baking powder
1/2 tsp. salt
sugar

1. In an electric mixing bowl, cream sugar and shortening together. Add egg, milk, and vanilla. Beat well.

2. In a separate bowl, mix dry ingredients together. Add to creamed mixture.

3. Stir well. Then work with hands until a stiff dough forms.

4. Lightly flour a work surface. Roll dough to 1/4" thickness. Cut with cookie cutters and place on ungreased cookie sheet. Sprinkle lightly with granulated sugar.

5. Bake at 375° for 8-12 minutes until lightly browned on edges. Cool on cooling racks.

Variation: Instead of vanilla, use 3/4-1 1/2 tsp. almond extract, according to your taste preference.
— **Barb Yoder**
Angola, IN

Crinkle Top Cookies

Esther J. Mast
Lancaster, PA

Makes 3 1/2-4 dozen cookies

Prep Time: 10-20 minutes
Chilling Time: 2 hours
Baking Time: 9-10 minutes
per cookie sheet

2 cups chocolate chips,
divided
1 1/2 cups flour
1 1/2 tsp. baking powder
1/4 tsp. salt
2 Tbsp. butter, at room
temperature
1 cup sugar
2 egg whites
1 1/2 tsp. vanilla extract
1/4 cup water
confectioners sugar

1. Melt 1 cup chocolate chips (3 min. at 60% power in microwave). Stir until smooth. Set aside.

2. In a mixing bowl, combine flour, baking powder, and salt. Set aside.

3. In a large mixing bowl cream together butter and sugar. Add egg whites and vanilla.

4. Stir in melted chocolate. Then add flour mixture alternately with water.

5. Stir in remaining 1 cup chocolate chips.

6. Refrigerate at least 2 hours until dough is firm. Roll into 1" balls and roll in confectioners sugar. Place on greased cookie sheet.

7. Bake at 350° approximately 10 minutes. Don't over-bake.

I got this recipe from a friend in my weight-loss group. Using egg whites and sugar substitute, plus eating only 1 cookie at a meal, allows you to enjoy dessert occasionally!

Cloud Cookies

Esther J. Mast
Lancaster, PA

Makes 6 dozen cookies

Prep Time: 15 minutes
Baking Time: 9-10 minutes
per sheet

4 cups flour, slightly
heaping
1 tsp. baking soda
3 tsp. baking powder
1 tsp. salt
2 sticks (1 cup) butter,
softened
2 cups sugar
3 eggs
1 1/2 tsp. vanilla
1 cup buttermilk

1. Sift together flour, baking soda, baking powder, and salt. Set aside.

2. In an electric mixing bowl, cream together butter and sugar.

3. Add eggs, one at a time, beating well each time. Add vanilla and mix well.

4. Add flour mixture alternately with buttermilk.

5. Drop by spoonsfuls onto greased cookie sheets. Make the cookies as large or small as you wish.

6. Bake at 350° for 9-10 minutes, until tops are slightly firm.

Tips:

1. The amount of flour is the key in this recipe. Too little makes them flat; too much gives them a biscuit texture.

2. Don't over-bake. When the tops are just firm enough not to indent, the cookies are perfect!

I received this recipe from Harvella Stutzman, my son's mother-in-law, now my friend. These have become my 10 grandchildren's favorite cookie!

Black and White Cookies

Joy Sutter
Perkasie, PA

Makes 2-3 dozen cookies

Prep Time: 30 minutes
Baking Time: 10 minutes, per
sheet

2/3 cup applesauce
1 1/2 cups flour
1 1/2 tsp. baking powder
1/2 tsp. salt
1 cup sugar
half a stick (1/4 cup) butter,
softened
1 1/2 tsp. vanilla
2 large egg whites

Frosting:
1 1/2 cups confectioners
sugar, *divided*
2 Tbsp. milk, *divided*
1/4 tsp. vanilla
4 tsp. unsweetened cocoa
powder

1. Place applesauce in a fine sieve and drain for 15 minutes.

2. With a whisk, combine flour, baking powder, and salt in a mixing bowl. Set aside.

3. In a large electric mixer bowl, combine drained applesauce, sugar, and butter with an electric mixer.

4. Beat in vanilla and egg whites.

5. Add flour mixture and beat until well blended.

6. Drop dough by tablespoonfuls onto an ungreased cookie sheet, 2 inches apart.

7. Bake at 375° for 10 minutes. Cool on racks.

8. For Frosting, combine 3/4 cup confectioners sugar, 2-3 tsp. milk, and vanilla in a bowl. Whisk until smooth.

9. Spread 1 tsp. white frosting over half of each cookie.

10. Combine 3/4 cup confectioners sugar and cocoa powder in a bowl. Add 2-3 tsp. milk and whisk until smooth.

11. Spread 1 tsp. chocolate frosting over other half of each cookie.

A Tip —

If you want soft cookies, try using all brown sugar.

Mexican Wedding Cakes

Leona Yoder
Hartville, OH

Makes 3 dozen dollar-size cookies

Prep Time: 15 minutes
Chilling Time: 2 hours
*Baking Time: 15-20 minutes
    per sheet*

2 sticks (1 cup) butter, at
    room temperature
1/2 cup sugar
1/2 tsp. salt
2 tsp. vanilla
2 cups flour
1 cup chopped nuts
confectioners sugar

1. Cream butter and sugar together in a large bowl with an electric mixer.

2. Add salt, vanilla, flour, and nuts. Mix well.

3. Chill dough for 2 hours.

4. Shape dough into balls. Place on lightly greased baking sheets. Flatten with the bottom of a drinking glass which has a design, dipped in flour.

5. Bake at 325° until lightly brown, about 15-20 minutes.

6. When cookies are cool, rub their tops lightly in confectioners sugar.

Butter Crescents

Janet Hardy
Arp, TX

Makes 3 dozen cookies

Prep Time: 10 minutes
*Baking Time: 10-14 minutes
    per sheet*

2 sticks (1 cup) butter,
    softened (no substitutes)
5 Tbsp. sifted
    confectioners sugar
1 tsp. vanilla
1 Tbsp. water
2 cups flour
1 cup chopped pecans
sifted confectioners sugar
    for dusting

1. Blend butter and sugar together in a mixing bowl with an electric mixer.

2. Mix in vanilla, water, flour, and pecans.

3. Shape into crescents and place on an ungreased baking sheet.

4. Bake at 350° just until slightly browned, about 10-14 minutes.

5. Remove from oven and allow to cool for 3 minutes. Then roll immediately in sifted confectioners sugar.

6. Place on wire racks and allow to cool fully. Watch them disappear!

Forgotten Cookies

Penny Blosser
Beavercreek, OH

Makes 2 dozen cookies

Prep Time: 10-20 minutes
Baking Time: overnight

2 egg whites
2/3 cup sugar
1 tsp. vanilla
pinch of salt
1/2 cup chocolate chips
1/2 cup chopped nuts

1. Preheat oven to 350°.
2. Beat egg whites until foamy in a large mixing bowl.
3. Gradually add sugar and beat until stiff.
4. Fold in remaining ingredients.
5. Line a cookie sheet with foil. Spray the foil with non-stick cooking spray.
6. Drop cookies by rounded teaspoonfuls onto foil-lined cookie sheet.
7. Place in oven. Turn oven OFF immediately!
8. Leave cookies in oven until oven is completely cool, or overnight.

I usually make these just as I finish baking. It's a sweet way to cool the oven.

A Tip —

To end up with soft, chewy cookies, remove them from the oven slightly unbaked.

Harvest Cookies

Sherlyn Hess, Millersville, PA

Makes 2-4 dozen cookies, depending on their size

Prep Time: 30 minutes
Baking Time: 15 minutes per sheet

1 1/2 cups raisins
boiling water
1 cup solid shortening
1 cup sugar
1 cup mashed pumpkin
1 egg
2 cups flour
1 tsp. baking soda
1 tsp. cinnamon
1/2 tsp. salt

Frosting:
2 Tbsp. butter
1/2 cup brown sugar
2 Tbsp. canned milk, *or* half-and-half
1 cup confectioners sugar
1 tsp. vanilla

1. Place raisins in a small bowl and cover with boiling water.
2. In an electric mixing bowl, cream together shortening, sugar, pumpkin, and egg.
3. In a separate bowl, mix together dry ingredients. Stir into creamed mixture.
4. Drain raisins and fold into batter. Drop by teaspoonfuls onto greased cookie sheets.
5. Drop by teaspoonfuls onto greased cookie sheets.
6. Bake at 350° for 8 minutes.
7. In a double boiler, heat butter, brown sugar, and milk

until sugar is melted. Stir frequently.
8. Add confectioners sugar and vanilla, mixing until well blended.
9. Drizzle or spread on hot cookies.

Apricot Bars

Jean Butzer, Batavia, NY

Makes 15-20 bars

Prep Time: 15 minutes
Cooking/Baking Time: 60-65 minutes

2/3 cup dried apricots
2 Tbsp., plus 1/4 cup, sugar, *divided*
1 stick (1/2 cup) butter, softened
1 1/3 cups flour, *divided*
1 cup brown sugar
2 eggs, well beaten
1/2 tsp. baking powder
1/4 tsp. salt
1/2 tsp. vanilla
1/2 cup chopped nuts
confectioners sugar

1. In a small saucepan, cover apricots with water. Stir in 2 Tbsp. sugar. Boil for 10 minutes.
2. Drain fruit, cool, and cut into bite-sized pieces. Set aside.
3. In a mixing bowl, combine butter and 1/4 cup sugar. Stir in 1 cup flour until crumbly.
4. Spread creamed mixture into greased 8 x 10 baking

pan, packing it down. Bake at 350° for 25 minutes.

5. Meanwhile, gradually beat brown sugar into eggs in a mixing bowl.

6. In a separate bowl, combine 1/3 cup flour, baking powder, and salt. Add to brown sugar/egg mixture.

7. Stir in vanilla, nuts, and apricots.

8. Spread over baked layer and bake an additional 25-30 minutes, or until lightly browned.

9. Cool in pan. Cut into bars and roll in confectioners sugar.

Polynesian Cookies
Wilma Haberkamp, Fairbank, IA

Makes 4-4 1/2 dozen cookies

Prep Time: 30 minutes
Baking Time: 8-10 minutes
*   per sheet*

1 1/2 cups sugar
2 sticks (1 cup) butter, at
    room temperature
1 large egg
1 tsp. vanilla
3 1/2 cups flour
1 tsp. baking soda
1/2 tsp. salt
8.5-oz. can crushed
    pineapple with juice
1 cup chopped nuts

1. In an electric mixer bowl, cream sugar and butter together. Add egg and vanilla.

2. In a separate bowl, sift together flour, baking soda, and salt.

3. Add dry ingredients to creamed mixture alternately with pineapple until mixed well. Add nuts.

4. Drop by teaspoonfuls onto ungreased baking sheet.

5. Bake at 375° for 8-10 minutes, or just until lightly browned. The finished cookies will be soft and cake-like.

Tips:

1. When storing cookies, use a sheet of waxed paper between layers to keep them from sticking together.

2. I often bake a sheet or two at a time and refrigerate the rest of the dough until I need it.

3. This dough will keep a week or more in the refrigerator.

Raspberry Almond Shortbread Thumbprints
Sherlyn Hess
Millersville, PA

Makes 3-3 1/2 dozen cookies

Prep Time: 35 minutes
Baking Time: 8-10 minutes
*   per sheet*

2/3 cup sugar
2 sticks (1 cup) butter,
    softened
1/2 tsp. almond extract
2 cups flour
1/2 cup raspberry jelly

Glaze:
1 cup confectioners sugar
1 1/2 tsp. almond extract
2-3 tsp. water

1. In an electric mixer bowl, combine sugar, butter, and 1/2 tsp. almond extract until creamy.

2. Add flour. Mix well.

3. Shape into 1" balls. Place 2" apart on ungreased cookie sheets.

4. With your thumb, make an indentation in the center of each cookie. Fill each indentation with 1/4 tsp. jam.

5. Bake at 350° for 8-10 minutes. Do not brown.

6. Remove from cookie sheets onto wire racks. Cool 10 minutes.

7. Combine confectioners sugar, 1 1/2 tsp. almond extract, and water. Drizzle over cookies. Cool completely.

Tip: I cool these cookies on racks. Then when I drizzle them with the glaze, the excess falls through the rack and the cookies have a nicer look than when the glaze puddles around them.

A Tip —

I usually make cookie dough and put it in the refrigerator instead of immediately baking it. Then I bake the cookies the next day. The dough is usually easier to work with when it's cold, and if I'm short on time, I've spread the job over two days.

223

Almond Bars

Darla Sathre, Baxter, MN

Makes 20 bars

Prep Time: 30 minutes
Cooling Time: 1-2 hours
Baking Time: 35 minutes

Crust:
2 cups flour
1/2 cup confectioners sugar
2 sticks (1 cup) butter, at room temperature

Filling:
8-oz. pkg. cream cheese, at room temperature
2 eggs
1/2 cup sugar
1 tsp. almond extract

Frosting:
1 1/2 cups confectioners sugar
half a stick (1/4 cup) butter, at room temperature
1 tsp. almond extract
2 Tbsp. milk

1. To make the crust, mix the flour and 1/2 cup confectioners sugar together. Then cut in butter with a pastry cutter or two knives until well mixed.

2. Pat into a lightly greased 9 x 13 baking pan. Bake at 350° for 20 minutes.

3. Meanwhile, prepare the filling by beating all 4 ingredients together with an electric mixer until fluffy.

4. Pour filling over baked hot crust.

5. Bake another 15 minutes. Cool for 1-2 hours.

6. Prepare frosting by creaming sugar and butter together until smooth. Stir in extract and milk until well blended.

7. Spread over cooled bars.

Pumpkin Pie Squares

Gina Hargitt, Quinter, KS

Makes 18-20 bars

Prep Time: 30 minutes
Baking Time: 45-50 minutes

1 cup flour
1/2 cup dry quick *or* rolled oats
1/2 cup brown sugar
1 stick (1/2 cup) butter, at room temperature
2 cups pumpkin
13 1/2-oz. can evaporated milk
2 eggs
3/4 cup sugar
1/2 tsp. salt
1/2 tsp. ginger
1 tsp. cinnamon
1/4 tsp. cloves
2 Tbsp. butter, at room temperature
1/2 cup brown sugar
1/2 cup pecans

1. In a mixing bowl, combine flour, dry oatmeal, 1/2 cup brown sugar, and 1 stick butter until crumbly.

2. Spread in a greased 9 x 13 baking pan. Bake at 350° for 15 minutes.

3. Meanwhile, combine

pumpkin, evaporated milk, eggs, sugar, salt, ginger, cinnamon, and cloves in the same mixing bowl.

4. Pour over baked crust. Return to oven and bake for 20 minutes.

5. Combine 2 Tbsp. butter, 1/2 cup brown sugar, and pecans. Sprinkle over pumpkin filling. Bake an additional 15-20 minutes.

Date Krumble

Marie Mahorney
Las Vegas, NV

Makes 18-20 bars

Prep Time: 25-30 minutes
Cooking/Baking Time:
50-55 minutes

Filling:
1/2 lb. pitted dates
1 1/2 cups water

Batter:
1/2 cup solid shortening
1 cup brown sugar
1 egg
2 cups flour
2 cups dry quick oats
1 tsp. baking soda
1 tsp. vanilla

1. Mix dates and water in a saucepan. Boil until thickened. Set aside.

2. In an electric mixer bowl, cream shortening, brown sugar, and egg together.

3. Mix in flour, dry oats, baking soda, and vanilla. Mixture will be crumbly.

4. Pat half of crumb mixture firmly into the bottom of a greased 9 x 13 baking pan.

5. Top with the date mixture.

6. Sprinkle remaining crumb mixture on top and press down gently.

7. Bake at 350° for 30-35 minutes.

Banana Cream Bars

Marsha Sabus, Fallbrook, CA

Makes 50 1½" x 2" bars

Prep Time: 15-20 minutes
Baking Time: 25-30 minutes
Cooling Time: 45-60 minutes

1 stick (½ cup) butter, at room temperature
1½ cups sugar
2 large eggs
2 tsp. vanilla
¾ cup sour cream
2 cups flour
¼ tsp. salt
1 tsp. baking soda
2 large, *or* 3 medium-sized, ripe bananas, mashed

Frosting:
3-oz. pkg. cream cheese, at room temperature
6 Tbsp. butter, softened
1 Tbsp. milk
1 tsp. vanilla
2 cups confectioners sugar
½ cup chopped nuts, *optional*

1. In a large electric mixer bowl, cream 1 stick butter and 1½ cups sugar together.

2. Add the unbeaten eggs and beat thoroughly. Add 2 tsp. vanilla and sour cream. Mix well.

3. In a separate mixing bowl, blend together flour, salt, and baking soda. Add alternately with the mashed bananas to the creamed ingredients. Mix well after each addition.

4. Spoon into a greased 15 x 10 x 1 baking pan. Bake at 350° for 25-30 minutes, or until toothpick inserted in center comes out clean. Cool on wire racks.

5. Meanwhile, make frosting by beating together cream cheese, 6 Tbsp. butter, milk, 1 tsp. vanilla, and confectioners sugar. Spread over cooled bars and sprinkle with nuts if you wish.

A Tip —

I just slightly underbake cookies for the best taste. When the cookies are cool, I put them into either gallon-size plastic bags or large plastic containers, with waxed paper between the layers. Then I freeze them.

When I'm ready to serve the cookies, I put them out on a plate for about 10 minutes, or I microwave them for a few seconds. Delicious!

Butterscotch Bars

Dottie Geraci, Burtonsville, MD

Makes 25 bars

Prep Time: 20 minutes
Baking Time: 40 minutes

6 Tbsp. butter, at room temperature
1½ cups brown sugar, *divided*
1¼ cups all-purpose flour, *divided*
2 eggs
1½ tsp. vanilla extract
1 tsp. baking powder
½ tsp. salt
½ cup chopped walnuts
1 cup butterscotch morsels

1. In a small mixing bowl, cream butter and ½ cup brown sugar together until light and fluffy. Blend in 1 cup flour and mix until crumbly.

2. Pat mixture into an ungreased 7 x 11 x 1½ baking pan. Bake at 350° for 10 minutes. Remove from oven.

3. In the mixing bowl, beat eggs until thick and lemon-colored. Add 1 cup brown sugar and vanilla. Continue beating.

4. In a separate bowl, combine ¼ cup flour, baking powder, and salt. Add to egg mixture. Stir in nuts.

5. Spread over baked crust. Sprinkle with butterscotch morsels.

6. Bake 30 minutes more. Cool and cut into 2 x 1½ bars.

Cheesecake Bars

Leona Yoder
Hartville, OH

Makes 12 bars

Prep Time: 10-15 minutes
Baking Time: 40 minutes

1 cup flour
1/3 cup brown sugar
1/3 cup butter, melted
8-oz. pkg. cream cheese, at
   room temperature
1/4 cup sugar
1 large egg
1 Tbsp. lemon juice
2 Tbsp. milk
1 tsp. vanilla

1. Mix flour, brown sugar, and butter together in an electric mixing bowl. Reserve 1 cup mixture. Press remainder into a greased 8 x 8 baking pan.

2. Bake at 350° for 15 minutes.

3. Meanwhile, in the mixing bowl, beat together the remaining ingredients. Spread on baked crust.

4. Top with reserved crumbs and bake for 25 minutes, or until set.

A Tip —

Use a pizza cutter to cut bar cookies into neat squares in half the time.

Philly Chippers

Erma Hoover
Lititz, PA

Makes 24 bars

Prep Time: 12-15 minutes
Baking Time: 15-30 minutes

1 cup butter, at room
   temperature
8-oz. pkg. cream cheese, at
   room temperature
3/4 cup sugar
3/4 cup brown sugar
1 egg
1 tsp. vanilla
1/4 cup milk
2 1/2 cups flour
1 tsp. baking powder
1 tsp. salt
12-oz. pkg. chocolate chips

1. In a large mixing bowl, cream together butter, cream cheese, and sugars.

2. Add egg, vanilla, and milk. Mix well.

3. In a separate bowl, combine flour, baking powder, and salt. Blend into creamed mixture.

4. Fold in chocolate chips.

5. Pour into a greased 9 x 13 baking pan.

6. Bake at 350° for 15-30 minutes, or until done in the center, but not dry around the edges.

Chocolate Peanut Bars

Andrea Zuercher
Lawrence, KS

Makes 2 dozen bars

Prep Time: 10 minutes
Cooking Time: 3-5 minutes
Chilling Time: 1 hour

1/2 cup light corn syrup
1/4 cup brown sugar
dash of salt
1 cup chunky peanut
   butter
1 tsp. vanilla
2 cups crispy rice cereal
1 cup cornflakes, slightly
   crushed
1 cup chocolate chips

1. Combine corn syrup, sugar, and salt in a heavy saucepan. Bring to a full boil.

2. Stir in peanut butter. Remove from heat.

3. Stir in remaining ingredients.

4. Press into a buttered 9 x 9 baking pan.

5. Chill about 1 hour before cutting and removing from pan.

Tips:
1. This recipe can be easily doubled for a larger quantity.
2. It's a nice no-bake treat during the hot summertime.

Chocolate Oatmeal Chews

Bertha Burkholder
Hillsville, VA

Makes 20 bars

Prep Time: 10 minutes
Baking Time: 15-18 minutes

3/4 cup butter, at room temperature
1 cup brown sugar
1 1/4 cups flour
1 1/2 cups dry quick oats
1/2 tsp. baking soda
1/2 tsp. salt
4 cups mini marshmallows
1 cup chocolate chips

1. In an electric mixing bowl, cream butter and sugar together.
2. In a separate bowl, combine flour, dry oats, baking soda, and salt.
3. Blend dry ingredients into creamy mixture thoroughly.
4. Set aside 1 1/2 cups batter. Press remainder into a greased 9 x 13 baking pan.
5. Sprinkle "crust" with mini marshmallows and chocolate chips.
6. Top with reserved batter.
7. Bake at 375° for 15-18 minutes, or until set in the middle and not dry around the edges. Cool and cut into bars.

Variatons:

1. After Step 4, sprinkle "crust" with 2 cups chocolate chips and 1 cup sliced almonds. In a mixing bowl, whisk 12-oz. jar caramel ice cream topping and 1/4 cup flour together. Drizzle over chocolate chips and nuts. Proceed with Step 6 above.
— **Stacy Schmucker Stoltzfus**, Enola, PA

2. After Step 4, spread "crust" with a mixture of a 14-oz. can sweetened condensed milk and 1/3 cup peanut butter. Combine reserved batter and 1 cup M&Ms. Sprinkle over top, pressing down lightly. Bake at 350° for 20 minutes.
— **Lawina Good**
Harrisonburg, VA

3. Follow Variation 2 immediately above, except add 1 cup chocolate chips to the reserved batter/M&M mixture.
— **Erma Rutt**
Newmanstown, PA

A Tip —

Need cookies for lunches? Plan a baking day with a friend. Divide and freeze what you've baked together.

Raspberry Walnut Shortbread

Joyce Nolt, Richland, PA

Makes 18-20 bars

Prep Time: 10-15 minutes
Baking Time: 40-45 minutes

2 1/2 cups flour
1 cup sugar
2 sticks (1 cup) butter, at room temperature
2/3 cup raspberry jam, beaten until softened
4 eggs
1 cup packed brown sugar
2 tsp. vanilla
4 Tbsp. flour
1/4 tsp. salt
1/4 tsp. baking soda
2 cups chopped walnuts

1. Combine 2 1/2 cups flour, sugar, and butter in a mixing bowl. Press into the bottom of a greased 9 x 13 baking pan.
2. Bake at 350° for 20 minutes. Remove from oven.
3. Spread raspberry jam over shortbread, being careful not to disturb the crust.
4. In the mixing bowl, beat together eggs, brown sugar, and vanilla.
5. In a separate bowl, combine 4 Tbsp. flour, salt, and baking soda.
6. Add dry ingredients to egg mixture. Mix well.
7. Spoon over jam and spread lightly to corners.
8. Sprinkle walnuts over top.
9. Return to oven. Bake 20-25 minutes longer. Cool before cutting into bars.

Pecan Squares

Louise Bodziony
Sunrise Beach, MO

Makes 4 dozen squares

Prep Time: 20-25 minutes
Baking Time: 45 minutes

Crust:
3 cups flour
1/2 cup sugar
2 sticks (1 cup) butter, softened
1/2 tsp. salt

Filling:
4 eggs
1 1/2 cups light *or* dark corn syrup
1 1/2 cups sugar
3 Tbsp. butter, melted
1 1/2 tsp. vanilla extract
2 1/2 cups chopped pecans

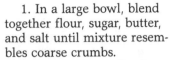

1. In a large bowl, blend together flour, sugar, butter, and salt until mixture resembles coarse crumbs.
2. Press mixture firmly and evenly into a greased 10 x 15 baking pan.
3. Bake at 350° for 20 minutes.
4. Meanwhile, in the mixing bowl, combine first 5 filling ingredients. Stir in pecans.
5. Spread evenly over baked hot crust.
6. Bake at 350° for 25 minutes, or until set.
7. Cool baking pan on a wire rack. Cut into squares.

Variation: After Step 6 above, remove baked squares from oven and immediately sprinkle with 1 cup chocolate chips. Return to oven for 5 minutes. Remove and spread melted chips over baked squares. Continue with Step 7.
— **Maria Archer**
Fort Defiance, VA

A Tip —

Always cut brownies with a plastic knife. It prevents clumping and ragged edges.

Deliciously Chocolate Brownies

Alice Whitman, Lancaster, PA
Michelle Martin, Ephrata, PA

Makes 10 servings

Prep Time: 10-15 minutes
Baking Time: 28-30 minutes

2 sticks (1 cup) butter, melted
1/2 cup, plus 2 Tbsp., unsweetened cocoa powder
2 cups sugar
4 eggs, beaten
1 1/2 cups flour
pinch of salt
1/2 cup chopped nuts
1 cup miniature chocolate chips

1. In a mixing bowl, combine butter and cocoa powder until well blended.
2. Add sugar, eggs, flour, and salt. Stir with a fork. (Stirring with a fork keeps the brownies from becoming too cakey.)
3. Stir in chopped nuts. Spread in a greased 9 x 13 baking pan.
4. Bake at 350° for 25 minutes. Do not over-bake.
5. Sprinkle with chocolate chips. Return to oven for 3-4 minutes, or just until chocolate melts.
6. Cool completely before cutting with a plastic knife—which will cut clean.

Microwave Brownies

Sandra Chang
Derwood, MD

Makes 16 brownies

Prep Time: 10 minutes
Cooking Time: 9-12 minutes

1 cup sifted flour
1/2 tsp. baking powder
1/2 tsp. salt
1 stick (1/2 cup) butter
2 1-oz. squares
    unsweetened chocolate
1 cup sugar
2 large eggs
1 tsp. vanilla extract
1/2 cup chopped nuts

1. Sift together flour, baking powder, and salt. Set aside.
2. Place butter and chocolate in an 8"-square glass baking dish. Microwave at 50 percent power for 3 minutes, or until melted.
3. Stir sugar into melted mixture. Add eggs and vanilla, beating well.
4. Gradually stir in dry ingredients, blending well. Add nuts.
5. Microwave on high for 5-6 minutes, or until the top is no longer wet, or a toothpick inserted in the center comes out clean. Rotate dish 1/4 turn every 2 minutes while microwaving.
6. Cool in baking dish, then cut into 2" squares.

Chocolate Chip Blonde Brownies

Vera Martin, East Earl, PA

Makes 18-20 brownies

Prep Time: 15 minutes
Baking Time: 25 minutes
Cooling Time: 20 minutes

10 2/3 Tbsp. (2/3 cup) butter
2 Tbsp. hot water
2 cups brown sugar
2 eggs
2 tsp. vanilla
2 cups flour
1 tsp. baking powder
1/4 tsp. baking soda
1 tsp. salt
1/2 cup chopped nuts,
    optional
1/2 cup chocolate chips

1. In a good-sized saucepan, melt butter. Add water and brown sugar. Cool for 20 minutes.
2. Add eggs and vanilla. Beat well.
3. In a mixing bowl, combine flour, baking powder, baking soda, and salt.
4. Add dry ingredients to egg/sugar mixture. Mix well and add nuts if desired.
5. Spread into a greased 9 x 13 baking pan. Sprinkle chocolate chips over the top.
6. Bake at 350° for 25 minutes. Cool slightly. Cut into squares with a plastic knife—which will make clean cuts.

Tip: These will be chewy in the center. Don't over-bake.

Chocolate Chip Peanut Butter Brownies

Monica Kehr
Portland, MI

Makes 36 brownies

Prep Time: 20 minutes
Baking Time: 20-22 minutes

2 cups flour
2 tsp. baking powder
1/2 tsp. salt
1 cup peanut butter
10 2/3 Tbsp. (2/3 cup) butter,
    at room temperature
1 cup sugar
1 cup brown sugar
4 eggs
12-oz. pkg. chocolate chips
2 tsp. vanilla

1. Mix flour, baking powder, and salt. Set aside.
2. In an electric mixer bowl, cream together peanut butter, butter, and sugars until fluffy.
3. Beat in eggs until well blended.
4. Stir in dry ingredients.
5. Stir in chocolate chips and vanilla.
6. Spread in a greased 9 x 13 baking pan. Bake at 350° for 20 minutes, or until slight imprint remains when pressed lightly in center. Do not over-bake.
7. Cool, then cut with a plastic knife—which will make clean cuts.

Apple Brownies

Wendy B. Martzall
New Holland, PA

Makes 18-20 brownies

Prep Time: 20-25 minutes
Baking Time: 40-50 minutes

2 sticks (1 cup) butter, at
    room temperature
2 cups sugar
2 eggs, beaten
2 cups flour
1 tsp. baking powder
1 tsp. baking soda
2 tsp. cinnamon
3 cups apples, peeled and
    thinly sliced
1 cup chopped walnuts,
    optional

1. In an electric mixing
bowl, cream butter and sugar
together.
2. Add eggs and mix well.
3. In a separate bowl, combine flour, baking powder,
baking soda, and cinnamon.
4. Stir into creamed mix-
ture, mixing well.
5. Fold in apples and walnuts thoroughly. Batter will
be stiff.
6. Spread in a greased
9 x 13 baking pan.
7. Bake 40-50 minutes at
350°, or until cake pulls away
from pan.
8. Cool in pan, then cut
into squares.

Cherry Brownies

Jolyn Nolt
Leola, PA

Makes 18-20 brownies

Prep Time: 5-10 minutes
Baking Time: 30 minutes

1½ cups flour
2 cups sugar
½ cup unsweetened cocoa
    powder
½ tsp. salt
1 cup vegetable oil
4 eggs
2 tsp. vanilla
½ cup chopped nuts,
    optional
2 cups cherry pie filling
confectioners sugar,
    optional

1. In an electric mixing
bowl, combine flour, sugar,
cocoa powder, salt, oil, eggs,
vanilla, and nuts. Beat with
mixer.
2. Stir in pie filling with a
spoon or spatula.
3. Pour into a greased 9 x
13 baking pan.
4. Bake at 350° for 30 minutes.
5. Remove from oven, cool
slightly, and sprinkle with
confectioners sugar, if you
wish. Cut when the brownies
have cooled.

Cakes

Moist Chocolate
Cake

Rosalie Duerksen
Canton, KS

Makes 9 servings

Prep Time: 15 minutes
Baking Time: 30 minutes

1 cup flour
1 cup sugar
1 tsp. baking powder
1 tsp. baking soda
½ cup unsweetened cocoa
    powder
1 cup hot water, *or* brewed
    coffee
1 egg
¼ cup butter, melted
½ tsp. vanilla
confectioners sugar

1. In a mixing bowl, com-
bine flour, sugar, baking powder, baking soda, cocoa powder, and hot water or coffee.
2. Add egg and butter. Mix
well.

3. Pour into a greased 8" square baking pan.

4. Bake at 350° for 30 minutes, or until toothpick inserted in center comes out clean.

5. Cool. Dust with confectioners sugar. Cut and serve.

Tip: This cake is just the right size for a small family, and very easy to make.

One Step Chocolate Cake

Brenda J. Marshall
ON, Canada

Makes 8 servings

Prep Time: 15 minutes
Baking Time: 40-45 minutes

1 cup sugar
1 egg
1/2 cup unsweetened cocoa
   powder
1 stick (1/2 cup) butter,
   softened
1 tsp. vanilla
1 1/2 cups flour
1 1/2 tsp. baking powder
1 tsp. baking soda
pinch of salt
1/2 cup hot brewed coffee

Frosting:
4 ozs. chopped semi-sweet
   chocolate
1/2 cup whipping cream
raspberries

1. Place sugar, egg, cocoa powder, butter, vanilla, flour, baking powder, baking soda, salt, and coffee in food processor or large electric mixer bowl. Process in food processor (or mixing bowl with mixer) until smooth.

2. Spoon batter into a buttered 8" springform pan with a round of parchment paper covering the bottom.

3. Bake at 350° for 40-45 minutes. Cool on rack. Remove cake from pan and place on serving plate.

4. To make frosting, combine chocolate and whipping cream in microwave-safe bowl. Cover and microwave for 1 minute on high. Stir to melt. Pour into center of cake and allow to run down the sides.

5. When cake is cooled, and just before serving, top with raspberries.

Chocolate Sheet Cake

Robin Schrock
Millersburg, OH

Makes 18 servings

Prep Time: 30 minutes
Baking Time: 20 minutes
Cooling Time: 1 1/2 hours

Cake:
2 sticks (1 cup) butter
5 Tbsp. unsweetened cocoa
   powder
1 cup water
2 eggs, beaten
1 Tbsp vinegar
1 tsp. baking soda
1 tsp. baking powder
1/2 cup sour milk, *or*
   buttermilk
1 Tbsp. vanilla extract
2 cups sugar
2 cups flour
1/2 tsp. salt

Frosting:
1 stick (1/2 cup) butter
5 Tbsp. unsweetened cocoa
   powder
1/2 cup milk
1 tsp. vanilla extract
confectioners sugar

1. To make cake, combine butter, cocoa powder, and water in a small saucepan. Bring to a rolling boil, stirring occasionally. Remove from heat and cool.

2. When cooled, pour slowly into mixing bowl. Add eggs, vinegar, baking soda, baking powder, sour milk, and vanilla. Mix well.

3. In a separate bowl, mix together sugar, flour, and salt. Add to liquid mixture and blend thoroughly.

4. Pour into a 13 x 16 x 1 1/2 cake pan. Bake at 350° for 20 minutes.

5. Allow cake to cool to room temperature.

6. When ready to ice, make frosting by combining butter, cocoa powder, and milk in the saucepan. Bring to a rolling boil.

7. When slightly cool, add vanilla. Gradually add confectioners sugar, 1/2 cup at a time, beating to make a spreadable consistency.

8. Ice cooled cake with frosting.

Chocolate Raspberry Cheesecake

LaRee Eby, Portland, OR

Makes 15 servings

Prep Time: 35 minutes
Baking Time: 50 minutes

Crust:
2 cups crushed Oreo
   cookies
1/4 cup butter, melted

Filling:
2 8-oz. pkgs. light cream
   cheese, at room
   temperature
1 cup sugar
2 eggs
1 tsp. vanilla
1 1/2 Tbsp. lemon juice
2 cups sour cream
1/2 cup powdered baking
   cocoa
3 cups fresh raspberries

Glaze:
2 cups raspberry, *or*
   blackberry, jelly
2 Tbsp. lemon juice
3 Tbsp. cornstarch
2 Tbsp. cold water

1. Mix crushed Oreos and butter together in a mixing bowl. Press into a lightly greased 9 x 13 baking pan.

2. Beat cream cheese with sugar in a mixing bowl until smooth.

3. Add eggs, vanilla, and lemon juice. Mix until well blended.

4. Add sour cream and cocoa powder. Beat 1 minute.

5. Spoon cream cheese mixture over the crumb layer, being careful not to disturb the crumbs.

6. Bake at 275° for 50 minutes on the middle shelf of the oven. Allow to cool slowly in the oven with the door ajar for up to an hour.

7. Place raspberries on top of cooled cheesecake.

8. While the cake is cooling, melt jelly in a small saucepan. Add lemon juice and bring to a boil, stirring constantly.

9. In a small bowl, dissolve cornstarch in cold water. Stir mixture into jelly mixture and cook until thickened. Remove from heat.

10. Pour glaze over raspberries. Refrigerate the cake for 4-8 hours, or overnight.

Chocolate Chip Zucchini Cake

Vonda Ebersole
Mt. Pleasant Mills, PA
Bernice Esau
North Newton, KS

Makes 12 servings

Prep Time: 20 minutes
Baking Time: 45 minutes

1 stick (1/2 cup) butter,
   softened
1/2 cup oil
1 3/4 cups sugar
2 eggs
1/2 cup buttermilk
1 tsp. vanilla
1 tsp. salt

1 tsp. baking soda
2 1/2 cups flour
4 tbsp. unsweetened cocoa
   powder
2 cups grated zucchini,
   peeled *or* unpeeled
1 cup chocolate chips

1. In a large mixing bowl, cream butter, oil, and sugar together.

2. Beat in eggs.

3. Add milk, vanilla, and salt.

4. In a separate bowl, sift together baking soda, flour, and cocoa powder. Stir into creamed mixture.

5. Gently stir in zucchini.

6. Grease a 9 x 13 baking pan. Sprinkle flour lightly over its bottom and sides. Pour in batter. Sprinkle with chocolate chips.

7. Bake at 325° for 45 minutes.

Black Bottom Cake or Cupcakes

Joleen Albrecht
Gladstone, MI

*Makes 15 servings of cake, or
about 18 cupcakes*

Prep Time: 20 minutes
Baking Time: 20-25 minutes

8 ozs. cream cheese, at
   room temperature
1 egg
1 1/3 cups sugar, *divided*
3/8 tsp. salt, *divided*
12 ozs. semi-sweet
   chocolate chips

1 1/2 cups flour
1/4 cup unsweetened cocoa
   powder
1 cup sugar
1/4 tsp. salt
1/2 tsp. baking soda
1 cup cold water
1/3 cup vegetable oil
1 Tbsp. vinegar
1 Tbsp. vanilla

1. Mix cream cheese, egg, 1/3 cup sugar, and 1/8 tsp. salt together with an electric mixer.

2. Stir in the chocolate chips by hand. Set aside.

3. Combine and mix the remaining ingredients in a separate bowl.

4. Pour cake batter into a greased 9 x 13 baking pan.

5. Spoon cream cheese mixture on top. Swirl with a fork.

6. Bake at 350° for 25 minutes, or until a toothpick inserted in the center comes out clean.

To make cupcakes, line cupcake pans with cupcake papers.

Spoon batter into the cups, making each about half-full. Put about 1 tablespoon cream cheese mixture on top of each. Bake at 350° for 20-25 minutes, or until toothpick inserted in centers comes out clean.

A Tip —

Do not open the oven door when baking an angel food cake. Use an electric knife in order to cut an angel food cake with a clean cut.

Angel Food Cake
Pauline Hindal, Grandin, MI

Makes 16 servings

Prep Time: 10-15 minutes
Baking Time: 35-40 minutes

2 cups egg whites, at room
   temperature
1 1/8 cups flour
2 cups sugar, *divided*
1/2 tsp. salt
1 1/2 tsp. cream of tarter
1 tsp. vanilla extract

1. Place egg whites in the large bowl of an electric mixer.

2. In a separate bowl, sift flour and 1 cup sugar together. Set aside.

3. Add salt to egg whites and beat on high speed until foamy, about half a minute.

4. Add cream of tarter to egg whites. Continue beating until whites are stiff, but not dry, approximately 2 1/2-3 minutes.

5. Quickly sprinkle 1 cup sugar into whites. Beat on a slower speed while sprinkling in the sugar. Then increase mixer to the highest speed, just until the sugar is blended in and very stiff peaks form.

6. Sprinkle in the flour/sugar mixture and vanilla. Blend in quickly by hand, using a spatula and a gentle folding motion from the sides toward the center of the bowl.

7. Spoon gently into an ungreased tube pan. Cut care-

fully through the batter—going the whole way around the pan—with a knife to release large bubbles.

8. Bake at 350° for 35-40 minutes, or until the top is springy when touched.

Tips:

1. Do not open the oven door while the cake is baking.

2. I like to use an electric knife to cut angel food cakes.

3. Strawberr-i-oca (page 203) is a great topping for this cake.

Sponge Cake
Cathy Boshart, Lebanon, PA

Makes 8-10 servings

Prep Time: 15 minutes
Baking Time: 35-40 minutes

4 eggs
2 cups flour
2 cups sugar
2 tsp. baking powder
1 cup hot milk
1 tsp. vanilla extract

1. In a mixing bowl, beat eggs well.

2. In a separate bowl, mix together flour, sugar, and baking powder. Add alternately with milk to the beaten eggs.

3. Stir in vanilla.

4. Pour batter into a greased tube pan or a 9 x 13 baking pan.

5. Bake at 350° for 35-40 minutes.

Strawberry Shortcake

Joyce Kreiser
Manheim, PA

Makes 15-18 servings

Prep Time: 8-12 minutes
Baking Time: 30-35 minutes

1½ cups sugar
¼ cup butter, softened
3 eggs
4 cups flour
4 tsp. baking powder
1 tsp. salt
1 cup milk
sliced strawberries

1. Beat together sugar and butter.
2. Add eggs and mix well.
3. In a separate bowl, sift together flour, baking powder, and salt.
4. Add to creamed sugar mixture alternately with milk.
5. Bake at 350° in a greased and floured 9 x 13 baking pan until lightly browned on top, about 30-35 minutes.
6. Serve topped with sliced strawberries and milk in bowls.

Tip: Another way to serve this cake is to slice 1½ qts. strawberries into a bowl, sprinkle the berries with 3 Tbsp. sugar, then cover and refrigerate the bowl for ½ hour or more before serving. The sugar over the sliced berries makes a great syrup.

Banana Nut Cake

Margaret Culbert
Lebanon, PA

Makes 12-15 servings

Prep Time: 15-17 minutes
Baking Time: 30-40 minutes

2 cups sifted flour
1 tsp. baking powder
1 tsp. baking soda
½ tsp. salt
1½ cups sugar
½ cup shortening
½ cup buttermilk
1½ cups sliced bananas
2 eggs
1 tsp. vanilla
½ cup walnuts

1. Sift flour, baking powder, baking soda, and salt together in a large bowl.
2. Combine sugar, shortening, buttermilk, bananas, eggs, and vanilla in a food processor. Cover and process on high until smooth.
3. Remove feeder cap and add walnuts. Continue to process only until nuts are chopped.
4. Pour these creamed ingredients into the dry ingredients. Mix just until combined.
5. Pour batter into a greased and floured 9 x 13 baking pan.
6. Bake at 350° for 30-40 minutes, or until toothpick inserted in center comes out clean.

Variation: Add this Frosting to the Banana Nut Cake:

1 stick (½ cup) butter, softened
1 tsp. vanilla
3½-3¾ cups confectioners sugar
¼ cup mashed bananas
1 tsp. lemon juice

1. Cream butter and vanilla together until well mixed, either by hand or with an electric mixer.
2. Gradually beat in sugar.
3. Stir in bananas and lemon juice.
4. Spread over cooled cake.
— **Kara Maddox**
Independence, MI

My Favorite Blueberry Cake

Mary E. Wheatley
Mashpee, MA

Makes 8 servings

Prep Time: 15 minutes
Baking Time: 1 hour, or more if using frozen berries

1 stick (½ cup) butter, at room temperature
1 cup, plus 2 Tbsp., sugar, *divided*
1 cup, plus 1 Tbsp., flour, *divided*
1 tsp. baking powder
½ tsp. salt
2 eggs
3 cups fresh blueberries*

2 Tbsp. freshly squeezed
    lemon juice
confectioners sugar

1. In a large bowl, cream the butter with 1 cup sugar until light and fluffy.

2. In another bowl, mix together 1 cup flour, baking powder, and salt. Beat into the butter mixture.

3. Beat in the eggs, one at a time. This will be a stiff batter.

4. Place batter into a lightly buttered 9" springform pan.

5. Toss berries with 2 tablespoons sugar, lemon juice, and 1 tablespoon flour. (*If using frozen berries, do not thaw them. And increase the amount of flour to 2-3 Tbsp.) Spread evenly over top of batter.

6. Bake 1 hour at 350°. (*Frozen berries may require more than an hour.) Check that the cake is done by inserting a toothpick in its center. It will come out clean if the cake is fully baked.

7. Cool cake in pan. Remove sides of pan and move onto a cake plate, berry-side up. Sprinkle lightly with confectioners sugar when serving.

Variation: If you'd like a very special finish, serve the cake with Lemon Sauce, which you can make while the cake is baking:
1 cup sugar
1 stick (1/2 cup) butter
1/4 cup water
3/4 tsp. fresh lemon zest
3 Tbsp. fresh lemon juice
1 egg, well beaten

1. Combine all sauce ingredients in a non-aluminum saucepan. Bring to a boil over medium heat, stirring occasionally.

2. Serve warm with warm squares of blueberry cake.

— **Stacy Schmucker Stoltzfus**, Enola, PA

Cajun Pineapple Cake

Jan Sams
Lancaster, PA
Kay Magruder
Seminole, OK

Makes 12-16 servings

Prep Time: 20 minutes
Baking Time: 50 minutes

3 cups flour
1/2 tsp. salt
1 1/2 cups sugar
1 1/2 tsp. baking soda
2 eggs
15-oz. can crushed
    pineapple, undrained
1/4 cup orange juice

Frosting:
3/4 cup sugar
1/4 cup evaporated milk
1 stick (1/2 cup) butter
1 cup chopped pecans
1 cup shredded coconut

1. Make the cake by combining the flour, salt, sugar, and baking soda in a large mixing bowl.

2. In a separate bowl, mix together eggs, pineapple, and orange juice.

3. Add wet ingredients to dry ingredients. Mix well.

4. Pour into a greased 9 x 13 baking pan.

5. Bake at 325° for 50 minutes, or until a toothpick inserted in the center comes out clean.

6. While the cake is baking, place the sugar, milk, and butter for the frosting in a saucepan. Bring to a boil. Continue simmering until the butter is melted. Cool.

7. Stir in pecans and coconut. Mix well.

8. Spread topping on hot cake. Place under broiler for a few minutes until lightly browned. But watch carefully so the topping doesn't burn!

Topping Variation:
1 stick (1/2 cup) butter, softened
8-oz. pkg. cream cheese, softened
1 1/2 cups confectioners sugar
1 tsp. vanilla
chopped walnuts

1. Cream together butter and cream cheese.

2. Stir in sugar and vanilla, stirring until well mixed and creamy.

3. Spread on lukewarm cake.

4. Garnish with walnuts.
    — **Erma Hoover**
       Lititz, PA
    — **Linda Overholt**
       Abbeville, SC

Unbelievable Carrot Cake

Sue Hamilton, Minooka, IL

Makes 16 servings

Prep Time: 5-10 minutes
Baking Time: 30 minutes
Cooling Time: 1 hour

Cake:
1 2-layer spice cake mix
2 cups (1/2 lb.) shredded carrots
1 cup crushed pineapples with juice
3 egg whites
1/2 cup All-Bran cereal

Frosting:
2 3-oz. pkgs. fat free *or* light cream cheese, softened
1 cup Splenda
1 tsp. vanilla
4 ozs. (1/3 of a 12-oz. container) fat-free frozen whipped topping, thawed

1. Combine all cake ingredients thoroughly.
2. Pour into a 9 x 13 baking pan sprayed with non-fat cooking spray.
3. Bake at 350° for 30 minutes. Cool completely.
4. Beat together cream cheese, Splenda, and vanilla.
5. Fold in the whipped topping. Frost cake and refrigerate.

Tip: There is no need to shred carrots yourself anymore, because you can now buy them in a bag all ready to use.

Carrot Cake

Janelle Myers-Benner
Harrisonburg, VA

Makes 13-15 servings

Prep Time: 45 minutes
Baking Time: 40-50 minutes

1 cup oil
1/3 cup sugar
1 scant cup brown sugar
4 eggs
1/2 cup applesauce
2 cups whole wheat pastry flour
1 tsp. baking soda
1 tsp. baking powder
1 tsp. salt
2 tsp. cinnamon
2 cups grated carrots, about 3 large carrots
3/4 cup grated coconut
1 cup crushed pineapple, drained
3/4 cup nuts, *optional*
2 tsp. vanilla

Cream Cheese Frosting:
2 3-oz. pkgs. cream cheese, softened
1/4–1/2 cup butter, softened
4 cups confectioners sugar
2 tsp. vanilla
milk

1. In a large mixing bowl, cream together oil, sugar, and brown sugar. Stir in the eggs and the applesauce.
2. In a separate bowl, sift together the flour, baking soda, baking powder, salt, and cinnamon. Add to creamed mixture.
3. Stir in the carrots, coconut, pineapple, nuts, if desired, and vanilla.
4. Pour into a greased 9 x 13 baking pan. Bake at 325° for 40-50 minutes, or until toothpick inserted in center comes out clean.
5. To make the frosting, mix cream cheese, butter, powdered sugar, and vanilla together. Add milk until you reach a spreadable consistency.

This is the cake my mom made for our wedding. We couldn't wait until our 1st anniversary to eat the top of the cake!

A Tip —

To keep a cake plate clean while frosting a cake, slide 6"-wide strips of waxed paper under each side of the cake. When the cake is frosted and the frosting is set, pull the strips away, leaving a clean plate.

Lemony Cheese Cake

Ruth Osborne
Carmichael, PA

Makes 8-12 servings

Prep Time: 10-20 minutes
Baking Time: 45-60 minutes

Crust:
2 cups graham cracker
   crumbs
2 Tbsp. sugar
5 1/3 Tbsp. (1/3 cup) butter

Filling:
4 eggs
3 8-oz. pkgs. cream cheese,
   softened
4 Tbsp. flour
2 Tbsp. lemon juice
1 cup sugar
1 tsp. vanilla
1/4 tsp. salt

1. Prepare crust by combining graham cracker crumbs and sugar.

2. Melt margarine and stir into cracker mixture.

3. Press combined ingredients around sides and bottom of a 9" springform pan.

4. Bake 2-4 minutes at 350°. Set aside.

5. Put eggs in an electric mixer bowl and beat slightly.

6. Add all other filling ingredients and blend with mixer until smooth.

7. Spoon over top of graham cracker crust, being careful not to disturb the crumbs.

8. Bake at 350° for 40-55 minutes, or until set in the middle.

Tip: To keep a cheesecake from cracking, either place a dish of water in the oven along with the cheesecake, or wrap the springform pan with foil and place the filled pan in a dish of water to bake.

Frozen Mocha Cheesecake

Stacy Schmucker Stoltzfus
Enola, PA
Ilene Bontrager
Arlington, KS

Makes 16-20 servings

Prep Time: 20-25 minutes
Freezing Time: 6 hours,
   or overnight

1 1/4 cups crushed chocolate
   wafer cookies
1/4 cup sugar
half a stick (1/4 cup) butter,
   melted
8-oz. pkg. cream cheese,
   softened
14-oz. can sweetened
   condensed milk
2/3 cup chocolate syrup
2 Tbsp. instant coffee
   granules
1 tsp. hot water
1 cup frozen whipped
   topping, thawed, *plus*
   extra for garnish
1 cup chocolate chips,
   optional
frozen whipped topping,
   thawed

1. Reserve a few cookie crumbs for garnish. In a small bowl, combine remaining cookie crumbs, sugar, and butter. Pat crumbs firmly on the bottom and up the sides of a 9 x 13 baking pan, or a 9" springform pan. Refrigerate while preparing rest of cake.

2. In a large mixing bowl, beat cream cheese until fluffy.

3. Add milk and syrup and combine well.

4. In a small bowl, dissolve coffee granules in hot water. Add to creamed mixture. Mix well.

5. Fold in whipped topping.

6. Pour into prepared pan. Cover and freeze about 6 hours, or until firm.

7. Meanwhile, melt chocolate chips in microwave (about 30 seconds). Stir. Place in plastic baggie, and cut off a small part of one corner.

8. Squeeze chocolate onto waxed paper into 16 or 20 shapes (hearts, fun squiggles, etc.). Place in refrigerator until firm.

9. Just before serving, place a dollop of whipped topping on each piece of cake. Gently lift chocolate shapes off waxed paper and lean each one into a dollop, so it stands up. Sprinkle with reserved crumbs, if desired.

10. Serve chilled.

Peaches and Cream

Becky Weaver
Ellsinore, MO
Krista Hershberger
Elverson, PA
Janeen Zimmerman
Denver, PA
Flo Quint
Quinter, KS

Makes 6 servings

Prep Time: 10-15 minutes
Baking Time: 35-45 minutes

3/4 cup flour
1/2 cup sugar
1 egg
1/2 tsp. baking powder
1/2 tsp. salt
3-oz. box instant vanilla
  pudding
1/2 cup milk
3 Tbsp. butter, softened
1 qt. sliced peaches, drained,
  3 Tbsp. juice reserved
8-oz. pkg. cream cheese,
  softened
1/2 cup sugar
3 Tbsp. sugar
1/2 tsp. cinnamon

1. Put first 8 ingredients in an electric mixer bowl. Beat well and pour into a greased 10″ pie plate.
2. Lay peach halves or slices on top.
3. Mix together cream cheese, 3 Tbsp. peach juice, and 1/2 cup sugar. Pour over peaches.
4. Mix 3 Tbsp. sugar and cinnamon together. Sprinkle over cream cheese mixture.

5. Bake at 350° for 35-40 minutes, or until toothpick inserted in center comes out clean.
6. Cool before slicing to serve.

Kiwi Pineapple Cheesecake

Mable Hershey
Marietta, PA

Makes 12-14 servings

Prep Time: 30 minutes
Baking Time: 8-10 minutes
Chilling Time: 7 hours,
  or overnight

13/4 cups crushed vanilla
  wafers (about 50 wafers)
1/4 cup sugar
1 stick (1/2 cup) butter,
  melted

Filling:
20-oz. can sliced
  pineapples, 1/2 cup juice
  reserved
1 envelope unflavored
  gelatin
2 8-oz. pkgs. cream cheese,
  softened
15 ozs. ricotta cheese
1 cup confectioners sugar
1 Tbsp. grated fresh orange
  peel
1 tsp. vanilla

Topping:
1/2 cup orange marmalade
1 kiwi fruit peeled, halved,
  and sliced

1. In a bowl, combine wafer crumbs and sugar. Stir in melted butter.
2. Press into the bottom and 2 inches up the sides of a 9″ springform pan. Bake at 350° for 8 minutes. Cool on wire rack; then refrigerate for 30 minutes.
3. Meanwhile, drain pineapple, reserving 1/2 cup juice.
4. Pour 1/2 cup pineapple juice into a small saucepan. Sprinkle gelatin over juice. Let stand for 1 minute.
5. Cook over low heat, stirring until gelatin is completely dissolved. Cool to room temperature, about 10 minutes.
6. While the juice is cooling, beat together the cream cheese and ricotta cheese in a large electric mixer bowl until smooth. Stir in confectioners sugar until smooth.
7. Gradually add gelatin mixture, orange peel, and vanilla to the cheese mixture. Beat on low speed until well mixed. Spoon half into crust.
8. Cut four pineapple rings in half and arrange in spoke-fashion over the filling.
9. Spoon remaining filling over pineapple.
10. Refrigerate in the baking pan for 6 hours, or overnight.
11. Beat marmalade until soft and spreadable. Brush 6 Tbsp. on top of thoroughly chilled cheesecake.
12. Cut remaining pineapple rings in half and arrange over marmalade.
13. Place kiwi slices between pineapple rings and

brush with remaining marmalade.

14. Just before serving, run knife around the edge of the pan to loosen. Remove sides of pan, cut cake into wedges, and serve.

Tip: To evenly press crumbs into a springform pan, place another round cake pan down on top of the crumbs, pressing gently. This will make the corner/bend from the bottom to the sides less thick and will help to make very straight sides. When you take the springform pan sides off, the sides of the cake will look even.

No-Bake Raspberry Cheesecake

Arlene M. Kopp
Lineboro, MD

Makes 10-12 servings

Prep Time: 30 minutes
Chilling Time: 4-5 hours

3-oz. pkg. raspberry gelatin
1 cup boiling water
8-oz. pkg. cream cheese, softened
1 cup sugar
1 tsp. vanilla
1 1/3 cups (19-20 crackers) graham cracker crumbs
1/4 cup melted butter
3 Tbsp. lemon juice
12-oz. can evaporated milk, chilled

1. Place a large mixing bowl in the fridge. (You'll need it later to whip the milk.)

2. Combine gelatin and boiling water in a small bowl, stirring until gelatin is dissolved. Cool.

3. In a medium-sized mixing bowl, cream together cream cheese, sugar, and vanilla. Mix well.

4. Add gelatin. Mix well. Chill until it begins to set.

5. Meanwhile, combine cracker crumbs and butter in a small bowl. Press two-thirds of crumbs into the bottom of a 9 x 13 pan.

6. Combine lemon juice and milk in the bowl you've been chilling. Whip until it's stiff and holds a peak.

7. Lightly fold gelatin mixture into whipped mixture.

8. Pour into crumb crust in pan, being careful not to disturb the crumbs. Sprinkle top with remaining crumbs.

9. Chill until set, about 2-3 hours.

A Tip —

When using fresh fruit to garnish a cake, be sure to pat it dry on a paper towel. This helps any juice from forming or puddling on the finished cake.

Coconut Cake

Michele Ruvola
Selden, NY

Makes 12 servings

Prep Time: 15-20 minutes
Baking Time: 30-35 minutes
Cooling Time: 1 hour

2 cups flour
1 tsp. baking powder
2 sticks (1 cup) butter, softened
1 1/3 cups white sugar
3 eggs
1 tsp. vanilla
1 cup milk
1-1 1/2 cups shredded coconut, according to your preference
confectioners sugar

1. In a medium-sized mixing bowl, combine flour and baking powder. Set aside.

2. Beat the butter with an electric mixer until creamy. Gradually add sugar. Blend until fluffy.

3. Add eggs, one at a time, beating well between each. Add vanilla.

4. Add flour mixture alternately with milk. Beat well after each addition.

5. Fold in coconut.

6. Spoon into a lightly greased 9" springform pan. Bake at 350° for 30-35 minutes, or until golden brown.

7. Sprinkle cooled cake with confectioners sugar before serving.

Moist Creamy Coconut Cake

Kathy Bless
Fayetteville, PA

Makes 20 servings

Prep Time: 10 minutes
Baking Time: about 30 minutes
Chilling Time: 8 hours,
    or overnight

1 pkg. yellow cake mix
1¼ cups milk
½ cup sugar
2 cups flaked coconut,
    divided
9-oz. container frozen
    whipped topping,
    thawed
1 tsp. vanilla

1. Prepare cake mix as
directed on package. Bake in
a greased 9 x 13 pan.
2. Cool 15 minutes. Poke
holes in the cake with a fork.
3. Meanwhile, combine
milk, sugar, and ½ cup
coconut in a saucepan. Bring
to a boil. Reduce heat and
simmer 1 minute.
4. Spoon evenly over
warm cake. Cool completely.
5. Fold together ½ cup
coconut, whipped topping,
and vanilla. Spread over
cooled cake.
6. Sprinkle remaining
coconut evenly over top of
cake. Chill overnight. Store in
refrigerator.

Mixed Fruit Cake

Merle E. Mast, Keezletown, VA

Makes 12 servings

Prep Time: 30 minutes
Cooking/Baking Time:
    90 minutes

3 cups chopped dried fruits
    (vary these as you like):
    ½ cup raisins *or*
        currants
    ½ cup dates
    1 cup figs
    ¾ cup dried apricots
    ¼ cup dried cranberries,
        or dried tart cherries
2 cups water
1 cup sugar
5 Tbsp. butter
3 cups flour
1 tsp. baking soda
2 tsp. cinnamon
½ tsp. cloves
½ tsp. salt
1 cup chopped nuts,
    optional

1. Combine chopped fruit,
water, sugar, and butter in a
saucepan. Bring to a boil,
cover, and simmer over low
heat for 20 minutes.
2. Meanwhile, stir together
flour, soda, cinnamon, cloves,
and salt in a mixing bowl.
3. Add fruit mixture, and
nuts, if you wish. Stir together
until well blended.
4. Spread mixture into two
greased 4½ x 8½ x 2½ loaf
pans.
5. Bake at 325° for 60 minutes, or until cakes test done.
Invert onto rack and cool.

Vicki's Lovely Lazy Daizy Cake

Dorothy Van Deest
Memphis, TN

Makes 12 servings

Prep Time: 30 minutes
Baking Time: 33-43 minutes

4 eggs
2 cups sugar
2 tsp. vanilla
2 cups flour
2 tsp. baking powder
1½ tsp. salt
2 Tbsp. butter
1 cup scalded milk

Topping:
½ cup, plus 2 Tbsp.,
    brown sugar
¼ cup, plus 2 Tbsp.,
    cream, *or* whole milk
6 Tbsp. butter
1 cup shredded coconut
1 cup chopped nuts

1. Beat eggs until light
in a large mixing bowl. Add
sugar, beating constantly. Add
vanilla.
2. Sift flour, baking powder, and salt together in a
separate bowl. Stir into egg
mixture.
3. Stir butter into scalded
milk, stirring until the butter
melts. Add to batter and mix
well.
4. Pour into a greased 9 x
13 cake pan. Bake at 350° for
30-40 minutes.
5. While the cake is bak-
ing, prepare topping. Mix all
topping ingredients in a

saucepan. Heat over medium-low heat until the butter melts and the topping is bubbling.

6. Test cake with toothpick. When done, spread immediately with topping.

7. Change oven to broiler and set cake under broiler until bubbly. Watch carefully; it doesn't take long!

8. Serve hot or cold.

Oatmeal Cake

Shari Jensen
Fountain, CO
Barb Yoder
Angola, IN

Makes 12 servings

Prep Time: 15 minutes
Baking Time: 50 minutes

1½ cups boiling water
1 cup dry quick oats
1 cup sugar
1 cup light brown sugar
½ cup shortening
2 eggs
1½ cups sifted flour
1 tsp. baking soda
½ tsp. salt
1 tsp. cinnamon

Topping:
1 cup light brown sugar
1 cup coconut, shredded *or* flaked
1 cup chopped walnuts
1 tsp. vanilla
5 Tbsp. melted butter
¼ cup evaporated milk

1. Pour boiling water over quick oats in a small bowl. Let stand a few minutes.

2. Cream together sugars, shortening, and eggs. Add oatmeal mixture.

3. In a small bowl, combine flour, baking soda, salt, and cinnamon. Add to egg/oatmeal mixture.

4. Pour into a greased and floured 9 x 13 baking pan. Bake at 350° for 40-45 minutes.

5. Meanwhile, make topping by combining sugar, coconut, walnuts, vanilla, butter, and evaporated milk in a mixing bowl.

6. Spread over cake as soon as it is comes out of the oven. Turn on broiler and place cake under broiler for 3-5 minutes, until golden and bubbly. Watch carefully so it doesn't burn.

7. Remove from broiler and let cool before serving.

Variation: Instead of finishing the cake with the topping above, in Step 4, after the cake is in the baking pan but before putting it in the oven, scatter 5 cups (6-oz. pkg.) peanut butter cups, chopped, over the batter. Bake at 350° for 40-45 minutes. Let cool before cutting into squares and serving.
— Joan Miller
Wayland, IA

A Tip —

Always use large eggs when baking cakes. They are a big part of the leavening process.

Poppy Seed Cake

Helen Goering
Moundridge, KS

Makes 15 servings

Prep Time: 20-30 minutes
Baking Time: 25-30 minutes

2 cups sugar
½ cup solid shortening
½ cup poppy seeds, finely ground
2 eggs
½ cup buttermilk
2 cups flour
1 tsp. baking soda
1 tsp. vanilla
1 cup boiling water

1. In a large mixing bowl, cream together sugar, shortening, and ground poppy seeds.

2. Add eggs and buttermilk. Mix well.

3. Sift flour and baking soda into mixture. Blend thoroughly.

4. Add vanilla and hot water. Blend in well.

5. Place in a greased 9" or 10" tube pan or a greased 9 x 13 baking pan.

6. Bake at 350° for 25-30 minutes, or until a toothpick inserted in center comes out clean.

Lemon Glaze Cake

Terry Stutzman Mast
Lodi, CA
Nancy Wagner Graves
Manhattan, KS

Makes 15 servings

Prep Time: 10 minutes
Cooking Time: 30-35 minutes

Cake:
1 yellow cake mix
4 eggs
3/4 cup oil
3/4 cup water
3-oz. pkg. lemon gelatin

Glaze:
juice and grated rind of
  2 lemons
2 cups confectioners sugar

1. In a large mixing bowl, mix together cake mix, eggs, oil, water, and gelatin.

2. Pour into a lightly greased 9 x 13 baking pan. Bake at 350° for 30-35 minutes, or until a toothpick inserted in the center comes out clean.

3. While the cake is baking, mix lemon juice, lemon rind, and confectioners together in a mixing bowl.

4. While the baked cake is still warm, poke holes all over it with a fork. Drizzle thoroughly with the glaze.

5. Allow cake to cool before cutting into squares and serving.

Ah, the annual summer picnic with folks from the church in Normal, Illinois, where I grew up. This was a regular contribution of Ruth Rowe, a family friend.

Variation: *Substitute a 3.4 oz. box of lemon instant pudding for the box of gelatin. Stir 1 tsp. almond flavoring and 1 heaping tsp. poppy seeds into batter in Step 1.*

Pour cake into a greased bundt pan and bake at 350° for 35 minutes, or until a toothpick comes out clean when inserted in the center.

— Beth Maurer
  Columbus Grove, OH

Orange Streusel Cake

Lori Newswanger
Lancaster, PA

Makes 16 servings

Prep Time: 20 minutes
Baking Time: 30-35 minutes

Streusel:
1 cup brown sugar
1 cup chopped nuts *or*
  sliced almonds
1/4 cup flour
3 Tbsp. butter, melted
1 tsp. grated fresh orange
  zest

Cake:
1 stick (1/2 cup) butter,
  softened
1/2 cup sugar

3 eggs
1 tsp. grated fresh orange
  zest
1/2 tsp. vanilla
2 cups flour
1 tsp. baking powder
1 tsp. baking soda
2/3 cup orange juice

Glaze:
2 1/2 tsp. orange juice
1/2 cup confectioners sugar

1. To make the streusel, combine brown sugar, nuts, flour, butter, and orange zest in a mixing bowl. Mix till crumbly and set aside.

2. To make the cake, beat together butter and sugar until creamy.

3. Beat in eggs 1 at a time. Add orange zest and vanilla.

4. In a separate bowl, combine flour, baking powder, and baking soda. Add to egg mixture alternately with orange juice.

5. Spoon half the batter into a greased 9" or 10" tube pan. Sprinkle with half the streusel. Top with remaining batter and then a layer of the remaining streusel.

6. Bake at 350° for 30-35 minutes, or until a toothpick comes out clean. Cool on a wire rack.

7. Prepare glaze by combining orange juice and confectioners sugar.

8. Turn cake right side up onto a serving plate. Drizzle with glaze.

9. Slice and serve.

Orange Lemon Pound Cake

Judi Manos, West Islip, NY

Makes 12-16 servings

Prep Time: 20 minutes
Baking Time: 45-60 minutes
Cooling Time: 15 minutes

2 sticks (1 cup) butter, softened
1/2 cup solid shortening
2 cups sugar
5 eggs, at room temperature
3 cups flour
1/2 tsp. salt
1/2 tsp. baking soda
1/2 tsp. baking powder
1 cup buttermilk, *or* 1 cup plain yogurt
1 tsp. vanilla
1 tsp. lemon extract

Glaze:
2 tsp. orange juice
2 tsp. lemon juice
1 cup confectioners sugar

1. In a large mixing bowl, cream together butter, shortening, and sugar until light and fluffy.
2. Add eggs, one at a time. Beat well after each addition.
3. In a separate bowl, combine flour, salt, baking soda, and baking powder.
4. Add dry ingredients to creamed mixture alternately with buttermilk. End with dry ingredients.
5. Stir in vanilla and lemon extract.
6. Spoon batter into a well greased and floured 10" tube pan. Bake at 350° for 45-60 minutes, or until cake tests done with a toothpick.
7. Combine all glaze ingredients in a mixing bowl. Blend well.
8. Cool cake on a wire rack for 15 minutes. Remove from pan. Place cake on the wire rack over a plate that is slightly larger than the cake. Punch holes in the still-warm cake with a toothpick and drizzle glaze over the cake until it is absorbed.

Variation: In addition to the vanilla and lemon extract in the batter, add 1/2 tsp. coconut extract, 1 tsp. almond extract, and 1/2 tsp. butter flavoring.
— **Ann Bender**
Fort Defiance, VA

Aunt Allie's Molasses Cake

Mary D. Smith, Moneta, VA

Makes 10-12 servings

Prep Time: 20 minutes
Baking Time: 40-45 minutes
Cooling Time: 45 minutes

2 eggs
1 cup sugar
2 sticks (1 cup) butter, softened
1 cup molasses
2 tsp. cinnamon
1 tsp. ginger
3 cups flour
2 cups boiling water
2 tsp. baking soda

Frosting:
8 Tbsp. butter *or* cream cheese, softened
2 cups confectioners sugar
orange juice concentrate

1. By hand, combine eggs, sugar, and butter. Mix well.
2. Add molasses, cinnamon, and ginger. Mix well.
3. Stir in flour. Mix well.
4. In a small bowl, combine boiling water and baking soda. Add to batter. Mix well.
5. Pour batter into a greased 9 x 13 baking pan.
6. Bake at 325° for 40-45 minutes. Cool.
7. In a mixing bowl, combine butter or cream cheese and confectioners sugar until smooth.
8. Add orange juice until of spreading consistency. Spread over cooled cake.

Variation: Instead of spreading frosting on the cake, serve the Molasses Cake with Lemon Sauce:
1/2 cup sugar
1/8 tsp. salt
1 1/2 Tbsp. cornstarch
1 1/2 cups boiling water
grated rind and juice of 2 lemons
2 Tbsp. butter

1. Combine sugar, salt, and cornstarch in a saucepan.
2. Add boiling water. Stir until smooth. Cook over low heat until thickened and clear, stirring constantly.
3. Remove from heat. Stir in lemon rind and juice and butter. Stir until well blended.
— **Virginia Bender**
Dover, DE

Sunny Spice Cake

Karla Baer, North Lime, OH

Makes 15-20 servings

Prep Time: 10 minutes
Baking Time: 35 minutes

1 spice cake mix
3 5/8-oz. pkg. butterscotch
   instant pudding
2 cups milk
2 eggs
peach halves, drained
frozen whipped topping,
   thawed

1. In a mixing bowl, blend together cake mix, pudding mix, milk, and eggs.

2. Pour into a greased 9 x 13 baking pan. Bake at 350° for 35 minutes.

3. Cool.

4. When ready to serve, cut into serving-sized pieces. Place a peach half on each serving of cake. Top each with a dollop of whipped topping.

A Tip —

Rhubarb is easy to freeze. Wash it, dry it, and slice it into plastic freezer bags by the cupfuls.

Bernice's Rhubarb Sour Cream Cake

Bonnie Heatwole
Springs, PA

Makes 15-20 servings

Prep Time: 20 minutes
Baking Time: 40 minutes

half a stick (1/4 cup) butter,
   softened
1 1/2 cups brown sugar
2 large eggs
1 tsp. vanilla
2 1/3 cups flour
1 tsp. baking soda
1 tsp. salt
4 cups rhubarb, cut in 1/2"
   slices
1 cup sour cream

Topping:
1/2 cup sugar
1 tsp. cinnamon
1 cup chopped nuts
frozen whipped topping,
   thawed, *optional*

1. In a large mixing bowl, cream together butter and sugar until fluffy.

2. Add eggs and vanilla. Mix well.

3. In a separate bowl, combine flour, baking soda, and salt. Add to creamed mixture. Mix well.

4. Stir in rhubarb and sour cream. Mix well.

5. Spread batter in a greased 9 x 13 baking pan.

6. To make the topping, combine sugar, cinnamon, and nuts in a small bowl. Sprinkle on top of batter.

7. Bake at 350° for 40 minutes, or until top springs back or toothpick comes out clean.

8. Serve warm with whipped topping for dessert or for breakfast as a coffee cake.

Pound Cake

Janna Zimmerman
Flemington, NJ

Makes 10 servings

Prep Time: 10 minutes
Baking Time: 1 1/4-1 1/2 hours

2 sticks (1 cup) butter,
   softened
3 cups sugar
1 cup sour cream
1 tsp. vanilla
1/2 tsp. baking powder
6 eggs
3 cups flour

1. In a large mixing bowl, cream butter and sugar together.

2. Blend in sour cream, vanilla, and baking powder.

3. Add eggs, one at a time, beating well after each addition.

4. Add flour and mix well.

5. Pour into a greased bundt pan. Bake at 325° for 1 1/4-1 1/2 hours, or until a toothpick inserted in the center comes out clean.

Pumpkin Yummy Dessert

LuAnna Hochstedler
East Earl, PA

Makes 15 servings

Prep Time: 15-20 minutes
Baking Time: 50 minutes

29-oz. can pumpkin
1/4 tsp. salt
2 tsp. cinnamon
1/2 tsp. ginger
1/4 tsp. cloves
1 cup brown sugar
3 eggs
14-oz. can evaporated milk
1 pkg. yellow cake mix
1 stick (1/2 cup) butter, melted
1-2 cups nuts
frozen whipped topping, thawed

1. In a large mixing bowl, combine pumpkin, salt, cinnamon, ginger, cloves, sugar, and eggs. Blend well.
2. Add milk and blend thoroughly.
3. Pour batter into a greased 9 x 13 baking pan.
4. Sprinkle batter with cake mix.
5. Pour butter over top.
6. Bake at 350° for 30 minutes.
7. Sprinkle with nuts. Bake for another 20 minutes. Cool.
8. Top with whipped topping just before serving.

Variations:
1. Instead of a yellow cake mix, use a spice cake mix.
— **Linda Simmons**
Gordonville, PA

2. Instead of topping the cake with nuts, proceed through Step 6, but bake for 50-60 minutes. Allow cake to cool thoroughly. Then frost with the following:

8-oz. pkg. cream cheese, softened
1/2 cup confectioners sugar
9-oz. container frozen whipped topping, thawed

In a mixing bowl, beat cream cheese until creamy. Fold in confectioners sugar and blend well. Fold in whipped topping. Spread over cooled cake.

— **Marolyn Minnich**
Westover, MD

Root Beer Cake

Charlotte Hill
Rapid City, SD

Makes 6 servings

Prep Time: 20-25 minutes
Baking Time: 30-35 minutes
Cooling Time: 1 hour

1 cup sugar
1/2 cup butter, softened
1/2 tsp. vanilla
2 eggs
2 cups flour
1 Tbsp. baking powder
1 tsp. salt
2/3 cup root beer

Frosting:
1/4 cup butter, softened
1/8 tsp. salt
2 cups confectioners sugar
2-4 Tbsp. milk
1/3 cup root beer, chilled

1. In a large electric mixer bowl, combine all cake ingredients and blend on low speed. Increase to medium speed and beat for another 3 minutes.
2. Pour into a greased and floured 8 x 12 baking pan and bake at 375° for 30-35 minutes.
3. To make frosting, beat together butter, salt, confectioners sugar, and milk in a medium-sized bowl. Blend in enough root beer to make frosting spreadable.
4. Spread on cooled cake.

Slightly Orange Frosting

Doris Zipp, Germantown, NY

Makes enough for one cake

Prep Time: 5 minutes

1-lb. box confectioners
   sugar
1 tsp. vanilla
dash of salt
2 Tbsp. butter, melted
orange juice

1. In a mixing bowl, combine confectioners sugar, vanilla, salt, and butter. Mix well.
2. Add enough orange juice until frosting becomes spreadable.

Sloppy Chocolate Icing

Linda Overholt
Abbeville, SC

Makes icing for 1 cake

Prep Time: 2-5 minutes
Cooking Time: 5-10 minutes

1 cup water
1 cup sugar
2 squares unsweetened
   chocolate, *or* 1/2 cup
   unsweetened cocoa
   powder and 1 Tbsp.
   butter, softened

2 Tbsp. butter, softened
2 1/2 Tbsp. cornstarch
couple of drops of vanilla

1. Stir together all ingredients in a saucepan, except vanilla.
2. Cook over medium heat, stirring constantly until thickened. Stir in vanilla.
3. Cool. Spread on cooled cake.

Tip: You can also serve this icing warm over vanilla ice cream as a great hot fudge sauce.

Almond Butter Cream Frosting

Barb Yoder
Angola, IN

Makes enough for one cake

Prep Time: 10 minutes

1/3 cup solid shortening
1/4-1/3 cup water
4 cups confectioners sugar
1 1/2 tsp. almond flavoring

Combine ingredients in order listed. Beat until smooth.

Variation: For a stiffer icing, add 1-2 Tbsp. flour.

Tip: You can store this in an airtight container in the refrigerator for 5-6 months.

Pies

Apple Cream Pie

Barb Stutzman
Carlock, IL

Makes 6-8 servings

Prep Time: 30 minutes
Baking Time: 60-65 minutes

Filling:
1 cup half-and-half
1 1/4–1 1/2 cups sugar
1/3 cup flour, *or more*
1 tsp. vanilla
dash of salt
4 cups baking apples,
   sliced thin
unbaked 9" pie shell

Topping:
1/2 cup flour
1/3 cup sugar
half a stick (4 Tbsp.)
   butter, cut in small
   pieces
cinnamon

1. Combine filling ingredients, except apples, in a mixing bowl.
2. Place apples in the unbaked pie shell. Pour filling mixture over apples.

3. To make topping, blend flour, sugar and butter together with a pastry blender until crumbs form.

4. Sprinkle crumbs over apples. Sprinkle cinnamon over apples to taste.

5. Bake at 450° for 15 minutes. Reduce heat to 350°. Bake an additional 45-50 minutes.

Variation: Substitute 1 cup sour cream for the half-and-half in the filling.

— Jeanne Heyerly
Chenoa, IL

Greatest Apple Pie
Lynette Nisly
Lancaster, PA

Makes 8 servings

Prep Time: 30 minutes
Baking Time: 45-55 minutes

Filling:
1 cup sugar
2 Tbsp. flour
1 tsp. cinnamon
dash of nutmeg
dash of salt
6 cups peeled and sliced apples (Rome is my favorite)
unbaked 9" pie shell

Crumb Topping:
1/4 cup brown sugar
1/4 cup sugar
3/4 cup flour
scant 1/3 cup solid shortening

1. To prepare filling, combine sugar, flour, cinnamon, nutmeg, and salt in a large bowl.

2. Add sliced apples and mix well. Put apple mixture in unbaked pie crust.

3. To prepare topping, combine sugars and flour in a medium-sized bowl.

4. Cut in shortening with a pastry blender or fork until crumbly. Sprinkle over apples.

5. Bake at 400° for 45-55 minutes.

When my husband and I were dating, I made this pie for him and he loved it. After that, he decided to think more seriously about our future together. He has convinced our children that I make the best apple pie, which they are not shy about stating whenever apple pie is served.

Harvest Cranberry Apple Pie
Janelle Reitz
Lancaster, PA

Makes 6-8 servings

Prep Time: 20 minutes
Baking Time: 55-60 minutes

1 cup sugar
2 Tbsp. cornstarch
1/2 tsp. allspice
2 tsp. cinnamon
4 large tart baking apples, pared, cored, and sliced
1 cup fresh, whole cranberries*
1/2 cup chopped walnuts
dough for a double-crust 9" pie
2 Tbsp. butter, cut into pieces
1 egg white, beaten

1. In a large mixing bowl, combine sugar, cornstarch, allspice, and cinnamon.

2. Add apples, cranberries, and nuts. (*Frozen cranberries also work in this pie. Allow them to thaw before stirring them into the mix.) Toss to coat.

3. Divide dough. Roll out one half. Fit into a 9" pie pan.

4. Fill with fruit mixture and dot with butter.

5. Roll out second half. Place pie crust on top. Seal, trim, and flute edges. Brush top with egg whites.

6. Bake at 400° for 55-60 minutes, or until crust is golden brown and filling is bubbly. (You may need to loosely cover the edges of the crust with foil to prevent it from burning during the last 30 minutes of the baking time.)

Blueberry Pie

Martha Ann Auker
Landisburg, PA

Makes 6-8 servings

Prep Time: *30 minutes*
Cooking Time: *10 minutes*
Chilling Time: *2 hours*

2-3 cups whole fresh blueberries, *divided*
water
1/2 cup sugar
2 Tbsp. cornstarch
2 Tbsp. lemon juice
half an 8-oz. pkg. cream cheese, softened
4 Tbsp. milk
9" deep-dish baked pie shell
9-oz. container frozen whipped topping, thawed

1. Mash 2 cups blueberries. Add enough water to equal 1½ cups. Pour into saucepan. Add sugar, cornstarch, and lemon juice.
2. Cook until thickened over low heat, stirring constantly. Remove from heat. Chill for 2 hours.
3. Meanwhile mix cream cheese and milk together until creamy. Put in bottom of baked pie shell.
4. Top with ½-1 cup whole blueberries.
5. Pour cooled, thickened blueberry mixture over top.
6. Top with whipped topping just before serving.

Crumb-Topped Blueberry Pie

Dawn Shertzer
Mechanicsburg, PA

Makes 6 servings

Prep Time: *15-20 minutes*
Baking Time: *25 minutes*
Cooling/Chilling Time: *4 hours*

1 cup water, *divided*
1 cup sugar
3 Tbsp. cornstarch
1 pint blueberries
8" pie crust, unbaked
3/4 cup flour
1/4 cup dry quick *or* **rolled oats**
1/4 cup sugar
1/4 cup brown sugar
6 Tbsp. butter, at room temperature

1. Pour 3/4 cup water into saucepan. Add sugar.
2. Heat over high heat, stirring until sugar is dissolved.
3. Pour remaining 1/4 cup water into a small bowl. Add cornstarch. Whisk until smooth. Add to sugar water.
4. Bring to a boil while stirring until thick and bubbly.
5. Add blueberries. Stir until heated through.
6. Pour into crust.
7. Combine flour, oats, and sugars in a mixing bowl. Cut in butter until crumbly.
8. Top pie with crumb topping.
9. Bake at 425° for 25 minutes.

10. Cool to room temperature, and then refrigerate 3 hours to allow filling to set.

Tips:
   1. You can use this recipe for other fruits, also.
   2. If the sugar syrup does not thicken as much as you like, add more cornstarch.

Cranberry Pie

Sandra Chang
Derwood, MD

Makes 6-8 servings

Prep Time: *20 minutes*
Baking Time: *35-40 minutes*

2 cups fresh cranberries
1/2 cup walnuts, chopped
1½ cups sugar, *divided*
half a stick (1/4 cup) unsalted butter, melted
1 cup flour
1 tsp. almond extract
2 eggs, slightly beaten

1. Pour cranberries and nuts into a greased 10" pie pan.
2. Sprinkle with 3/4 cup sugar.
3. In a mixing bowl, add remaining sugar to butter and blend together thoroughly.
4. Stir in flour and almond extract and mix together.
5. Add eggs and blend well.
6. Pour over cranberries and nuts.
7. Bake at 325° for 35 to 40 minutes.

Fruit and Cream Pie

Mary Jones
Marengo, OH

Makes 8 servings

Prep Time: 15 minutes
Chilling Time: 4 hours

half an 8-oz. pkg. cream cheese, at room temperature
1/2 cup confectioners sugar
1/2 cup frozen whipped topping, thawed
9" graham cracker crust
3-oz. pkg. gelatin (flavor to match fruit)
3.4-oz. box instant vanilla pudding
1 1/4 cups water
2 cups sliced fruit of your choice—strawberries, peaches, etc.
whipped topping

1. Mix together cream cheese and sugar until smooth.
2. Fold in whipped topping. Spread in crust. Refrigerate.
3. In saucepan, combine gelatin, pudding mix, and water until smooth. Stir constantly over medium heat until mixture comes to a boil. Remove from heat.
4. Stir in fruit. Spoon over cream-cheese layer.
5. Refrigerate 4 hours. Garnish with whipped topping just before serving.

Easy Peach Cream Pie

Doyle Rounds
Bridgewater, VA

Makes 8 servings

Prep Time: 15 minutes if using a bought pie crust; 30 minutes if making your own
Baking Time: 40-50 minutes

3 cups peeled and sliced fresh peaches
9" unbaked pie shell
2 eggs
1 cup sugar
1/4 cup flour
dash of salt
1 cup heavy cream
1 tsp. vanilla extract
cinnamon, *optional*

1. Fill pie shell with peaches.
2. In mixing bowl, beat eggs slightly. Blend in sugar, flour, and salt.
3. Stir cream and vanilla into sugar/flour mixture. Blend well and pour over peaches.
4. Sprinkle with cinnamon if you wish.
5. Bake at 375° for 40-50 minutes, or until center shakes slightly when moved. Don't over-bake.
6. Serve warm. For a firmer pie, chill before serving. Refrigerate leftovers.

Tips:
1. If the pie crust can't accommodate all the filling, put the extra in a small greased baking dish. Bake it along with the pie until the filling is set.
2. To prevent the crust edges from becoming too brown, cover the edges with foil after baking 30 minutes.

Southern Peach Cobbler Pie

Lori Showalter
New Hope, VA

Makes 6-8 servings

Prep Time: 15 minutes
Baking Time: 1 hour

6-8 fresh peaches, peeled and sliced
1 scant cup sugar
1 stick (1/2 cup) butter, softened
1 egg, beaten
1 tsp. vanilla
1 cup flour

1. Fill a 9" pie pan with sliced peaches.
2. In a mixing bowl, cream together sugar and butter.
3. Add egg and vanilla. Beat well.
4. Gradually add flour to creamed mixture.
5. Spread over peaches.
6. Sprinkle with additional sugar and cinnamon, if desired.
7. Bake at 350° for 1 hour, or until golden brown and bubbly.
8. Serve warm with ice cream.

Fresh Peach Pie

Lavon Martins
Postville, IA
Darlene E. Miller
South Hutchinson, KS

Makes 6-8 servings

Prep Time: 15 minutes
Cooking Time: 10 minutes
Chilling Time: 30 minutes

¾ **cup sugar**
½ **tsp. salt**
1 **cup water**
3 **Tbsp. cornstarch**
2 **Tbsp. white corn syrup**
3-oz. pkg. peach gelatin
4-6 peaches
9″ **baked pie crust**

1. In a saucepan, combine sugar, salt, water, cornstarch, and syrup. Cook until clear, stirring constantly.
2. Add gelatin and stir until dissolved. Cool in fridge for 30 minutes.
3. Slice peaches. Place in pie crust.
4. Pour filling over peaches. Chill until ready to serve.
5. Serve with whipped cream or ice cream.

If you want to make your own crust, try this:
1½ **cups flour**
½ **tsp. salt**
1½ **Tbsp. sugar**
2 **Tbsp. milk**
½ **cup oil**

Mix all ingredients together in a mixing bowl. When blended, simply press into a 9″ pie plate. Jag with a fork to keep it from buckling while baking. Bake at 350° until golden brown. Cool thoroughly before filling with fruit.
— **Darlene E. Miller**
South Hutchinson, KS

Variation: Replace the peach gelatin with strawberry gelatin. And use 1 qt. strawberries, fresh or frozen, instead of the peaches.
— **June S. Groff**
Denver, PA

Mile-High Strawberry Pie

Violette Harris Denney
Carrolton, GA

Makes 12 servings

Prep Time: 20-25 minutes
Freezing Time: 4 hours, or overnight

10-oz. pkg. frozen strawberries, chopped, but not thawed
2 **egg whites**
1 **cup sugar**
2 **Tbsp. lemon juice**
8-oz. carton frozen whipped topping, thawed
10″ **crumb pie crust— graham cracker or Oreo crumb**

1. Combine strawberries, egg whites, sugar, and lemon juice in an electric mixer. Beat at high speed until very stiff, 10-15 minutes.
2. Fold in whipped topping.
3. Pile into crust. Freeze at least 3-4 hours.
4. Remove from freezer 30 minutes before serving.

Frozen Strawberry Pie

Betty Salch, Bloomington, IL

Makes 6 servings

Prep Time: 20 minutes
Freezing Time: 3-4 hours

8-oz. pkg. cream cheese, at room temperature
1 **cup sugar**
1 **tsp. vanilla**
4 **cups chopped fresh strawberries**
12-oz. carton frozen whipped topping, thawed
½ **cup chopped pecans, toasted**
2 **9″ chocolate crumb crusts**

1. In a large bowl, beat the cream cheese, sugar, and vanilla until smooth.
2. Beat in the strawberries. Fold in whipped topping and pecans.
3. Pour mixture into crusts. Cover and freeze for 3-4 hours, or until firm.
4. Remove from the freezer 15-20 minutes before serving.

Gingerberry Lattice Pie

Jan Sams
Lancaster, PA

Makes 8 servings

Prep Time: 30 minutes
Baking Time: 50 minutes

15¼-oz. can crushed
   pineapple, juice reserved
3 cups fresh *or* frozen
   cranberries
1⅓ cups sugar
¼ cup cornstarch
1-2 Tbsp. chopped
   crystallized ginger,
   or ½ tsp. ground ginger
dough for a 9" double-
   crust pie

1. Drain pineapple, reserving juice.
2. Add water to pineapple juice to make 1 cup.
3. In a medium saucepan, combine cranberries and pineapple juice. Bring to a boil. Reduce heat. Simmer, uncovered, for 5 minutes, or until cranberries pop.
4. In a small bowl, combine sugar and cornstarch. Stir into cranberries. Cook until bubbly, stirring constantly. Remove from heat.
5. Stir in drained pineapple and ginger.
6. Fit half the pie dough into a 9" pie plate.
7. Pour filling into pie crust. If there's more filling than will fit in the crust, grease a small baking dish and place the extra filling in

it. Bake it alongside the pie.
8. Cut strips from the other half of the pie dough to make a lattice. Arrange the strips over the filling. Cover the lattice-topped pie with foil.
9. Bake at 375° for 25 minutes. Remove foil. Bake an additional 20-25 minutes until golden brown.

Hawaiian Delight Pie

Freda Imler, Eldon, MO
Josephine Earle, Citronelle, AL

Makes 6 servings

Prep Time: 10 minutes
Baking Time: 50 minutes

3 large, *or* 4 medium-sized,
   eggs, beaten slightly
1 cup sugar
1 cup grated *or* flaked
   coconut
1 cup drained crushed
   pineapple
½ stick (4 Tbsp.) butter,
   melted
pinch of salt
unbaked 8" pie shell

1. Mix first 6 ingredients in a mixing bowl.
2. Pour into unbaked pie shell.
3. Bake at 350° for 10 minutes, and then at 325° for 40 minutes, or until lightly browned and knife inserted in middle comes out clean.

Tip: If you use a foil pie pan, fill it, and then place it on a cookie sheet to bake. That will help the bottom crust to bake more fully.
— **Jeanne Heyerly**
Chenoa, IL

Lemon Sponge Pie

Jean H. Robinson
Cinnaminson, NJ

Makes 6 servings

Prep Time: 20 minutes
Baking Time: 25 minutes

1 cup sugar
3 Tbsp. flour
2 Tbsp. butter, melted
2 eggs, separated
¼ tsp. salt
1 cup milk
grated rind and juice of a
   large lemon
9" unbaked pie shell

1. In a mixing bowl, combine sugar, flour, and butter.
2. Beat egg yolks in a small bowl. Add to filling mixture. Blend well.
3. Add salt, milk, lemon rind, and juice. Mix well.
4. In a separate bowl, beat egg whites until stiff. Fold into pie filling.
5. Pour into pie shell.
6. Bake at 425° for 10 minutes. Reduce heat to 350°. Bake an additional 15 minutes, until top is golden brown. Cool.

Lemon Sour Cream Pie

Lilli Peters
Dodge City, KS

Makes 6-8 servings

Prep Time: *15 minutes*
Cooking Time: *20-30 minutes*
Cooling Time: *1 hour*

1 cup sugar
3½ Tbsp. cornstarch
1 Tbsp. finely grated
   lemon rind (reserve
   juice and several slices)
½ cup fresh lemon juice
3 egg yolks, slightly beaten
1 cup milk
half a stick (¼ cup) butter,
   softened
1 cup sour cream
9-inch deep baked pie shell
1 cup heavy cream,
   whipped
lemon twists for garnish

1. In a heavy saucepan, combine sugar, cornstarch, lemon rind, lemon juice, egg yolks, and milk. Cook over medium heat until thickened. Stir frequently.

2. Stir in butter until melted. Cool to room temperature.

3. Stir sour cream into pie filling. Pour into pie shell.

4. Cover with whipped cream. Garnish with lemon twists.

5. Refrigerate until ready to serve.

Microwave Lemon Pie

Jean Butzer
Batavia, NY

Makes 6 servings

Prep Time: *20 minutes*
Cooking Time: *10-12 minutes*
Cooling Time: *2 hours*

baked 9″ pie shell
1 cup sugar
4 Tbsp. cornstarch
¼ tsp. salt
1¾ cups water, *divided*
3 egg yolks, slightly beaten
2 Tbsp. butter, at room
   temperature
⅓ cup lemon juice
whipped cream *or*
   whipped topping

1. Combine sugar, cornstarch, salt, and ¼ cup water in a 1½-qt. microwavable casserole.

2. Microwave remaining water on high for 2-3 minutes until boiling. Stir into sugar mixture. Microwave on high 4-6 minutes until very thick. Stir every 2 minutes.

3. In a separate bowl, add a little hot mixture into egg yolks. Then blend yolks well into sugar mixture. Microwave on high 1 minute.

4. Stir in butter. Then add lemon juice. Cool slightly and turn into pie shell.

5. Serve cooled, topped with whipped cream or whipped topping.

Tips:

1. To make a large deep-dish pie, you can double this recipe.

2. This is also good served in custard cups as a pudding with no crust.

3. The microwave is a wonderful way to make the lemon filling—no need to worry about it sticking to the bottom of the pan as it thickens.

Key Lime Pie

Norma I. Gehman, Ephrata, PA

Makes 1 10″ pie

Prep Time: *20 minutes*
Baking Time: *25-28 minutes*
Chilling Time: *8 hours,
   or overnight*

1½ cups graham cracker
   crumbs
½ cup firmly packed light
   brown sugar
1 stick (½ cup) butter,
   melted
2 14-oz. cans sweetened
   condensed milk
1 cup key lime juice
2 egg whites
¼ tsp. cream of tartar
2 Tbsp. sugar

1. Combine first 3 ingredients. Press into a 10″ pie pan.

2. Bake at 350° for 10 minutes, or until lightly browned. Cool.

3. In a mixing bowl, stir milk and lime juice together until blended. Pour into crust.

4. In a clean mixing bowl, beat egg whites with cream

of tartar at high speed until foamy.

5. Gradually beat sugar into the egg whites until the sugar dissolves and soft peaks are formed, about 2-4 minutes.

6. Spread egg-white meringue over filling. Bake at 325° for 25-28 minutes.

7. Chill 8 hours, or overnight.

Pumpkin Pie

Wafi Brandt, Manheim, PA

Makes 6-8 servings

Prep Time: 15-20 minutes
Baking Time: 40-50 minutes

9″ unbaked pie shell
3 eggs
scant 1/2 cup brown sugar
1/3 cup sugar
1/4 tsp. salt
1 1/4 tsp. cinnamon
1/4 tsp. ginger
1/4 tsp. nutmeg
dash of allspice
2/3 tsp. vanilla
1 1/3 cups pumpkin
1 1/3 cups milk
2 tsp. cornstarch

1. Beat eggs in a large mixing bowl. Add all remaining ingredients as listed. Whisk until very smooth.

2. Pour into unbaked pie shell.

3. Bake at 350° for 40-50 minutes, until set and browned.

Sour Cream Raisin Pie

Kay Magruder
Seminole, OK

Makes 6 servings

Prep Time: 20 minutes
Cooking/ Baking Time:
30 minutes
Cooling Time: 45-60 minutes

1 cup sour cream
1/2 cup raisins
1 cup, plus 2 Tbsp., sugar, *divided*
1/4 tsp. ground cloves
1/2 tsp. cinnamon
dash of salt
4 eggs, separated and *divided*
1 9″ baked pie crust, cooled

1. In a medium-sized saucepan, blend together sour cream, raisins, 1 cup sugar, spices, salt, 1 egg white, and 4 egg yolks. (Reserve the 3 other whites for the meringue.) Cook over low heat until raisins plump and are tender.

2. Let pie filling and crust cool completely before pouring the filling into the crust.

3. Prepare the meringue topping by beating the 3 reserved egg whites until stiff.

4. Fold in 2 Tbsp. sugar, beating gently until the sugar is incorporated. Then increase beating to top speed until meringue turns glossy and stiff peaks form.

5. Pile meringue on cooled pie filling in crust. Bake at 350° for about 12 minutes, until golden brown.

Oatmeal Pie

Edna Beckler
Mt. Pleasant, IA

Makes 8 servings

Prep Time: 30 minutes
Baking Time: 50 minutes

half a stick (1/4 cup) butter
1 cup brown sugar
2 eggs, beaten
dash of salt
1 tsp. vanilla
3/4 cup milk
3/4 cup light corn syrup
1/2 cup unsweetened, grated *or* flaked, coconut
3/4 cup dry quick, *or* rolled, oatmeal
1/4 cup chopped nuts
9″ unbaked pie crust

1. Melt butter. Mix with sugar in a large mixing bowl.

2. Add beaten eggs, salt, and vanilla.

3. Add remaining ingredients in order given.

4. Pour into unbaked 9″ pie crust and bake at 350° for 50 minutes.

French Rhubarb Custard Pie

Carol Findling
Princeton, IL

Makes 8 servings

Prep Time: 25 minutes
Baking Time: 40-50 minutes
Cooling Time: 1-2 hours

2 egg whites
2 whole eggs
3 Tbsp. milk
1½ cups sugar
¼ cup flour
¾ tsp. nutmeg
4-6 cups rhubarb, cut into
    ½" pieces
pie dough for 1 single
    deep-dish crust

Topping:
⅓ cup butter, at room
    temperature
½ cup brown sugar,
    packed
1 cup flour

1. In a large bowl combine egg whites, whole eggs, milk, sugar, flour, and nutmeg. Beat thoroughly.
2. Add cut-up rhubarb.
3. Put pie dough into deep pie pan and flute crust above rim of pie pan. Pour rhubarb mixture into unbaked crust.
4. Blend butter, brown sugar, and flour in food processor until crumbly. Sprinkle over pie filling.
5. Bake at 425° for 10 minutes. Reduce heat to 350° and bake for an additional

30-40 minutes, until nicely browned.
6. Cool and serve.

Tip: This pie may seem runny while it's warm, but it will thicken as it cools.

German Sweet Chocolate Pie

Hazel Lightcap Propst
Oxford, PA

Makes 8 servings

Prep Time: 10 minutes
Baking Time: 35 minutes

13-oz. can evaporated milk
4-oz. package German
    sweet chocolate, melted
¼ cup butter, softened
3 eggs
½ cup sugar
1⅓ cups unsweetened,
    grated *or* flaked,
    coconut
½ cup chopped nuts

1. In an electric mixer bowl, blend evaporated milk, melted chocolate, butter, eggs, and sugar for 15 seconds on medium speed.
2. Pour into a greased 9" pie pan. Sprinkle with coconut and nuts.
3. Bake at 350° for 35 minutes.

Chocolate Chess Pie

J. Stefl
East Bethany, NY

Makes 8 servings

Prep Time: 15 minutes
Baking Time: 35-45 minutes
Cooling/Chilling Time:
    4-5 hours

Filling:
1 cup sugar
1 Tbsp. flour
⅓ cup dry baking cocoa
    powder
2 egg yolks
1 egg
3 Tbsp. water
1 tsp. distilled vinegar
2 sticks (1 cup) butter,
    melted

9" pie crust

Ganache:
2 cups chocolate chips
1 cup whipping cream

Topping:
1 cup whipping cream
2 Tbsp. confectioners sugar

1. Mix together filling ingredients until thickened and smooth.
2. Pour into pie shell and bake at 350° until set, about 35-45 minutes. Cool.
3. Combine ganache ingredients in a double boiler until smooth and thickened. Cool.
4. While ganache cools, whip the cream for the topping. When soft peaks have

formed, fold in sugar. Continue whipping until stiff.

5. Pour cooled topping over baked filling. Top with ganache. Refrigerate for several hours before slicing and serving.

Tips:

1. You can cut this pie and freeze individual pieces.

2. Serve this rich pie with fresh raspberries.

Fudge Pie

Vicki Hill, Memphis, TN

Makes 8-10 servings

Prep Time: 10-20 minutes
Baking Time: 25 minutes
Cooling Time: 1 hour

2 squares unsweetened chocolate
1 stick (1/2 cup) butter
1 cup sugar
2 eggs
1/4 cup flour
1 tsp. vanilla
1/8 tsp. salt
1/2 cup pecans, chopped

1. Melt chocolate and butter over water in top of double boiler.

2. Add remaining ingredients in order listed. Mix well.

3. Pour into a greased 9" pie pan.

4. Bake at 350° for 25 minutes.

5. Allow to cool before cutting into wedges to serve.

White Chocolate Pie

Jeanne Allen
Rye, CO

Makes 6 servings

Prep Time: 15-30 minutes
Chilling Time: 6 hours

8 ozs. white chocolate
20 large marshmallows
1/2 cup milk
1/2 pt. whipping cream
1/2 tsp. vanilla
1/2 cup toasted almonds, cut in half *or* coarsely chopped
9" baked pie crust

1. Over hot water in double boiler, melt chocolate and marshmallows over medium heat.

2. Stir in milk. Cool completely.

3. Whip cream in a chilled bowl until stiff.

4. Fold in vanilla.

5. Fold cooled chocolate mixture into flavored whipped cream.

6. Fold in almonds. Pour into pie shell.

7. Chill several hours before serving.

White Christmas Pie

Carolyn Bell
Quinter, KS

Makes 8 servings

Prep Time: 30 minutes
Chilling Time: 1-2 hours

14-oz. can sweetened condensed milk
1/3 cup lemon juice
1/3 cup grated coconut
1/2 cup chopped pecans
16-oz. can crushed pineapples, drained
1/2 tsp. pineapple flavoring
12-oz. carton whipped topping
2 8" baked pie shells

1. In a large mixing bowl, combine milk, lemon juice, coconut, pecans, pineapple, and pineapple flavoring.

2. Fold in whipped topping. Pour into pie shells. Chill at least 1 hour before serving.

A Tip —

To keep the crust from becoming overdone when baking pies, loosely wrap the edge of the pie plate with aluminum foil after approximately 30 minutes of baking, at about the time the crust is turning golden brown.

Peanut Butter Pie

Nadine Martinitz
Salina, KS
Trudy Kutter
Corfu, NY

Makes 8 servings

Prep Time: 15 minutes
Freezing Time: 6 hours,
  or overnight

8-oz. pkg. cream cheese,
  softened
1/2-1 cup peanut butter
1/2 cup milk
1 cup confectioners sugar
8-oz. container frozen
  whipped topping,
  thawed, *divided*
prepared graham cracker
  pie crust
1/4 cup chopped peanuts

1. Combine cream cheese,
peanut butter, and milk,
using an electric hand mixer.
2. Add confectioners sugar
and mix well. Fold in 3/4 of
the whipped topping (reserve
the rest).
3. Pour into graham
cracker crust and freeze until
firm.
4. Just before serving, edge
the top of the pie with the
remaining whipped topping.
Sprinkle the peanuts in the
center of the pie.

Variation:
  1. Instead of milk, use 12-oz. jar marshmallow cream.
    — **Sharon Leali**
    Jackson, OH

*2. Instead of a graham cracker
pie crust, use a chocolate gra-
ham cracker crust.*
  — **Sharon Leali**
  Jackson, OH
  — **Bernadette Veenstra**
  Rockford, MI

*3. Spread 1/4 cup hot fudge sun-
dae topping over the bottom of
the pie crust before adding the
rest of the pie filling.*
  — **Stacy Petersheim**
  Mechanicsburg, PA

Pecan Dream Pie

Jeanne Allen
Rye, CO

Makes 8 servings

Prep Time: 20-25 minutes
Baking Time: 45-50 minutes
Cooling Time: 2 hours

9" unbaked pie crust
1 stick (1/2 cup) butter,
  softened
1 cup sugar
2 eggs, separated
2 Tbsp. vinegar
dash of salt
1 tsp. vanilla
1/8 tsp. nutmeg
1/2 cup pecans
1 cup golden raisins

1. Jag pie crust with sharp
fork all over its surface to
prevent it from buckling
while pre-baking it. Bake the
empty crust at 400° for 10
minutes. Remove from oven
and set aside.

2. In a mixing bowl, cream
together butter and sugar
until smooth.
3. Add egg yolks, vinegar,
salt, vanilla, nutmeg, pecans,
and raisins.
4. In a separate bowl, beat
egg whites until stiff.
5. Fold stiff whites into filling mixture. Pour into crust.
6. Bake at 350° for 35-40
minutes, or until golden.
7. Cool to room tempera-
ture before serving.

Southern Pecan Pie

Mary Ann Bowman, East Earl, PA

Makes 6 servings

Prep Time: 10 minutes
Baking Time: 50-60 minutes

unbaked 8" pie crust
1 cup chopped pecans
3 eggs
1/3 cup brown sugar
1 cup light corn syrup
2 Tbsp. butter, softened
1/8 tsp. salt
1 tsp. vanilla

1. Place pecans in pie
crust.
2. Beat eggs in a mixing
bowl.
3. Add remaining ingredi-
ents and mix well.
4. Gently spoon filling
over pecans.
5. Bake at 350° for 50-60
minutes, or until browned
and set in the middle.

Variation: Instead of brown sugar and corn syrup, use 3/4 cup honey.

— **Charlotte Hill**
Rapid City, SD

Lemon Pecan Pie

Betsy Chutchian
Grand Prairie, TX

Makes 6-8 servings

Prep Time: 10 minutes
Baking Time: 30-40 minutes
Cooling Time: 1-2 hours

3 eggs
2²/₃ Tbsp. butter, softened
1-1¼ cups sugar, according to your preference
¾ cup chopped pecans
1 tsp. lemon extract
juice of half a lemon
8″ unbaked pie shell

1. Mix first 6 ingredients in order listed in a large mixing bowl. Stir with a spoon, not a mixer, just enough to incorporate all ingredients.
2. Pour into pie shell.
3. Bake at 350° for 30-40 minutes, or until crust is brown and pie filling is set.
4. Allow to cool before slicing to serve.

Cream Cheese Pecan Pie

Martha Bender
New Paris, IN

Makes 8-10 servings

Prep Time: 30 minutes
Baking Time: 35-45 minutes

8-oz. pkg. cream cheese, softened
½ cup sugar
1 egg, beaten
½ tsp. salt
1 tsp. vanilla
10″ unbaked pie shell
1¼ cups chopped pecans

Topping:
3 eggs
1 cup light corn syrup
½ tsp. vanilla

1. In a large mixing bowl, cream together cream cheese, sugar, egg, salt, and vanilla.
2. Spread over bottom of pie shell.
3. Sprinkle pecans over cream-cheese layer.
4. Make topping by combining 3 eggs, corn syrup, and vanilla. Beat until smooth. Pour over pecans.
5. Bake at 375° for 35-45 minutes, or until golden brown.

Crispy R-Ice Cream Pie

Lavina Hochstedler
Grand Blanc, MI

Makes 8 servings

Prep Time: 10-15 minutes
Chilling Time: 1 hour
Freezing Time: 3 hours

⅓ cup corn syrup
⅓ cup peanut butter
2 cups crispy rice cereal
1 qt. vanilla ice cream, slightly softened
sliced, sweetened fresh peaches, *or* peaches and blueberries

1. Measure corn syrup and peanut butter into a large bowl. Stir until thoroughly combined.
2. Add crispy rice cereal and mix well.
3. Firmly press mixture evenly into the bottom and up the sides of a greased 9″ glass pie plate. Chill 1 hour.
4. Fill with vanilla ice cream. Freeze until firm.
5. Place pie in fridge ½ hour before serving. Cut into slices. Top each piece with fresh fruit.

Peanut Butter Banana Pie

Joy Sutter, Perkasie, PA

Makes 8 servings

Prep Time: 45 minutes
Baking/Cooking Time:
    27 minutes
Cooling/Chilling Time:
    5-6 hours

Crust:
1 cup graham crackers, crushed
2 Tbsp. butter, melted
1 Tbsp. sugar

Filling:
2/3 cup sugar
3 1/2 Tbsp. cornstarch
1/4 tsp. salt
1 1/3 cups milk
2 large eggs, slightly beaten
2 Tbsp. creamy peanut butter
1 tsp. vanilla extract
2 1/2 cups sliced bananas
1 1/2 cups frozen whipped topping, thawed

1. In a mixing bowl, combine crust ingredients. Press into a 9" pie plate.
2. Bake at 350° for 10-12 minutes. Cool.
3. Make the filling by combining sugar, cornstarch, and salt in a saucepan.
4. Gradually add milk, stirring until well blended.
5. Bring to a boil and cook for 1 minute, whisking constantly.
6. Place the eggs in the mixing bowl. Gradually add about one-third of the hot creamy filling to the eggs, stirring constantly to blend and to keep the eggs from scrambling.
7. When the eggs have been incorporated well, return the creamy egg mixture to the pan. Stir constantly over low heat, until thickened.
8. Remove from heat and stir in peanut butter and vanilla. Cool slightly.
9. Arrange banana slices on top of graham cracker crust.
10. Spoon in filling.
11. Press plastic wrap onto filling to prevent skin from forming. Chill 4 hours.
12. Remove plastic wrap and top with whipped topping. Chill until ready to serve.

Shoo-Fly Pie

Sharon Anders, Alburtis, PA
Arlene M. Kopp, Lineboro, MD

Makes 8 servings

Prep Time: 15-20 minutes
Baking Time: 40 minutes

Crumbs:
1 cup flour
2/3 cup brown sugar
1 Tbsp. butter, softened

Filling:
1 cup molasses
1 egg
1 tsp. baking soda
1 cup boiling water
unbaked 9" pie shell

1. In a mixing bowl, stir together flour, brown sugar, and butter. Reserve 1/2 cup of crumbs, and set aside.
2. Add molasses and egg to crumb mixture remaining in the mixing bowl. Mix well.
3. Dissolve soda in boiling water. Then add to the mixing bowl, mixing until blended.
4. Pour filling into pie shell and top with remaining crumbs.
5. Bake for 10 minutes at 375°; then for 30 minutes at 350°.

No-Roll Pie Crust

Annabelle Unternahrer
Shipshewana, IN

Makes 1 10" pie crust

Prep Time: 5-10 minutes
Baking Time: 12 minutes

1 1/2 cups flour
1/2 cup oil
1/4 tsp. salt
2 Tbsp. sugar
2 Tbsp. milk

1. Blend ingredients in a large 10" pie pan.
2. Press into shape with the back of a spoon.
3. Bake at 400° for 12 minutes.
4. During baking time prepare whatever filling you wish to use.

Snacks, Candies and Beverages

Sugared Almonds and Pecans

Linda Hartzler
Minonk, IL

Makes 28 1/4-cup servings

Prep Time: 15 minutes
Baking Time: 1 hour

1 egg white
1 Tbsp. water
1-2 tsp. cinnamon, according to your taste preference
1 tsp. vanilla
1 cup sugar
1 lb. almonds and/or pecans

1. In a large bowl, beat together egg white and water until fluffy.
2. Stir in cinnamon, vanilla, sugar, and nuts.
3. Spread in a single layer on a baking sheet with sides.
4. Bake at 200° for 1 hour, stirring every 15 minutes.
5. Cool completely before storing.

Pretzel Treat

Sheila Heil
Lancaster, PA

Makes lots!

Prep Time: 10 minutes per 8-oz. bag
Baking Time: 4-6 minutes per cookie sheet

1 bag Hershey Kisses *or* Hershey Hugs
1 bag waffle-shaped pretzels
1 bag M&Ms

1. Unwrap Hershey Kisses.
2. Preheat oven to 170°.
3. Place pretzels in a single layer on a baking sheet.
4. Top each pretzel with 1 Hershey Kiss.
5. Bake for 4-6 minutes, until chocolate feels soft when touched.
6. Remove from oven. Quickly press an M&M candy into the center of each Hershey Kiss.
7. Allow to cool before storing.
8. Refrigerate if necessary.

Tips:

1. Use green and red M&Ms for Christmas.
2. Use multi-colored M&Ms for birthdays.
3. This is a good activity for children or senior adults who need supervision!
4. To share as gifts, place handfuls of these pretzel treats into clear or colored plastic wrap and tie with colorful ribbon.

Cheesy Pretzels

Kim Jensen
Thornton, CO

Makes 16 pretzels

Prep Time: 10-15 minutes
Baking Time: 20 minutes

1½ cups flour
⅔ cup milk
½ cup cheddar cheese,
   shredded
2 Tbsp. butter
2 tsp. baking powder
1 tsp. sugar
1 tsp. salt
1 egg, beaten
kosher salt

1. In a large bowl, mix the first 7 ingredients with a fork until blended.
2. Divide dough into 16 equal pieces. With your hands, roll each portion into a rope about 12-14" long. Lay them on greased cookie sheets, forming each into a pretzel shape as you do so.
3. Brush each pretzel lightly with beaten egg and sprinkle with salt.
4. Bake at 400° for 20 minutes, or until golden brown.

Tip: You can substitute onion or garlic salt for the kosher salt.

Fiddle Sticks

Cova Rexroad
Kingsville, MD

Makes 20 servings

Prep Time: 15 minutes
Baking Time: 10 minutes

2 cups pretzel sticks,
   broken in half
1½ cups raisins
1½ cups lightly salted
   peanuts
½ cup pecans, *optional*
12-oz. pkg. white chocolate
   chips
2 Tbsp. butter

1. Mix together pretzels, raisins, and nuts in a large mixing bowl or 9 x 13 baking pan.
2. Place in a warm 200° oven for about 10 minutes.
3. Melt the chocolate chips and butter in a double boiler over hot water, or in the microwave (50% power for 1 minute; stir; 50% power for 30 seconds; stir. Continue microwaving at 50% for 30-second time periods, stirring between each one, until the mixture is melted).
4. Pour melted chocolate and butter over the warmed pretzel mixture. Stir well to coat.
5. Spread out on a baking sheet to cool.
6. Break up and serve or store.

White Chocolate Crunch

Becky Harder
Monument, CO

Makes 20 ½-cup servings

Prep Time: 10 minutes
Cooking Time: 5-10 minutes

1 whole block of white
   chocolate
6 cups Chex cereal
2 cups M&Ms
2 cups small pretzels

1. Chop the white chocolate block into pieces. Place in a microwave-safe bowl. Microwave at 50% power for 2-3 minutes. Stir. Heat again at 50% power for 15 seconds. Stir. Continue heating for 15-second periods, following each by stirring, until the pieces around the edges are melted and the center of the bowl feels hot. Let stand for a minute and then stir. If solid pieces remain, continue the heating for 15-second periods, followed by stirring.
2. When the chocolate is fully melted, stir in cereal, M&Ms, and pretzels.
3. Spread out on waxed paper and let harden.
4. Break into chunks/pieces to serve.

Crunchy Peanut Bark

Doyle Rounds, Bridgewater, VA

Makes about 60 pieces

Prep Time: *5 minutes*
Cooking Time: *5 minutes*
Standing Time: *4-6 hours*

2 lbs. white confectionery coating
1 cup creamy peanut butter
3 cups crisp rice cereal
2 cups dry roasted peanuts
2 cups miniature marshmallows

1. Place confectionery coating in a large microwave-safe bowl and microwave at 50% power for 1 minute. Stir. Microwave at 50% power for 30 seconds. Stir. Continue microwaving at 50% power for 30-second periods until the coating is melted.

2. Stir peanut butter, rice cereal, peanuts, and marshmallows into melted coating.

3. Drop by heaping tablespoonful onto waxed paper.

4. Let stand on counter for several hours until very dry. Store in refrigerator or freeze. The bark keeps well.

Notes:
1. White confectionery coating can be found in the baking section of most grocery stores. It is sometimes labeled "Almond Bark" or "Candy Coating." It is often sold in bulk packages of 1-1½ lbs. in disc or block form.

2. I always make this special snack at Christmas. It's a great give-away gift.

Party Mix for a Bunch

Barbara Yoder
Christiana, PA

Makes 80 cups!

Prep Time: *20-30 minutes*

12-oz. box Rice Chex
12-oz. box Corn Chex
17-oz. box Crispix
12-oz. bag cheese curls
1-lb. bag small pretzels
10-oz. box Ritz Bits
1 box Wheatables
1 box White Cheddar Cheez-its
1 lb. mixed nuts
12.5-oz. box goldfish crackers
16-oz. jar dry roasted peanuts
2 pkgs. Hidden Valley Ranch dry salad dressing mix
1 bottle butter-flavor popcorn popping and topping oil

1. Pour all ingredients, except oil and salad dressing mix, into a large garbage bag.

2. Add some oil and salad dressing mix. Tie bag shut and shake.

3. Continue to add oil and salad dressing mix, shaking after each addition until well blended.

Tips:
1. Place one garbage bag inside another to cut down on possible leaks.

2. You can freeze the finished Mix.

3. If you can't find the popcorn popping and topping oil, you can substitute 1 cup olive oil and 1 Tbsp. butter flavoring.

A Tip —

When measuring honey, corn syrup, or molasses, first lightly spray the measuring cup with non-fat cooking spray. The liquid will slide right out.

Caramel Popcorn

Janelle Reitz, Lancaster, PA
Starla A. Diem, Denmark, SC

Makes 12 1-cup servings

Prep Time: 10 minutes
Cooking/Baking Time:
75-80 minutes
Cooling Time: 1 hour

12 cups popped plain
    popcorn, unsalted, air-
    or oil-popped
1 cup brown sugar
1/2 cup light corn syrup
half a stick (1/4 cup) butter
1/2 tsp. salt
1/2 tsp. baking soda
1/2 tsp. vanilla

1. Place popped popcorn
in two 9 x 13 greased baking
pans. Preheat oven to 250°.
2. Combine sugar, corn
syrup, butter, and salt in a
heavy saucepan.
3. Cook 7-10 minutes, stirring constantly, bringing mixture to a boil over medium
heat. Boil 4 minutes. Do not
stir.
4. Remove from heat. Add
baking soda and vanilla. Pour
over popcorn, stirring to coat
evenly.
5. Bake for 1 hour, stirring
every 15 minutes.
6. Cool on waxed paper.
Break apart into pieces. Store
in tightly-covered container.

Variaton: For a real treat, add
1 1/2 cups broken cashews to the
popcorn in Step 1.
    — Dawn Derstine
    Souderton, PA

Sweet Snack Mix

Ruth Ann Penner
Hillsboro, KS

Makes about 20 cups

Prep Time: 10 minutes
Cooking Time: 2-5 minutes
Cooling Time: 2-3 hours

14 cups popped popcorn
3 cups crisp rice cereal
2 cups salted peanuts
1 lb. white almond bark
3 Tbsp. creamy peanut
    butter

1. In a large bowl, com-
bine popped popcorn, cereal,
and peanuts.
2. Place bark and peanut
butter in a microwave-safe
bowl. Heat on high for 1
minute. Stir. Heat on high for
15 seconds. Stir. If the mixture isn't yet melted, continue
heating on high for 15-second
periods, stirring between
each.
3. Pour melted mixture
over popcorn mixture, stirring
to coat.
4. Spread on waxed paper.
Allow to stand for at least 2
hours.
5. Break up and store in
an airtight container.

Tip: Look for the almond bark
in the baking section of the gro-
cery store.

Granola Bars

Barbara Kuhns
Millersburg, OH
Kim Stoll
Abbeville, SC
Lydia Stoltzfus
East Earl, PA
Christine Weaver
Reinholds, PA

Makes 20 servings

Prep Time: 5-10 minutes
Cooking Time: 5-10 minutes

2 cups (1 pkg.) graham
    crackers, crushed
5 cups dry quick oats
4 1/2 cups crisp rice cereal
1 1/2 sticks (3/4 cup) butter
1/2 cup peanut butter
3/4 cup honey
2 10-oz. pkgs.
    marshmallows
1 cup M&Ms, frozen
1 cup chocolate chips,
    frozen

1. In a large bowl, com-
bine crushed graham crackers, dry oats, and crisp rice
cereal.
2. In a saucepan, combine
butter, peanut butter, and
honey. Stir frequently, heating
until butter is melted.
3. Add marshmallows.
Heat until marshmallows are
melted, stirring constantly.
4. Pour over dry mixture.
Mix well.
5. Add M&Ms and choco-
late chips. Mix well.
6. Press onto a greased
baking sheet. Cut into 20
pieces.

Variations:

1. Add 1 cup each of any of the following to Step 1: grated coconut, almonds, raisins, other dried fruit.

— **Lori Showalter**
New Hope, VA

2. Add 2 tsp. vanilla to Step 2.

— **Julie Newman**
Sidney, BC

3. Add 1 cup all-bran cereal, 1/4 cup sunflower seeds, and 1/4 cup sesame seeds to Step 1.

— **Frances Schrag**
Newton, KS

— **Esther Zimmerman**
Ephrata, PA

Salted Peanut Squares

John D. Allen
Rye, CO

Makes 20-24 servings

Prep Time: 5 minutes
Cooking Time: 5 minutes
Chilling Time: 1 hour

16-oz. jar salted peanuts
3 Tbsp. butter
10-oz. pkg. peanut butter chips
2 cups miniature marshmallows
14-oz. can sweetened condensed milk

1. Cover the bottom of a greased 9 x 13 baking pan with half the salted peanuts.

2. In a saucepan, melt butter and peanut butter chips.

3. Stir in marshmallows and milk. Heat until melted.

4. Pour over peanuts.

5. Top with remaining peanuts.

6. Chill. Cut into squares.

Peanut Butter Clusters

Ruth Ann Gingrich
New Holland, PA

Makes 4-5 dozen pieces

Prep Time: 5-10 minutes
Cooking Time: 3-5 minutes
Cooling Time: 1 hour

2 cups light corn syrup
2 cups peanut butter
2 cups sugar
1 12-oz. box cornflakes, or 12 cups cornflakes

1. Mix corn syrup, peanut butter, and sugar in a large saucepan.

2. While stirring constantly over medium heat, bring to a boil.

3. Immediately remove from heat and stir in cornflakes until coated evenly.

4. Drop by spoonfuls onto waxed paper.

5. When fully cooled, store in airtight container, placing a sheet of waxed paper between each layer.

Tip: You must stir constantly in Step 2 so the mixture doesn't burn. As soon as it reaches the boiling point, remove from heat!

Cranberry Clusters

Edwina Stoltzfus
Narvon, PA

Makes 24 clusters

Prep Time: 5-10 minutes
Cooking Time: 2-4 minutes
Standing Time: 1 hour

2 cups (12-oz. pkg.) semi-sweet chocolate chips
2/3 cup craisins
2/3 cup peanuts

1. Place chocolate chips in a microwave-safe bowl. Microwave at 50% for 1 minute. Stir. Microwave at 50% for 15 seconds. Stir. Continue microwaving at 50% for 15-second periods, followed by stirring, until the chips are melted.

2. Stir in craisins and peanuts.

3. Drop by teaspoonfuls onto waxed paper. Let stand until set.

Variations: Use white chocolate chips instead of chocolate chips, cashews instead of peanuts, and raisins or dried cherries instead of craisins.

Honey Milk Balls

Sherry Goss Lapp
Lancaster, PA

Makes 28 balls

Prep Time: 10 minutes

½ cup honey
½ cup peanut butter
1 cup powdered milk
1 cup dry quick oats

1. In a large mixing bowl, mix together honey and peanut butter.
2. Stir in milk and oats, mixing well.
3. Roll mixture into small balls.

This is a great, healthy snack that children can help to make.

Easy Fudge

Barbara Tenney
Delta, PA

Makes 36 servings

Prep Time: 5 minutes
Cooking Time: 12-15 minutes

⅔ cup evaporated milk
1⅔ cups sugar
½ tsp. salt
1½ cups mini marshmallows, *or* diced large marshmallows
1½ cups semi-sweet chocolate chips

1 tsp. vanilla
½ cup chopped nuts

1. Place first 3 ingredients in saucepan. Mix and heat over medium heat. Bring to a boil, stirring continuously.
2. Boil 5 minutes and remove from heat.
3. Add remaining ingredients and stir until marshmallows and chocolate chips melt.
4. Pour into a buttered 9 x 9 pan. Cut into squares while still warm and chill.

Variations: Replace chocolate chips with peanut butter chips.

Chocolate Peanut Butter Fudge

Meredith Miller
Dover, DE
June S. Groff
Denver, PA

Makes 36 servings

Prep Time: 10-15 minutes
Chilling Time: 4-6 hours, or overnight

2 sticks (1 cup) butter, softened
½ cup peanut butter
½ cup unsweetened cocoa powder
1 tsp. vanilla
4 cups confectioners sugar

1. Mix together butter, peanut butter, cocoa powder, and vanilla. Stir in sugar.

2. Line an 8 x 8 pan with waxed paper. Pat mixture into pan.
3. Refrigerate 4-6 hours or overnight.
4. Cut into small squares.

Tip: It's easier to mix these ingredients together using your clean hands rather than a spoon.

Since this is such a simple recipe, my siblings and I enjoyed making this candy by ourselves at a very young age. The hardest part was to wait until it got firm. We often ate our share (and more) before then. We also served it at quite a few parties.

— **Meredith Miller**
Dover, DE

Raspberry Truffles

Dawn Ranck
Lansdale, PA

Makes 18 balls

Prep Time: 10 minutes
Cooking Time: 10 minutes
Freezing Time: 2½-3 hours
Standing Time: 1 hour

1 Tbsp. butter
2 Tbsp. whipping cream
1⅓ cups semi-sweet chocolate chips
7½ tsp. seedless raspberry jam
6 ozs. white *or* dark coating chocolate
2 Tbsp. solid shortening

1. In a heavy saucepan, combine butter, cream, and chocolate chips. Cook over low heat 4-5 minutes, or until chocolate is melted. Remove from heat.

2. Stir in jam. Transfer to freezer container. Cover and freeze 20 minutes.

3. Drop by teaspoonfuls onto foil-lined baking sheets. Freeze 15 minutes.

4. Roll into balls. Freeze until firm.

5. Melt chocolate and shortening together, stirring frequently. Dip balls. Place on wire rack over waxed paper. Let stand until firm. Store in refrigerator.

Fruity Yogurt Ice Pops

Paula King, Flanagan, IL

Makes 10 servings

Prep Time: 5 minutes
Freezing Time: 8 hours,
or overnight

2 16-oz. cups strawberry
  yogurt
8-oz. can unsweetened
  crushed pineapple,
  undrained
1 Tbsp. honey

1. Combine yogurt, pineapple, and honey in a blender or food processor, blending until smooth.

2. Pour into 10 plastic molds or 3-oz. paper cups.

Top with holders or insert wooden sticks.

3. Freeze until firm, about 8 hours or overnight.

Tip: You can use other flavors of yogurt and other fruits. Just make sure you use the correct amounts of each.

Mochaccino

Jenelle Miller
Marion, SD

Makes 10 servings

Prep Time: 15 minutes

12 Tbsp. freshly ground
  coffee
10 cups water
3/4 cup nondairy powdered
  creamer
1/2 cup chocolate syrup
1/2 cup caramel syrup
1/3 cup sugar
crushed ice
whipped cream and
  additional syrup, *optional*

1. Brew coffee (with 10 cups water) in coffeemaker. Pour into a 2-qt. pitcher.

2. Add creamer, syrups, and sugar. Whisk together. Cool in refrigerator.

3. To use, place 1 cup coffee mix in blender with 1 cup crushed ice. Blend for 1 minute.

4. Pour into a tall glass. Top with whipped cream and drizzle with syrup, if you wish.

Tip: Coarsely crushed ice blends better than finely crushed ice.

3-2-1 Lemonade

Tabitha Schmidt
Baltic, OH

Makes 1 gallon

Prep Time: 15 minutes

3 lemons
2 cups sugar
water and ice to make a
  gallon

1. Thinly slice lemons, discarding tips.

2. Place in a one-gallon pitcher and add sugar. Stir thoroughly until lemon slices are well-covered with sugar. Let stand for 10 minutes.

3. Add ice and water to make one gallon.

4. Serve immediately or within hours, putting a lemon slice in each glass if desired.

Tips:
1. If you have left-over lemonade, remove the lemons if you won't be using it within 24 hours. The rinds can turn bitter if left in too long.

2. To get the maxium flavor from the lemons, mash the sugar and lemon slices together (Step 2) until well blended.

Mint Lemonade Concentrate

Stacy Schmucker Stoltzfus
Enola, PA
Virginia M. Eberly
Loysville, PA

*Makes about 2 quarts
of concentrate*

Prep Time: 10 minutes
Cooking Time: 10 minutes
Cooling Time: 1-2 hours

2 cups fresh tea leaves
(stems are okay to use,
too)
1 qt. water
1½ cups sugar
12-oz. can frozen lemonade
concentrate
6-oz. can frozen orange
juice concentrate

1. Wash tea leaves and put
in a large bowl.
2. Combine water and
sugar in a saucepan. Boil for
10 minutes.
3. Pour over tea leaves.
Cover and let cool. Squeeze
water out of leaves, remove
them, and compost.
4. Add juice concentrates
to tea. Stir until thawed.
5. To serve, mix 1 part
concentrate to 3 parts water.

*Tip: At the end of the growing
season, I make quantities of the
concentrate and freeze it to use
in the winter.*

Mint Tea

Carol Eberly
Harrisonburg, VA

Makes 1 gallon

Prep Time: 15-20 minutes
Steeping Time: 10 minutes

4 cups water
3 Lipton family-size tea
bags (only Lipton!)
8-10 stalks fresh mint tea,
or 2 Boston's mint tea
bags, or 8-10 stalks
dried mint
1¼ cups sugar

1. Heat 4 cups water to
boil in the microwave or on
the stove.
2. Remove from heat and
add family-size tea bags and
mint tea or tea bags.
3. Let steep at least 10
minutes.
4. Remove tea bags and
mint.
5. Add sugar. Stir until dissolved.
6. Add enough water to
make a gallon.
7. Serve over ice in glasses.

*Tip: In the summer when the
tea grows, I cut it off and dry it
for use in the winter.*

Indian Tea

Terry Stutzman Mast
Lodi, CA

Makes 4 servings

Prep Time: 5 minutes
Steeping Time: 5-10 minutes

4 cups water
3 black (regular or decaf)
tea bags
3 whole cloves
1" piece of gingerroot,
chopped
3 pods cardamom, opened
for seeds
1 stick cinnamon, chopped
6-oz. can evaporated skim
milk
¼ cup sugar

1. Bring water to a boil in
a covered saucepan. Turn off
heat.
2. Place tea bags in to
steep for 5 minutes. Keep
covered.
3. In a tea ball or muslin
bag (tied shut) place cloves,
gingerroot, cardamom seeds,
and chopped cinnamon. Place
into steeping tea.
4. After 5 minutes, remove
tea bags. (If you prefer a
stronger tea, allow the tea
bags to steep a few more
minutes until tea is darker.)
5. Stir in evaporated milk.
6. Add sugar, stirring until
dissolved.
7. Remove tea ball or spice
bag and serve.

Red Velvet Punch
J.B. Miller
Indianapolis, IN

Makes 24 8-oz. servings

Prep Time: 15 minutes

8 cups cranberry juice
  cocktail
1 cup each, thawed frozen
  concentrate of orange
  juice, lemon juice, and
  pineapple juice
2 cups grape juice
block of ice
2 qts. ginger ale
lemon and lime slices

1. Mix all ingredients
together in large punch bowl.
2. When well blended, add
a block of ice.
3. Just before serving add
2 quarts ginger ale.
4. Garnish with slices of
lemon and lime.

*Tip: Instead of a solid block of
ice, substitute an ice ring with
slices of citrus and cherries
inbedded in the ice.*

Sugar-Free
Holiday Nog
Norma I. Gehman
Ephrata, PA

Makes 8 servings

Prep Time: 10 minutes

7 cups skim milk, *divided*
1-oz. pkg. instant sugar-
  free vanilla pudding mix
1-2 tsp. vanilla, *or* rum,
  extract, your choice of
  amount
sugar substitute equivalent
  to 4-8 tsp. sugar,
  according to your taste
  preference
1 cup evaporated skim
  milk

1. Combine 2 cups milk,
pudding mix, extract, and
sugar substitute in a bowl.
Mix according to directions
on pudding package.
2. Pour pudding mixture
into a 1/2-gallon container
with a tight-fitting lid. Add 3
cups skim milk and shake
well.
3. Add evaporated milk
and remaining skim milk,
shaking well after each addition.
4. Chill and serve.

Strawberry
Refresher
Helen R. Goering
Moundridge, KS

Makes 1 gallon

Prep Time: 20 minutes

10-oz. pkg. frozen
  strawberries
6-oz. can frozen lemonade
  concentrate
8-oz. can crushed
  pineapple, undrained
3 qts. ginger ale
fresh strawberry slices, if
  available

1. Place frozen strawber-
ries, frozen lemonade concentrate, and crushed pineapple,
into blender. Blend on high
speed.
2. Pour into punch bowl.
3. Add ginger ale just
before serving.
4. If serving in a punch
bowl, garnish with fresh
strawberry slices.

Orange Julius

Janet Derstine
Telford, PA
Arlene Leaman Kliewer
Lakewood, CO
Krista Hershberger
Elverson, PA

Makes 3-4 servings

Prep Time: 5 minutes

6 ozs. frozen orange juice
  concentrate
1 cup water
1 cup milk
1/2-1 tsp. vanilla, according
  to your taste preference
1/2 cup sugar
12-14 ice cubes, *or* 3 cups
  crushed ice

1. Mix all ingredients in
blender.
2. Serve immediately.

Orange Crème Smoothie

Dale Peterson
Rapid City, SD

Makes 2 servings

Prep Time: 5 minutes

2 cups milk
1/2 cup plain *or* vanilla
  yogurt
1/2 cup frozen orange juice
  concentrate
4 tsp. sugar *or* honey
1 banana, sliced

1. Blend all ingredients in
blender or food processor.
2. Serve cold.

Variations:

*1. Add 4-6 ice cubes to the
blender to make the smoothie
slushy.*
*2. Make the smoothie with-
out adding any sweetener.*
   — **Annabelle
     Unternahrer**
     Shipshewana, IN

Strawberry Banana Smoothie

Ann Bender
Fort Defiance, VA

Makes 4-5 servings

Prep Time: 5 minutes

1 banana
1 cup frozen strawberries
1/2 cup orange juice
1/4 cup sugar, *or* honey
1/2 cup pineapple, crushed
  or cubes
1 tray of ice cubes
1 cup yogurt, *optional*
peaches *or* **blueberries,**
optional

1. Place ingredients in a
blender in the order listed.
2. Blend until ice is dissolved (1-2 minutes).

*This is exceptionally good—
and welcome—on a hot day or
night.*

A Tip —
   Keep hot dishwater in
the sink so you can clean
up the kitchen as you go
and while the food is baking or cooking.

Abbreviations used in Fix-It and Enjoy-It Cookbook

lb. = pound
oz. = ounce
pkg. = package
pt. = pint
qt. = quart
Tbsp. = tablespoon
tsp. = teaspoon
9 x 13 baking pan = 9 inches wide by 13 inches long
8 x 8 baking pan = 8 inches wide by 8 inches long
5 x 9 loaf pan = 5 inches wide by 9 inches long

Assumptions

flour = unbleached or white, and all-purpose
oatmeal or oats = dry, quick or rolled (old-fashioned), unless specified
pepper = black, finely ground
rice = regular, long-grain (not minute or instant)
salt = table salt
shortening = solid, not liquid
spices = all ground, unless specified otherwise
sugar = granulated sugar (not brown and not confectioners)

Equivalents

dash = little less than 1/8 tsp.
3 teaspoons = 1 Tablespoon
2 Tablespoons = 1 oz.
4 Tablespoons = 1/4 cup
5 Tablespoons plus 1 tsp. = 1/3 cup
8 Tablespoons = 1/2 cup
12 Tablespoons = 3/4 cup
16 Tablespoons = 1 cup
1 cup = 8 ozs. liquid
2 cups = 1 pint
4 cups = 1 quart
4 quarts = 1 gallon
1 stick butter = 1/4 lb.
1 stick butter = 1/2 cup
1 stick butter = 8 Tbsp.
Beans, 1 lb. dried = 2-2 1/2 cups (depending upon the size of the beans)
Bell peppers, 1 large = 1 cup chopped
Cheese, hard (for example, cheddar, Swiss, Monterey Jack, mozzarella), 1 lb. grated = 4 cups
Cheese, cottage, 1 lb. = 2 cups
Chocolate chips, 6-oz. pkg. = 1 scant cup
Coconut, 3-oz. pkg., grated = 1 cup, lightly filled
Crackers, graham, 12 single crackers = 1 cup crumbs

Crackers (butter, saltines, snack), 20 single crackers = 1 cup crumbs
Herbs, 1 Tbsp. fresh = 1 tsp. dried
Lemon, 1 medium-sized = 2-3 Tbsp. juice
Lemon, 1 medium-sized = 2-3 tsp. grated rind
Mustard, 1 Tbsp. prepared = 1 tsp. dry or ground mustard
Oatmeal, 1 lb. dry = about 5 cups dry
Onion, 1 medium-sized = 1/2 cup chopped
Pasta
    Macaronis, penne, and other small or tubular shapes, 1 lb. dry = 4 cups uncooked
    Noodles, 1 lb. dry = 6 cups uncooked
    Spaghetti, linguine, fettucine, 1 lb. dry = 4 cups uncooked
Potatoes, white, 1 lb. = 3 medium-sized potatoes = 2 cups mashed
Potatoes, sweet, 1 lb. = 3 medium-sized potatoes = 2 cups mashed
Rice, 1 lb. dry = 2 cups uncooked
Sugar, confectioners, 1 lb. = 3 1/2 cups sifted
Whipping cream, 1 cup unwhipped = 2 cups whipped
Whipped topping, 8-oz. container = 3 cups
Yeast, dry, 1 envelope (1/4 oz.) = 1 Tbsp.

Substitutions—for when you're in a pinch

For one cup **buttermilk**—use 1 cup plain yogurt; or pour 1⅓ Tbsp. lemon juice or vinegar into a 1-cup measure. Fill the cup with milk. Stir and let stand for 5 minutes. Stir again before using.

For one cup **cake flour**—fill 1-cup measure with all-purpose flour. Remove 2 Tbsp. flour. Add 2 Tbsp. dry cornstarch. Pour into small bowl and stir together lightly.

For 1 oz. **unsweetened baking chocolate**—stir together 3 Tbsp. unsweetened cocoa powder and 1 Tbsp. butter, softened.

For 1 Tbsp. **cornstarch**—use 2 Tbsp. all-purpose flour; or 4 tsp. minute tapioca.

For 1 **garlic clove**—use ¼ tsp. garlic salt (reduce salt in recipe by ⅛ tsp.); or ⅛ tsp. garlic powder.

For 1 Tbsp. **fresh herbs**—use 1 tsp. dried herbs.

For ½ lb. **fresh mushrooms**—use 1 6-oz. can mushrooms, drained.

For 1 Tbsp. **prepared mustard**—use 1 tsp. dry or ground mustard.

For 1 medium-sized **fresh onion**—use 2 Tbsp. minced dried onion; or 2 tsp. onion salt (reduce salt in recipe by 1 tsp.); or 1 tsp. onion powder. Note: These substitutions will work for meat balls and meat loaf, but not for sautéing.

For 1 cup **self-rising flour**—use 1 cup all-purpose flour plus 1½ tsp. baking powder plus ½ tsp. salt. Pour into bowl and stir together lightly.

For 1 cup **sour milk**—use 1 cup plain yogurt; or pour 1 Tbsp. lemon juice or vinegar into a 1-cup measure. Fill with milk. Stir and then let stand for 5 minutes. Stir again before using.

For 2 Tbsp. **tapioca**—use 3 Tbsp. all-purpose flour.

For 1 cup **canned tomatoes**—use 1⅓ cups diced fresh tomatoes, cooked gently for 10 minutes.

For 1 Tbsp. **tomato paste**—use 1 Tbsp. ketchup.

For 1 Tbsp. **vinegar**—use 1 Tbsp. lemon juice.

For 1 cup **heavy cream**—add ⅓ cup melted butter to ¾ cup milk. Note: This will work for baking and cooking, but not for whipping.

For 1 cup **whipping cream**—chill thoroughly ⅔ cup evaporated milk, plus the bowl and beaters, then whip; or use 2 cups bought whipped topping.

For ½ cup **wine**—pour 2 Tbsp. wine vinegar into a ½-cup measure. Fill with broth (chicken, beef, or vegetable). Stir and then let stand for 5 minutes. Stir again before using.

Kitchen Tools and Equipment You May Have Overlooked

1. Get yourself a salad spinner.
2. Make sure you have a little electric vegetable chopper, the size that will handle 1 cup of ingredients at a time.
3. Don't try to cook without a good paring knife that's sharp (and hold its edge) and fits in your hand.
4. Almost as important—a good chef's knife (we always called it a "butcher" knife) with a wide, sharp blade that's about 8 inches long, good for making strong cuts through meats.
5. You really ought to have a good serrated knife with a long blade, perfect for slicing bread.
6. Invest in at least one broad, flexible, heat-resistant spatula. And also a narrow one.
7. You ought to have a minimum of 2 wooden spoons, each with a 10-12 inch-long handle. They're perfect for stirring without scratching.
8. Get a washable cutting board. You'll still need it, even though you have an electric vegetable chopper (#2 above).
9. A medium-sized whisk takes care of persistent lumps in batters, gravies, and sauces when there aren't supposed to be any.

Three More Hints

1. If you'd like to cook more at home—without being in a frenzy—go off by yourself with your cookbook some evening and make a week of menus. Then make a grocery list from that. Shop from your grocery list.
2. Thaw frozen food in a bowl in the fridge (not on the counter-top). If you forget to stick the food in the fridge, put it in a microwave-safe bowl and defrost it in the microwave just before you're ready to use it.
3. Let roasted meat, as well as pasta dishes with cheese, rest for 10-20 minutes before slicing or dishing. That will allow the juices to re-distribute themselves throughout the cooked food. You'll have juicier meat, and a better presentation of your pasta dish.

Index

Index

Index

Index

Index

Index

Index

About the Author

Phyllis Pellman Good is a *New York Times* bestselling author whose books have sold more than 8.5 million copies.

Good has authored the national #1 bestselling cookbook ***Fix-It and Forget-It Cookbook: Feasting with Your Slow Cooker*** (with Dawn J. Ranck), which appeared on *The New York Times* bestseller list, as well as the bestseller lists of *USA Today, Publishers Weekly,* and *Book Sense.* And she is the author of ***Fix-It and Forget-It Lightly: Healthy, Low-Fat Recipes for Your Slow Cooker***, which has also appeared on *The New York Times* bestseller list. In addition, Good authored ***Fix-It and Forget-It Recipes for Entertaining: Slow Cooker Favorites for All the Year Round*** (with Ranck) and ***Fix-It and Forget-It Diabetic Cookbook*** (with the American Diabetes Association), also in the series.

Good's other cookbooks include *Favorite Recipes with Herbs, The Best of Amish Cooking,* and *The Central Market Cookbook.*

Phyllis Pellman Good is Senior Editor at Good Books. (Good Books has published hundreds of other titles by more than 125 different authors.) She received her B.A. and M.A. in English from New York University. She and her husband, Merle, live in Lancaster, Pennsylvania. They are the parents of two young-adult daughters.

For a complete listing of books by Phyllis Pellman Good, as well as excerpts and reviews, visit www.GoodBks.com.